Separating With Children 101

3rd edition

Editors

Rebecca Giraud and Bob Greig

Consulting editors

Dr Angharad Rudkin and Emma Nash

First edition published January 2019

Second edition published October 2020

Third edition published May 2023

ISBN 978-1-7393103-0-1

Text © Original authors and contributors

Typography and design © Bath Publishing

All rights reserved. No part of this publication may be reproduced in any material form (including photocopying or storing it in any medium by electronic means and whether or not transiently or incidentally to some other use of this publication) without the written permission of the copyright holder except in accordance with the provisions of the Copyright, Designs and Patents Act 1988 or under the terms of a licence issued by the Copyright Licensing Agency (www.cla.co.uk). Applications for the copyright owner's written permission to reproduce any part of this publication should be addressed to the publisher.

The authors and contributors assert their rights as set out in ss77 and 78 of the Copyright Designs and Patents Act 1988 to be identified as the authors of this work wherever it is published commercially and whenever any adaptation of this work is published or produced including any sound recordings or films made of or based upon this work.

The information presented in this work is accurate and current as at April 2023 to the best knowledge of the authors. The authors and the publisher, however, make no guarantee as to, and assume no responsibility for, the correctness or sufficiency of such information or recommendation. The contents of this book are not intended as legal advice and should not be treated as such.

Bath Publishing Limited
27 Charmouth Road, Bath
BA1 3LJ
Tel: 01225 577810

email: info@bathpublishing.co.uk

www.bathpublishing.co.uk

Bath Publishing is a company registered in England: 5209173

Registered Office: As above

This book is dedicated to

Saskia Giraud-Reeves

Priya Greig

Anya Greig

Three outstanding young women

MD Communications is proud to be a pro-bono campaign partner for OnlyMums & Dads. We see the vital work they do around protecting children and supporting parents, during and after separation, as a major factor in defending mental health and resilience of the next generation.

Introduction from the editors to the 3rd edition

Since setting up our not-for-profit social enterprise OnlyMums & Dads over a decade ago, the vast bulk of our work has involved pointing separating parents in the right direction when they encounter problems during their divorce / separation. Parents not agreeing what happens to the children after a separation is, sadly, not unusual.

Many separating parents have similar questions: What happens to the children and how will they cope? Do they live with one parent or both? How long do they spend with their other parent? How are handovers best arranged? Such questions form a part in almost all interactions we have. Concerns about the welfare of the children when staying with the other parent too are frequent.

These questions (and others) have been answered fully in this book with the helpful contributions from over one hundred leading family justice sector professionals. There are valuable contributions from health professionals too. All the content in this book is aimed to help parents put their children at the heart of their decision-making.

This 3rd edition sees some important updates. The welcome arrival of no-fault divorce has resulted in legal information in this book being updated. Following the publication of **(Almost) Anything But Family Court** by Jo O'Sullivan in 2022 we have taken the opportunity to strengthen the messaging about the real upside of parents avoiding the family courts wherever possible. We also welcome Emma Nash onto the editorial team. Emma runs the Language Matters Project on top of her day to day work as a family solicitor.

Dr Angharad Rudkin, Bob Greig, Rebecca Giraud and Emma Nash

On 23 March 2023 the Government announced proposals that will see mediation become mandatory in all suitable low-level family court cases excluding those which include allegations or a history of domestic violence. This will mean separating couples have to attempt to agree their child and financial arrangements through a qualified mediator with court action being a last resort. This demonstrates the commitment of the Government and others within the family justice sector to try and keep couples out of the family courts where possible.

Finally, whatever your situation, it is our hope that this book will bring you direction and greater clarity. We wish you and your family well.

Rebecca, Bob, Angharad, and Emma.

Spring 2023

Foreword to the third edition by The Rt. Hon. Sir Andrew McFarlane, President of the Family Division

The publication of **Separating with Children 101** is aimed at those who are facing the daunting and at times bewildering prospect of picking up and reforming their lives after a separation. The guidance on parenting and finances after separation could not be more welcome, coming, as it does, at a time when more and more are having to cope with these major life-challenges without professional advice or guidance.

For many, separation from a spouse or long-term partner sufficient to trigger the need to engage with the issues covered in this book will be a once in a lifetime event. They will be facing the significant challenges that separation generates for the first time and without any experience or understanding of what may be involved. Expectations of entitlement and of what is 'right' and 'just' may run high; emotions may well be both raw and powerful. A common view amongst the judiciary is that there is a need for a range of interventions aimed at assisting those who come to the Family Court by managing their expectations at an early stage as to what the court can and cannot do for them. This book is therefore both welcome and timely simply because it is most likely to succeed in meeting this very need.

A parent in a family case who is hungry for hard information, sound realistic advice and a 'feel' for the court process will find much to feed on in these pages; they may also consume them knowing that they have been compiled from a gender-neutral perspective, with the aim simply of providing practical and legally accurate information without any underlying agenda.

Most 'self-help' books seem to be penned by a single author or a small team. In contrast, each question in this book is answered by a different expert. This, obviously, has the benefit of enhancing the quality of the individual answers, but, in my view, there is a greater value when the book is read as a whole. Each specialist contribution, like a pixel, builds up to a bigger picture. Whether the question is about pension sharing or a worry about the alcohol consumption of the other parent, the author, being experienced in working with families and the Family Court across the board, when describing how best to approach the micro-issue, is also contributing to an overall understanding of how the legal system engages with the issues generated by separation more generally. It is this latter aspect, which is, in my view, of great value and marks this work out from others. Irrespective of the current pressing problem that may have caused a parent to pick this book up, any reader would be well advised to invest the time in reading it from cover to cover, thereby gaining a real 'feel' for the approach of family law professionals and the courts in general to these important and difficult problems.

The Rt. Hon. Sir Andrew McFarlane

President of the Family Division

13 February 2023

Acknowledgements

We would like to acknowledge the thousands of parents who have come through our organisation over the years. We have learned so much from their experiences and this book would not be on the shelves without them.

Big thank you's to Director of Training Dr Angharad Rudkin, Emma Nash and Adele Ballantyne for their contributions and helping us to shape this book.

Our Publishers, Helen and David at Bath Publishing who support our organisation in many ways and continue to be such a pleasure to work with.

There are many individuals and organisations that we work with that play a key part in the work we do. In particular, we would like to thank Jo O'Sullivan for her time, knowledge and wisdom in writing **(Almost) Anything But Family Court**; all those involved in delivering the **'What About Henry'** training for professionals; the team at Resolution; our co-founders of the Parent Promise Alliance, James Hayhurst and Melissa Davis; and the lovely Claire and Adrian who support us with all our last-minute printing and design needs.

We want to particularly acknowledge the help, support, and encouragement of Richard Wain and Dominic Cooper from Vu-online. They have been our tech wizards and project partners in the delivery of the Family Separation Support Hub. Their commitment to developing this holistic website for those going through a separation has been nothing short of inspiring.

x

How to use this book

This book contains answers to the questions frequently coming through to OnlyMums & OnlyDads CIC. All the questions have been answered by our team of experts; solicitors, barristers, mediators and other professionals.

The book also has information about useful organisations including Samaritans, NSPCC and Relate.

Dotted throughout the book are quotes, one-liners and top tips from parents, solicitors, children and therapeutic personnel.

A useful list of organisations has been included at the back.

This advice has been written by Adele Ballantyne (Family Consultant, MA Relationship Therapy, Director at Eleda Consultancy), Mike Flinn (Counsellor and Family Therapist) and Dr Angharad Rudkin (Programme Tutor / Child Clinical Psychologist within Psychology at the University of Southampton).

The main priority for separating parents is their children. We have collected together some real life quotes from children who have accessed Voices in the Middle.

A number of solicitors, barristers and paralegals have contributed dozens of handy tips and helpful nuggets of wisdom throughout the book.

Some words of wisdom from parents who've been through the separating journey. There are some regrets, words of advice and hopes for the future.

Rebecca and Bob work with separating parents every day and they have added in their top tips.

Contents

Introduction from the editors to the 3rd edition	v
Foreword to the third edition by The Rt. Hon. Sir Andrew McFarlane, President of the Family Division	vii
Acknowledgements	ix
How to use this book	xi

Why this book matters

Fresh hope for separating families Dr David Curl	1
Language Emma Nash	4
What does it mean to put children first? Dr Angharad Rudkin	6
Is it over? Adele Ballantyne	8

We are separating

Separating: are there any practical steps I should take? Emma Cordock	12
How do I tell the children we are separating? Claire Field	14
I have children but I am just about to separate. Do I need legal advice? Yanoulla Kakoulli	16
We're not married. Does this mean mum gets the children? James Maguire	19
I have decided to leave the family home. Does this have implications? Jessica Palmer	21
Common law marriage is a common myth Catherine Bell	23
What 'no-fault' divorce means and how it is different from how things were before Sarah Whitelegge	25
What is the law relating to the unmarried/cohabiting family? Paul Summerbell	27
My ex is a narcissist – do you have any tips for dealing with this personality type? Dr Supriya McKenna Karin Walker	30
Divorce/separation and the use of social media Amanda Adeola	33

Contents

My partner is having an affair and wants to divorce. What are my options? — 35
Helen Pittard

What is the role of friends in separation? — 39
Charlotte Friedman

Recognising and dealing with stress — 41
Dylan Watkins

Samaritans — 43

How can technology help parents and children cope after separation? — 45
Melanie Bataillard-Samuel
Tom Brownrigg

How can conversations be transformed into a problem-solving approach? — 47
Norman Hartnell

Domestic abuse

What are the effects on children who witness domestic violence? — 52
Dr Angharad Rudkin

What is Coercive Control? — 54
Phillippa Kum
Polly Atkins

What is gaslighting and how do I deal with it? — 56
Irena Osborne

Domestic violence: a checklist? — 58
Beverley Watkins

Help for victims of domestic abuse in the Family Court — 60
Lucy Todd

No one believes me - how do I prove I am telling the truth? — 63
Jennifer Williamson

What will happen if I contact a solicitor about a domestic abuse concern? — 65
Ruth Hawkins & Irena Osborne

Can I get legal aid? — 67
Derek Jordan

Can I change the locks on my house to keep my ex from just wandering in? — 69
Melanie Westwood

My partner has told me he will take the children away if I report his abuse. What are my options? — 71
Angela Parsons

What about dads coping with an abusive female partner? — 73
Dr Elizabeth Bates & Dr Julie Taylor

It's been suggested I get a Prohibitive Steps Order. What is that? — 76
Bernadette Hoy

What is a Non-molestation Order? — 78
Inayat Nadat

The Independent Domestic Violence Advisor (IDVA) Marilyn Selwood	81

Children

Effects of marital discord on children Dr Angharad Rudkin	84
Teenagers, young adults and parental separation Angela Lake-Carroll	86
How can I help my children cope with stress and recognise when professional help is needed? Dr Sabina Dosani	89
Should we ask the children where they want to live, or is that unfair? Emma Taylor	91
I really don't think my ex is well enough mentally to look after the kids. What can I do about it? Kate Barton	93
I'm really concerned that my ex does not look after the children properly. What can I do? Sabrina Bailey	96
My children have come home reporting inappropriate sexual behaviour. What should I do? Emma Benyon-Tinker	98
Has my child been kidnapped? Imran Khodabocus	101
Can you answer some of my concerns about child contact centres? Phil Coleman	103
My ex has changed the kids' school and doctor without telling me anything. What should I do? Rachel Duke	106
Is my ex allowed to change my child's surname? Marc Etherington	108

Drugs & alcohol

I am sure my ex is drinking too much when looking after the kids. What should I do? Heather Broadfield	112
How do I leave my alcoholic partner? Luke Chester-Master	114
I am sure my ex is taking drugs when looking after the kids. What should I do? Carol-Anne Baker	117
DNA, hair drug & alcohol tests in families - what do you need to be aware of? Dr Salah Breidi	119

Contents

Mediation and non-court options

What are the benefits of a mediated settlement? *Jo Edwards*	124
Family Mediation Government Voucher Scheme for separated parents *Sushma Kotecha*	127
How can I get the most out of mediation? *Sarah Hawkins*	129
Top tips which may help you before your first joint mediation meeting *Sheena Adam*	131
Can I refuse to go to mediation? *Deborah Butterworth*	133
How do you expect me to mediate? My ex is a total nightmare *Paul Kemp*	135
I have an abusive ex. Is mediation right for me? *Anna Vollans*	138
How should I prepare for a MIAM? *Sarah England & Karen Shirn*	140
How does child mediation work? *Angela Lake-Carroll*	141
Are arrangements made in mediation legally binding? *Rebekah Gershuny*	144
(Almost) Anything But Family Court *Jo O'Sullivan*	146
How to choose professional support *Claire Colbert & Rachael Oakes*	148

Money

My soon to be ex-husband has money all over the place. Where do I start? *Rachael Oakes*	152
What is child maintenance? *Gingerbread*	154
My partner owns the house but I have done all the improvements and upkeep. Where do I stand? *Emma Dewhurst*	157
What should I do if I am going through a divorce and one party has cryptoassets? *Victoria Clarke*	160
What if we are separating and have a joint business? *Natalie Sutherland*	163
Can you advise me on pension sharing? *Mary Shaw*	165
How can people deal with debts when they divorce or separate? *Hasan Hadi*	167

How can I move from a 2-income to a 1-income household? Tom Farrell	169
Are assets split equally on divorce? Andrew Meehan	172

Going through the family court

The Children Act paradox Kathryn McTaggart	176
How should I prepare for court? James Belderbos	179
Top tips on the day of court Nicola Sully & Scott Sharp	182
Should I appoint a barrister? Lucy Reed KC	184
What does it mean to 'instruct' a solicitor? Melanie Bataillard-Samuel	187
Can I get the Judge to speak directly with my children? Jon Armstrong	189
The children's guardian and children's solicitor Sarra Gravestock	190
What is the Welfare Checklist and do I need to know about it? David Starkey	192
Advocate	194
Can I change my Cafcass Officer? Mark Leeson	196
Have you any tips for dealing with an abusive partner at a court hearing? Claire Fitzgerald Sue Scott	197
What is a C100? Rajan Thandi	200
Representing yourself in court Olivia Piercy	202
How should I prepare for a meeting with a professional to save time and money? Ursula Rice	206
What are directions orders? Norman Hartnell	208
What happens at a fact-finding hearing? Fiona O'Sullivan	210
What is a Child Arrangements Order? Shanika Varga-Haynes	212
What is a Parenting Co-ordinator? Claire Webb	214

Contents

Do courts automatically think kids are better off with mum? *Gillian Bishop*	217
How will the court decide on where the children will live? *Ruth Hawkins*	219
My ex is threatening to take our children abroad. What should I do? *Emine Mehmet*	221
What is a Leave to Remove application? *Fiona Turner* *Lottie Tyler*	223
I've been ordered to attend a SPIP by the court. What should I expect? *Laura Beech*	226
Broken court orders: what are my options? *Dawn Gore* *Grant Cameron*	228
Cafcass	230
What records can I keep and can I make secret recordings? *Shivi Rajput*	232
Can my ex withhold our child's passport? *Caroline Young*	234
What is the law in Scotland? *Rachael Noble*	236

Parental alienation

What is parental alienation? *Dr Sue Whitcombe*	240
How do I recognise and deal with the first stages of alienating behaviour? *Alison Bushell*	242
My children don't want to see their dad. What should I do? *Anthony Jones*	246
How does the court deal with parental alienation? *Jeremy Ford*	247

Co-operative parenting

What makes a successful handover? *Ashley Palmer*	252
Do I have to do all the driving? *Chris Fairhurst*	254
Co-parenting with your ex-partner *Marcie Shaoul*	256
What should I do about an unreliable ex? *Louisa Dickson*	258
Practical strategies to help children cope with two homes *Kate Daley*	260

Contents

Grandparents

The importance of the grandparents' relationship with children ... 264
Jane Jackson

How can I retain contact with my grandchildren after their parents have separated? ... 266
Alun Jones

I don't see my grandchildren. What rights do I have? ... 268
David Kendall

My grandchildren are telling us worrying things and it sounds like neglect. What should we do? ... 269
Kimberley Bailey

We have ended up as parents to our grandchildren. Can we make it official? ... 271
Camilla Fusco

Profiles

The family solicitor ... 276
Paul Linsell

The family barrister ... 278
Stephanie Heidjra

The solicitor neutral ... 280
David Lister

The chartered legal executive ... 282
Emma Taylor

The arbitrator ... 284
Claire Webb

The family mediator ... 287
Jo O'Sullivan

The child inclusive mediator ... 289
Louisa Whitney

The divorce specialist financial planner ... 291
Tamsin Caine

The Pensions on Divorce Expert (PODE) ... 293
Ian Hawkins

The family consultant ... 295
Kim Crewe

The counsellor ... 297
Lesley Edelstein

The divorce consultant ... 298
Rhiannon Ford

Last words

How to be successful separated parents ... 302
Angela Lake-Carroll

Final reflections ... 305
Claire Molyneux

Notes

ONLY Mums & Dads

Why this book matters

Fresh hope for separating families

Dr David Curl

David is CEO of Two Wishes, an international foundation dedicated to transforming how we think about, and deal with, family separation

Family life can be tough - financially, emotionally and in so many ways. But it can also be the most treasured and rewarding experience of our lives. So, it's hardly surprising that if your own family seems to be falling apart, or cherished dreams seem to be disappearing before your eyes, it can be one of the toughest times of all.

Times, though, are changing. 50 years ago, partly in response to escalating divorce rates, a wave of legislation swept the globe: "family law" put legal proceedings and family courts firmly at the heart of family separation and divorce. Today, there's an increasing recognition that the breakdown or change of relationships within a family should not be primarily a matter of law, especially when children are involved. It's a matter of health and wellbeing, first and foremost. Occasionally, even, it's a matter of life and death.

It's a time when children and families can be at their most vulnerable and need compassionate, non-judgmental help and support as a matter of urgency, not torturous, terrifying processes in a court of law. Remarkably, the past few years have seen some of the world's top judges step out beyond their own family court systems to make impassioned pleas for a fresh approach too.

The UK's top family court judge Sir Andrew McFarlane, along with his predecessor Sir James Munby, have both challenged the dominant place that their own family courts retain in the landscape of divorce and suggested there are better ways to separate than in courts. Accessible, compassionate support, education and mediation should not be considered "alternatives" to court; these should, quite simply, be the best-known, best-marketed and universally used elements of any modern family separation.

In Australia, former Chief Justice John Pascoe, went even further in suggesting that his own institution needed the broadest of reviews, a Royal Commission; "tinkering" with family law was not enough to address what's become a public health crisis. We need a very different approach, a different way of thinking even.

Maybe you saw the photo (reproduced below) that went viral in 2017 of an extended family with two sets of parents supporting their 4-year-old daughter at a soccer match in the USA? Maybe you've raised an eyebrow, or thought it bizarre - inconceivable even - to hear stories of families where ex-partners join each other for Christmas or family holidays. Maybe 'conscious uncoupling', a term popularised in 2014 by actress Gwyneth Paltrow and the title of a book by Katherine Woodward Thomas who invented it, sounds like a trendy bridge too far.

But contrast those positive images with the language of divorce of past decades. The very term 'divorce' itself retains a stigma to this day; it's not really the topic of polite dinner party conversation. We still talk casually about 'custody', a term otherwise reserved for those in prison. The word 'ex' is

Why this book matters

rarely uttered with unbridled joy. Even words that might seem polar opposites like 'up' and 'down' become equally depressing and negative when used in the context of family break-ups or breakdowns.

Getting separated or divorced still lingers near the top of many lists of most traumatic life experiences. It comes with some of the strongest feelings we'll ever experience, ranging from grief, humiliation, sorrow or just sheer numbness and bewilderment, to anger - even rage - or desperation - even terror - about the future. This isn't generally a moment when we need people judging, lecturing or, worse still, trying to diagnose us. "Sometimes," to quote the admirable resource for families Hey Sigmund, "the only diagnosis is 'human'".

It's human nature too that, when any sort of relationship - business or personal - breaks down, we want people to be on our side and our side alone. We want them to share our view of what happened. Family friends and bystanders often get caught up in that and provide well-meaning but uncritical support; few are brave or experienced enough to give the help that's really needed and challenge thinking that may not be constructive, or behaviours that may not be best for children.

When families split up, there's simply one side we must all be on together: the children's.

For other widespread social issues or human frailties - especially when lives are at stake, as they are here - society has recognised what's needed: accessible help; compassionate support; and signposts to navigate the road ahead and warn of dangers, step-by-step. Adults and children alike need someone to hold their hand.

Most of us have heard of groups like Alcoholics Anonymous, which provides support of this kind. Many of us are aware of how treating drug addicts with compassion, and using health-focused not law-based approaches, can transform lives for the better. And we've all seen signposts or orange flags as we drive through school zones warning distracted drivers of acute danger to children on the road ahead.

Not so with divorce. At this time of intense emotions and high risk to children and parents, we have to embark on a life-changing journey that many of us will do once, and once only, in our lives. And, we have to do so without any standard road map - and with no orange flags to warn us of potentially life-threatening dangers to our children on the road ahead. If navigated well, this journey can lead to new and unexpected joys and avoid great and unimaginable tragedy.

This book provides one of the nearest things you'll get to the road map that every separating couple should have. In simple, relatable terms, it helps explain how to get through one of the toughest challenges that some of us will face in our entire lives.

Some things go without saying. We all know that children benefit from developing positive relationships with all who love and

Why this book matters

care for them. And we shouldn't be surprised to find out how precious every parent-child connection is; among other things, they're 'the most powerful mental health intervention known to mankind', helping give children the resilience they need to get through life in general, and a family break-up in particular.

For many children, their parents' separation can be the most frightening and lonely time of their lives. Even if there's no extreme or overt conflict, it can be the first time they find themselves truly alone - with no-one they feel they can talk to, no-one who'd understand. Their parents, suddenly, are pre-occupied with something else. Whatever age they are, though, children's lives and futures can be transformed if their family gets the help it needs and avoids being sent off in the wrong direction, as so many are today.

I think there are many words of wisdom in this book that can help, guide and support and that can direct families to people and resources that will help give children the brightest possible future when their parents split up. Someday, they may even help the rest of us to think of this moment not as families breaking up or down, but as families changing, growing new branches, and even thriving.

But, for anyone going through a separation right now, don't be too hard on yourself. Or your ex. Compassion doesn't come easy during such a family crisis, but more of it is needed wherever it can be found - especially for the sake of children. One day, your own children will really thank you for that.

Humans have developed various ways of adapting to change, but it still takes up a lot of energy, resources and time. When an unexpected, traumatic event occurs such as being told that your partner is leaving, your body and brain responds with fight, flight response or freeze response.

During these responses, the brain ensures that you are in optimum survival mode. It shuts off certain aspects of functioning and heightens others, with adrenaline cortisol surging through the body.

To counteract this natural physiological reaction, you need to stay as calm and relaxed as possible. Now is not the time to make any major decisions and you will need all the support from family and friends you can.

Once you start to feel safe and contained, your brain will stop sending alarm signals. Having recovered from the acute stress, you can take small steps in thinking about the future, planning and making decisions. As with any loss, you will move through stages of different feelings - numbness, anger, depression, acceptance. There are no time limits, so trust that you will work your way through these stages at your own pace.

Angharad Rudkin

Why this book matters

Language

Emma Nash
Partner at Rayden Solicitors and Founder of the Family Law Language Project

How we communicate and the language we use is fundamental to all of our lives. How parents talk about the world, their problems and relationships and how they talk to each other will significantly impact on the health, wellbeing and development of their children. This is all the more important for parents who are separating or for separated families or families facing significant changes such as divorce, re-marriage or a move to another part of the world. Even normal life events, such as children starting secondary school or the birth of a new step-sibling, can be a source of friction which may lead to negative language and an increase in tension and parental conflict.

We know that parental conflict causes harm to children. This harm can be devastating and far reaching. Research published in the Department of Work & Pensions **Reducing Parental Conflict Programme** shows that children who are exposed to parental conflict are more at risk of having problems at school, with their physical health, with smoking and substance abuse and mental health problems. This can negatively impact their life chances in all areas including relationships, academically, in employment and can put them at risk of long term health problems such as depression and anxiety.

Language that creates, increases or perpetuates parental conflict is therefore capable of putting children at real risk. That is the case whether that language is being used by a parent at school pick up, by a professional in correspondence or by the media on television.

Here are some tips to help you improve the language and reduce conflict for separated and separating families:

- Avoid fighting language. Resolving family issues does not have to be a battle. You are not at war with the other parent. You need to work together and confrontational language will only make that more difficult;

- Think about how you talk about the other parent in front of your child and in front of others. You may not like the other parent anymore. You may not trust them. But like it or not they are an important part of your child's life and putting them down, criticising them or humiliating them will not only impact your child's relationship with them but it will make co-parenting more likely to end in disagreement and conflict and may even damage your own relationship with them;

- Think about using a technical term, especially if you are not sure what it means. People often misuse terms as 'shared care', 'parental alienation' or 'primary carer'. These can be very loaded terms which can often raise tensions and make resolving disagreements more difficult;

- Don't believe everything you see on television! Who doesn't love a good TV drama but be careful about how family breakdown and family

Why this book matters

legal problems are portrayed. Most family cases resolve out of court through careful discussion and negotiations. It may not be exciting but if you come expecting a fight because that's what happens on TV then you are already making things more difficult. Also, be careful about the language used in foreign media. Many US programmes use the terms 'custody,' 'visitation' and 'access' whereas we have taken a conscious decision to remove those words from the law in England & Wales as they immediately create an imbalance between parents which causes conflict and does not adequately focus on what is best for the child;

- Keep your language child focussed. Try to avoid language that makes it about you. It is not 'your weekend' or 'your turn' to attend parents evening. The focus should be on the arrangements for your child to have a relationship with both parents. Sometimes that means putting what is best for them over what you think is fair for you and using language that acknowledges this may help reduce conflict.

Another way you can help to improve the language of family law for everyone is to get involved in the debate around the use of language and help identify incorrect or inappropriate use of language in the media. The **Family Law Language Project** was launched in November 2021 with the aim of doing just that. You can get involved and follow the Project at thefamilylawlanguageproject.co.uk and on social media @TheFLLProject.

It is not just about using language that reduces conflict. The family legal system is there to help families and children. It is not there to help lawyers, judges or any other professional. It therefore needs to be as accessible and understandable as possible to those families and children and put their needs first. At the moment, the law is full of technical terms, acronyms, abbreviations, procedures and traditions which can make those who are not familiar with it feel alienated and excluded. Whilst there will always be some need for technical language this has to be balanced against ensuring an inclusive and accessible legal system particularly when, as with many family law cases, vulnerable people such as children and victims of domestic abuse are relying on that system to support them during a time of crisis.

If you do find yourself needing to engage with the family legal system and there is something that you do not understand then remember it is ok to ask for an explanation, and that can be from your own lawyer, the lawyer for another party, a Judge, social worker or another professional. We are ultimately all there to help families and should be providing a system that is open, supportive and helps families to resolve issues in a positive and child focussed manner.

Whatever you do, please think carefully about the language you use and the impact it may have on you, your family and the wider community.

Language boxes

Throughout the book are scattered some language boxes:

STOP – these terms are either outdated, inflammatory or inappropriate.

THINK – these terms may be appropriate in some circumstances but could cause problems in others.

GOOD – this language is correct, appropriate and promotes positive parenting.

Why this book matters

What does it mean to put children first?

Dr Angharad Rudkin
Clinical Psychologist, MA (Oxon), CPsychol, AFBPsS

It is so easy to be told that you need to put your children first, but what does that mean exactly?

We need to return to the notion proposed by Winnicott in the 1950s that the best kind of parents is +the "good enough parent". This doesn't mean being a perfect parent - it means being a parent who trundles along doing an adequate job for most of the time, who sometimes messes up and occasionally outdoes themselves. This, of course, is not quite so straightforward before, during and after a separation for two reasons. Firstly, your child is dealing with an enormous change and therefore needs a lot more from you at the very time that, secondly, you are dealing with an enormous change and just getting out of bed is difficult enough. Being a good enough parent during a separation can feel like a superhuman effort.

Caring quota

Imagine everyone has a 'caring quota' i.e. an amount of love, care, organising, listening to, feeding and nurturing you can give (to yourself, your child and others in your family). Let's say the absolute maximum you can give is 100%. On an average kind of day your child may need about 25% and you may need about 25% for yourself. The rest is free to give if anyone needs it. When your child is in the middle of exams or being bullied at school, they may need 75% of your caring quota, which leaves less for you and anyone else around you. When your parent is very ill or you've just been made redundant, you need a lot of your own caring quota to get through each day (say, 80%) leaving just 20% for your child and everyone else. During a separation your child may need 100% of your caring, at the very same time you need 100% in order to function. You don't have to be a mathematician to realise that 200% isn't possible.

Getting the balance right

The key to getting through this time is balance. Getting a balance between caring for you and caring for your child. Remember, there is no such thing as a perfect parent, and there is definitely nothing like perfection

---

My child/my children/my family – STOP

If you have a child with someone then whatever you think of them or whatever they might have done they will still have an important role to play in the life of your child. Exceptions to this are rare. Possessive language that excludes or minimises the role of the other parent can negatively impact the relationship between that parent and the child and can increase conflict and make it more difficult to co-parent.

during separation. To get the balance, we need to think about another area of research looking at parenting. Studies have shown that being a 'responsive' parent is one of the most important keys to a contented child. Being responsive means that you are open to, and aware of, your child's needs. It doesn't mean that you always have the answer or that you know exactly what to do. But it does mean listening, watching and communicating with your child in a flexible way, so that you are moving with your child's changing needs. This may be where the concept of putting your child first can be useful - responding to your child as they are right now may mean letting go of your expectations about how they *should* be. If they're not upset when you expect them to be, then respond to their happiness. If they're upset when you really don't expect them to be, then respond to their sadness rather than your belief that they should be absolutely fine.

Some people are better at being responsive than others, but what is universal is that we find it easier to respond appropriately to others when we are being cared for. Talk to friends and family about your feelings, spend time with people who make you feel happy. Being able to relax and download some of your feelings will mean that you have more head and heart space to respond to your children.

Child's point of view

The final aspect of putting your child first is to imagine how things feel from their point of view. Remembering our own childhood can help us to understand our own children. If you find it hard to tap into memories of your childhood, read books about children so that you can understand how they see the world. And if you are in doubt, ask them how it feels to be them right now. They may not give you an answer, but the fact that you're asking will help them feel valued.

Conclusion

So, should you put your child first? There are no 'shoulds' at a time like this. Instead, aim to be responsive to your child. Try to understand how they are feeling while accepting that their feelings and needs will change rapidly. Look for a balance between what you require to get yourself through, and what they need. Listen, watch and communicate with openness. The rest will then take care of itself.

> ***Putting Children First*** is a phrase you will hear a lot. It trips off the tongue. It sounds obvious and straightforward. We have found that parents who recognise that they might not always know what is in their children's best interest and are willing to question their own instincts are probably those who end up really making the best decisions for their children. Don't be afraid to ask for help/advice. Separating with children is rarely easy or straightforward.

Why this book matters

Is it over?

Adele Ballantyne
Relationship Therapist, Eleda Consultancy

Deciding to end a relationship is a complex and difficult process and is not arrived at easily. Equally, being told your relationship is at an end is often a shocking and emotionally traumatic event.

It is common for those leaving and for those being left to experience similar feelings despite how it might look on the outside.

Depending on what has been happening in the relationship, and every couple relationship is unique, the ending might feel inevitable and expected or a complete surprise.

Some might describe the initial event as a car crash. Life speeds up and thoughts run away turning life upside down. Others might say it's like everything is in slow motion and they are devastated.

Loss & uncertainty

There are, however, certain processes that couples go through when a relationship is over - both experience *loss* and both are 'pushed' into a period of *uncertainty*.

"So, is it really over?"

"I can't believe it's over"

"I didn't see it coming"

"Why didn't you tell me you were this unhappy?"

"I'll do anything, let's just try again"

"I tried to tell you, you wouldn't listen"

"You know we haven't been happy"

"We've been arguing for ages, you just storm off"

As a therapist I hear these questions again and again from couples who are about to separate or have already separated.

Coming to terms with losing someone whom you thought you would be with forever is one of the most difficult journeys a mum or dad can take; knowing that you will never again be the love of their life; that they no longer 'want' you; and they have already found someone, or will go on to find someone, who will have what you no longer have, is one of the hardest things to acknowledge. How long it takes to accept and move on depends on the individual.

Mums and dads often find it difficult to separate their couple relationship feelings from their parenting feelings and it is this dichotomy that invariably gets in the way of allowing continued relationships with the children for the non-residential parent.

So, let's talk about the two processes you will both have in common; loss and living with uncertainty.

The loss cycle

Whether you are a mum or a dad, whether you have initiated the separation or not, you will both go through loss. It is the same process that you might go through if a loved one dies and it is common for one of you to be at a different stage than the other.

Imagine this. You are in a relationship, it's been good, then OK and now it's not working. You can't talk to each other, you might feel unloved, criticised, disrespected, not wanted or needed, taken advantage of. Maybe you feel like something is going on but are afraid to ask. You've tried to talk but got nowhere. Sound familiar?

When issues like this occur in a relationship, if they are not resolved then each of you begins to exhibit different behaviour. Sometimes it's subtle, sometimes it's obvious.

Usually for one person the loss cycle begins. There are 5 stages:

- denial/shock
- anger
- bargaining
- depression/sadness
- acceptance

As one person begins to make their way through the 5 stages, the relationship may continue to deteriorate. After a time, there is often a catalyst that will force a major change. Commonly when this occurs the relationship has ended for one person. The mum or dad is at stage 5 and accepts that, for them, it is over.

Then comes the car crash for the other person and they begin their journey through the loss cycle. No wonder it's difficult for them to accept that it's ended.

Uncertainty

Once this has happened both mum and dad are thrown into a period of uncertainty.

Identities are changing from couple to single, from mum and dad together as a family unit to mum with children and dad with children. Depending on the circumstances and who decides to leave the family home, there are many questions that arise during this time.

"Will we have to sell our home?"

"I haven't worked since we had children - how will we manage financially?"

"What will our friends and family think?"

"How much will divorce cost?"

"Will I cope on my own?".

There seems to be so much to sort out both practically and emotionally and it comes at a time when at least one of you will be 'all over the place' emotionally due to the loss you are experiencing. This can make decision-making seem impossible. Who wants to agree the practicalities of legal issues and more importantly organise the children when they are devastated, angry and confused by loss? It can turn otherwise rational, clear-thinking mums and dads into what appears to be belligerent, stubborn, unreasonable people.

Being honest with yourself about the relationship whilst you are emotionally upset is, for many extremely hard. It is important when struggling to accept that a relationship is over to get some help. There are many professionals out there who can help you on this journey.

Don't compare your family to others. It makes it seem like your family is completely broken but in reality a new family can be made again. Cerys-Sophie (16)

1 in 3
parents separating
are going to court

(Family Solutions Group 2020)

We are separating

The early days of separation can feel hazy, fast and yet, at the same time, painfully slow. The world as you knew it is changing, and you have to take your life and your children's lives into an unfamiliar future. No one stands at the altar expecting to divorce. The worlds of finance, law and mediation can feel intimidating. As with any major crises, now is the time to lean on the support of your friends and family. Look after you own needs as well as you possibly can so that you can then look after those who are dependent on you. Remember that even a few days can make a big difference, so keep your focus on the short-term. The long-term will then look after itself.

We are separating

Separating: are there any practical steps I should take?

Emma Cordock
Director, AFG LAW

For many people it can feel overwhelming when a relationship comes to an end. This checklist is not legal advice but a list of practical steps designed to try and make things a little easier and help you during this difficult time.

End of the relationship
Firstly, make a note of the date that you decided the relationship was over, even if you are still living in the same property. This date will be needed by different agencies and by your lawyers.

Children
How are you going to tell your children about your separation? Discuss this with your partner and reach an agreement on what the children should be told and how. Remember that it is a difficult time for your children as well as for you and your partner; it is important that they are not put in a position where they are aware of parental conflict or feel they have to choose between their parents. This can have a lasting impact on children's emotional welfare and development. Try to put the children's needs first.

On a practical basis think about:

- who the children will live with;

- how the children will share their time between the parents;

- whether it is possible for the children to stay in the family home so they have stability;

- whether the arrangements for the children are practical;

- getting the children to school, employment or other commitments.

If it is not possible to reach agreement, then consider getting legal advice or trying mediation.

Living arrangements
This can be a really difficult, emotional decision. Ask yourself:

- What will happen to the family home?

- Are you married or cohabiting? The legal position is different, so you might need to think about taking legal advice.

- Can you afford to stay in the house? Think about the rent or mortgage as well as the running costs.

Dividing your belongings
Sometimes this can be straightforward if it is clear you own an item, but if you have purchased things together think about making a list and try and reach a compromise. Think about what the children will need.

Managing money
This needs to be carefully approached and as always you need to think about your children's needs first. For most separating couples the

priority is trying to maintain the family home for the children. This may involve the person leaving contributing to mortgage or rent payments. Separating finances can be complicated and you may need to take legal advice.

- Think about your banking arrangements. Do you have sole or joint accounts? Do you need to set up a separate account? Think about which account the bills and rent/mortgage are paid from and be careful you don't cause any problems with missed payments or any overdrafts.

- It may be worth speaking to your mortgage provider to see if they can offer any help whilst you sort out the details e.g. moving to an interest only mortgage or taking a payment break.

- If you have joint debts such as credit cards or loans think about how you will meet these obligations between you.

- Do you need to consider maintenance?

- Are pensions involved? If you are married or in a civil partnership an ex-partner could be entitled to a share of the other person's pension(s).

- Has your benefit position changed? Do you need to speak to the DWP or HMRC? You could be entitled to further benefits.

Updating your personal information

Think about the practicalities involved and update your information now that you are no longer a couple:

- Update your emergency contacts.

- Decide on your next of kin for medical purposes.

- Review passwords and PIN numbers for banking purposes, email accounts, social media, online accounts or apps.

- Organise mail redirection for the person who leaves the shared home.

Informing people that you've separated

Think about who needs to know you have separated or moved address:

- Children's School;

- GP / Health Professionals;

- Employers;

- Bank or Building Society, credit card or loan companies;

- HMRC;

- DVLA;

- Insurance policies;

- Council Tax;

- Telephone / broadband providers;

- Utility providers.

Getting legal advice

Solicitors can help during this difficult time. It is important to know your legal rights at the start to ensure that you achieve the best outcome for yourself and your children.

We understand that our clients worry about legal costs spiralling. You can keep legal costs down by agreeing matters through negotiation and attending mediation rather than going to court. Solicitors can then formalise the final agreement by creating a legal document so you are protected.

A lot of our clients prefer to get some initial advice prior to entering into discussions and many solicitors (as I do) offer competitive fixed fee services to help keep your costs down.

We are separating

How do I tell the children we are separating?

Claire Field
Managing Director,
The Parenting Apart Programme

Telling your children about separation or getting a divorce will never be easy, but there are definitely things to consider before you have that particular discussion with them.

Here are some of our most important tips on how to tell your children about a divorce or court order:

- If possible, talk to your ex-partner and make sure you are both sharing the same information with your children;

- If possible, tell your children about your divorce at the same time. They need to hear it together so that they all are told the same thing in the same way. This will allow the children to ask questions and these can be addressed together;

- It is important that children are told as soon as possible to avoid the heartache of them finding out from others or older siblings;

- Most importantly be polite and civil with your ex-partner while you are telling your children about your divorce. Show your children that you can be civil to each other despite the emotional situation you are going through.

Language

- If you have children of different ages, plan to share the basic information at the initial meeting and follow up with the older children during a separate conversation;

- It is important to agree in advance the language you will use, depending on the age of the child (there are storybooks available for younger children to help them to understand the change);

- Know the limits of what you think is suitable for them to hear and how much they will understand. Try not to say too much or justify why you have made this decision. Keep the information bitesize, allowing your child space to ask questions;

- Tell your children where they will be living, with whom and those areas of their lives which may change such as school, friends, home and routine;

- Tell them when, where and how often they will meet the non-resident parent;

- Children need to understand that the decision to live apart is an adult decision and that they are not to blame;

- Try to incorporate the word "we" when you're explaining the decisions that have been made;

- Reassure them that no matter what happens, and no matter where anyone lives, they will still be loved and cared

14

We are separating

for by both parents;

- Make sure other significant adults are aware of the information shared with your children – children may ask others to check out if what they've been told is the truth.

When and where to tell your children

- Timing is important – when both parents have enough time (preferably not a school day) allow a few hours to share the news to allow your children to process it and ask questions;

- Consider an environment with which the children are familiar, possibly their main residence so that they have other spaces to go to if the situation becomes upsetting for them;

- Do not plan other activities after you have shared the information – the children may need time to absorb and talk through what you've just told them;

- Consider asking another significant adult (grandparent, uncle, aunt) who is close to the children to be present to offer support.

> Remember that you won't both approach a separation at the same pace. If it was your decision to permanently separate, you'll be much further ahead in grieving for your broken relationship than your ex-partner.
>
> Be mindful of this and allow them the space and time they need to come to terms with the relationship breakdown. Don't rush.
>
> *Louise Buttery, Family Law Partners*

Even if one parent is not present, as we know that this can be quite a challenging and emotive situation, it is important the absent parent is told, possibly in writing, exactly what was said at the meeting.

> *There are people and support lines you can contact, ordinary teens just like me that will always be a shoulder to cry on. Jade (17)*

We are separating

I have children but I am just about to separate. Do I need legal advice?

Yanoulla Kakoulli
Senior Associate, Judge & Priestley LLP

If you and your ex-partner agree on all aspects of your children's lives, including where they are to live and the amount of time they are to spend with the non-resident parent, the short answer to this question is you probably do not need legal advice.

However, if you are a father, it is important to find out whether you have parental responsibility. Parental responsibility is defined in section 3(1) Children Act 1989 as being:

> "All the rights, duties, powers, responsibilities and authority which by law a parent of a child has in relation to the child and his property".

In practical terms, when certain important decisions about the child's upbringing need to be made, all those with parental responsibility for the child are allowed to have a say in that decision. This includes but it is not limited to consenting to taking a child abroad for holidays or extended stays, deciding the child's education and where they go to school, consenting to a medical operation or certain treatment and deciding what religion a child will be brought up to practice. Mothers automatically have parental responsibility as do fathers who were married to the mother. Parental responsibility is not lost if the mother and father get divorced. Unmarried fathers do not automatically have parental responsibility but they can obtain parental responsibility by:

- having his name registered or re-registered on the birth certificate if his name is not already on the birth certificate as the father;

- entering into a parental responsibility agreement with the mother;

- obtaining a parental responsibility order from the family courts;

- having obtained a residence order prior to 22 April 2014;

- being named on a child arrangements order as a person with whom the relevant child is to live.

If you do not have parental responsibility and you wish to continue to be involved in your child's life, you should take legal advice to help you to obtain parental responsibility.

Parenting agreements

If you and your ex-partner do not agree on issues relating to the children, it is important to get legal advice early on so that you can be informed about your rights and how to achieve the best possible outcome for you and your children as quickly as possible. It is also helpful to get the assistance of a solicitor if you and your ex-partner are not on good terms. A solicitor can try to come to an agreement on your behalf by writing to your ex-partner setting out your proposals. If an agreement is reached this

We are separating

way, a solicitor can prepare a parenting agreement, which is sometimes referred to as a parenting plan. It is a written agreement between parents covering practical issues regarding the children such as living arrangements and when the children see the non-resident parent. Parenting agreements are not legally binding documents. However, they are helpful as they set out the arrangements clearly if they are prepared well. The general idea is that if arrangements are set out in black and white then they are less likely to break down and lead to disagreements. If the arrangements do break down and a court application needs to be made later on, a parenting agreement can also be a helpful way to clearly evidence you and your ex-partner's intentions at that time.

Mediation

Another way to try to come to an agreement with your ex-partner might be mediation. Mediation is when separated parents try to agree on the future arrangement of the children with the assistance of a neutral and trained third party. Often, a mediator will also have a legal background. Mediation is voluntary and so both parties need to be willing to participate for it to work. If you are not comfortable sitting with your ex-partner, many mediators offer "shuttle mediation", whereby you and your ex-partner will be in separate rooms. A mediator will take your proposals first then attend on your ex-partner in another room with your proposals in order to try to reach an agreement. If you are able to reach an agreement during mediation, a mediator can draw up your agreement in a document called a "memorandum of understanding". You should seek legal advice on this document before signing and agreeing to any final version. What is agreed and discussed during mediation is strictly confidential and will not be allowed to be placed before the court if court proceedings occur at a later stage. However, a solicitor can prepare a parenting agreement based on the memorandum of understanding. This parenting agreement can be disclosed to a court at a later stage if necessary.

There will be instances when mediation is not appropriate, for example if your matter is very urgent or if you are a victim of domestic abuse. Otherwise, before making an application to the court, you must first contact a mediator and arrange for a mediation, information and assessment meeting, commonly known as a "MIAM". You are required to attend this meeting to show that you have at least attempted to resolve the matter without going to court.

Before trying to reach an agreement whether through solicitors, in person or through mediation, it is important to approach the issues in a child focused way and be guided by what is in the children's best interests. Your children's welfare will also be the court's first consideration, above what you or your ex-partner want, on any application made in relation to them. In general, it will be in a child's best interests to spend time with both parents unless there are safeguarding issues whereby the child could be

> **Custody battle – STOP STOP STOP**
>
> This is the one of the worst phrases anyone can use when talking about child arrangements. The word 'custody' is outdated, incorrect and focusses on one parent having control over the other. The word 'battle' is aggressive and perpetuates the misconception that separated parents have to fight with each other to sort things out. Please stop using this language!

17

We are separating

at risk of harm if they were to spend time with a parent. If you believe there are safeguarding issues, you should immediately seek legal advice.

Of course, there may be instances where you will not be able to reach an agreement with your ex-partner or trying to reach an agreement without the court's assistance is not appropriate. If this is the case, you will need to make an application under section 8 of the Children Act 1989. Any court application should be a last resort as it is often expensive, time consuming and stressful. If you are thinking of applying to issue court proceedings, it is always better to get legal advice and representation as a solicitor will know the law and procedure. They will be best placed to prepare your application and represent you so as to achieve the best outcome.

Reaching agreement

At court, negotiations often take place before hearings outside the courtroom. Having legal representation can help to reach an early agreement between you and your ex-partner if possible. If an agreement is reached at court, it can be drafted into a consent order and the court can make it legally binding. It is crucial that this document is drafted clearly and well. Having a solicitor to draft such an order is extremely helpful as they will have the relevant drafting skills. An order drafted vaguely at court can lead to disagreements in the future - the matter may have to return to court to have issues clarified and the order re-drafted, all of which will incur further expense.

A mum once said to me;

"So he dropped this bombshell two weeks ago, he's leaving. Ever since then we've been talking more than we have in years and we seem to be closer than ever; but, he's still leaving. I'm so confused".

This is not uncommon, often the relief for the partner who's leaving is so great that they become more amenable to conversation. Sometimes the guilt of leaving creates an atmosphere of understanding and even closeness that may have been absent for years.

A mum or dad who wants to leave knows they have hurt their partner and this initial to-ing and fro-ing seems to be a way, for many to limit that hurt. However it is usually short lived as the reality sinks in.

Adele Ballantyne

I couldn't believe that my father, the man that taught me to love and to care, could leave my mother. I cried and cried for hours. Isaac (15)

We're not married. Does this mean mum gets the children?

James Maguire
Managing Director, Maguire Family Law

There is no automatic presumption that the children would stay with their mother if an unmarried couple separate. The focus should be on looking at the arrangements which best suit the children and always taking decisions which are in the children's best interests.

The court has recently introduced a new provision which means that if they are asked to decide the arrangements for a child, the court shall presume, unless the contrary is shown, that involvement of that parent in the life of the child concerned will further the child's welfare.

What can sometimes complicate matters is if the mother and the father have a different legal status in relation to the children. A mother always has parental responsibility for her child or children. This is not automatic for a father. Whether a father does or does not have parental responsibility can impact on the practical arrangements for a child's care. This does not, however, mean that the father should be excluded from the child's life.

What is Parental Responsibility?

Parental responsibility (PR) is defined as all the rights, duties, powers, responsibilities and authority which by law a parent of a child has in relation to the child and their property.

This includes all fundamental decisions as to what the child does presently and in the future; for example, where the child goes to school, what medical treatment the child can or cannot receive and what religion the child should follow.

The more significant a decision regarding a child's welfare, the more cooperation and discussion there should be between the adults who have PR.

If a father does not have PR then this could make it more difficult for him to ensure the child or children attend medical appointments or are enrolled at school, and he may find that he has to

---

Win/Lose – STOP

Family law is not about winning losing or scoring points against each other. The last thing families going through difficult times need is to feel like they are in a contest. Language like this increases the conflict between parents and can make the whole process much more stressful for everyone. The evidence that parental conflict damages children is overwhelming. We all need to start thinking about child focussed solutions and not which parent is going to come out on top.

We are separating

obtain the mother's authority.

How do I know if I have PR?
All mothers have PR.

All fathers who are married to the mother have PR even if their name is not on the birth certificate.

Unmarried fathers with children whose birth was registered after 1 December 2003 and whose name appears on the birth certificate have PR.

Those unmarried fathers who are not on the birth certificate or whose children had their births registered before 1 December 2003, do **not** have PR.

How can I acquire PR?
All is not lost for a father who does not have the automatic right to PR. It can be obtained in one of the following ways:

- Entering into a Parental Responsibility Agreement with the mother. The agreement must be in a prescribed form, signed and witnessed by a court official. This is the most straightforward option, but it does require cooperation from the child's mother.

- Re-registering the child's birth and having the father's name added. Again, an element of cooperation from the child's mother would be required.

- Applying to the court for PR. This may be a standalone application or it may be made as part of an application for a child arrangements order (see page 210 for more).

  When making a Parental Responsibility Order the court will look at the father's degree of commitment to the child, the state of the father's current relationship with the child and his reasons for making the application.

- A Child Arrangements Order providing that a child lives with their father (for any amount of time) also confers PR. Any decision taken by the court about where a child lives has to have regard to the child's welfare.

- Being appointed as a guardian either by the mother or the court, although in these cases the father will only assume PR on the mother's death.

- By marrying the mother. This grants PR to the father, even if the child was born before they got married.

Summary
The issues relating to PR and the rights of a parent can be complex. The law and court practice procedure can be difficult and it would be advised that where a person is confused about the rights they have as a parent they should seek family law advice from a solicitor.

There are no fixed presumptions as to who will care for a child or children once a relationship breaks down. In many cases, it is about dealing with the practicalities first - for example, one parent may mainly stay at home to provide care whilst the other parent works long hours, possibly away from the family home.

I have decided to leave the family home. Does this have implications?

Jessica Palmer
Partner, Streathers

Upon separation, it can often be tempting to leave the family home to avoid tension and conflict but there are a number of reasons why you should think very carefully before doing so. It can cause various issues financially, practically and emotionally which you should always consider before deciding to leave.

Economy of scale

Unless you are able to stay with friends or family, you will have to pay rent and utilities on a second property which for many people is unaffordable and the money spent will not be recoverable at a later stage. This situation could continue for a prolonged period of time which could lead to significant debts being incurred. This is not in anyone's best interests as it decreases the amount of assets available to meet both parties' needs.

Practical and emotional consequences

If you have children and they remain with your spouse in the family home then in some cases it can lead to difficulties with contact arrangements. You are no longer seeing your children every day and the parent they are living with is likely to automatically be seen as the primary carer which could put you at a disadvantage should there ever be a dispute about who the children should live with. The children will also have emotional ties to the family home so it can lead to them preferring to spend more time there than in temporary accommodation they are not used to.

If your spouse has a new partner, there is a danger that they could end up moving into the home or spending a significant

> "Allow your children to have a different opinion to your own. In fact, allow anyone (friends, family and your children) to have their own opinion on both your ex-partner and the circumstances of your separation. They can't share your hurt and trying to make them do so will only harm them as well as your relationships.
>
> *Diane, Mum*"

amount of time there. This could create an increased level of hostility between you and your spouse which in turn impacts upon the children.

You will lose control over the practical care of the home which could lead to it deteriorating into a state of disrepair and there being a decrease in value of the property, the loss of which you would struggle to recover in the long run. As well as the deterioration in value, it could also make the property more difficult to sell leaving you in a state of limbo for a longer period of time.

We are separating

If the property is to be sold as part of the financial settlement, the spouse living there could cause difficulties with arranging viewings and presenting the property for sale which can create further delay.

Many people leave the property without taking all of their personal belongings with them. This is usually for practical reasons such as lack of storage or the means to transport them. However, you may find that it becomes tricky to get these items back as they are no longer in your possession. Although legally you own them, you could face yourself being denied access to obtain them or they could be disposed of without your permission. Often these items have sentimental value and cannot be replaced.

Tactical implications

Often you can end up being 'out of sight out of mind.' The spouse remaining in the property can lose all incentive and impetus to resolve the longer term financial issues because they remain comfortable where they are.

If this is the case, you could find yourself having to make an application to court for the property to be sold or transferred which is not only a long process but can also costs thousands of pounds. If you are in the home still, you are more likely to ensure that your spouse has the same desire to resolve matters sooner rather than later for the benefit of everyone involved.

Are there other options?

It is important to consider whether there are any other options available to you first before moving out of the home. For example, is there a spare room? Are you able to shift the living arrangements around to accommodate sleeping somewhere else?

If you are thinking of leaving the home as a result of your spouse's abusive behaviour then you should seek advice first on whether you could apply for an occupation order which forces them to leave and allows you to stay in the home.

Steps to take if you feel you have no option but to move out

Be sure of your legal standing with the property. If your name is not on the legal title then you must register your matrimonial home rights over the property.

Gather any documents for you and the children that you think you may need going forward such as your marriage certificate, birth certificates, bank statements etc. It is also useful to take an inventory of items that are there when you leave and you should take any personal items, particularly those of sentimental value, in case your spouse disposes of them without consent. If you are an international couple then it is also important to consider where the children's passports should be kept.

Before leaving, try and begin putting in place a pattern of time you spend with the children i.e. certain days at the weekend or during the week. This will then make the transition when you have left easier and be more natural for the children.

Ensure that your new accommodation is attractive and adequate for the children to stay in or it could create difficulties with contact going forward.

Manipulation and mistruths are common - get proper advice to make informed decisions.

Carol-Anne Baker, Bridge Law Solicitors Limited

Common law marriage is a common myth

Catherine Bell
Consultant, Hall Brown

Many people believe that 'common law marriage' is a legally binding entity. Sadly, it's just a myth, and the reason that's sad is because many unmarried couples rely on it.

The truth is that unmarried couples who live together have few rights in relation to each other's property, regardless of how long they've been cohabiting. If a couple in a marriage or civil partnership have a relationship breakdown, the courts will aim to divide the party's assets 'fairly'. This isn't the case when an unmarried cohabiting couple separate. In this situation, the person who owns the property in their name will be entitled to it (subject to some limited situations where the other person could make a claim).

If you separate, and the property you share with your partner is not in your name, then you could find yourself, at worst, homeless. This would be particularly devastating if you've been with your partner for many years and you have children together. You could be left with very little.

Yet there is a solution.

A cohabitation agreement can give you security

The solution is to make a cohabitation agreement at the beginning of your relationship and when you consider the relationship serious, for example, buying a property together, when you have children, in case you ever separate.

People often don't think about what could happen to them if their relationship were to break down until it's too late. That's why it's a good idea for both of you to make a cohabitation agreement now, while you're still enjoying a good relationship. Think of it as an insurance policy; it covers something you don't want to happen but means you'll be protected if it does.

A cohabitation agreement records what you and your cohabiting partner have agreed should happen if your relationship ends and you no longer want to live together. The agreement will be unique to you and

---

All parents dread telling their children that they are separating.

"Tell them the truth and what they need to know" is good advice.

So too is acknowledging that this will be a process and that you may have the same or similar conversations with your children over the forthcoming weeks and months as they discover for themselves what this really means.

We are separating

your partner and it should at least cover property ownership, finances and arrangements for any children from your relationship. Provided you both agree, you can include whatever matters to you - including who keeps the pets!

For the agreement to be legally binding, it's important that each of you has independent legal advice in case the other person later alleges the agreement was made under duress, and you were forced into it. There also should be time for each of the parties to consider the terms with their advisers, including their accountant/tax adviser, if necessary.

Incidentally, you don't have to be in a relationship with the person you are living with to have a cohabitation agreement. If you're sharing a house with someone, it's still a practical safeguard, for example if two friends buy a house together.

Other ways to protect your future

Making a cohabitation agreement is not the only step you can take to ensure both you and your partner are protected if you separate. It's worth thinking about a declaration of trust and you must also look at your wills.

A declaration of trust concerns property ownership. It sets out who owns what and in what proportion, and can be very important if you and your partner are buying a property but not both contributing the same amount to the purchase price.

The reason each of you should make a will is because the intestate rules (which apply when someone dies without a will) don't provide any right of inheritance for a cohabitee. So, if you want your estate, which includes your property, to pass to your partner on death, you need to specifically state this in your will. And of course, your partner will need to do the same.

Happy ever after

Cohabiting couples are often unaware they have fewer rights than their married counterparts. However, I hope this article has shown you that there are safeguards you can put in place and how important it is to get advice.

The lack of public awareness about the limited rights of cohabiting couples, and what can be done to provide peace of mind, led Resolution to spearhead a national campaign. rights and avoiding disputes.

Go to https://resolution.org.uk/campaigning-for-change/awareness-raising-week/ so you can look at when Cohabitation Awareness week is in their raising awareness week campaign.

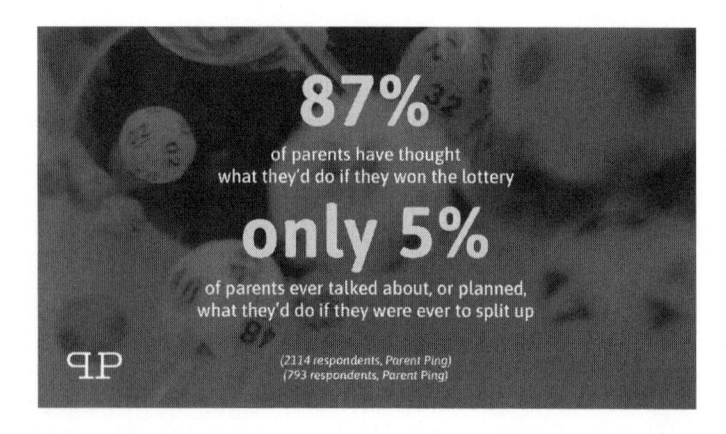

87%
of parents have thought what they'd do if they won the lottery

only 5%
of parents ever talked about, or planned, what they'd do if they were ever to split up

(2114 respondents, Parent Ping)
(793 respondents, Parent Ping)

What 'no-fault' divorce means and how it is different from how things were before

Sarah Whitelegge
Senior Consultant, Myerson

The introduction of the Divorce, Dissolution and Separation Act 2020 has changed the law relating to divorce and dissolution of civil partnerships.

The Act came into force on 6 April 2022 and introduces 'no-fault divorce' in that it is now possible to apply for a divorce or dissolution of a civil partnership by providing a simple statement of irretrievable breakdown of the marriage or civil partnership.

With the introduction of no-fault divorce, most applications will likely be undisputed and the court will not need to consider the reason for the breakdown of the marriage or civil partnership.

Old Law
Divorces that started on or before 5 April 2022 will continue to progress under the old law.

Prior to no-fault divorce, in establishing the irretrievable breakdown of the marriage, the person applying for a divorce had to rely upon one of five facts:

- Adultery
- Unreasonable behaviour
- Desertion
- Two years separation with consent
- Five years separation

Unless you had been separated for two years or more and your spouse consented to the divorce, or you had been separated for five years or more, the party applying for the divorce was required to show grounds for divorce.

Do both parties have to agree to a no-fault divorce?
It is no longer possible to defend an application for a divorce or dissolution of a civil partnership, save in circumstances where there is a dispute in respect of jurisdiction or the validity of a marriage or civil partnership.

This means that one party can make an application on their own, even if their spouse or civil partner does not necessarily agree with the divorce.

What has changed?
Some of the other changes introduced include the following:

- Joint applications can be made, and couples can apply together for a divorce or a dissolution of a civil partnership.

- There is a new timeframe of six months. This is made up of a minimum period of 20 weeks from the application being issued until the conditional order can be applied for, and a further

We are separating

six week period from the conditional order and when the order can be made final.

- The language relating to divorce and dissolution has been updated. 'Petitioner' has been renamed 'Applicant', 'Decree Nisi' has become 'Conditional Order' and 'Decree Absolute' becomes 'Final Order'.

Can behaviour be taken into consideration when sorting out the finances or arrangements for the children?

When couples are going through a marriage or civil partnership breakdown, it is a highly emotive time. One party may blame the other if there has been adultery or if that party does not want to separate.

One party may feel that the outcome of the financial settlement should reflect the fact that their spouse or civil partner has behaved badly but the reasons for the breakdown of the marriage or civil partnership very rarely have an impact on the financial settlement.

When considering the arrangements for children, the starting point is that it is important for the children to have a relationship with both parents unless there are clear reasons as to why this would not be safe or in their best interests.

Can I claim costs?

Under the old law it was commonplace for the person applying for a divorce based on the fault of the other party (because of adultery, unreasonable behaviour or desertion) to ask the court to make an order that the other party pay the costs of the divorce.

With the introduction of no-fault divorce, the court's decision about whether to make a final divorce or dissolution order will not depend on the court making any findings about the responsibility of either party for the breakdown of the marriage.

This means that while the court will retain a discretion to make a costs order, the circumstances in which an order for costs will be appropriate are likely to be very limited.

It may still be relevant for the parties' litigation conduct to be considered, particularly if the court considers that the conduct of one party has been unreasonable.

Aside from cases where one party has behaved unreasonably in terms of their litigation conduct, a costs order will likely be inappropriate in an application for divorce or dissolution of a civil partnership where the parties have conducted the proceedings in a reasonable manner.

The new divorce and dissolution applications do not include any provision for applying for a cost order. This means that if you are seeking to apply for costs you will need to prepare a separate application notice and provide written evidence in support, setting out the grounds on which a cost order is sought.

An end to the blame game

Separated couples may have previously been reticent to start proceedings due to not wanting to place blame on their spouse or civil partner.

Now that the law has changed with the introduction of no-fault divorce, you may now feel that separating from your spouse or civil partner will be less acrimonious.

It is anticipated that no-fault divorce will help to reduce conflict and allow couples to focus on important matters, such as sorting out the arrangements for the children or finances. It is hoped that the new law will allow separating couples to work together collaboratively to resolve issues that arise on separation.

What is the law relating to the unmarried/cohabiting family?

Paul Summerbell
Senior Family Solicitor, Reeds LLP

There is a common public misconception that the unmarried/cohabiting couple enjoy similar rights to married couples. This is sometimes referred to as 'common law marriage' or 'common law husband/wife'. This is not the case and has no foundation in law. In financial terms those couples who marry and subsequently divorce have the benefit of the legal protections of the Matrimonial Causes Act 1973. Same sex couples enjoy the protections of the Civil Partnership Act 2004. There is no equivalent coherent body of law available to cohabitants. The law relating to cohabiting couples has developed in a piece meal fashion to deal with their arrangements on relationship breakdown. The legal position of a cohabitant on relationship breakdown *in financial terms* is as follows:

- There is no legal process to end the relationship.

- There is no legal duty to provide financial support (maintenance).

- Property issues (home) are addressed by taking civil proceedings in property and trust law (see below).

- There is no statutory right to occupy the home.

- Cohabiting couples do not inherit each other's property under the intestacy rules.

- Transfer of tenancy orders can be made in some circumstances under the Family Law Act 1996.

- Occupation of the home can be obtained by establishing a contractual licence or obtaining a property order in favour of children under the Children's Act 1989 or temporarily by an occupation order under the Family Law Act 1996.

- If a partner becomes bankrupt the sale of the home can be delayed only if there are dependent children and only for 12 months.

The legal position of a cohabitant on relationship breakdown *regarding children* is as follows:

- At birth the natural mother will have automatic parental responsibility for the children but the father does not unless he is named on the child's birth certificate, or by agreement with the mother or through a court order.

- Either parent can issue proceedings under the Children Act 1989 for an order relating to the children if they are the natural parent.

- Both parents have a duty to maintain the children and can make an application to the Child Support Agency or Child Maintenance Service and Schedule 1 of the Children Act 1989 for financial support.

We are separating

The main issue for many cohabitants, and the children, is what happens to the family home on the relationship breakdown. This depends on how the property is owned. If the property is held by both parties jointly as legal co-owners then the property cannot be sold or transferred without the consent of both parties. If it is not owned equally a declaration of trust should be used to specify the respective shares in the property. The TR1 form completed to convey the property can be crucial as it requires details of how the property is to be owned. It should be completed to reflect that ownership and the parties should be fully advised about how the property is to be held before completing this document. This is often referred to as an **express trust** as the details are fully or expressly documented.

The ownership of property is in two parts:

- Legal title - the person in whom the legal estate is vested.

- Beneficial interest - the person with co-ownership rights even though their name may not appear on the legal title of the property.

If the property is owned by one party the non-owning party must then establish a **constructive trust, resulting trust** or **proprietary estoppel**. In the **constructive trust** the non-owning party must establish by both words and conduct that they were led to believe that they had a beneficial interest in the property and that the non-owning party acted in reliance on this to their detriment. This could be by way of mortgage payments or improvements to the home. It can also be by deferring home security in the completion of the "occupier" form for the mortgage company financing the purchase of the home that allows the non-owning party to postpone those rights as against the mortgage company. This is a common form required by mortgage companies.

If a financial contribution was made to the purchase of the property the beneficial interest in the property will be allocated accordingly. This is known as a **resulting trust**.

Proprietary estoppel has been used to grant property rights in the past. Three preconditions apply:

- An assurance of an interest in property;

- Reliance on that assurance;

- Detriment suffered as a result.

This must be such as to allow the court to make an additional finding that it would be unconscionable to deny the claimant the relief sought. It is said to be easier to establish than a constructive common intention trust as it relies on a mere assurance rather than a common intention.

In deciding the share of the property which both parties may be entitled to in circumstances where a trust is found to exist there is wide discretion to look at the whole course of the dealings between the parties and to concepts of what is fair.

If legal action is required to determine an issue concerning the property of cohabitants i.e. where they cannot agree what is to happen to the property, proceedings are issued under section 14 of the Trusts of Land and Appointment of Trustees Act 1996. In reaching any decision the court will consider:

- The intention of the parties who created the trust;

- The purpose of the trust;

- The welfare of any minor who occupies the property as his home;

- The interest of any secured creditor.

It is worthy of note that in case law it has been stated that:

"The onus is on the person seeking to show that the beneficial ownership is different from the legal ownership. So in the non-owner cases, it is upon the non-owner to show that he had any interest at all".

How to protect the cohabitant (and children)

1. Enter into a Declaration of Trust when the property is purchased, specifying the shares in the property.
2. Make sure the TR1 form conveying the property is properly completed to reflect the ownership of the property.
3. Enter into a living/cohabitation agreement at the time of cohabitation to specify property ownership.
4. Negotiate to execute a transfer of property to properly reflect ownership of property.
5. If disagreements arise, negotiate the ownership of the property prior to using legal proceedings.
6. Ensure what life insurance provisions exist and that the cohabitant is catered for.
7. Ensure that each cohabitant has an up to date will.

Death

If the property is owned as joint tenants the property will pass to the other joint owner and the survivor becomes the sole owner of the property. If there is no will the cohabitant has no rights to inherit under the intestacy rules. However, if the survivor can show that they were maintained by the deceased before death a claim can be brought under the Inheritance (Provision for Family and Dependants) Act 1975.

THE FIRST CHAT ABOUT SEPARATION

This is a life changing moment; give it, and more importantly your partner, the time and respect they deserve.

- Pick a time and place where you can have an uninterrupted conversation.
- Prepare your partner by explaining that the conversation is important and essential.
- Try not to 'blurt it out' during a heated conversation. If possible choose a time when both of you are calm.
- Ensure that you have thought about what you want to say beforehand.
- Keep calm and breathe slowly, it will help!
- Try not to interrupt each other, wait until the other person has spoken.
- Really listen to each other.
- Check you have heard correctly by repeating what you thought you heard.
- Correct if it's not accurate.
- If either person becomes heated or angry call a time out and try again once you are both calm.
- Give your partner some space, allow the information to sink in, expect an outrage or silence.
- Talk again when they are ready to talk.

Adele Ballantyne

We are separating

My ex is a narcissist – do you have any tips for dealing with this personality type?

Dr Supriya McKenna
The Life Doctor

Karin Walker
KGW Family Law

Your views have been invalidated and ignored; your boundaries overstepped. You have been exploited, compared to others, argued with and demeaned. You are wondering who you even are, questioning your ability to make decisions. Perhaps you are worried you might be lured again by their charm? Perhaps, confused, you are wondering whether it is actually you who is the narcissist, as many do.

These days the word 'narcissism' is a buzzword. We use it to mean anyone who is a bit vain, mean or selfish. But true narcissism is actually Narcissistic Personality Disorder (NPD), and it is really important not to label your ex incorrectly, because separating from a real narcissist will mean you have a specific behaviour pattern to follow. Underlying that sense of superiority and entitlement is actually a person with a very fragile sense of self-esteem. They construct a false self (often a larger than life persona) to hide behind, an 'armour' which needs to stay intact. This armour is kept strong by validation from others; it prevents them having to face their own lack of self-worth. They need constant attention, all the time, in the form of adoration, drama or conflict. This is known as narcissistic supply. If this is the situation you are dealing with you have a rocky road ahead.

In separation, suddenly this armour has been breached and their less than perfect life, exposed. This causes 'narcissistic injury' triggering narcissistic rage. And everything that follows is as a result. Awareness of what is likely to happen is key to coping.

As this uncontrollable rage pores forth, a narcissist will try to annihilate their former partner in every way they can – financially, mentally, spiritually, even using the children as pawns to do so, weaponising them against you. They will bad mouth you to alienate the children from you. They may refuse to pay for them in order to financially punish you, not caring about the effect on them. They might enlist them to take items from your home or to feedback information about you. They may suggest that they live with them, even though very often they are terrible parents – selfish, demanding of attention and immature. They may even make false allegations of abuse.

Narcissists lack empathy – although they can pretend

> Separation can be a moment of crisis, and whilst it is important to draw on friends and family for support at this difficult time, it is also crucial to get sound professional advice.
>
> *Rob Parker, Lamb Brooks*

to feel another's pain, they actually just *can't care*. You will have to model empathy for your children, so that they develop it themselves.

Limiting contact to the bare minimum is essential. Only communicate in the written word, preferably by email, not in real time to their face or by phone. Never respond to communications immediately – calm down first, and see the ranting accusations for what they are – a ploy to rope you in to the drama you need. Consider whether you even have to reply at all, even to lies and attempts to discredit you. Do not be fooled by pity plays – they are just attempts to pull you back into the game that they must win.

Employ the 'grey rock technique': become as boring as you can to them, so that they slink off to find new sources of supply instead of you. If you have to see them, don't make eye contact. Speak in a dull monotone using as few words as possible. Take away all emotion, from the spoken and written word. They will most likely ramp up their bad behaviour at first, but do not be drawn in or let them push your buttons.

Finding the right lawyer to represent you is essential if you are divorcing a narcissist. You are looking for someone who understands what you are dealing with. If they don't, find someone who does. Ideally you would want to instruct a senior family lawyer, who has also trained further in mediation, hybrid mediation or arbitration. Your lawyer needs to have a *specific* understanding of NPD so that:

- they can *pre-empt* the behaviour which your ex will demonstrate rather than just react to them when they arise.

- they are aware of the financial and emotional abuse tactics that will be used.

- they do not unwittingly become tools of the narcissist's abuse.

- they can advise you on which 'out of court' methods of dispute resolution will work best (hybrid mediation and arbitration), giving you the best chance of staying out of court and minimising legal costs.

- they understand the emotional impact on you, and that you will be in a state of flight, fight or freeze which will hamper your decision-making ability.

- they recognise that the best outcome for you might be to get out of the relationship as quickly as possible rather than the best financial outcome which could take a long time to achieve.

- they can ensure that court orders are as 'loophole free' as possible to prevent the narcissist from exploiting you in the future.

- they understand the importance of achieving a 'clean break'.

- they understand the need for you not to react to the behaviour of the narcissist if you are to reduce the supply which you provide to them.

- child arrangements plans/orders are detailed and 'loophole free' to prevent the narcissist from using the children as weapons of post-separation abuse.

31

We are separating

It is essential that your lawyer understands that your ex does not want a quick resolution to the divorce, but rather to cause delay at every opportunity, providing them with more time to cause drama and chaos – a 'better than nothing' form of narcissistic supply.

When negotiating with your ex, your lawyer needs to understand that the narcissist needs to feel in control. Allow them to make decisions (such as selecting the hybrid mediator or arbitrator) when that decision does not make a difference. Ultimately the narcissist needs to feel as though they have won (or at least had the last word). If you are aware of this and stay 'two steps ahead', in reality it is you who have taken control away from them.

Narcissists are rule breakers, and have little respect for the law. In practice they are rarely punished for such course of action. The family court does not deliver retribution for bad behaviour unless it is really extreme. Narcissists can be charming and plausible. They play the 'victim' with aplomb – and sadly, are likely to be believed. So if you can, stay out of court.

Breaking free from a narcissist is a momentous act of courage and, although there is no true justice in divorce with a narcissist, there is a huge opportunity for growth and true happiness. Be strong. It will be worth it.

Supriya and Karin are the co-authors of '**Divorcing a Narcissist – The Lure, The Loss And The Law**' and '**Narcissism and Family Law – A Practitioner's Guide**' both published by Bath Publishing in 2020.

When relationships go wrong and arguments occur it can be worrying for both parents, especially when children are around.

Deciding to leave is a big upheaval but for some it is the only option, especially if there is violence or emotional abuse.

There are a few strategies to try if there is no violence/abuse, before you move out;

- Agree not to argue when the children are around

- If you are talking and things begin to escalate, agree to take a 'time out'

- Perhaps relationship therapy might help you to have the most difficult conversations

Reassure your children that although you are not getting on at the moment you are trying to resolve things. Remind them it's not their fault and that you both love them.

Adele Ballantyne

I'm still learning about the mistakes my parents made and I'm still learning how to better myself. Anonymous (20)

Divorce/separation and the use of social media

Amanda Adeola
Partner, BHP Law

As a family lawyer who uses social media to inform and educate my audience, I have seen, and I am sure many of you would also have come across, posts, comments and opinions on various family law related issues which are shared and adjudicated upon by the court of public opinion.

In any discussions with my clients, I always stress, at the outset, the importance of keeping matters private, with your family law related issues remaining just that - within your family. Using social media as a tool to antagonise, elicit support and reaction, abuse and indirectly attack your spouse/partner should be avoided and more significantly so where children are concerned. The internet never forgets as they say - you may post something in the heat of the moment and later delete it - however, somewhere in the abyss it can be found, so be mindful.

A paramount consideration should be how any child of the relationship will feel in the future coming across posts where their parents have been disparaging towards each other or waging a war of words indirectly to draw attention to the fact that there is a breakdown of the relationship.

Do not get me wrong - social media has its advantages such as raising awareness of important issues in real time and sharing of information that can support many in various aspects of the law, for example highlighting key issues such as domestic abuse and the support available to survivors. But it also has its disadvantages. In family disputes, there are many disadvantages to its use which must always be at the fore of the minds of all individuals. Issues I have come across over the years have included the following:

1. Providing details of an ongoing case including names of children and the location of a hearing, which is prohibited;

2. A celebratory post about a recent job role being acquired when dealing with issues around maintenance, but this information was not voluntarily disclosed, despite the ongoing duty to disclose in these types of cases;

3. An update of relationship status which was crucial information in a financial remedy matter;

4. An abusive post which had a negative impact on the person who was a target of the post;

> It's your life; be careful who you take advice from as others may have their own agenda.
>
> *Carol-Anne Baker, Bridge Law Solicitors Limited*

We are separating

5. Posting photographs of children of the family which is not agreed by all those involved with concerns around the impact of this.

These are just a few examples which caused the court a great deal of concern and indeed those involved.

So, before you take to social media to seek for spectators to be judge and jury of your family law dispute, I would urge all individuals to pause, breathe, and reflect. Consider the impact the action you are about to take will have and the ripple effect of this on all. Remember that what you post may be admitted as evidence and it just takes one person to take a screenshot before you delete it. Think of the long-term implications of that post, comment, or narrative that you are presenting about your circumstances. What you share may also undermine your case.

My view remains that sharing personal details of your family law issue on social media should be avoided when a relationship breaks down. Anger can get in the way as emotions are often high. I am not suggesting that you do not use social media at all - just be cautious about what you share and if you have any concerns about your case, then speak to your lawyer who will be able to provide you with advice tailored to your circumstances.

Do you need help with your situation? Understanding your legal and mediation options could save time, money and unnecessary stress.

Check the OnlyMums/Dads Panel www.thefamilylawpanel.org to find the leading family law and mediation specialists and a range of pricing options and free family law clinics.

The Panel member will set out your options and stop you taking the M6 when you could be on the M4!

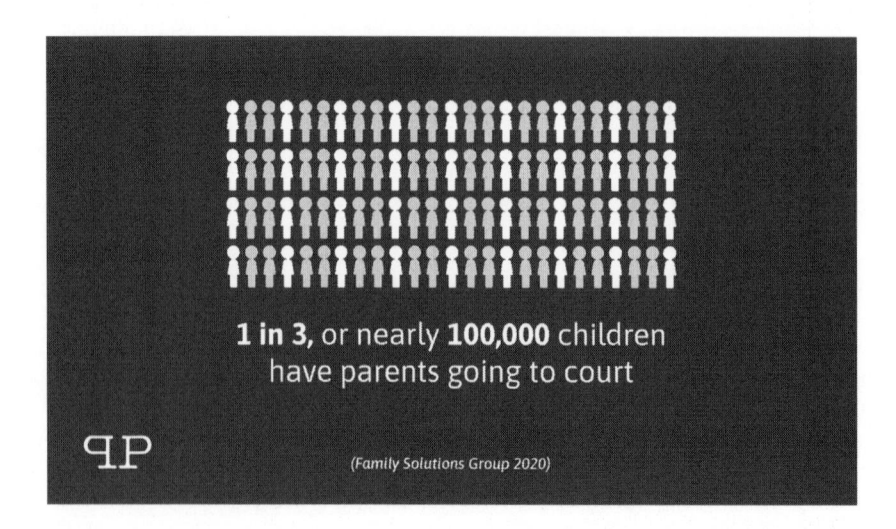

---

1 in 3, or nearly **100,000** children have parents going to court

(Family Solutions Group 2020)

My partner is having an affair and wants to divorce. What are my options?

Helen Pittard
Director, 174 Law Solicitors

We have had the biggest overhaul of our divorce system for over 50 years which came into force in April 2022, the aim of this being to introduce a "no-fault" divorce process, so as to remove any element of blame and reduce conflict. The overriding objective is to minimise the risk of emotional harm on children which is often caused by parental conflict, and prevent the legal process from adding to the heightened emotions otherwise associated with allegations previously needed within the old system.

There are always pros and cons with any legal changes and with the new divorce process, if one spouse wishes to divorce the other, then they can proceed under the new regime in any event. The only ground for a divorce is that the marriage has irretrievably broken down and there is no defence to this. So, if your partner intends to proceed with this then there is very little that can be done unless there is a jurisdictional defence preventing the divorce from proceeding.

The question is therefore: if there is to be a divorce, what role do you wish to play in it?

Under the new regime you can have a sole Applicant or you can both apply as joint Applicants. This can again help to reduce any animosity and help you to work together when you are looking to address matters such as the children or your financial affairs. If you start the process as joint Applicants then you must work together throughout the whole of the divorce process unless you apply to the court for a change to a sole application.

> " Once you've decided there is no going back, stop trying to score points over your ex and concentrate on the positives for the children.
>
> *Vicki, Mum*

Either way, whoever issues, there will be a one off divorce issue fee (currently £593) which will need to be paid unless you are exempt due to you being on a low income. In this case you will need to apply for an application for exemption from fees when you submit your application for the divorce. If your application is successful, all of your fees or some may be remitted.

I want to issue divorce proceedings. Can I get my partner to pay my legal and court fees?

Under the new procedure, you cannot make an application for your partner to pay your legal fees. However, there is no reason why you cannot engage in dialogue with your partner

We are separating

to try and agree how you are to divorce and how this is to be funded. It may be you can agree for this to be funded between you equally or if it is your partner who wants the divorce they may well be prepared to fund the whole process. If you don't feel you are able to have this dialogue between you directly then this could be done in mediation.

Do I need a lawyer to help me issue proceedings?

No you don't. The system is now all online and has been simplified immensely. It is therefore a matter for you as to whether or not you wish to be supported by a lawyer through this process. However, it is always important to remember the divorce has legal implications which affect your financial rights and therefore you need to ensure you protect your interests in this respect. There may well be jurisdiction issues you need to be aware of or there may be benefits to you issuing proceedings in a different country where appropriate, so in these sorts of cases, I would always suggest you seek some legal advice before you embark upon any legal process.

How long will a divorce take?

Once the application has been made online the court will notify your partner who will be given access to the online portal to see the application and acknowledgement service, confirming that the documents have been received and whether they believe there are any jurisdictional grounds upon which they can base a defence. Once this has been done your partner does not need to play any further role within the divorce unless of course you make a joint application.

The next steps are for you to apply for a conditional order which is a declaration that your marriage has irretrievably broken down. You cannot apply for this until 20 weeks has elapsed since the date your application was issued and the application has also been acknowledged or you can otherwise prove to the court that your ex has been served with the application. You may need to ask the court for an order for deemed service if this is the case. The court will notify you of the dates upon which you can make this application but it is wise to diarise such dates in any event.

It is hoped this 20 week period gives you sufficient time to address any arrangements and co-parenting plans for your children, and your financial affairs such as what will happen to the family home and pensions. You are encouraged to resolve such matters via an out of court dispute resolution process such as mediation and to seek some legal advice. The courts are

---

MAKING HASTY DECISIONS

It can be really easy to make a hasty decision, especially during an argument.

When making decisions, remember that one of you is coping with a bombshell, even if you think it's been obvious for ages that things are not OK.

Take time when making important decisions - there is no hurry to decide in the moment. Waiting a week or two and having conversations will really help in the long run.

Often hasty decisions are made when feelings are running high. We often see things differently once we have calmed down.

Adele Ballantyne

not in a position to approve any financial arrangement you agree between you until you have your conditional order so it is always important to remember these time frames.

You cannot apply for the final stage of the divorce, called the final order, until 6 weeks and one day after the date your conditional order has been made. Once your final order is made, you are no longer a spouse. This impacts upon many financial issues such as a widow/er's pension within any pension scheme, inheritance tax, who your next of kin is and also any will you may have made. This is why it is important to understand the legal implications of the dissolution of your marriage or civil partnership and to seek some legal advice in this respect.

It is always important to remember that, from a legal perspective, when you refer to a divorce this relates solely to the status of your marriage or civil partnership and does not deal with matters relating to your children or your finances.

Orders relating to children

Although children are not parties to the divorce, they are often deeply affected by the breakdown of the marriage or civil partnership. Since April 2014, the consideration of any children has been removed from the divorce process itself. Consequently, parents are left to pursue appropriate remedies separately in the event of there being a dispute. If there is a dispute in relation to the children following the divorce, it is open to either party to make an application under s8 Children Act 1989 and there are three different types of orders which can be applied under this:-

1. Child Arrangements Order – used to regulate when or with whom a child is to live or spend time with.

2. Prohibited Steps Order – an order that no step that could be taken by a parent in meeting their parental responsibility for a child, and which is of a kind specified in the order, shall be taken without consent of the court.

3. Specific Issue Order – giving directions for the purpose of determining a specific question which has arisen or which may arise in connection with any aspect of parental responsibility for a child.

Each of these orders will determine a particular matter relating to the child's upbringing and last until the child reaches the age of 16 (or 18 in exceptional circumstances). However, you are encouraged, where

> Time is never on your side. Getting the right advice at an early stage is crucial to a separation.
>
> Inayat Nadat, Nadat Solicitors

appropriate, to try and resolve these matters between yourselves or through mediation, and the Government have recently introduced a family mediation voucher scheme which will contribute up to £500 towards your mediation costs to help you to resolve your child arrangements. This voucher is non-means assessed. Legal aid is also available for mediation for those who qualify.

When parties separate, it is necessary to also consider your financial affairs in order to sever any financial ties. There are a number of financial orders available to spouses and/or children under the MCA 1973 upon marriage breakdown. However, as financial provision between spouses is closely linked with provision for any children, it is also important to appreciate the impact of the Child Support Act 1991 in that the court does not have jurisdiction to make child maintenance orders save for

We are separating

a significant minority of cases. The Child Maintenance Service is the body responsible for assessing child maintenance in the absence of any agreements and we would recommend you visit their website for more details relating to the calculation of child maintenance (www.gov.uk). The court, therefore, retains jurisdiction to deal with cases in which the CMS has no jurisdiction, for example, in relation to step-children and children who are too old to be qualifying children.

Orders relating to finances

The powers of the court to make financial orders fall into two main categories; income orders and capital orders.

Income orders are:

- maintenance pending suit;
- periodical payments; and
- secured periodical payments.

Capital orders are more diverse and include:

- lump sum orders;
- property adjustment orders;
- orders for sale;
- pension sharing orders; and
- pension sharing compensation orders.

Spouses may apply for any of these orders, or indeed all of them, on or after filing of the divorce petition. However, with the exception of maintenance pending suit, orders cannot be made until the conditional order and no order will take effect until the final order. By contrast, most applications for provision for children may be made and heard at any time, and such orders take immediate effect. Again, we would encourage mediation as a means of addressing such issues where appropriate.

In most cases, the arrangements for financial provision for a spouse are finalised after the divorce itself has gone through. However, parties should take care to apply for financial provision before remarrying otherwise you may be debarred from making any such applications.

Parents: Whenever possible, stick to the plans you make that involve your children. Bridie (22)

Family Separation Support Hub
A national signposting service

The starting point for anyone going through a separation or divorce.

www.familyseparationsupporthub.org

What is the role of friends in separation?

Charlotte Friedman
Psychologist, Author of Breaking Upwards

One of the definitions of a friend is someone you can rely on.

Before you separate you believe that your friends will remain with you giving unconditional support. It probably never occurred to you that any of your friends would be a casualty of separation - understandably, it is something that you never gave any thought to.

Friendships during a long term relationship are complicated. Some of them might have grown out of the relationship i.e. friends you made together as a couple and other friends might be those that each of you brought with you.

Unfortunately there are so many other unforeseen losses involved in separation apart from the relationship and often one of them is that some friends fall by the wayside. Of course, that is particularly painful when, pre-separation, you had no reason to doubt them.

It is truly painful and shocking when you discover that good friends aren't as available to you as they have been or that they seem more interested in pursuing a friendship with your ex rather than you. It is difficult but not terminal if you can see it as part of the shake-up of separation.

Concentrate on those people who are loyal to you who deserve your appreciation and thought, not the ones who can't accommodate change. Those 'friends' who see their bread buttered by choosing your ex rather than you don't really understand the meaning of true friendship. It is important not to become preoccupied by it.

Some friends are simply too short sighted to maintain a friendship post-separation. When you come up for air you will see that the friends who have stayed are the important ones and there are many more waiting in the wings willing to share their experiences and their similar values with you and create with you new stories and memories.

Change

Change is extremely painful and frightening but out of it comes new choices and life. There is a choice to be made

---

Support yourself. Confide in close friends and relatives while going through the process of separation. Don't be afraid of telling them what they can do to help you - they will want to help in any way they can. Factor in some 'me time' each day, even if it's just a few minutes to sit and read a book or go for a walk to clear your head.

Louise Buttery, Family Law Partners

We are separating

when you are a bit further down the line from the shock or grief of new separation. That choice is how you wish to live your life which includes the type of people that you want to have in it. Those friends who have deserted you are probably not as good as you thought they were.

There are all sorts of friendships and some people are only in it for what you provide for them. Once that is turned around and you need something from them, you may not see them for dust. You don't need people like that in your life. It is a matter of adjusting to the new order of things.

Real friends stick around, can bear you telling the story of your pain over and over again and go out of their way to support you. Those friends need to be celebrated, a story of real connection and meaning. Real friends know how to give and take and can stay around when the chips are down. It doesn't matter if you are left with one or ten; the quality of your friendship is what is important.

What is important in a friend?

Make a list of what is important to you in a friend. Match that list against those you know and value the ones that meet your needs and wishes. Everyone else is unimportant. Sometimes people need you more than you need them but when you separate it is your turn to call in the help. If a really important friend of yours has fallen short and just can't be there for you, it is part of the loss of separation and something to be mourned. Inevitably, there are casualties but it is not just the end of something - it is truly the beginning of something new.

Your friend's job post-separation is to help you get back a sense of self-esteem and remind you that you matter to them and others. It is their role to listen to you and be there for you, whatever you need. If they can't do that, they are not worth it. They need to listen without pushing their own agenda. They may have all sorts of views about what you should feel about your ex, but it is more helpful to you if they can give you the space to express what you feel.

'Friendly' advice?

Friends, also without meaning to be hurtful, can try to get you to 'get over it' or 'move on'. Although they may have good intentions, it would help if you could tell them what you need from them and that you will be ready to get over it, but only when you feel you are.

Sometimes even a good friend needs guidance on how to manage you in a crisis. A good friend will adapt to what you need.

If you have a friend who is dependable, non-judgemental and willing to listen, then you are going to be just fine.

> I fell out with friends, they didn't understand. Anon (20)

Recognising and dealing with stress

Dylan Watkins
GP at Leatside Surgery, Totnes

What do they say the big life stresses are?

Moving house, having a child, divorce, bereavement, losing a job... People commonly quote them but it is hard to pin down actually which ones are worse - there seem so many.

The first for most I think is the life stress of having kids. Having a family can be unbelievably stressful. The kids are of course our greatest joy and delight too but the strain that parenting can put on a relationship is a great risk.

The second is then the separation. If you've got to the point where that is the best option then you have usually tried various means of compromise and getting along: perhaps been to Relate or a counsellor. By the time you get to separation this has been going on a while and you will invariably be suffering the strain of a stressful situation.

Third then is negotiating terms with your ex-partner: the house, finances and access rights.

Fourth is moving house. It happens so much in any separation and is hugely disruptive in your lives but stressful emotionally too.

How do you recognise that you are stressed though?

It isn't like being stressed for an exam - that, I think, you feel as a stressed brain. In life-stresses the body often reveals the stress more than the mind. You can be so busy telling yourself you are OK in a situation that you don't recognise the tightness in the chest, the tremor and sweaty palms or the butterflies in the stomach for what they are. Disturbed sleep begins to kick in and tiredness with it. Fatigue just exacerbates the response to the stresses you are under.

Once stress begins to take hold, it can get out of control unless some kind of help is sought.

The pressures can tip over into depression, depression being more than just some sad, bleak thoughts, but something deeper and more pervasive.

The Royal College of Psychiatrists has made a list of typical symptoms someone with clinical depression might suffer. They might:

- feel unhappy most of the time (but may feel a little better in the evenings);
- lose interest in life and can't enjoy anything;
- find it harder to make decisions;
- not be able to cope with things that they used to;
- feel utterly tired;
- feel restless and agitated;
- lose appetite and weight (some people find they do the reverse and put on weight);
- take 1 to 2 hours to get off to sleep, and then wakes up earlier than usual;
- lose interest in sex;
- lose their self-confidence;
- feel useless, inadequate and hopeless;

We are separating

- avoid other people;
- feel irritable;
- feel worse at a particular time each day, usually in the morning;
- think of suicide.

I think it is a pretty good list. If you scan down the list going "Yes, yep, that one too…" then it really is time to consider getting some advice.

As a GP people come to discuss their problems with me at all sorts of points along this line.

I couldn't say if it is right or wrong to go to the GP earlier or later. We are all individuals with different backgrounds and we each, individually, seek help when we need to. A high proportion of GPs have been divorced or separated so they can usually empathise pretty well: and if they haven't themselves been through it they will likely have a colleague who has.

It doesn't have to be the GP that you talk to of course. Anyone who is a good listener can be great to offload on. There is something more though, I think, to be gained from talking with someone trained to listen and help you find your way forward. Whether that is a counsellor, doctor or priest… it doesn't matter.

I know what I do as a GP though. I will try to understand the problem and get its context. I will try to gauge where on the scale of anxiety or depression or stress scale my patient is at that point. I will then attempt to tailor my suggestions to the individual: in terms of helping them understand where they are at emotionally and understand how this might have come about. I'm not trying to be a marriage guidance counsellor, but I might try to ascertain what my patient really wants as an outcome and to try to see if it feels achievable.

GPs can signpost patients on to support: counselling especially. If the stress symptoms are stronger, then most places now in the UK have easy access to psychological therapies; especially Cognitive Behavioural Therapy (CBT). This is often accessible by self-referral. Check your GP's website or search for "CBT self referral" in your local area.

Often I do prescribe some sort of medication.

Sleeping pills seem most helpful in the short term. Getting some sleep can be terribly regenerative.

SSRI antidepressant drugs are demonised in the press sometimes, but in my experience really can bolster your emotional state. I don't like to prescribe them long term, but find that using them for a spell when the stresses are most high can make a real difference. They counteract anxiety as well as lift mood a little. In my experience they can begin to work within just a day or two. They seem to have very few side effects, especially when used for shorter spells.

For severe anxiety there is diazepam. I don't tend to prescribe it a whole lot but it can be used for situational stress. (Mostly for fear of flying or going in an MRI scanner). My worry with diazepam is that it may cloud the mind or judgement more than the SSRI pills so perhaps not best if you are stressed about attending court or similar.

I know GPs say they are busy, but you are the patient and if you recognise stress in yourself then starting to talk about it sooner rather than later with your GP is probably best.

We don't judge anyone, ever, for coming in feeling the effects of stress, so get talking sooner in the process.

Samaritans

About Samaritans

Samaritans offer a safe place for you to talk any time you like, in your own way - about whatever's getting to you. You don't have to be suicidal.

Samaritans volunteers are available any time, from any phone. You can call the free helpline number, 116 123, and it will not appear on your phone bill. You can also contact Samaritans volunteers via email at jo@samaritans.org or go to www.samaritans.org/branches to find details of your nearest branch.

Reaching out for help when you are feeling low can be extremely hard. The feelings that can push you into (and keep you) in a low place - shame, loneliness, depression, low self-esteem, anger - can act as barriers to stop you opening up and getting the help you need.

Ironically, this is the time you particularly need support and someone to listen to you. It can be the first step on the path that leads to a better life. Suicide and suicidal feelings are very complex, and vary from individual to individual, but generally they grow in isolation and are fed by silence.

Volunteers

Samaritans has more than 20,000 volunteers who are available to help anytime, and can be contacted free from any phone. They know it is difficult to reach out, sometimes particularly for men, and they do their best to make it easier.

The charity, which was set up more than 60 years ago to prevent suicide, not only has a free-to-callers helpline, available night and day, but you can also contact the volunteers by email, or visit your nearest for branch for face-to-face help (see the side panel for contact details).

Samaritans' volunteers keep what you tell them confidential and they don't judge, and you can choose what you tell them and what you don't. They say that is one of the main reasons people get in touch, because they feel safer talking to someone who does not know them and does not have the emotional expectations associated with family and friends.

Suicidal thoughts

Often there isn't one main reason why someone decides to take their own life, and suicidal thoughts are common - one in five people who responded to the NHS Mental health and Wellbeing (2014) said they had felt suicidal. It's how you manage feeling low that is a key thing.

Often feeling suicidal it is a result of problems building up to the point where you can't see past them, and you can think of no other way to cope with what you are experiencing. There is also a critical voice that can sit on your shoulder and compares your life to others, to your detriment.

A suicidal crisis will pass - feeling this way often only lasts for a short period of time. Talking can really help you to find a way through, and this is why Samaritans would encourage anyone who is feeling low to reach out for help.

Another issue that affects men is that they tend to compare themselves to a 'gold standard' of masculinity and when they don't achieve this, they can experience a sense of shame

Organisations

and defeat. There is also evidence that men find it more difficult to reflect on what's happening to them, which stops them reaching out for help.

Other factors, such as financial pressures, can also raise the risk of someone becoming suicidal. Deprivation, poor education, income, housing and unemployment can all contribute to suicide risk; men from lower socio-economic groups are at ten times greater risk of suicide.

Psychiatric illness such as depression can also increase suicide risk; but it is important to remember that the majority of those who suffer from depression will not take their own lives - suicide is not an inevitable outcome of mental illness.

Relationship difficulties

Relationships difficulties are in the top five most quoted reasons for contacting a Samaritans volunteer. Our close relationships are fundamental to our well-being - especially those with partners, spouses and children.

If relationships go wrong, you can be thrown into turmoil, and it can be difficult to function normally. Emotional pain is as real as physical pain and getting through the day can become a major undertaking if you are dealing with a breakup or separation.

Another consequence of relationship problems and separation is that you may not live with your children full time, so there is the emotional pain of missing them to deal with, plus the practical arrangements and the challenge of sustaining the relationship with them.

When you are in a difficult place emotionally it can be hard to see your life objectively and realise you need help. You don't need to feel lonely and isolated when there is help available, and the message to remember is that you might feel very alone, but you are not.

Once you have made the decision to leave, you may not understand that your partner is at a completely different point. They may think there's nothing wrong with the relationship or may believe that you are both still working on it.

'Theory of mind' refers to the ability to put yourself in someone else's shoes. That is, to see the world from their point of view. Use this innate ability to help you manage the conversation about leaving.

Be clear, be concise, don't use clichés, don't be disingenuous. Explain what has been going through your mind preceding your decision, but try not to use blaming statements, shun responsibility or excuse.

All of this will make your partner feel less attacked and therefore less defensive, and they will be more able to listen and process the information. It is so tempting to keep talking, but leave silences so that your partner can ask questions. You are also less likely to talk yourself into a difficult position.

Finally, write down your main points so that you can refer to them should you start feeling fuzzy headed as the emotional heat goes up.

Adele Ballantyne

We are separating

How can technology help parents and children cope after separation?

Melanie Bataillard-Samuel
Family Law Solicitor, MBS Family Law

Tom Brownrigg
Partner, Goodman Ray Solicitors

We live in an era where the way in which we live would be unrecognisable 20 years ago. Technology is intended to be there to make processes more efficient and to make your life easier. It goes to follow that it should make the separation process easier too. For every action there is an equal reaction though, and technology can be more trouble than it is worth.

Set out below are some examples of how innovations in family law can hopefully help people navigate through separation and keep up with their children's lives.

I've just separated - what happens next?

Get advice and learn about your options. The internet is a helpful tool, especially if you know what you are looking for but it is no substitute for understanding what your options are for your particular circumstances, or taking legal advice.

Finding a solicitor, mediator, therapist or barrister to speak to has never been easier - you do not have to just Google your local family solicitors. More detailed information is available online through:

- their professional bodies;

- organisations like Resolution whose members are committed to taking an amicable approach;

- legal directories such as Chambers & Partners and the Legal 500.

Some of the old ways are the often the best though, and it is always worth considering a personal recommendation.

Do your homework

Make sure that you don't just know your options, but that you understand them too. It can be helpful to read and learn about your options along side this, provided it is from a professional and reputable source. There are a number of good free, or cheap, resources. Resolution's website has guides and there are various other helpful videos, podcasts, interactive websites and online guides (such as Law for Life) which help talk you through the process.

There are other online resources which can help you and your children deal with the emotional strain of separation. Websites like the Parent Connection help parents with the separation process and Voices in the Middle can help children share their experiences with other children from separated families.

How are we going to work this out?

Over the last thirty years or so there has been a sea

45

We are separating

change in how family law issues are resolved. Alternative Dispute Resolution (ADR) is focused on adapting the family law process to discussions taking place in the right environment to ensure that parents can hopefully agree upon a solution amicably, instead of having to rely on a judge to make a decision.

Mediation is a voluntary way of enabling couples to have constructive confidential discussions with an impartial mediator. Mediators come from a variety of backgrounds, and can be therapists, solicitors, family consultants or barristers.

Solicitors have also adopted different approaches for advising their clients and working with other solicitors, with a greater use of face to face meetings. Collaborative law has developed where parents will commit not to go to court and to have a series of face-to-face meetings involving both parents and their solicitors.

Arbitration has been recognised to resolve most children and financial disputes. Unlike court, you can both choose an arbitrator with the skills to decide on your case, and it can be quicker than court.

How are the children going to cope?

In the 2011 census, one third of children in England and Wales came from families with separated parents. There is more pastoral support in school now, and support through child consultants or family therapists is far more integrated into the way lawyers work too. They can also work with the parents to aid communication with the children.

The child's voice is now far more audible in the decision-making process. The government published a paper outlining its commitment to this in 2015 called "The Voice of the Child". It is increasingly common for children to be consulted as part of mediation, and the training process for Child Inclusive Mediation was overhauled substantially in September 2018.

Handovers

Handovers can be difficult for one, or both parents, especially when there has been a difficult separation. Where parents are struggling to communicate helpful information, there are now better resources to enable parents to share this information positively. There are shared online diaries or books such as The Handover Book, which is a more creative way of sharing information.

Depending on what arrangements the parents make, they could be going a long time without seeing the children. Video calling using Facetime or Skype has made this easier.

It was hard enough keeping track of arrangements when we were in one house. How do we manage it now we are in separate homes?

Many children's diaries are more jam-packed than their parents'. Keeping diaries in sync used to be a very difficult process, with misunderstandings causing friction between parents. There are now specialist online calendars for separated families, as well as programs like iCal which have share functions so that both parents can put plans into calendars to be accepted by the other parent.

There is no right or wrong answer to how to manage a child's expenses post separation, especially if parents are sharing the cost of a school trip or extra-curricular activities. Apps such as Splitwise can help keep track of expenses and how these need to be shared.

How can conversations be transformed into a problem-solving approach?

Norman Hartnell
Joint Managing Director,
The Family Law Company
by Hartnell Chanot

Words can wound or words can heal. In the context of a relationship breakdown it is often the case that the expression of unresolved hurt arising from the breakdown is reflected verbally, in letters either direct or with the added volume of solicitors letters, emails and text messages.

Any attack, whether verbal or in writing naturally evokes a flight or fight response; the first could result in either disengagement and capitulation to the person who is seen as the more powerful, or the second might trigger a response which may be of equal or even greater hostility, leading to an escalation of conflict.

Either way it results in one or both feeling angry, trying to re-exert the control over their lives they feel they are at risk of losing. Response leads to further response. The whole basis of litigation encourages a point-scoring, blame-attributing approach to justify one's own actions and undermine that of the other person. Yet Judges almost always express dismay at the inability of parents to understand that their conflict is harming their children, apparently oblivious of the fact that the very system of which they are a part encourages this adversarial approach.

So how on earth can this vicious cycle be broken?

How can conversations, whether direct or though legal channels, be transformed into a problem-solving approach?

I may not have all the answers but have found the following to be effective in many situations.

> I would have done things differently by accepting the family break-up sooner, de-attaching myself emotionally and not being too reactive.
>
> *Craig, Dad*

Receipt of aggressive communication
When receiving an aggressive or angry communication in any form, first listen to your natural internal response. It is likely to be one of protest, anger, a desire to respond and justify your own stance. It is the equivalent of being slapped across the face. Put into words how it makes you feel. I find it helpful to highlight or underline the provocative words which evoke your strongest response. They may be overtly rude or manipulative.

Give vent to your feelings
Put into words how you would have instinctively

We are separating

wanted to respond - in other words give vent to your feelings in a private note, **which will not be sent**. It is good to get the instant feelings out and acknowledged. Until that first step is done, it will prevent any further progress.

Review
Having paused and had a cup of tea, then review the communication again from a different perspective. This time you will be searching to ascertain whether the other person is being purely controlling or manipulative or whether, despite the words used, part of what they say is indicative of a valid point of view, worry or grievance which is being expressed poorly, in a childish way.

Considering your response
This is the time to separate the wheat from the chaff. Your challenge is to determine which parts of the communication you wish to respond to and which you do not. You do not have to answer everything.

Which parts require a response?
So, some parts of the communication will be gratuitously rude or hurtful. They are designed to get you hooked into an argument on their terms which they enjoy, their territory. The more insecure someone is the more they will seek to control their world, by pulling the strings or pushing the buttons they have learned are likely to get a response. Don't respond to these parts of the communication - you **can** choose not to.

Other parties may be motivated by something different. They may be simply angry about something - perhaps the other person is fearful and is trying to exert control themselves in a situation where they are fearful of loss and trying inappropriately to secure their position by threats.

You now have a choice as to how to respond to the different elements
In relation to the provocative hurtful gratuitous comments, the basic law you need to understand is you get what you reward. If you respond to those words, then you are likely to achieve nothing apart from to add fuel to the fire. Even a put-down of the other person by shaming them or remonstrating with them for their use of language will be seen as a response which will justify a further response from them - and so it goes on.

Therefore, the right response is to ignore such comments. Should you wish, you can record them to demonstrate later to a Judge or other person what language has been used on

> By engaging in the mediation process parties can create building blocks on how to communicate in the future to ensure that any animosity is limited and that both parents remain focused on the child or children's needs rather than their own agenda.
>
> *Sarah Manning, Consilia Legal*

you to demonstrate their coercive approach. This provides you with the best possible evidence of the approach adopted by the other person, as it comes from their own hand. If you read such words in that way, their power to hurt can be transformed into the satisfaction that they themselves have provided the best possible evidence should you need it later. Keep it.

Re-writing the communication
If there are concerns which are genuine to them but badly expressed and, which if expressed differently would have evoked an adult response from you addressing any concerns, then do the following:

- Re-write their communication in the way they should have expressed it. It should have started politely with "Dear ..." using your first name; and it should have been worded to express the following:

  - What they are worried about;

  - What they are asking you to do about it;

  - Asking for a response within a reasonable timescale.

- Now draft your response to your reworked communication. You will also start with "Dear...." and you will end with "Regards" because you will be writing to them to model what good communication looks like politely as parent to parent.

You will acknowledge their worry and not dismiss it and you will put it into the words they should have used. You'll then go on to respond in the way you can to address any concerns. If there is a matter on which you are not going to agree, you should take this opportunity to explain why in non-emotive language, showing that your approach is one which meets the needs of all concerned children and adults alike. If you can provide some alternative choices and explain the pros and cons and why you recommend your preferred suggestion, then that will provide them with the opportunity to respond in kind. Your communication should model a good boundary-setting structure as follows by;

- setting out clearly factually what happened;

- explaining what its effect on you and/or the children was (factual);

- saying what now needs to happen;

- explaining when it needs to happen by (setting a reasonable deadline and agreeing to any justified request for an extension);

- explaining the consequence of it not happening by that deadline. The consequence will not be worded as a threat - it will be an expression that you are left with no alternative, in the absence of a positive response, to any other course of action to resolve the situation.

As this will be a new form of communication between you it may well take some time to take effect and bring about a change in response. The exercise may have to be repeated many times; but sooner or later the difference between your communication and theirs should dawn on them, showing them to be unreasonable. They will come to realise that anyone seeing such communications (such as a Judge) will quickly come to the conclusion which parent is reasonable. That accountability will in most cases be the conversation. Your role is to set a good example of what communication between parents should look like and not respond to provocation.

Your children need you to be the one to take responsibility for being the adult. Hopefully using the above method, you will have educated the other parent to follow your lead for the benefit of the children.

Notes

Domestic abuse

Recognising and acknowledging that you, and your children, are a victim of Domestic Abuse (DA), also referred to as Domestic Violence (DV), can take time. Your expectations are so undermined by DA that a whole new idea of 'normal' develops. But once you separate, patterns of behaviour that were suffered and tolerated before, are seen in a different light. Coming out of a relationship where there was DA will impact on the process of separation. The control, threat and suppression that pervaded the relationship may well increase after separation, leading to sky high levels of anxiety and fear. But this chapter highlights all of the legal structures and emotional support available to you, so that you can feel strong about making the break and starting a new, healthy life.

Domestic abuse

What are the effects on children who witness domestic violence?

Dr Angharad Rudkin
Clinical Psychologist, MA (Oxon), CPsychol, AFBPsS

> The best response to unreasonable behaviour is to be unerringly reasonable.
>
> *Matthew Richardson, Coram Chambers*

We will never really know how many children and families experience Domestic Violence (DV) as so many of these incidents go unreported. But what we do know for certain is that witnessing DV has an adverse effect on children.

Witnessing DV

Over half of known DV incidents happen when a child is present, and half of these happen when a child is under the age of 6. Most of the time, children are not directly physically hurt during these incidents, but the lasting impact on their development is significant. For example, children who have witnessed DV are more likely to have difficulties in their friendships, find it harder to concentrate at school, do fewer activities outside school, act in an aggressive way and will have symptoms of trauma such as nightmares and flashbacks.

This all makes sense when you think of how children learn. Children, especially younger ones, learn predominantly by observing and imitating. As any parent will tell you, you could tell your child to do something a hundred times and they won't. Show them how to do it and they are far more likely to copy you. Watching your parents physically hurt each other is a terrifying experience for children. The two people you love the most and who guide you through life are doing the very things you know are wrong. These children go back into school the next day and will act out what they've seen. They get into trouble for it, and yet their parents don't. They get into trouble at school and they go home to a house that scares them. There is little wonder they don't blossom.

What does research tell us?

But, research is helping us to understand how we can best support children who have witnessed DV. There are a few clues coming out of studies, with the most significant one being that the child needs a mother with 'good enough' parenting skills and a mother who is functioning as well as she can despite the DV. That is, having a pillar of strength, hope and comfort in the form of a responsive mother can build up the child's resilience to help them get through this period of time (NB: The research has focused mainly on male to female DV as that is still the most common form. It will be interesting to see what is found when researchers begin to study female to male DV). Being a family who is active, sociable and organised is also a protective factor. As you would expect, being exposed to DV for a shorter period of time, and it being the first time it's occurred, will also mean that you are better able to cope with it.

Intervention and support

Given that a child can be buffered from the effects of DV by the continuing care of a 'solid' parent, it follows that any effective intervention should involve the parent as well as the child. Studies have looked at the impact of teaching children social skills as well as coping skills. The main difference in how children did was still determined by how their parent was functioning. So again, the message is clear that the more the parent is coping and functioning the more the child will be able to keep going.

Parents need to get all the support they can so that they can in turn be that pillar of strength for their child. Acknowledging and admitting to the DV is the first step. Accessing support and networks is the second. These are difficult to do as DV seeps into the very core of a person's belief in themselves and the future. But, knowing that how you as a parent copes is the biggest determiner of how your child copes may give you the drive you need to change things.

COULD I BE A VICTIM OF DV?

JOT DOWN WHAT BEHAVIOURS YOU THINK ARE ACCEPTABLE OR NOT IN THE FOLLOWING 3 COLUMNS AND ASK YOURSELF IF YOU HAVE EXPERIENCED ANY LISTED IN THE 3RD COLUMN

Behaviours that are acceptable	Behaviours that are acceptable occasionally	Behaviours that are never acceptable

Domestic abuse

What is Coercive Control?

Phillippa Kum
Associate at Hunters

Polly Atkins
Associate Solicitor at Hunters

Coercive and controlling behaviour is often a covert form of abuse. It can be insidious and difficult to evidence but causes serious harm to the victim. Since 2015, coercive control has been a criminal offence in England and Wales.

Am I experiencing coercive control?

Whilst the term 'coercive control' has become familiar, they are in fact two separate behaviours which constitute an offence of domestic abuse.

Controlling behaviour is an act or series of acts intended to make you feel dependent, isolated or subordinate.

Examples of such behaviour include:

- Isolating you from your family, friends and support system;
- Controlling your finances;
- Depriving you of your independence and basic needs, for example, not letting you have access to a vehicle or denying you access to support;
- Repeatedly putting you down by being critical of your worth, or by name calling; or
- Regulating your everyday behaviour by monitoring your activities and movements by, for example, hacking into your accounts.

Coercive behaviour is an act or series of acts that an abuser uses to make you feel punished, scared and frightened.

For example:

- Threatening to harm or kill you or your loved ones, or to publish information about you, or reporting you to the police or authorities;
- Damaging your property;
- Intimidating and/or humiliating you, for example, through the enforcement of unnecessary and demeaning rules or comments in front of others or privately;
- Assaulting you; or
- Forcing you to participate in criminal activity or child abuse.

To fall within the criminal definition of coercive control, these behaviours must come from someone who is personally connected with you. This includes someone you have an intimate personal connection with, such as a spouse or partner. If you both live under the same roof, a personal connection also includes a family member, or someone who you have had a previous intimate relationship with.

If it is safe to do so, you may find it useful to keep a diary of key behaviours to establish a pattern of events which could help you to tell others about your experience and also to demonstrate patterns of behaviour which emerge.

What happens when I report coercive control?
Your abuser will be guilty of this criminal offence if:

a. They repeatedly or continuously engage in the controlling or coercive behaviour against you;

b. You both are personally connected at the time of the behaviour;

c. This behaviour has a serious effect on you; and

d. They know or ought to know that the behaviour will have a serious effect on you.

In this context, serious effect means that the behaviour causes you to:

- Fear, on at least two occasions, that violence will be used against you, or

- Experience serious alarm or distress which has a substantial adverse effect on your usual day-to-day activities. For example, your physical and/or mental health has deteriorated, your social life has changed, or you have changed the way you behave within the house by having to implement safeguarding measures. These effects could also be in your workplace such as your working patterns and journey.

If convicted, an abuser could be jailed for up to five years, or made to pay a fine, or both. In addition, they may also be guilty of other criminal offences. For example, if the controlling or coercive behaviour involved the breaking of your electronic devices or personal possessions, they would have also committed the offence of criminal damage.

Protection in the Family Court
The Family Court has a range of powers to deal with coercive control. It can make a non-molestation order which protects you and any relevant child from harassment or violence. It can prohibit certain behaviours from your abuser, such as contacting you or being violent towards you. The breach of a non-molestation order is a criminal offence, so you are able to report the breach of the order directly to the police. The Family Court can also make an occupation order dealing with who lives at the family home. If appropriate, this could order your abuser to move out of the property or to keep a certain distance away from it. Some occupation orders have a power of arrest attached to it, which allows police officers to arrest the respondent if they breach the order.

Coercive and controlling behaviour is frequently alleged within children proceedings as a factor relevant to the determination of a child's welfare. The Family Court has a continuing duty to consider whether domestic abuse is an issue, and this includes coercive and controlling behaviours. It is important to raise the fact that you have experienced coercive and controlling behaviour early on to ensure the court is aware of this potential safeguarding issue. The court may decide to hold a fact-finding hearing if it considers the truth of your allegations need to be determined in order to make welfare decisions in relation to your children.

What do I do in an emergency?
If you are unable to speak due to fear for your safety, and are calling 999 from a mobile, you can press 55 when prompted. This is known as the "silent solution" and will transfer your call to a police call handler who will try to communicate with you.

In the event of a non-emergency, you can contact your local police force by dialling 101. The charity, Refuge, also runs a 24-hour National Domestic Abuse Helpline on 0808 2000 247.

Domestic abuse

What is gaslighting and how do I deal with it?

Irena Osborne
Partner, Boardman Hawkins & Osborne LLP

> "My mother told me, after I left my husband, that she was relieved but I shouldn't forget that, because we had a child together, I was with him for life!
>
> *Caitlin, Mum*

Gaslighting is a form of emotional abuse and the Domestic Abuse Act 2021 is clear that emotional abuse is a form of domestic abuse.

Gaslighting is a kind of emotional manipulation when the perpetrator slowly alters the perception the victim has of him or herself and world around them.

Gaslighting may include (but it is not limited to) persistent lying; undermining victims' confidence, thinking, reasoning and intelligence; encouraging feelings of guilt; questioning the victim's sanity and their perception of reality, including past and present events; questioning the victim's perception of other people and their actions; and encouraging feelings of inadequacy. It may focus on criticising the victim's looks, choices or set of beliefs. Perpetrators may switch between charm and anger making the victim feel constantly on edge and encouraging the feeling that the victim is responsible for the perpetrator's change of mood. It generally affects the victim's self-esteem and as it is perpetrated over a long period of time the victim may not even be aware that it is happening.

It can start with the perpetrator making small, seemingly insignificant suggestions and corrections to the victim's way of behaving, thinking, likes and dislikes, and slowly but surely it's likely to grow and expand to encompass many (if not all) of the victim's thinking and perceptions about themselves and about the world around them.

It is hugely difficult for victims themselves to recognise the perpetrator's actions as gaslighting as with time their perception of the world and themselves can become entirely aligned with that of the perpetrator and therefore in the victim's own eyes, they are at fault. They are the ones that need to change their behaviour and actions.

It is not unusual for victims to disbelieve anyone and everyone that attempts to point out emotionally abusive and manipulating behaviours of the perpetrators to them and completely side with the perpetrator against any outside influences.

Eventually, gaslighting is likely to achieve social isolation of the victim, loss of their self-esteem and even loss of their own identity. It will achieve complete and unhealthy reliance on the perpetrator, making any breaking away from the perpetrator harder and harder.

Breaking the cycle of abuse, however, is not impossible. It is undoubtedly a hard and difficult step for the victim to take, making them feel worse, helpless and at rock bottom, before they can start re-building themselves.

Due to its very nature, it is difficult for victims to pursue allegations of gaslighting in court. It is difficult for victims to describe individual instances of the perpetrator's manipulating behaviours, or particularise and compartmentalise manipulations that have become part of their own being and their own belief system.

However, with careful analysis of the perpetrator's past behaviours and descriptions of the victim's changed life experiences and perceptions, it is possible to show to the court that the victim has been subjected to gaslighting.

The case of *Re: H-N and others (Children) (Domestic Abuse: finding of fact hearing)* [2021] EWCA Civ 448 is particularly significant in my view, demonstrating a victim's ability to pursue allegations of gaslighting in court. It is no longer necessary for victims to plead and give evidence of individual and specific allegations of domestic abuse. Instead, the courts are now encouraged to consider the perpetrator's behaviour in a wider context, looking for patterns of the perpetrator's actions that amount to coercive, abusive, controlling and gaslighting behaviour. It is no longer necessary to plead individual actions of abuse in a schedule of allegations, which would make pleading gaslighting behaviour almost impossible. It is now possible to seek findings on wider patterns of abusive behaviours which, in their totality, may amount to gaslighting.

In my view the above case made the ability of the victim to plead gaslighting behaviour in the family court that little bit easier.

Victims should be encouraged to talk about all the perpetrator's behaviours with their lawyers, support workers and others assisting them in working through the abuse they suffered. In my view, only with discourse around the perpetrator's actions and understanding the change in the victim's life experiences, will patterns of behaviours that amount to gaslighting behaviour be identified. Victims should be encouraged to speak about their experiences in abusive relationship as a whole, rather than focusing on actions and behaviours they themselves consider abusive.

I felt very alone and as if I had nobody to turn to. It knocked my confidence and changed my behaviour. I started messing about at school and not listening in class, but I realised this wasn't the person I wanted to be known as. Cerys (17)

Domestic abuse

Domestic violence: a checklist?

Beverley Watkins
Managing Partner,
Watkins Solicitors

The Family Court has the power to make a "Non-Molestation Injunction" which is an order of the court usually prohibiting the following:

- Using or threatening violence;
- A person from contacting the applicant;
- A person from going to a home or within 100 metres of a home.

In order to make an application in the Family Court, the Applicant must be "related" in some way, for example married, previously co-habited, parent of a child together, parent, son, aunt, uncle, grandparent etc. Family Non-Molestation Injunctions cannot apply to parties who are not related such as neighbours or former friends.

If there has been a recent serious threat or if there has been recent violence (there is no time limit on what is regarded as "recent"), a party can apply for what is known as an emergency injunction without notice to the other party of the hearing. When dealing with an emergency injunction the court is unlikely to challenge or question the evidence of the applicant. If an order is made there is likely to be a review hearing one or two weeks later when the court will reconsider the matter. This will give the opportunity for the other party to make representations as to why a Non-Molestation Order should not continue. However, at the review hearing often the other party does not attend.

Breach of a Non-Molestation Injunction

Breach of a Non-Molestation Injunction is in itself a criminal offence for which a person could be punished by a term of imprisonment of up to 5 years. The difficulty, however, is that the police seem extremely reluctant to take action in respect of a breach of a Non-Molestation Injunction.

Non-Molestation Injunctions are usually made for 6 months or a year. If, however, there is a breach of a Non-Molestation Injunction during the period when it is in force, it is possible to apply to the court to extend the period of the injunction.

Occupation Orders

Occupation Orders are orders which regulate whether a person can occupy a property when they are entitled to. Often they will prohibit a party from entering or attempting to enter a property even if they are entitled to.

Occupation Orders are often made for 6 months to 1 year. During that period, parties are expected to resolve

> If you are unsure about the way forward think about what advice you would give to your friend if they were in your situation/dilemma. Courses of action advised to a friend are often more measured than one driven by personal emotion.
>
> *Ceri Thomas, KBL Solicitors*

Domestic abuse

issues concerning the occupation of property. For example, if parties were married, they are expected to deal with the property and financial matters.

Legal Aid
Legal Aid is available to apply for a Non-Molestation Injunction. However, it must be remembered that there are tests which an Applicant must meet:

- Disposable needs should be below a certain figure;
- Capital needs should be below a certain figure (equity in a home is taken into account).

Applying for a Non-Molestation Injunction.
There is no court fee payable to make a non-molestation injunction. An application form must be completed and a statement must be signed by the applicant.

The statement should contain the following information;

- Details of the relationship between the parties;
- Details of any children;
- Details of where the parties are living;
- Details of the first incident of violence or threats;
- Details of the worst incident of violence or threats;
- Details of the most recent incident of violence or threats;
- Details of any medical treatment, if any;
- Details of witnesses, if any.

The above is not an exhaustive list.

Legal aid and other proceedings
If a non-molestation injunction is granted, it can act as 'gateway evidence' for other legal services such as finance and children matters but an applicant must still be financially eligible.

> Divorce for any child is one of the most defining moment of their lives. Sure, it gets better with time, but it never ever leaves you. Jess (17)

Domestic abuse

Help for victims of domestic abuse in the Family Court

Lucy Todd
Associate Solicitor, Irwin Mitchell

> My four children became so hard-wired to abuse that they normalised it like toast and honey.
>
> *Kitty, Mum*

Embarking on a journey through the Family Court is often a stressful and emotional experience. The strain will be worse for those who are survivors of domestic abuse. However, there are things which the court can do to make things a little easier, and these are called "special measures".

Special measures are provisions which help a party or witness in family proceedings participate or give evidence. The family court has the power to make 'participation directions' to assist a person during proceedings. These can include:

- A separate court entrance;
- Separate waiting rooms for the parties;
- Allowing the survivor to leave first after a hearing takes place;
- Using screens in court (to prevent the witness from seeing the perpetrator and vice versa);
- Giving evidence via video/live link;
- Assistance of a supporter or McKenzie friend.

The Law
Practice Direction 12J says that if, at any stage, the court is advised by the applicant, by Cafcass or otherwise that there is a need for special arrangements to secure the safety of any party or child attending any hearing, the court shall ensure that appropriate arrangements are made for the hearing and for all subsequent hearings in the case, unless it considers that these are no longer necessary.

The Family Procedure Rules 2010 say that victims of domestic abuse are eligible for special measures if the court is satisfied that the quality of their evidence (or ability to participate in the proceedings) is likely to be diminished due to their vulnerability.

Section 63 of the Domestic Abuse Act 2021 says that where a party is, or is at risk of being, a victim of domestic abuse, they will automatically be eligible for special measures in family proceedings because the court will assume their ability to participate or give evidence and the quality of their evidence will likely be diminished.

There is acknowledgement by the President of the Family Division, Sir Andrew McFarlane, that victims of domestic abuse should always be consulted as to their preferred mode of participation in proceedings - whether that be in person, or by telephone or video.

What you can do?
It's important to take steps

Domestic abuse

at the start of your case to make sure that things are set up properly. Set out below are some key tips:

Be proactive
Contact the court and request details about what special measures they offer and the processes they have in place.

Communicate with the court
Tell the court about the special measures you are requesting as soon as you know the hearing date so that the court has time to respond. If you don't hear back from the court, you should chase this up 7 days before the hearing, and then again 2 days prior to the hearing. If you haven't given the court plenty of notice, then you must let them know 48 hours prior to the hearing at the very latest.

Don't attend alone
Decide who you would like to attend the hearing with you to support you. The court should usually allow either party to be accompanied in any hearing by a supporter (whether or not you are legally represented) or a McKenzie Friend (if you are not legally represented), though the Judge has discretion to exclude any supporter who disrupts the hearing. The supporter should ideally not be directly involved in the proceedings. A suitable person may be a domestic abuse support worker or friend. The supporter/McKenzie Friend should be permitted to sit quietly in the same room as you, whether physically present in court or joining the hearing remotely.

Think about your arrival and safe space
Avoid arriving at court alone. Attend with your legal representative, supporter or McKenzie Friend. If arranged, use a separate entrance.

Request the use of a conference room or separate waiting room to the other party. Think about arriving slightly earlier than scheduled to give you plenty of time to find a safe space and alert court staff to your requirements.

Cross-examination - know what the law says
There is a new law in place (Section 65 of the Domestic Abuse Act 2021) which says that where a party has been found to be an abuser, they cannot cross-examine their victim. Instead, the court will appoint a solicitor or barrister to cross-examine instead. The victim can't cross-examine the perpetrator either, and again this would need to be done by a court-appointed solicitor or barrister. This is a huge step forward, and saves victims having to be subjected to questioning by someone who has abused them.

Planning is key
Provision for special measures/participation directions should be included in the case plan for all hearings and recorded on the order arising from your hearing. You should raise this with your legal representative or the court directly.

Remote Hearings

It is just as important to put measures in place for remote hearings, and the Family Court recognises that just because the parties aren't attending in person, it doesn't mean that a survivor will automatically feel safe.

You may find it comforting to know that you should never be put in a situation where you are alone with the perpetrator, whether in or outside of a courtroom, on a telephone line, or in a video conference. Either a member of court staff should activate the hearing and remain on the line at least until the Judge has joined, or the Judge should activate the hearing and admit the other parties.

The court recognises the importance of the perpetrator not seeing details of your private, safe space via a screen. If you are unable to attend from a neutral space i.e. a lawyer's office, and are joining the link from your home, ask the court to distort your background or request permission to join by audio only or have your video turned off.

Domestic abuse

You may seek permission to be excused from attendance at the hearing, if you are legally represented and the hearing is not one at which evidence will be given (as long as you are available to your representative to provide instructions throughout the hearing via telephone).

Conclusion

When it comes to court proceedings, planning is key, and this is especially important if you are a survivor of domestic abuse. Communication with your legal adviser, the court and your support network is crucial, and will help to make the whole process feel a lot less daunting.

One thing is certain, from a relationship perspective - unless there is coercive control, we cannot make anyone do anything that they don't want to.

It is extremely difficult when couples continue to have heated, unresolved arguments, especially in front of the children.

It might be more empowering to take control of 'your end' of the conversation.

Arguments can only happen if you both engage. I don't mean one of you should storm off - in fact the opposite. Rather than getting caught up in the argument, call a 'time out'.

Calmly say "I understand that this conversation is important but I'm feeling stressed/upset/angry at the moment so I'm going to make a cup of tea so I can calm down. Can we talk when the children aren't around?"

Adele Ballantyne

I felt like I was torn in the middle as I didn't want to take one's side over another. Sophie (16)

No one believes me - how do I prove I am telling the truth?

Jennifer Williamson
Partner, Punch Robson

Domestic violence! Bruised, battered, broken women (and men) - pretty self-evident right? But, of course that was never the whole story. Setting aside those perpetrators manipulative enough not to leave physical marks, abuse can be psychological, emotional, financial, or any combination of these. It was in recognition of these equally powerful forms of abuse that the government changed its terminology from 'domestic violence' to that of 'domestic abuse'. A large proportion of victims will have experienced all of the above aspects of abuse and many will find that the psychological and emotional abuse is the worst but usually the most difficult to 'prove'.

It's a sad fact that many victims will not, themselves, realise or appreciate the extent of the abuse they have been subjected to, until they have escaped from that relationship and/or engaged with counselling or support services. An even sadder fact is that, even in this climate of campaign and awareness, the vast majority of victims will not report the abuse that they have been subjected to, out of fear or shame.

Often, a perpetrator of abuse can convince you and perhaps everyone around you, that it is you who is the problem, or even that it is your fault that they are subjecting you to that behaviour, that you deserve it, you drive them to it. Frequently, this can result in disclosures being made by victims and the person whom they have entrusted that information to, not recognising the seriousness of the abuse or not believing the victim. The helplessness a victim of abuse can feel as a result of not being believed can have significant impairments upon a victim's mental health, and further enmesh them in the perpetrator's web. The disbelief or disregard of others reinforces the victims feeling of worthlessness, that they deserve this, that it's normal. It isn't normal and we as a society need to change our thinking; hopefully with campaigns and education this will come about in the longer term, but until then ...

How do you prove that you are telling the truth?

There are various ways in which you can gather evidence to demonstrate that you are telling the truth.

- Consider keeping a diary, thus keeping a chronology of the abusive behaviour; when, where and how it happened. A diary should only be kept if it is safe to do so - think about keeping it electronically on a device, your phone, a tablet, a laptop, where it can be password protected.

- Retain any evidence of domestic abuse that has been perpetrated by way of indirect communication (i.e. text message, letter, voicemail etc.). Don't delete them, no matter how hurtful they are. Use them to

Domestic abuse

show that you are right.

- Consider whether to confide in your GP or seek support through counselling as a way of evidencing through independent professionals that you are suffering abuse. All GP's have training in domestic abuse, and even if they can't help you directly, they can direct you to someone who can.

- Speak to friends and relatives. Have they noticed a change in you? Do they feel you have been isolated from them? Often their views and descriptions will point out things that you have never even noticed.

- Even if you feel that no one believes you, still report the abuse to the appropriate authorities, whether that be the Police or Social Services, should there be children involved in the domestic abusive situation. It is so important that you let people know what is happening to you. Police officers are trained to deal with domestic abuse; even if it seems trivial to you at first, have it recorded.

- Lastly, seek help and support from a domestic abuse support group who will be able to listen but also offer services to help you in dealing with the domestic abuse you have been subjected to. You can find their details online, at your local library, Citizen's Advice or at your GP surgery.

Sometimes you will need protecting. If the police are unable or unwilling to take action, you can use the courts to obtain an injunction. Again, this where victims often feel they won't be believed. The courts are very experienced in dealing with domestic abuse, and very sympathetic to applications.

Legal aid

Legal aid is still available to help you get representation (albeit with some qualifications), and there are specialist solicitors trained in domestic abuse - look for Resolution Accredited Specialists.

It may be worth noting that such an application is made within the family court whereby the burden of proof is on the balance of probabilities. Therefore, even if the domestic abuse is unreported, or disbelieved by friends or professionals such as the Police due to lack of 'evidence', the family court will listen to the evidence you wish to put forward, usually by way of a signed witness statement and oral evidence and decide, on the balance of probabilities, whether the incident has, or has not occurred. Your word is as good as anyone else's - just tell the truth.

The most important way to evidence that you are a victim of domestic abuse is to speak out and to continue speaking out, until someone listens. We are trying to hear you and are here to help.

For a while I was scared of talking to someone but it really does help. School, teachers, friends, parents and siblings are always great people to turn too. Imogen (11)

Domestic abuse

What will happen if I contact a solicitor about a domestic abuse concern?

Ruth Hawkins & Irena Osborne

Founding partners of Boardman Hawkins & Osborne LLP

There are a number of steps that can be taken, including various applications that can be brought through the family court, to protect someone experiencing domestic abuse.

It's really important to look at the client's needs as a whole, and just because it is possible to make an application for a protective order, that might not always mean that it is the right thing to do, as it could have a 'knock-on' effect on other family issues, such as arrangements with the children. A specialist family lawyer can therefore look at the situation holistically, and advise on the best course of action.

All professionals involved in the family justice world are cautious about the safety for victims of domestic abuse and the practical difficulties and danger to their personal safety that seeking legal advice could bring. That, alongside the stress of the situation, including financial worries particularly in the current cost of living crisis, undoubtedly puts them in greater danger than normal. Many people might find themselves trapped in a situation due to financial worries.

What legal protection can a victim obtain?

The court can provide a number of different options to protect a victim of domestic abuse, both through the family courts and criminal courts;

- Non-molestation orders can help prevent the perpetrator's violence, abuse and harassment;

- Occupation orders can exclude the perpetrator from your home;

- Prohibited steps orders, can prevent the perpetrator from removing the children from your care without your consent;

- The police can also assist with removing the perpetrator from your home and give warnings and cautions;

- Protection from harassment orders;

- Domestic violence protection notices.

These are just a few orders that may be appropriate to consider.

Lawyers are able to take instructions over the telephone or in person or via web conferencing, from which they can prepare the

65

Domestic abuse

necessary paperwork, and this can be sent to clients electronically for their approval.

Before speaking to a lawyer, it might be really helpful, if you're able to, to make some notes about what has been happening, who is involved, and other useful information, such as the names, ages and other key information of any children of the family. It might be helpful to have an idea - if you know it - about any financial issues, including any family assets, debts, income and expenditure. But don't worry if you don't know about this, as your lawyer will advise you about what information they need.

Even in domestic abuse cases, there might be other ways of ensuring protection or of resolving your issues, without court proceedings, and a specialist lawyer can help you look at the pros and cons of other ways including mediation, and ways of ensuring issues can be dealt with safely and sensibly.

If any application is to be made to the court your lawyer can give you advice about the options, and consider the best timing for the application too. It might be important, for example, to make sure you are in a safe place before any application is made or any correspondence is sent.

Since the pandemic, hearings have been a mixture of remote or in person hearings. 'Special measures' around safety, can also be considered by the lawyer, in conjunction with the court office.

After the hearing, the lawyer will draft the court order and email it to the Judge who can then approve or amend. A process server can be instructed and provided with the information to make sure that the order is served on the perpetrator.

Other help

Many organisations and businesses have become more aware of domestic abuse. For instance, more than half of UK pharmacies are signed up to the **'Ask for ANI'** scheme, (including Boots the chemist, Lloyds pharmacies and some independent pharmacies) where anyone alerting staff that they need help would be taken into a separate room, and offered immediate assistance. Many pub chains are signed up and aware of a similar scheme, **'Ask for Angela'**. Rail companies across the country are working in conjunction with Women's Aid to offer the **'Rail to Refuge'** scheme which provides free travel for victims fleeing their home and travelling to a safe place.

The police have also taken a very proactive approach to assisting victims of domestic abuse, and have introduced a way to seek emergency assistance if it is not safe to speak on the phone. After dialling 999 on a mobile, dial 55 when prompted and this will alert the call handlers that there is an emergency that needs dealing with (but this will not allow location tracking). If calling from a landline, the call will automatically be transferred to the police where they will be able to hear background noise and track the location.

I found speaking to someone who didn't know me was better because then they couldn't judge me.
Emily (16)

Domestic abuse

Can I get legal aid?

Derek Jordan
Director, The Family Law Company by Hartnell Chanot

If you are suffering any form of domestic abuse within or following the breakdown of a relationship, you are likely to feel extremely unsettled, frightened for your future and unsure of your options. An additional concern is very often the thought that to obtain specialist legal advice would be very expensive. The provision of legal aid in England and Wales has changed significantly in recent years but where a person or a relevant child has suffered or is at risk of suffering some form of domestic abuse they may still be able to access legal aid to meet the costs of legal advice and assistance.

Eligibility for legal aid has always relied on satisfying two elements:

- the merits of the case - is there an issue that is sufficiently serious that legal aid should be granted to assist that person? and

- whether they qualify financially for legal aid.

In addition to those elements, however, The Legal Aid, Sentencing and Punishment of Offenders Act 2012 (LASPO) introduced the requirement for there to be either:

- a need for urgent protective orders (Non-molestation Order or Occupation Order), or;

- evidence of previous domestic abuse or a risk of domestic abuse from the other party to the applicant or of abuse of a child in other family law cases such as applications concerning children, divorce or separation and the financial matters arising from relationship breakdown.

There is a range of evidence (known as gateway evidence) that the Legal Aid Agency will accept in applications for legal aid. The evidence can include the fact that the other party has a criminal conviction or formal police caution for a domestic abuse offence or child abuse offence, or that there have been previous protective orders made to protect against the behaviour of the other party.

In addition, evidence can come from assessments by professionals such as social workers or from a medical professional (including GPs, health visitors and midwives) or from domestic violence support organisations or support workers. It is not possible to set out every type of gateway evidence here. For a full list of the acceptable gateway evidence one should go to the Legal Aid Agency's website at www.gov.uk/legal-aid.

The rules and procedure for assessing financial eligibility for legal aid are quite complex and again we would refer you to the Legal Aid Agency's website where guidance can be found on financial eligibility. Essentially, income is assessed on the basis of the total income from all sources and the total income is then reduced by deducting allowable expenses against the gross income. The allowable deductions include housing costs, a fixed allowance for dependents and children, any tax and National

Domestic abuse

Insurance deductions from gross earnings, childcare costs incurred because of working or studying and any maintenance paid for children who do not live with the applicant.

If a person's gross income is in excess of £2,657 per calendar month they are automatically ineligible for legal aid. If the disposable income after the allowable deductions are made is £733 per calendar month or less then they may qualify on the basis of income.

In addition to qualification on income, however, the applicant will also need to qualify on the basis of capital. The capital limit for qualification for legal aid is currently £8,000 although the value of properties can be disregarded in certain circumstances as can the value of any assets that might be in dispute between the parties.

A person in receipt of legal aid is under a duty to inform the Legal Aid Agency of any significant change in their financial position - it is possible that a person begins by qualifying for legal aid but then due to a change of circumstances may find that they move outside of eligibility for legal aid and legal aid will cease. Similarly, a person may not qualify financially for legal aid when they are first assessed but may then become financially eligible.

Legal aid funding is not always completely free. The Legal Aid Agency do apply a sliding scale where a full legal aid certificate has been granted which means that, depending on the income and capital a person has within the overall eligibility limits, they may be required to make a regular contribution from their income during each calendar month the certificate is in force or they may be required to make a one-off payment out of any capital they have. There are also circumstances in which a person who has received the benefit of legal aid will be required to repay to the Legal Aid Agency the fees paid to the person's lawyers. Again, the rules and circumstances under which a person may have to repay the Legal Aid Agency are very detailed.

Broadly speaking, a person may have to make a payment under the Statutory Charge whereby a person who has recovered or preserved any money, property or costs as a result of the case is required to repay the legal costs paid on their behalf or if the legal aid certificate has been revoked. A legal aid certificate may be revoked if the Legal Aid Agency considers that the legal aid funding has been obtained fraudulently by, for example, providing false financial information.

Legal aid funding is therefore very much still available but is subject to rigorous eligibility conditions. Anyone who is dealing with the difficult circumstances of relationship breakdown who has suffered domestic abuse or who needs help to be protected from domestic abuse should always take specialist advice.

My parents told me 'you'll understand when you're older'. Now I'm older I've experienced all the good things about it.
Ben (16)

Domestic abuse

Can I change the locks on my house to keep my ex from just wandering in?

Melanie Westwood
Senior Associate Solicitor, Howes Percival

When you separate from your partner, spouse or civil partner, and they leave the family home, you may wish to change the locks to stop them coming back.

Can you do this?
It all depends on how you both own or rent the property. If:

- you are renting the property and both names are on the tenancy agreement; or
- you own the property in joint names,

you **cannot** exclude your ex from the home without an order from the court. Your ex is entitled to live in the property and if you do change the locks, they are entitled to break back into the property as long as they make good the damage. This means that they can get a locksmith in or break into the property themselves but they must repair any damage they make and give you a key if the locks are changed.

If your ex is violent or abusive towards you, you can apply to the court for a non-molestation order and an occupation order. You will need to show that you are at risk of being intimidated, harassed or pestered and that you need to be able to enjoy peaceful occupation of your home. It also helps to show that your ex has somewhere else to live whilst the order is in place.

If:

- you rent the property in your sole name; or
- you own the property in your sole name,

you **may be able** to change the locks. However, if you are married or have been living with someone for a long time, they may have rights to live in the property and you must be very careful before stopping them from coming back in. In these circumstances, they could apply to the court to get an order to regain entry to the property and even for an order to exclude you.

There are very limited circumstances in which you can change the locks without any consequences and you should take legal advice if you are thinking about doing this. Changing the locks without having an order in place may mean that your case starts on an aggressive footing and it may stop you being able to deal with other issues in an amicable matter.

Other issues
You may want to think about the other issues that separating from your ex may bring. Are you able to pay the rent or mortgage and bills on your own? What other financial support are you entitled to if you are now living on your own?

Domestic abuse

It is now a good time to try to talk about Child Maintenance (cmoptions.org can help) and you can look at whether you are entitled to tax credits or other benefits if you are on a lower income or you are working part time.

You can also look at arrangements for your ex to see the children and think about your long-term plans i.e. whether you wish to get divorced and how you might go about separating your assets.

It's extremely difficult to prove you're telling the truth. All you can do is continue to tell the truth. Remember there are two sides to every story, and if you're in court, it's the judge's responsibility to establish proof, either beyond reasonable doubt, or on the balance of probability.

Try to keep calm if others aren't telling the truth and practice calming exercises (e.g. mindfulness). If you feel you're getting frustrated then ask for a recess to calm down, and say why, calmly and clearly.

Mike Flinn

All me and my brother were thinking was this is our fault.
Sammie (17)

My partner has told me he will take the children away if I report his abuse. What are my options?

Angela Parsons
Senior Associate Solicitor, Wolferstans

As a parent you have a duty to safeguard your children from harm.

Being in a home where there is domestic abuse puts children at risk of harm. Whether they are subjected to domestic abuse themselves, or witness one of their parents being violent or abusive to the other parent, children may suffer direct physical, psychological and/or emotional harm, and may also suffer harm indirectly.

You could be seen to be failing to safeguard your children from harm if you do not take appropriate action to protect them from this exposure. However, taking action to safeguard and protect them is understandably difficult when you are scared.

There are some practical steps you can take to protect yourself and the children in the first instance:

- Keep a list of emergency numbers;
- Keep a diary of events;
- Seek medical attention if you have suffered any injury and make a note of the date you visited the GP;
- Keep the police informed; and
- Inform your children's school.

Support
The very nature of domestic abuse can make a person feel that they are isolated, but there are a number of organisations such as Woman's Aid and local Domestic Abuse Services and refuges that can offer practical advice and support.

The details for such organisations can be found online, or your local children's centre, council, health centre, or GP surgery should be able to provide details of such organisations or alternative support.

The family court
It is highly unlikely that a domestic abuser would be able to 'take' your children away if you make an application to court. There are orders that the court can make to protect you and your children. Safeguarding

---

Do NOT make negative comments about your ex on social media however tempting this may seem. It will only exacerbate an already difficult situation. Best advice is to resist posting updates and avoid making personal comments at all.

Emma Alfieri, Greene & Greene

Domestic abuse

the children will always be the court's paramount consideration.

Children Act Orders

In law, a parent with parental responsibility should be able to see their children providing it is in the child's best interests. The mother who gave birth to the child will automatically have parental responsibility and a father will have parental responsibility if he is named on the child's birth certificate or the parents are married. However, where there is an allegation of domestic abuse the court will only consider making an order for the child to see a parent who has been abusive if it can be satisfied that the physical and emotional safety of the children and the parent with whom the children are living will not be subjected to further controlling or abusive behaviour.

The court is required to give special consideration to cases in which there are allegations of domestic violence or abuse. In such cases the court must decide whether it is necessary to conduct a fact-finding hearing in relation to any allegation of domestic violence or abuse.

There are a number of factors the court must take into consideration which include the following;

- The views of the parties and Cafcass;
- Whether any allegations have been admitted;
- Whether there is any evidence available to the court to allow the court to proceed i.e. in non-molestation (injunction) proceedings; and
- The nature of the evidence.

Protective orders

The courts can protect you and the children by making one or more of the following orders:

Non-molestation Order

This is an Order where a party is ordered not harass or intimidate you or your child, not to use or threaten to use violence and in some circumstances it can even limit their ability to contact you or come near you or your home.

Occupation Order

An Occupation Order deals with the occupation of the home and can for example include the exclusion of the domestic abuser.

Prohibited Steps Order

A Prohibited Steps Order prevents a person from removing a child from a parent's care or from removing a child from their school or nursery.

Costs

If you are a victim of domestic abuse you may qualify for Legal Aid. When you contact a solicitor for advice, they will be able to assess whether you are eligible for Legal Aid and if you are not, then they will be able to provide you with an estimate of the likely costs involved.

If you are concerned about any of the issues raised above, you should seek support and the advice of a solicitor.

Don't ever think that your emotions and how you feel aren't valid. Don't ever stay silent. Ensure there will ALWAYS be someone there to confide in. Jess (17)

What about dads coping with an abusive female partner?

Dr Elizabeth Bates & Dr Julie Taylor
University of Cumbria

From the 1970s onwards, domestic violence researchers have adopted a gendered model of men's perpetration and women's victimisation and have focused on explanations that have their roots in norms of patriarchy. Historically this has excluded male victims from much of the research and consequently the societal narrative. When this issue is explored without a gendered lens, we see a very different picture emerge. Research using more representative samples has revealed not only the extent of men's victimisation but also the bidirectional nature of some violence. The findings reveal that in relationships women can be just as violent as men, and this violence is not motivated purely by self-defence as some would purport.

Whilst there is, relatively speaking, less research exploring men's experiences, our understanding of the prevalence, severity and outcomes for male victims is growing. A study based in the United States utilised data from a national helpline for abused men; of the 190 callers analysed all reported physical abuse included being punched, kicked and choked. A similar study in the Netherlands found the most common kinds of abuse were stabbing with an object, kicking, biting and seizing by the throat. Despite differences that exist for size and strength that lead to the perception that women are unable to injure men, the violence often seen includes the use of a weapon/object, and is often seen to cause injury, for example in a US sample 80% reported injuries with 35% reporting a serious injury (e.g. a broken bone).

There is a tendency within the research to focus on physical aggression as it is seen as more injurious and life threatening. More recently however, there has been increased interest in exploring the impact of coercive control, specifically since the introduction of this into the UK Serious Crime Act (2015). Coercive control (or emotional/psychological abuse as it is often known as) is seen in relationships more commonly than physical aggression. Coercive control can include behaviours such as economic abuse and deprivation, possessive and jealous behaviour, insults and name calling, threats and intimidation, degradation and isolation, and manipulation and control over everyday activities. This has been seen frequently in women's accounts of their abuse, but more recently has been seen in men's experiences. It is seen in the account of men in the aforementioned international studies, but also in a recent UK based study. A non-help-seeking sample was recruited to try and understand men's

Domestic abuse

experience more broadly, the men reported experiences of gaslighting (i.e. the manipulation of someone by psychological means into doubting their own sanity) and being manipulated through the use of false allegations, coercion around sex and pregnancy, being isolated from friends and family, and a range of threats relating to their children.

Experiencing domestic violence is a traumatic event, and trauma is known to increase the risk of developing mental health issues and psychiatric disorders. Domestic violence is known to have a long-term impact on both physical and mental health; indeed, this has been seen in both men and women who have experienced it. More specifically the literature that has explored men's experience suggests that men typically externalise their psychological distress; men report impacts such as binge drinking, post-traumatic stress disorder symptoms, a loss of self-worth and self-esteem, substance use, and suicide ideation. Despite this, the status of "victim" does not seem to apply to men and women equally. Women's violence and men's victimisation is not construed as serious or in need of intervention. This female to male perpetration is seen as less serious and less in need of support services than any other gender combination. These attitudes are thought to have their roots in socially constructed gender roles, and how synonymous aggressive behaviour is with the male gender role, with women generally being less aggressive in non-intimate contexts. These perceptions have been found to have an impact on men in terms of their well-being and their help-seeking decisions. A recent UK study revealed that experiences of domestic violence coupled with these perceptions had left men with feelings of anxiety and depression, and also left them reluctant to help seek; indeed, men commented that they felt they were weak and they would not be believed. Furthermore, these men had felt further victimised from services when they had sought help, they commented they had been ridiculed, blamed for their victimisation, and accused of being the perpetrator of the violence.

Whilst there is overlap in men's and women's experiences of abuse, there are also experiences that are unique and gender-based. A specific type of abuse that seems to be experienced overwhelmingly by men is legal and administrative aggression; this is described as the manipulation of legal and other administrative systems in a way that is harmful to the other partner. One particular aspect of this that has been seen in the research is around the use of children. Men described incidents where their female partner has made, or threatened to make, false allegations of either domestic violence or violence towards the children in order to manipulate their parental relationships, or prevent access. This can be a further barrier to leaving the current abusive relationship, or indeed a post-separation experience that can result in parental alienation.

Indeed, there is mounting evidence to suggest that child victims of domestic violence have, like male victims, been silenced by the pervasive social narrative. For many years children have been construed as passive witnesses to abuse and as such have been assumed to be less harmed than the 'direct victim' (typically identified as the mother). More recent research challenges this construction, suggesting that children are affected directly and indirectly from living in homes where domestic violence is present, and a number of mutually reinforcing negative outcomes may follow such exposure. Unfortunately, the ubiquitous gendered lens and the rudimentary binaries it reproduces have produced support service responses that are partial and fail to meet the needs or safeguard certain victim groups within our

Domestic abuse

communities, in particular, adult male victims and male children aged 13 and above.

Support

For men experiencing domestic violence: ManKind Initiative, Abused Men in Scotland (AMIS), and Amen in Ireland.

For anyone interested in reading more about men's experiences: *Abused Men: The Hidden Side of Domestic Violence* by Phillip W. Cook.

For more information about the research in domestic violence including male victims, women's aggression and the impact on children: *Intimate Partner Violence: New Perspectives in Research and Practice* edited by Elizabeth A. Bates and Julie C. Taylor.

TELLING THE CHILDREN

Separation and divorce is a difficult time for all those involved. There are so many decisions that have to be agreed, including telling the children.

Children have told us what they need during this difficult time and following these simple steps will help to reduce anxiety and upset for your children:

- Be as prepared as you can before you talk to your children.

- Tell them what's happening in a simple language without all the 'intimate' details.

- Children often worry about the practical things, so make sure you have agreed who they will live with, including contact arrangements, before you tell them.

- Reassure them that it's not their fault and that you will continue to be their parents and be involved in their lives.

- Most importantly, LISTEN to your children and reassure them that you are still 'Mum and Dad' and will continue to be a part of their lives.

- Reassure them that you love them.

Adele Ballantyne

Notes

It's been suggested I get a Prohibitive Steps Order. What is that?

Bernadette Hoy
Partner, Collins & Hoy Solicitors

In cases where there is a genuine fear and evidence that someone may take certain action in respect of a child which you would not agree with, you may require the intervention of the court and it is important to seek urgent legal advice.

What is a Prohibited Steps Order?

A Prohibited Steps Order (PSO) is an order of the court providing that certain action cannot be taken by a parent in meeting their parental responsibility (PR) for a child without express permission of the court. In broad terms, the exercise of PR relates to any decisions that are made concerning the welfare, development and upbringing of a child.

Essentially, a PSO restricts the exercise of PR and forbids a person from taking certain steps, such as:

- Removing a child from your care or other approved care giver;
- Taking a child out of the UK;
- Moving the child to another location within the UK;
- Removing a child from their school;
- Bringing a child into contact with certain people;
- Changing a child's name or surname;
- Making decisions in respect of a child's medical treatment, etc.

A court can make a PSO during the course of ongoing family proceedings, in conjunction with another court application (such as a Child Arrangements Order providing for a child to live with you) or as a free-standing application.

Application process

Any parent, person with PR or guardian in respect of a child can make an application for a PSO with the required court fee of £215. The person applying may not have to pay the court fee, or may get some money off, subject to an assessment of their means, for example if you have no or limited savings, if you are in receipt of certain benefits or if you are on a low income. You can find out more about applying for help with court fees at the Gov.uk website.

Before making an application to the court, it is a requirement that you attend a Mediation Information and Assessment Meeting (MIAM), unless you qualify for an exemption from attending (which will often be the case in urgent cases). See page 140 for more information on MIAMs.

Involvement of Cafcass

After making an application to the court, a Children and Family Court Advisory and Support Service (Cafcass) Officer will be appointed. Cafcass will meet with the parties to see if agreement

Domestic abuse

can be reached and prepare a letter to the court setting out the outcome of initial safeguarding checks undertaken as to any potential welfare issues and their recommendations going forward. If welfare issues are highlighted and/or if no agreement can be reached, the court may ask Cafcass to investigate further and prepare a report (called a 'section 7' report) to the court with their recommendations. This will be considered carefully and given significant weight by the court in making a decision.

Urgent applications

In an emergency, you can apply to the court for an urgent PSO without the other person being given notice of the hearing. In this case, the court may make a temporary or interim PSO and arrange for there to be another hearing when the other person can attend and put their case forward. This will also allow an opportunity for the Cafcass initial safeguarding enquires to be made.

Welfare of the child is paramount

When considering whether or not a PSO should be made, the court's paramount consideration will be the welfare of the child. In cases where the other party contests the application, the court must have regard to the 'welfare checklist', which is a list of 7 criteria which must be considered before a decision is made (see page 192 for more information on the welfare checklist):

In addition, the court must have regard as to whether any delay in making a PSO will be prejudicial to a child and it must be satisfied that in the circumstances, making a PSO would be better for a child than making no order at all. In the event the court decides that a PSO is required, consideration will always be given to the duration of the order and in some cases, an order can be made to last indefinitely.

Notes

Domestic abuse

What is a Non-molestation Order?

Inayat Nadat
Principal Solicitor, Nadat Solicitors

For years victims of domestic abuse have suffered in silence and have had limited knowledge of the protection that can be afforded to them by the courts (and other authorities).

What is a Non-molestation Order?

In essence, a Non-molestation Order is exactly what the term describes. It is a civil order obtained by a victim of domestic abuse from a Judge (or Magistrates) through the Family Court. The term molestation has a wide interpretation - it can include, but is not limited to, physical, emotional, financial and sexual abuse, and can also cover coercive and controlling behaviour, intimidating behaviour and harassment. The abuse can be once or over a sustained period.

A victim of such abuse can apply to the court for a Non-molestation Order against someone described as an 'associated person'. Such a person(s) can include spouses, ex-spouses, civil partners, ex-civil partners, cohabitees and former cohabitees; it can also include various family members.

The person applying for an order is referred to as the 'applicant' and the person against whom orders are sought is known as the 'respondent'.

By obtaining a Non-molestation Order the court proclaims that the abuser (a perpetrator of the abuse against a victim) cannot do or take certain actions, for example, not to approach the victim, not to act in a threatening manner or use violence or abuse towards a victim (in some cases the child(ren)) or attend any property occupied by the victim. The Non-molestation Order would usually specify that the abuser cannot use or threaten violence but may also prohibit other, more general behaviours, which amount to harassment or cause distress to a victim. An example might be unwanted and frequent contact with the victim by numerous means, through social media and text messages and not just telephone calls. In short, the Non-molestation Order, if granted, prohibits the abuser from 'molesting' the victim.

A Non-molestation Order is time limited and provides protection to a victim. However, a victim can ask for the order to be extended just prior to its expiry if the victim needs to continue with the protection.

Such an order not only provides protection but also empowers a victim with some sense of control in relation to uncalled for actions from their abuser.

Where an order is made by the court and this is breached by the abuser, either by themselves or by instructing any other person to do so, then the victim in such circumstances can contact the Police who can arrest the perpetrator(s) and take them through the criminal justice process. If found guilty of a breach of the terms of a Non-molestation Order the abuser can face charges for a criminal offence and can be dealt with by a fine or up to 5 years imprisonment, although an initial and/or minor breach may not attract a custodial sentence. Any persistent or serious breaches may well do.

The victim also has the option of referring the matter back to the Family Court as well and follow the civil process.

In addition to seeking a Non-molestation Order a victim may also seek to remain in the family home to the exclusion of the abuser. In such circumstances, the option available would be to seek an Occupation Order to maintain some stability for the victim and any child(ren). Such an order is available to an 'associated person' (see above). The court has the power to remove the abuser, for example your spouse or partner, from the family home. There are also additional powers available to a Judge making an Occupation Order, such as requiring one party to be responsible for maintenance of the home and paying the rent or mortgage and other outgoings such as rates and utility bills affecting the home.

Occupation Orders can in some circumstances be complicated as they affect one party's right to live in the family home and are sometimes considered to be 'draconian' orders. To consider the options of seeking such an order it is important to get the right advice at an early stage for your circumstances.

A court may or may not attach a power of arrest to an occupation order depending on the circumstances. Therefore, an important factor to consider is 'safety' and 'stability', not just for the victim but also for a child(ren).

When would I seek a Non-molestation Order?

In simple terms, you should apply to the court if your abuser falls into the category of an 'associated person' and you are a victim of domestic abuse, as described above.

A victim does not deserve the abuser's conduct or behaviour tantamount to undermining the victim, nor do they deserve to suffer a physical assault or be afraid for their own safety.

It is important that a victim acts expeditiously if there is any risk that the victim (or any child(ren)) will suffer harm through the conduct and behaviour of their abuser.

Research has shown that domestic abuse witnessed by children and young people can cause serious harm to them and is tantamount to child abuse.

Therefore, do not hesitate. The sooner the victim applies for a Non-molestation Order the better, as this will afford some safety to the victim (and the child(ren)) and will control the conduct and behaviour of the abuser as the court will place restriction(s) on the abuser.

Top tips - some do's and don'ts

- Do ensure you understand the terms of the Non-molestation Order, that it adequately safeguards you (and any child(ren)) and provides the necessary protection you seek.

- Do keep a copy of the Non-molestation Order handy in case you should need to refer to it when you are out and about or in case it is breached.

- Do make sure you provide as much detail of the abuse in your application to the court.

- Do make sure your evidence of abuse is in a clear and concise format in your application to the court. Don't be afraid to ask for assistance. Use examples, such as text messages.

- Do use appropriate options to maintain an avenue of communication where there are contact arrangements for children, such as a contact diary.

- Do keep a diary or a notebook with emergency contact details for the Police,

Domestic abuse

Social Services, support agencies and other important contacts. It can also be used to keep a written record.

- Do remember you are worth so much more than having to put up with an abusive relationship and you can move on from it.

- Don't stay quiet.

- Don't continue with being a victim of abuse for yourself and any child(ren)) because you are afraid of what to expect if you move on.

- Don't blame yourself (or the child(ren)). Remember it is not your fault. The abuser is the one at fault.

- Don't dismiss the severity of the abuse or its long-term affect on you (and any child(ren)).

- Don't make an application to gain an advantage on the other party, for example, in contact arrangements or financial & property matters. It should be made to seek protective measures.

- Importantly, don't be afraid to seek help. There are various support agencies and lawyers who specialise in this area of work.

- Finally, do remain positive for you and any child(ren). There is life outside of an abusive relationship.

It is the view of the author that the above article provides some insight into this particular area of the law. It is simply an overview and the author would recommend the reader to seek advice and assistance from a specialist family lawyer who would be better placed to provide advises specific to your own circumstances. However, it is hoped that it provides some valuable information.

> Heartbreak - yes there's nothing worse, it haunts you, like an evil curse.
> A quote from a poem by Kat (15)

280,000
children experience their parents separating every year

(Family Solutions Group 2020)

Domestic abuse

The Independent Domestic Violence Advisor (IDVA)

Marilyn Selwood
Services Associate for ManKind Initiative

IDVAs are advocates who work with domestic abuse victims e deemed to be at high risk of harm or homicide. In addition to safety planning and advocacy, part of the IDVA's role is to empower the victim, enable them to access the right support and allow them to recover from their experiences.

The role of an IDVA can vary as some specialise in certain areas, for example health or courts, so they will not necessarily work in the community in the same way as other IDVAs. Some may also undertake this role as part of their wider job. IDVAs usually work for a commissioned domestic abuse service where their role will be funded by the Local Authority and sometimes other funding streams such as grants or specifically contracted pieces of work. Some IDVAs are individually funded by agencies such as health trusts and young peoples' services to specifically work with certain cohorts of victims or in certain areas. Young People's Violence Advisors (YPVAs) usually work with young people aged 13 to 18, sometimes older, in the same way as an IDVA but also have specialist skills for working with young people and supporting them to form healthy relationships in the future. Some IDVAs and YPVAs will also deliver group work and training as part of their role.

IDVAs will liaise with other organisations and professionals such as children's social care, police, courts, solicitors, housing officers, education officers and health & wellbeing professionals to build a network around the victim and their family. It is important that the safety plan promotes good multi agency working, transparency and reduces duplication. IDVAs may attend regular MARAC (Multi Agency Risk Assessment Conference) Meetings where a team of practitioners discuss high risk cases and try to put a plan in place to support them, their children and the alleged perpetrator.

When a victim/survivor needs to attend court to provide evidence or give statements to the police they can often be supported by their IDVA. The IDVA will arrange for them to attend pre-court visits so that they are familiar with the building and know what to expect on the day; and also to arrange a safe place for them to wait (entrances/exits etc). The IDVA may also support the victim to apply for special measures such as screens or video links.

When the risk reduces, IDVAs will very often refer the survivor on to other support services such as pattern changing courses or The Freedom Programme.

The Challenges....

It can be really difficult to get some victims to engage as they are often very fearful of repercussions such as having their children taken away or having to leave their home. It is really important for the IDVA to reassure them that they are independent whilst being clear about confidentiality and the IDVA's duty to safeguard

Domestic abuse

if necessary.

The Best Bits....
To see a survivor a few months or even a year or so after you have supported them in a safe and happy place is really rewarding. To know that they have broken the cycle of abuse and hopefully that they and their children will go on to have healthy relationships is the ultimate goal.

ONLY Mums & Dads
parents meet professionals

This book outlines the people and processes you need to know about to sort things out and avoid family court. It has been written to increase confidence, reduce stress and avoid wasting time and money.

Find out more at: www.familyseparation.shop

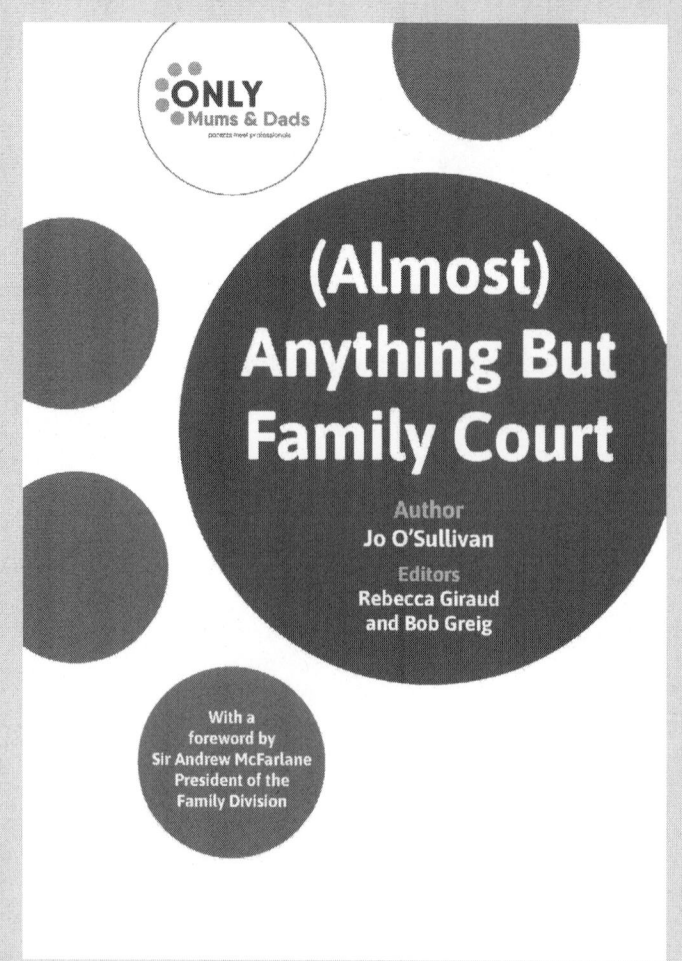

(Almost) Anything But Family Court

Author
Jo O'Sullivan

Editors
Rebecca Giraud and Bob Greig

With a foreword by Sir Andrew McFarlane President of the Family Division

Children

Separation and divorce are difficult processes in themselves, but when you add children to the mix, the process enters a whole new level of complexity. This chapter covers important legal and emotional aspects of separating as parents such as arranging contact and visits, contact centres and liaising with schools. Communication between parents is key to an impact-minimising separation, as is an awareness of legal requirements. Relationships are the scaffolding of our lives. Knowing what support and guidance is out there will help parents maintain a positive, healthy relationship with their children.

Children

Effects of marital discord on children

Dr Angharad Rudkin
Clinical Psychologist, MA (Oxon), CPsychol, AFBPsS

Before having children, we dream of a family home full of love, harmony and peace. Sadly, reality often doesn't work out that way. Two parents, running a busy house together while keeping their own work and social lives going, is a difficult task and one which can lead to high tension and stress. Children can deal with their parents making the odd snipe at one another, a short sulk in the front of the car, or a shirty comment or two. Children can even deal with relatively heated arguments that arise from a forgotten holiday suitcase, a car running out of petrol or a burnt dinner. What children really struggle with though is chronic, nasty arguments between their parents.

Arguing in front of children

In children's black and white worlds, arguing is bad and being nice is good. Parents and teachers reinforce this message when they guide children through friendships. However, it is not quite so clear cut. Arguments that are quickly and generously made up don't necessarily harm children. They can, in fact, help children to understand that parents can have a difference of opinion, feel cross, but can then resolve the issue. However, when children hear their parents arguing regularly, their view of the world changes. Disagreement becomes risky, they view conflict as dangerous and happy relationships seem impossible.

Children's levels of the stress hormone cortisol rises when they witness arguments. Seeing an argument is one thing, but witnessing the two people you love most shouting at one another, and yet be completely helpless to change this, can lead to sadness, worry and stress. Think back to a time you've been with adults who are arguing. The rational part of your brain tells you that this isn't a major problem, that everyone's different and that part of being an adult is not having to think something just because someone else does. But the emotional part of your brain switches into high alert. It automatically sends signals of escape or avoidance in order to get you out of the situation. In response, you look at the floor, play with your phone, anything instead of having to watch the argument playing out in front of you. Children are just the same. However many times you tell them it was just a little argument and that it doesn't mean anything, your child will still feel the automatic surge of anxiety and panic that comes with witnessing conflict.

Conflict and relationships

Arguments between parents not only affects the parent's relationship, it also affects their relationship with their child. Before and after divorce, conflict between parents will be high. Caught up in the vicious cycle of resentment, anger and frustration, parents struggle to find the resources to bear in mind their child's needs. Parents who live with a high amount of conflict are likely to be colder and use harsher discipline with their children. Perhaps it's become so normal to argue that they don't even notice they are also arguing with their children. Or it may be that parents dealing with high conflict just don't have the capacity to understand their children need a different approach. Children living in families with high levels of arguments are also more likely to experience "minimal parenting" where parents don't set routines, structures or boundaries. They can go to bed when they want or eat whatever they want. While this may feel fun to the child in the short term, it can quickly make children feel unsettled and uncared for. This can lead to low self-esteem and low mood.

1 or 2-parent households?

Children usually fare better living in a single-parent low conflict house than remaining in a two-parent high conflict house. However, the long-term psychological impact of parental discord on a child has been well established, and adults who remember their parent's relationship as being an unhappy one are more likely to describe their own marital relationship as unhappy too. Research suggests that boys struggle more in the aftermath of a divorce. Boys tend to be more impulsive and defiant by nature, but these characteristics are exacerbated when they live with parents in conflict.

After a divorce, boys are left trying to cope with few coping skill and limited resources. While most children's school work will suffer as a result of divorce, boy's school work suffers most. Boys also receive less emotional support than girls after a divorce, which just maintains the false belief that boys are not affected, don't need to talk about it and aren't overwhelmed with emotions.

Minimising the impact of conflict

Returning to my first point, no one aims to bring their children up in unhappy households. While witnessing conflict is stressful and life changing for children, there are things parents can do to minimise the impact.

- Maintain a loving relationship with your child, which involves pouring understanding, interest and consistency into your time and communication with them.

- Seek support from friends and family to help manage your stress so that you are less likely to unwittingly take your frustration and sadness out on your child.

- Work with your child's school to ensure that relevant people know and understand your child's needs, so that they feel understood and contained.

- Being emotionally close to parents is one of the most important protective factors for a child as they move through life. Do all you can to create and maintain yours, and your ex-partners, relationship with your child.

- Most importantly, try as hard as you can to be civil to your ex-partner in front of your children. If this means acting "as if" you really like them, then this is a role play worth doing.

Don't let their break-up change any ambition or expectation or goal that you have! Anonymous (20)

Children

Teenagers, young adults and parental separation

Angela Lake-Carroll
Consultant, Cambridge Family Law Practice

Many parents worry about how older children will deal with the separation of their parents. Adolescents are dealing with a great many things - they are changing physically and emotionally, they are trying to become adults and make their first steps towards independence and they may be starting to have relationships of their own. All these things can affect how they deal with their parents separating. Below are some hints and tips for parents which you may find useful.

Be respectful
Older children and young adults have the right to respect for their feelings. They are often struggling with growing up and may find your separation particularly difficult at a time when they need your attention and support. Try to put yourself in their shoes and not expect that they will be able to put themselves in yours

Think back
You were an adolescent once. Try to think about what that felt like, how you behaved and what would have helped you most - and what you found difficult as far as your relationship with your parents was concerned

Difficult behaviour is not always associated with your separation
Your child may be exhibiting normal adolescent behaviour rather than behaving badly because you are separating. Try not to assume that everything is connected with your separation. Adolescents need to test boundaries, have mood swings, be uncommunicative and spend time alone or with friends

Keep things balanced
It is tempting when you separate to try to make things up to children by being overly generous, allowing changes to well-established routines or providing two very different

> "Find someone to talk to in confidence - the turning point for me was going to see a counsellor on my own. I hadn't realised you could do this but it helped me recognise what was happening and gave me the courage to start to take practical steps towards leaving.
>
> *Tanya, Mum*"

models for discipline once separated. Try, wherever possible, to keep a balance. You may not agree on discipline, but you need to ensure that you are delivering a united front to your children, especially to teenagers who need continuing security at a time when they may feel that their life is changing and may be feeling insecure and different. Young adults can be particularly adept at playing their parents off against each other - although this may score some early benefits for them, invariably, they can end up frightened by the sense of power they have and ultimately blamed as the instigator of conflict between their parents. Best not to go there in the first place!

Don't criticise their other parent

Often it can be easy to fall into assuming that an older child or near adult is old enough to understand the differences between you and their other parent and can be an ally or confidante for you. This is very damaging for all children. You are the people whom they love best in the world - they don't want to take sides and may be distressed or angered by your behaviour in trying to get them on side or leaning on them too heavily emotionally

Try not to nag

When you are dealing with a difficult and emotional time yourself, a difficult teenager can feel like the last straw. Try to hold on to the fact that teenagers need to be difficult and to challenge as they struggle to become adults. They may also need extra sleep, time to be alone and to think and they may be uncommunicative. Make sure that they know you are available to them if they want to talk, that you understand how difficult things feel for them and that as their parents, you love them. Acknowledge to them that this is a difficult time for everyone but that you and their other parent will continue to work together to make things as best you can for them and their siblings. If things boil over, make sure you say sorry too - and be honest with them about how, when things are tough for everyone, it is easier to get into arguments.

Risk taking behaviour

Adolescence is a time for experimentation. Be watchful for risk-taking behaviour. Some young people take risks as a means of dealing with unhappiness or insecurity. Others risk take as part of their growing up process. If you think your child is involving themselves in risk taking behaviour. Don't panic. Remember that many young people are going to experiment or take risks as part of a growing up process and don't feel that your child is the only one. If possible, talk to your child, without accusing them, about your worries and concerns for and about them. Risk taking behaviour includes experimenting with alcohol, smoking, involvement with soft drugs and inappropriate sexual relationships. More serious risk- taking behaviour, which may indicate a need for professional support includes self-harming, eating disorders and regular or heavy drug use. Try to get some sense of whether the child or young person has simply experimented or whether the behaviour is more frequent than a one-off experiment. If you're worried, get professional advice and support (see sources of help and support at the end of this book). Try not to blame yourself - you need to stay confident in your role as their parent in order to help them through a difficult and confusing time.

Someone to talk to

Try to make sure that you keep communications open with your child - keep them informed about what is happening as far as you can and appropriate to their age and understanding. Offer them opportunities to talk to you about how they are feeling by giving them your time. If they are finding it difficult to talk to you, think about to whom, in the family or amongst your friends, may be someone they could talk about their feelings. Make sure that person is someone who can take a neutral view of the situation and suggest that your child might spend some time with them, or have that person make contact with the child to take them out. Encourage your child to find other ways of dealing with their inability to communicate their feelings - keeping a private journal or computer diary perhaps. If your adolescent child is having difficulty communicating their anger or sadness, think about activities that might help them to discharge some of those feelings - sporting

Children

activities, karate, judo, circuit training etc. are good ways of letting off steam

New families
If you are in a new relationship and/or may be forming a new family be careful to talk to your child about how you hope that will work for everyone and seek their views. Do not assume that children from different families will get on and try to put yourself in the children's shoes as to how it might feel to be joined together because of a new parental relationship. For teenagers, privacy is very important - don't assume or expect that they will share their room or belongings easily and try wherever possible to avoid expecting that. Older children can also be very difficult with new partners - this is a normal reaction and you and your new partner will need to work closely together to agree how you will deal with day-to-day living issues and with discipline. Be aware that your former partner may also find your new relationship very difficult, at least initially, and may resent someone else having a 'parenting' role.

Accepting independence
Young people form social communities of their own. They will want to be with their friends, continue their activities, go to parties or see their boy or girlfriend. This can be difficult when you are sharing time with them. Arrangements that might have worked when they were younger are likely to be less do-able as children get older. Don't insist that they must spend time with you as per an existing arrangement. They will resent you for it and are not likely to be communicative or happy if they have been forced to be with you. As children mature, time spent with either of you should be their choice - not your right. Give them their freedom and they are much more likely to choose to spend time with you, but remember as they grow up they will naturally grow away as they become adults. Be proud that you have raised an independent young adult rather than resentful that you're not getting your quota of time with them.

Don't bottle it up, don't keep it to yourself - TELL SOMEONE!
Tyla (15)

Notes

How can I help my children cope with stress and recognise when professional help is needed?

Dr Sabina Dosani
Consultant Child & Adolescent Psychiatrist, MBBS MSc MRCPsych

Stressed people are often the last to recognise what is happening. Our children are no exception.

Could my child be stressed?

Just because your daughter isn't complaining about finding your divorce stressful, it doesn't mean she's not suffering. If your toddler seems to be behaving differently: irritable, crying more than usual, having nightmares and regressing, chances are she's stressed. Likewise, if younger children are permanently tired, not sleeping, whinging and doing badly at school, they too may be stressed. Teenagers, on the other hand, may surprise you with outbursts of anger, missing school and generally feeling bad and miserable about themselves and the rest of the world.

Children who have ongoing stress are more likely to develop colds, digestive problems, anxiety disorders, headaches and obesity. Unless they learn to cope with stress, they're more likely to misuse drugs and alcohol in their teens and adult life and become depressed and even suicidal.

What kicks off stress?

It could be almost anything. Common sources of stress include the death of a pet, arrival of a new brother or sister, dad being made redundant, parental separation, moving home, changing school, exams, university applications, being bullied, the death of a grandparent or an unresolved family argument.

What helps?

Sound, confiding relationships with adults are

> "If you can possibly afford counselling for yourself, do it. It really helped me see that my family of 4 was still a real family and not incomplete without 5 of us.
>
> Vicky, Mum"

enormously helpful. It doesn't matter who they are: parents, grandparents, aunts, uncles, godparents, family friends or teachers. Stressed children may not know what is causing them to feel awful and behave differently to usual. The trigger may be divorce, but ongoing stress in children often overwhelms them when there is more than one difficulty. What helps is being an active listener and being prepared to ask open questions to tease out what is wrong.

Being heard and taken seriously by a parent helps children of all ages cope better with stress.

89

Children

What else helps?
- Breathing slowly and deeply
- Having a long warm bath and listening to favourite music
- Exercise
- Hobbies to retreat into
- Relaxation exercises

Even very young children can learn a relaxation exercise called progressive muscle relaxation.

When to seek professional help

All children and adults feel stressed from time to time. Experiencing some anxiety in childhood and beyond is normal. As parents know, most toddlers are afraid of monsters and many children show some signs of anxiety on their first day at school.

Anxiety becomes a problem when it interferes with a child's life. For instance, fear of contamination can lead to avoidance that gets in the way of friendships, fear of being away from home often affects a child's ability to go to school and fear of the dark stops a child going to sleep. Children and young people with anxiety disorders experience extreme fears, worries or a sense of dread that is out of proportion with a real or imagined threat, and impacts on many aspects of life.

Anxiety disorders change how children and young people think, often affecting their ability to make logical decisions. Although historically thought to be harmless, these disorders can interfere with academic, social and family life.

Although anxiety disorders are so common in children and teenagers, they are also one of the least well understood conditions in this age group. Most anxiety disorders begin between the ages of 12 and 21, although they are often first diagnosed later in life. Anxiety disorders affect between one in five and one in ten children and teenagers at some stage of their lives. There is good evidence for early intervention and self-management for children and young people with anxiety disorders. Delays in diagnosis, failure to involve patients in treatment and poor follow up can lead to further deterioration.

When to see a specialist?

1. Does your child worry or ask for reassurance almost every day?
2. Does your child consistently avoid certain age-appropriate situations or activities, or avoid doing them without a parent?
3. Does your child frequently have tummy ache, headaches, or episodes of hyperventilation?
4. Does your child have daily repetitive rituals?

Ask for specialist assessment and therapy if:

1. Your child or teenager has persistent worries or intrusive thoughts, extreme clinging, avoidance, or repetitive behaviours that interfere with school performance, friendships or family life.
2. Your child has palpitations, chest pain, abdominal pain, vomiting, shortness of breath or sleeping problems for which no physical cause can be found.

Children

Should we ask the children where they want to live, or is that unfair?

Emma Taylor
Partner, Goodlaw Solicitors

When parents separate, children are inevitably affected. What is important to remember is that they should not be drawn into any adult conflict. However, this needs to be balanced with ensuring that they are listened to and kept informed to some degree about the plans which are going to be put in place for their care so that they do not feel too anxious about their own future.

Far too frequently, children can feel stuck in the middle of their parents as if they have to choose one or the other. Whilst it is important to engage with the children and listen to what they want, it is also vital to reassure them and ensure that they do not assume the weight of responsibility for decisions regarding their care.

Child's voice

A child's ability to express their wishes and feelings accurately, with an understanding as to the implications of those wishes and feelings, depends on how old they are. Indeed, a court, when making a decision for a child, will apply the 'welfare checklist' found in Section 1(3) of the Children Act 1989, which states that wishes and feelings should be considered in light of the child's age and understanding (see page 192 for more help on the welfare checklist). What this means is that, for example, an older child within any court proceedings may be given more of an opportunity to write a letter to the Judge or to express their views than that afforded to a younger child because they are more able to understand the consequences of what they are communicating.

Practical steps you can take when deciding on where the child lives

By directly asking a child where they want to live, it is possible that this will put them in an unfair situation where they feel they have to choose. It may be more appropriate, depending on their age, to have an open discussion with them as a family to invite and listen to their wishes and feelings rather than asking direct questions.

Cafcass, (Children and Family Court Advice and Support Service) provide guidance on their website about how to listen to the child's voice after separation. Cafcass also provide a template parenting plan document, which may help separating parents to consider how best to approach discussions concerning the arrangements for the children.

Some parents also like to consider whether some form of family therapy is suitable to help guide parents and children through the emotional impact of a separation with practical plans also being established during the course of that therapy. Family mediation is another service that may assist parents. Within mediation you can discuss the arrangements for the children but also agree how best to talk to the children and listen to what they want.

Children

ONLY Mums & Dads
parents meet professionals

Communication between parents

Ultimately, the majority of child arrangements cases that end up in court arise because there is a lack of communication between the parents. It is undoubtedly a difficult and stressful time for parents when separating but it is important to remember that the children must be protected; they love both as their parent and, whilst the parents are ultimately responsible for the decision as to where they live, they must feel listened to without being forced to choose.

Further information can be found on our family law website at www.familylaw-brighton.com/children.

REFLECTIONS ON THE FIRST TWO WEEKS

The first two weeks can often be the hardest; getting used to a massive change in your relationship and your life, working out how to organise seeing the children, thinking about the practicalities of where you're going to live, financial and legal issues and employment. These are just some of the thoughts that will dominate this time.

Feelings of abandonment, rejection and humiliation are very real for most mums and dads and reeling from the shock of it all can leave you feeling emotionally and physically bruised. Don't be surprised if eating and sleeping are affected and that you feel exhausted.

Self care at this time is really important. Ensure you have support.

Adele Ballantyne

The amygdala is a little almond shaped structure in your brain which responds to threat. It fires off within milliseconds of a stressful situation and triggers the release of cortisol, the stress hormone.

When your brain is flooded with stress hormones, it is harder to use all the logical parts of your brain to make decisions. Instead, decisions tend to be based on feelings - especially unpleasant feelings such as fear, anxiety, panic, which you want to escape or avoid. Emotional decisions are useful in some aspects of life and at certain times in life e.g. falling in love.

But when it comes to making logic based decisions around finance, legality, and especially child care and contact arrangements, emotions need to be second to clear thinking, logic and understanding of your children's needs.

Angharad Rudkin

I really don't think my ex is well enough mentally to look after the kids. What can I do about it?

Kate Barton
Managing Partner, Boyce Hatton

After a relationship breakdown, it can sometimes be difficult to let go and allow your former partner to look after the children you had together. This can be for several reasons, many of which are often unrelated to the children themselves. For example, you may have been emotionally hurt by your ex-partner, or you may be trying to agree what's going to happen to the house, or what will happen with child support and maintenance. This is all part of the emotional and legal fall out when a relationship ends.

However, what happens if you have a genuine concern over your ex-partner's mental health?

Welfare of the children
The starting point must always be the welfare of your children. If contact or care cannot be agreed and it becomes necessary to ask the court to make a decision, this will be the court's paramount consideration. The court will also look at a range of other important factors, and it is helpful to start thinking about them at this stage.

The most relevant considerations in this situation would be:

- the emotional needs of the child;
- any risk of harm that the child has suffered or is at risk of suffering;
- how capable your ex is of meeting your child's needs.

Your child has an emotional need to have a relationship with their other parent, so they should be seeing them unless there is a reason *not* to. This reason could be any risk of harm they could suffer, or whether your ex is capable of meeting their needs.

For example, are they well enough to prioritise the children, feed them, stimulate them and generally make sure that they are safe and secure during contact? If someone is mentally ill they may not be able to do so. If they are suffering from delusions, psychosis or depression then this could be frightening for children, and may cause emotional harm.

What should you do?
Firstly it is important to identify whether this is a *genuine* concern. It is natural to be nervous, or even unhappy about childcare arrangements after a relationship has broken down, but do you *really* feel that your ex is too ill to look after the children?

Psychiatric illness covers a whole range of conditions and severities, not all of which impact on the ability to care for children.

Consider whether your ex

93

Children

has a history of mental illness. If they have, how has this been managed in the past? Were they taking medication or undergoing treatment? If so, are they continuing to do this? If properly managed, this should not prevent your ex from looking after the children.

Consider your ex's presentation and demeanour. What is it about them that makes you worried? Is it something that they may be able to manage while they are looking after the children, perhaps for a short period of time, if necessary?

Supporting your ex
Is there anyone who could support your ex during their time with the children? For example, a grandparent, a sibling or family friend who may be able to assist. Having someone else present may help to minimise any risk to the children without them even realising that such steps have been necessary. If you are able to share your concerns with your ex's parents or a trusted friend, then this could also help them to access further support. They may accept advice from other people in a way that they no longer feel able to do from you.

Whether or not your ex realises that they are unwell is also crucial. Do they recognise that they may be a risk to the children? If they understand this, and are willing to take steps to ensure that the children are safe in their care, the risk may reduce significantly.

Consideration should also be given as to whether this is a short or long-term situation, even if that is not clear at the outset. If contact does not take place for some time, this in itself can present problems later down the line, even when the mental health issues have been resolved.

Stopping contact
If you have tried all of the above and your ex still wants to see the children, but you feel that they are not mentally well enough to do so, you may need to consider stopping contact. This is a big step and not one that should be taken lightly. However, if you have concerns that your children are at risk of harm if your ex was to look after them then you have no alternative.

Applications to the court
Do you think that if you stop contact your ex may try to see the children anyway, for example by trying to collect them from school without your knowledge or agreement? If this is the case then you should make an application to the Family Court for a Child Arrangements Order, and a Prohibited Steps Order.

A Child Arrangements Order confirms who a child should live with, when they should see the other parent and whether this contact should be supervised. A Prohibited Steps Order means that the person named in the order is forbidden from doing something. In this scenario, it could prevent a child being removed from your care by your ex-partner.

If the children are already in your ex-partner's care, you may need to collect them yourself if you genuinely feel that there is a risk of harm. If your ex will not allow them to come with you, you need to consider making an urgent application to court for a Child Arrangements Order stating that the children should live with you and outlining what contact they should have with their other parent. In that situation, the court may decide that it needs evidence of the risk of harm that you are alleging, for example by obtaining a report from your ex's GP or any treating psychiatrist.

Evidence
The court needs to be convinced that there is a risk of harm to the children before removing them from your ex's care or restricting contact, which takes us back to the questions raised earlier about how any mental health issues actually affect your ex's ability to care for the children.

The sad truth is that contact

Children

arrangements after the breakdown of a relationship are often highly charged and difficult for both parties to come to terms with. If your ex has mental health issues then this can make a difficult situation even more stressful and confusing, especially when you only want to do what is best for the children.

It is always helpful in these circumstances to see a solicitor to explain your concerns and obtain guidance on the best way forward for you and your family.

TALKING AND LISTENING TO YOUR CHILD

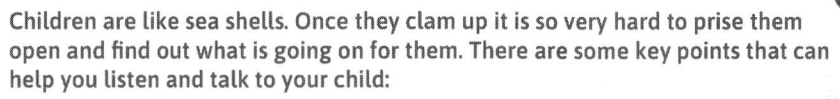

Children are like sea shells. Once they clam up it is so very hard to prise them open and find out what is going on for them. There are some key points that can help you listen and talk to your child:

- Practice *really* listening. Use your non-verbal communication to show you're listening (e.g. nodding your head) but don't say anything. Even when they've just stopped talking, give it a moment before you speak. It's amazing how much information you can get out of someone when you don't fill up the spaces with your own words and thoughts.

- Children, even older ones, have shorter attention spans than adults. They can concentrate for perhaps 5 or 6 sentences before drifting back into a daydream. Don't talk to them with long monologues and don't pack lots of information into one speech.

- Children often open up at the least opportune moment. More often than not this is because they know you aren't over-prepared and that you won't 'make a big deal' at these times. Sometimes it could be because they just want to reach out to you and have some of your time and attention. Keep conversations low key. If you care less than they do about having the conversation then they are more likely to talk openly (even if you are just feigning this casual approach).

- Children find it easier to talk when you are not sitting face to face, perhaps when you're in the car, on a walk, while you're cooking. Being physically close, but not having to look at one another's faces, helps conserve brain capacity so that you can both process the conversation more easily.

I blamed myself and I let my anger take control and I did cut myself. That is the one action that I deeply, deeply regret because I now have scratches on my body that can never be removed. Kay (16)

Children

I'm really concerned that my ex does not look after the children properly. What can I do?

Sabrina Bailey
Managing Partner, Allard Bailey Family Law

When parents separate it is inevitable there will be occasions where mums and dads will disagree about parenting styles and the way in which each of them cares for the children. However, it is important to keep this in perspective and keep in mind that there will be diverse styles of parenting (unless you believe the children are at risk of harm). If there is an issue it should be approached in a non-confrontational way and not in the children's presence in order to have a minimal impact on them.

Communication
The first step you can take is to talk to the other parent, as communication is key in co-parenting when there are two different households. If you have concerns such your child's hygiene, dietary issues and/or lack of routine, these could be an indication that the other parent is not managing adequately, and they may need a wider support network around them or assistance and advice from professionals. It could be that, if they have never looked after the children by themselves prior to the separation, they may benefit from some third party support such as attending a parenting course.

If it is difficult to discuss such issues with your ex-partner, perhaps a neutral family member or a mutual friend could be there to support such a conversation, to ensure it remains focused on the children and isn't seen as a personal attack.

However, it can often be easier to have this conversation with a completely impartial person such as a mediator or a family therapist. They can act as an independent neutral third party who can help you talk through the issues and try to reach an agreement with the other parent.

Contact book and parenting plans
It may be wise to set up a contact book between you and the other parent so that you can continue to raise any concerns in a non-confrontational way. Producing a parenting plan can also ensure that your children's practical day-to-day needs are being met and not missed by either party. The plans can include who is responsible for taking them to the doctors, dentist and for vaccinations. It can even include expectations for meals and set bed times, so that the children can expect the same routines and rules in each household. There are several online tools available to help create a plan, including on the Cafcass website. Having a parenting plan which can be referred to can avoid any future conflict over arrangements as it clearly sets out the agreement reached.

Children

Safeguarding concerns

If your concerns are of a serious nature such as suspected abuse in any form, whether physical, emotional or neglect, it is essential that you act quickly in gaining help.

In an emergency, you should contact the police. You can approach your GP for any troubling concerns about a child, even if that concern is about the child's care with the other parent and they will be able to advise and refer to you other agencies such as social workers depending on the circumstances.

It would also be helpful to speak to the children's school or nursery to see if they have noticed any changes in behaviour and/or presentation. Each school will have a Designated Safeguarding Lead and will have received specialist training, so they can talk to you about your concerns. If they feel it is necessary, they have access to a number of services and can ensure the right help and support for your children.

If you believe your children have been, or are likely to be, at serious risk from their time with the other parent, it may be that contact with them should stop until any serious concerns have been properly investigated and advice from professionals received and followed. Depending on the situation it may be possible to arrange some supervised contact at a contact centre whilst matters are ongoing (see page 112 for more).

Asking the court for help

If you are unable to resolve the issues with the other parent, you may wish to ask the court to look at the circumstances and make a decision in the best interests of your children. This could include who spends time with your child, where your child lives and the amount of time a child spends with each parent. Any decision a court makes will have to be applied to criteria known as the welfare checklist under s1(3) Children Act 1989. This will consider:

- the ascertainable wishes and feelings of the child concerned;
- the child's physical, emotional and educational needs;
- the likely effect on the child if circumstances change as a result of the court's decision;
- the child's age, sex, background and any other characteristics which will be relevant to the court's decision;
- any harm the child has suffered or may be at risk of suffering;
- capability of the child's parents (or any other person the courts find relevant) at meeting the child's needs;
- the powers available to the court in the given proceedings.

The court may ask Cafcass to meet you, the other parent and your children and produce a detailed report with recommendations to provide the court with a better understanding of the situation, whether the children's needs are being met and how they feel about contact.

Court orders

If there is a court order already in place setting out how both parents spend time with the children, and you have concerns about how they're being looked after, you will need to return the matter to court and ask for the order to be varied. In doing so, you can bring to the court's attention any concerns you have about the children.

If it is a serious concern and the child is in risk of immediate danger Children's Services or the NSPCC may do this themselves to protect the child. If you are concerned that a court order needs to be stopped or varied in any way you can seek some initial advice from a solicitor.

Children

My children have come home reporting inappropriate sexual behaviour. What should I do?

Emma Benyon-Tinker
Associate Solicitor, Dunn & Baker

Your children have come home from spending time with their other parent, and they make a comment that leads you to believe that there has been some sort of inappropriate sexual behaviour.

What steps do you need to take?

It will depend on the precise nature of the allegation but as a parent you have a duty to safeguard your children, even from their other parent, if there has been any sort of inappropriate sexual behaviour. This could be the children being exposed to adult sexual behaviour that they are too young to understand or witness; or it could be that something inappropriate has happened to your child.

If there is a Child Arrangements Order in force determining what time your children should spend with each parent, then this is potentially a conflict with your duty to safeguard the children. In that case you need to inform the other parent that you are going to stop complying with the order due to your concerns, and you must then immediately seek an urgent order from the court. This might be a Prohibited Steps Order which is an order which would prevent your children from coming into contact with the person against whom the allegation is being made.

The court will then review the allegations and consider what level of contact may be appropriate between the parent and the child, not only if the allegation is proved but whilst the court is investigating the allegation itself.

Fact finding

The court may undertake a

> "When I look back I cringe at how I got everything off my chest to anyone who would listen. I was hurting so much. It may have helped me deal with it, but I would aim to be more measured with my emotion if I went through it again.
>
> Dom, Dad"

finding of fact hearing. This is a hearing where the court hears the relevant evidence and, using the civil test for the burden of proof, determines whether or not the allegations are proved.

It is important to note that the test for burden of proof in civil courts is whether the allegation is proved on the balance of probabilities. This is very different from the criminal burden of proof where the court and jury must be satisfied beyond all reasonable doubt. That is why you can have the same case and the same evidence with the criminal courts saying the allegation is not proved and the civil courts saying it is proved!

Will the court allow contact?

Depending on the seriousness of the allegation, the court may still order that there should be some contact between the parent and the child. The court is under a duty to consider the welfare of the child and contact will only be ordered if it is safe. This might mean there is supervised contact. It might mean that there is indirect contact only, for example the parent is allowed to send cards and gifts to their child. If the allegation is extremely serious then it is unlikely that any contact would be ordered.

What if there is no court order in place?

If there is a court order in force, you cannot simply decide to ignore the order and not return the matter to court. You must comply with the court order which is why an urgent application to the court is required.

What should you do however if there is no court order in force? You still have a duty to safeguard your children from harm.

You may still need to suspend any informal arrangement that you have with the other parent whilst the matter is being investigated. You would need to report the matter to your local social services and your GP. They will initially undertake what is known as a section 47 investigation. The local authority has a duty to investigate where they believe a child has suffered or is likely to suffer harm in their area. They can also involve the police if they deem it necessary. Social services may ask that the parents make the necessary application to the court and the court would then decide the issues as set out above.

In some cases social services may decide that they need to take court proceedings themselves to protect the children from harm if the allegations are serious.

What if a criminal offence is suspected?

What should you do however if the allegation is so serious that a criminal offence potentially has taken place? In those circumstances, you will also need to make a report to the police. The police will want to interview your children and this will take the form of what is known as an achieving best evidence ('ABE') interview. The police will then decide whether or not a criminal offence might have been committed, and the CPS will decide whether or not there should be a prosecution. If the police are investigating an allegation, it does not stop the family courts being involved and determining the arrangements for your children. Often criminal proceedings and family proceedings are happening at the same time on the same facts.

It is important that you seek urgent legal assistance if you believe your children have suffered from some sort of inappropriate sexual behaviour.

I've looked everywhere for support, even at school, but I haven't really found anything helpful. Imogen (11)

Children

I always tell my clients that they must never regret the relationship that has ended as it has produced fantastic children.

Therefore they have to find a way to communicate as there are going to be sports days, birthdays, school plays, graduations etc where they will need to be in a room together and their children won't thank them if they have to have two top tables at their wedding because mum and dad still can't be near each other.

It's hard, and there will be bumps in the road but it can be done, and it's great for everyone when it happens.

Julie Hobson, Gullands Solicitors

SKYPE SESSIONS ARE BEING OVERSEEN BY MY EX

You can't control anyone but yourself. It would be reasonable to ask your ex prior to the session, politely, if they wouldn't mind leaving the children alone whilst they talk to you.

Additionally, open up a discussion so ground rules are agreed between you, if you can (e.g. discuss the children's lives and not how they're getting on with your ex). If not then it's better to have some Skype than none, so if none of the above works then just live with it.

Remember; you're a role model, so display the behaviour you'd like them to learn.

Mike Flinn

> "I have many friends where their parents have broken up badly and I can see how **severely** they have been affected by this."
>
> *Nerys, aged 19, Woking*

Children

Has my child been kidnapped?

Imran Khodabocus
Director, The Family Law Company

This article offers some advice to parents who believe that their child has been kidnapped. It aims to set the record straight when it comes to some of the misconceptions about this complex subject.

What is kidnapping?
Kidnapping is a 'common law' offence. This basically means that there is no statutory definition of kidnapping. Therefore, we have to look at those cases that a court has deemed a kidnapping to help us define it. However, essentially, kidnapping is the unlawful removal of someone against their will.

What might kidnapping be confused with?
Kidnapping is not the same as **child abduction**. Child abduction is a specific criminal offence in accordance with the Child Abduction Act 1984 and refers to an instance when a person connected with a child (not necessarily a parent) takes or sends a child under 16 outside of the UK without the appropriate consent. Usually this means the written consent of everyone with parental responsibility for the child, or a court order.

However, those who have a Child Arrangements Order (which confirms the child lives with them) or a Special Guardianship Order, can legally remove a child for up to one month or three months respectively.

Kidnapping is also different to **false imprisonment**, which involves someone being detained against their will.

What situation is not a kidnapping?
Many parents believe that kidnapping has taken place if:

1. a child hasn't been returned to their care; or

2. a child isn't made available for contact.

But these are common misconceptions.

1. If a parent does not return a child to the other's care following

> I'd have explained things more clearly and honestly to the children throughout. I didn't always do that and I've caused confusion down the line.
>
> *Kelly, Mum*

contact this does **not** constitute kidnapping. If there is a court order regulating contact arrangements then, in the absence of a reasonable excuse, it is a breach of the court order so can be enforced through the family courts. It is not, however, a criminal offence.

But what if there is no court order? If this is the case and both parents share parental responsibility, a parent who doesn't return the child is not breaking the law. They are entitled to do this in the exercise of their parental responsibility. The other parent has to apply to the court for a 'without notice' (emergency) court order - possibly a

Children

Child Arrangements Order or Specific Issue Order - seeking the return of the child. They may also decide to apply for a Prohibited Steps Order, which prevents the subsequent removal of the child by the other parent.

In either scenario, not returning the child does not constitute an abduction unless it involves the child leaving the UK.

2. I am often asked, if a child is not being made available for contact does this mean they are being kidnapped? The answer is no, they are not. The child is not being 'removed' from anywhere.

In addition, in the absence of a court order such as a Child Arrangements Order there is no legal obligation for one parent to make the child available for contact, therefore it is not a crime. For the same reason, neither does it count as false imprisonment. Even if there was a breach of a Child Arrangements Order, this a is a family court order, not a criminal court order.

When is it appropriate to introduce my new partner to my children?

The first thing to say here is that your children's thoughts and reactions to a new partner are going to be different from yours.

This is their mum or dad moving on, not their partner.

Age plays a big part in this process. Often younger children will adapt more quickly than say teens, but every child is unique and it's very much dependent on the circumstances surrounding the initial separation as to how they might present a reaction towards a new partner.

Although there are no hard and fast rules, it is a good idea only to introduce a new partner when you are sure (as you can be) the relationship is becoming more committed.

A gradual introduction on neutral territory for a short period of time initially and then building up to more contact is often a good way of introducing children.

Adele Ballantyne

I am happy that I never chose a side, because I knew my parents could teach me valuable lessons and morals in life. Isaac (15)

Can you answer some of my concerns about child contact centres?

Phil Coleman
Manager at National Association of Child Contact Centres (NACCC)

> It does get better; the world is not ending so take care of your emotional well-being.
>
> *Vincent, Dad*

A question we hear a lot is: *"I can't imagine seeing my kids in a strange place and being watched - won't it be awkward?"*

It is quite normal to feel this way - spending time with your children in an environment which you are not used to can seem very daunting and intimidating. Many parents have not come across child contact centres before and so can feel apprehensive. If you are going to be using a supported centre the volunteers and staff are generally in the background and do not sit with you watching or listening to what you are saying. They want you and your children to have a positive experience and spend good quality time together. The volunteers and staff will go out of their way to make you as comfortable as possible.

An environment to help you have quality time with your children

We aim to create a warm, sociable atmosphere where you and your children can relax and enjoy yourselves. Contact centres have toys, games and books for children of all ages. Tea, coffee and other refreshments are provided.

Research your local centre!

Find out as much as you can about the centre so that it is more familiar when you go for your pre-visit. There may be photos on your local centre's website showing what the various rooms look like and you should also be sent a leaflet from the centre explaining what it is like and how they run.

Pre-visits

If your local contact centre is accredited by NACCC you will have already been invited to the centre for what we call a 'pre-visit'. This gives you the opportunity to discuss your worries with the person who runs the centre before the first session when you'll be seeing your kids.

During the pre-visit you'll get a chance to look round and the co-ordinator will go through some paperwork which helps them to double check that the service their centre offers is going to be appropriate for your situation.

Your ex-partner and children will also be invited for a pre-visit on a different occasion to you. In this respect it can be compared to the preparation visits when a child is first starting school or nursery.

Again, part of their visit will include a look round the centre so that the

Children

environment can become more familiar and your kids can see the types of toys and games that the centre has.

For more information about accredited contact centres please check the NACCC website.

My children don't like going to the contact centre

It is important to find out why your children are not enjoying coming to the contact centre. It might be a good idea to speak to the coordinator, volunteers or team leader at the centre to see if we can make things more comfortable for your children. We may be able to help by providing toys that your children particularly like.

Parents can also support their children with the emotions related to contact centres by making it 'OK' to talk about contact in a positive and exciting way. Children are very perceptive and will feed off the emotions and anxieties of the resident parent.

Helping your children express their feelings

Your centre may have a way of your children giving feedback if they find it hard to put into words how they are feeling. For example, centres in Yorkshire have developed some 'Buzz my feeling' sensory boxes (in consultation with the Family Justice Young People's Board) which support children particularly if they lack the confidence to verbalise their emotions and feelings. It is hoped that this tool can help volunteers, staff and parents to pick up on issues sooner, so that appropriate encouragement, reassurance or other relevant follow-up can take place.

Reviews

You will not be using the contact centre forever. Ideally, contact centres provide a stepping stone to having contact in a more natural environment. In due course you should move on to perhaps just using the centre as a place to pick up/drop off (known as a 'handover') and then to make your own independent arrangements for your children without needing the centre at all. The centre co-ordinator will organise a review to help you prepare for this. If this seems too daunting there are some great free online resources to help you make this next step.

Cafcass produce a range of information that will support you when experiencing separation and/or accessing a contact service. We particularly like the Parenting Plans that support separated parents to consider how they might be able to co-parent in a way that puts the needs of children first.

I haven't seen my kids for ages and am going to see them for the first time in our local contact centre. I am very nervous!

It's normal to feel nervous and many parents think that their kids will have forgotten them but when they see their kids they realise they haven't. It's a special time for you and your kids so take deep breaths and enjoy it.

One dad shared his experience with us:

"I was shown in the hall... suddenly the boys came in running to me, their arms open, both shouting 'Daddy, daddy, daddy!' Big hugs for each one. It was like a rugby scrum only for once I was crying. They had not forgotten me."

Will my kids be safe in the contact centre?

All centres on the NACCC website are accredited and inspected by NACCC to ensure they provide a safe and neutral environment. This endorsed accreditation process demonstrates that the centre is working to agreed and approved national standards, ensuring the safety of you and your children. The national standards are updated by NACCC in line with legislation and good practice.

Which contact service is best for your kids?

There are a range of contact

Children

services which can be used depending on your situation and the level of risk.

Supervised contact

Is there a potential risk of harm? Supervised contact ensures the physical safety and emotional well-being of children in a one-to-one observed setting.

Supported contact

Supported contact keeps children in touch with parents if trust has broken down or communication is difficult. Parents or family members do not have to meet and several families use the facilities at the same time.

Handover service

This is when the centre is used for a short period as a drop off/pick up point. Again, family members do not have to meet.

Ways to help your contact run smoothly

The centre has strict rules which are there to make the contact run as smoothly and safely as possible for your children. Typical rules at a supported contact centre would normally include the following:

- Parents are responsible for the safety and supervision of their children at all times while at the centre. No child may be left without a parent in attendance.

- The resident parent must leave a contact number when leaving children at the centre.

- A child can only be taken from a centre during a visit if this is stated on the referral form, or with written consent of both parents.

- Relatives or friends can only attend if they are named on the referral form.

- There must be no arguing in front of any of the children. Abusive or aggressive behaviour and racist or other offensive remarks will not be tolerated. Any visitor acting in such a way will be asked to leave.

- No mobile phones, photographs (unless agreed with the coordinator) portable computers or pets are allowed.

- Alcohol, drugs or anyone under the influence of these will not be allowed on the premises.

> Always be there and be honest to your children. Never put down the other parent and teach your kids it's wrong to say bad things about people.
>
> *Philip, Dad*

> I now have no involvement in any argument between my divorced parents, and I feel a lot more comfortable to contact and see either of them without feeling like I'm betraying one.
> Sophie (16)

Children

My ex has changed the kids' school and doctor without telling me anything. What should I do?

Rachel Duke
Partner, Aletta Shaw Solicitors

The first key question here is whether you share something called 'parental responsibility' (PR) (see page 91 and page 19 for more information). Sharing parental responsibility means that both parents have to consult each other about important decisions relating to bringing up their children. That doesn't mean that you have to do this in relation to routine, everyday decisions, but it does include changing a child's school or doctor's surgery. So, if you share parental responsibility then in theory you should never be in this situation.

But if it does, what should you do?

Act quickly
The first thing to do is to make sure that you act quickly. The law sets out certain factors that are relevant to deciding these kinds of issues. One of those factors is to consider the effect upon a child of a change in their circumstances. If you leave it too long to object after the change has been made, then you could find yourself in a situation where it won't be in your child's best interests for the change to be reversed because a new 'status quo' has been established. There could also be an issue with losing the place at the previous school or surgery.

Communicate with the other parent
You should immediately notify the other parent that you don't agree to the change. You should also notify both schools or the GP practices and the relevant education/health authority.

It is generally worth trying to sort these issues out by agreement if possible. You should try to find out why

> *Take personal responsibility for improving your parenting skills and learn how to co-parent without criticising your ex.*
>
> Andy, Dad

> *Maintain your network of friends. Don't hide away into a new boyfriend/girlfriend.*
>
> Lucilee, Mum

your ex has done this. Is the GP surgery more convenient? Does it have a wider range of services? Does it have better reviews? Although you should have been consulted, it may be that it is in fact better for your child. That is the question that you should ask yourself. If you still don't agree then you should explain your reasons and request that the change is immediately reversed.

Children

Getting the court involved

If the other parent is not willing to cooperate, then you can apply to court for a specific issues order. This type of order does what it says on the tin. In this case the issue is the proposed change of school or doctor. The court will have to decide if the change is in your child's best interests. The court will want to see a good reason for it.

You should research and compare both schools including reading the latest Ofsted inspection reports. If you don't already have them, you should get copies of your child's recent school reports to see how they were doing at the previous school. You should speak to the teachers also. Is the new school more difficult for you to get to, so that you won't be able to pick up your child, or drop them off anymore? Is the new school fee-paying and if so, who is going to pay the fees? You will need to be able to explain all the reasons why you don't believe that the proposed change is better for your child.

If you don't have PR then the other parent does not have to consult you before changing your child's school or doctors. This is one of the reasons why PR is very important for both parents. But you can still apply to the court for a specific issues order if you don't think that the change is in your child's best interests.

If you get wind that a change of school or doctors is proposed but hasn't yet happened, then you should immediately get legal advice. It may be that you want to apply to court for something called a prohibited steps order to stop the change happening in the first place.

Ultimately it is far better to avoid these situations happening if possible. It may be worth considering why your ex didn't consult you. Mediation might help the two of you improve your communication, trust and joint parenting.

> Sharing the driving to and from handovers is the best thing to do. Many parents mention how that time in the car allows for one-to-one time with your children which can aid that (sometimes difficult) transition from one home to another. It also avoids unnecessary arguments about "one parents doing all the driving". It also demonstrates to your children that you are working together for their benefit.

> For a while I was scared of talking to someone but it really does help. School, teachers, friends, parents and siblings are always great people to turn too. Imogen (11)

Children

Is my ex allowed to change my child's surname?

Marc Etherington
Legal Director, Rayden Solicitors

To answer the question, you first need to know who has parental responsibility. I have assumed this issue concerns the child's biological mother and father as is often the case.

What is Parental Responsibility and who has it?

Parental responsibility is defined by section 3(1) Children Act 1989 as 'all the rights, duties, powers, responsibilities and authority which by law a parent of a child has in relation to the child and his property'. This means if you and/or your ex-partner have parental responsibility for your child, you are recognised by law as having a responsibility to make day-to-day and important decisions on their behalf.

The mother of the child automatically acquires parental responsibility for each child from their birth. The father does not have the same automatic right unless he was married or in a civil partnership with the mother on the day that child was born.

Nevertheless, there are various ways the father can acquire parental responsibility. This article won't cover all of these options because there are quite a few, but the most common ways are:

- Being registered on the child's birth certificate as the father provided the child was born after 1st December 2003;

- The father entering into a parental responsibility agreement with the mother; or

- The father obtaining a court order granting him parental responsibility.

Once you understand who has parental responsibility, this should help you identify the law's position in your case.

We both have Parental Responsibility

Section 13(1) of the Children Act 1989 makes it clear that when there is a court order regulating who the child lives with (called a Child Arrangements Order), the written consent of all those with parental responsibility must be obtained in order to change the child's surname.

If you have no court order regulating who the child lives with, the same rule still applies because judges in a number of reported cases have confirmed all those with parental responsibility must be consulted and give their consent for a surname to be changed.

Therefore, if you don't agree to the surname of your child being changed, your ex-partner is forbidden from doing so, even if they want the surname hyphenated. The only way they can then change your child's surname would be for them lodge an application to the family court asking a judge for permission to do so.

Only one of us has Parental Responsibility

The party with parental responsibility, most likely to be the mother because she has that automatic right as mentioned earlier, can act independently and change the child's surname without consulting the other parent. Yet, if the party without parental responsibility does object to the change of the surname, they can make an application to the family court asking for an order preventing the party with parental responsibility from taking this step.

What should I do next?

If there is a dispute as to the surname of your child, explore first of all whether a resolution can be found with your ex-partner. Each of you giving your reasons for adopting your respective positions and listening to the other may help find that solution. Mediation or a roundtable meeting, for example, may be tools you could explore.

If no agreement can be found, regardless of who the child lives with and whoever has or has not got parental responsibility, this issue should be determined by a third party before any action regarding the surname is taken because this is a such fundamental decision concerning a child's welfare.

As already explained, a judge could be the individual who makes the final decision. If you want to avoid court proceedings but still need someone to make the decision, an alternative option is to ask an arbitrator. To do this, you need to go through the arbitration process. These are private proceedings where you pay the arbitrator a fee for using their services. The decision of the arbitrator can then be made into a court order. If you want further information about arbitration, go to the Institute for Family Arbitrators website at http://ifla.org.uk/.

What approach would a judge or arbitrator take at any final hearing in my case?

The outcome of your case, as with any other case, would be treated on its own merits with the decision being made on what is in the best interests of your child. However, when cases concerning a change of surname have been reported, it appears that successfully changing a child's surname can be difficult to achieve, especially when it is opposed by the other parent. As said in the report case of *Dawson v Wearmouth* [1999] 1 FLR 1167, a change of surname should not be permitted without evidence that it would improve the welfare of the child.

My parents' divorce has been a positive change, and although it may initially seem hard, once you get into that routine, everything will start feeling homely and normal again. Stephanie (17)

Notes

Drugs & alcohol

Navigating separation can be even more complex for parents when there are concerns about drug and alcohol use. The impact can be detrimental to children and the wider family. The pages that follow offer guidance and support on looking after you and your children.

Drugs & alcohol

I am sure my ex is drinking too much when looking after the kids. What should I do?

Heather Broadfield
Solicitor, Slater Heelis

This is a difficult issue to address without knowing the reasons behind the concerns and how the suspicion has arisen. If there is evidence in support of the suspicion, or the children are already being affected by a parent's alcohol consumption, the issue needs to be addressed at the earliest opportunity.

It is OK for a parent to enjoy a couple drinks with their meal or at a family party for example. Parents need to remember, however, that alcohol affects different people in different ways and need to have an awareness as to how alcohol affects them personally. For example, one person may have a couple of alcoholic drinks at a family BBQ and it does not affect their behaviour or awareness in anyway. Another person may consume the same amount of alcohol and become sleepy which could pose a risk to younger children if left unsupervised, or become louder, agitated or start to use bad language, all of which would be upsetting for children.

How much is too much?

There are no specific laws or guidelines as to how much is too much and common sense must prevail. Moderation is the key and ensuring that as a parent, you are in control and able to care for children without putting their safety at risk. A parent should always be alert to any potential risks to children and ensure that in the event any child was about to, or had hurt themselves, they can act as quickly and appropriately as possible. Consuming alcohol to excess can delay reaction times, can make people drowsy or sleep deeper which can put children's safety at risk. Excessive alcohol consumption is also often linked to violence and domestic abuse which are dangerous and damaging for children to become caught up in.

If you have a relatively amicable relationship with your ex-partner, it could be a good idea to broach this subject in a sensitive way, when the children are not present of course. This would enable you to ascertain further information, voice your concerns and potentially put your mind at ease. This does of course require the other parent to be open and honest about their alcohol consumption. If there is an acceptance on their part that they do consume alcohol, a short-term solution could be that the children no longer stay overnight until the issues have been addressed. There could be an agreement that alcohol will not be consumed prior to or during contact and contact could take place at a children's play area or swimming pool for example, where the temptation of alcohol is not there.

Safeguarding your children

In situations where it isn't possible to have these frank discussions with the other parent or there is an obvious denial, you must ensure that you safeguard your children if you believe they are at risk of harm. This does not necessarily mean to prevent the children from seeing the other parent as this can also be emotionally damaging for them, but to have appropriate safeguarding in place. This could be, for example, having another family member to supervise to ensure that the other party has not consumed alcohol prior to contact and does not do so during contact.

If the children are overnight with the other parent and you are led to believe that the other parent is intoxicated and placing the children at risk of harm, for example one of the children contacts you by telephone upset, you should make arrangements to collect the children. If this is not welcomed by the other parent and they become abusive or refuse you entry, the police can be contacted to carry out a welfare check. It is extremely important to note however that this is only in emergency situations and is not to be used as a means of 'checking up' on parents without good grounds to do so.

If the other parent does not accept the concerns raised and therefore does not agree to any reduction in contact with the children, an application to the court may be necessary to ensure that the concerns are fully investigated and the appropriate level of contact is taking place.

If drinking alcohol to excess is raised during the course of court proceedings, the court can order that testing is carried out which will be followed with a report setting out whether the results are consistent with excessive alcohol consumption. In the event that tests show excessive/chronic alcohol consumption, the court may wish to see further testing in say 3 months time as evidence that the issue is being addressed. In the meantime, contact may be restricted to visiting contact as opposed to overnight and possibly supervised, depending on the seriousness of the concerns.

If you do have concerns and are unsure as to the best way to deal with the issue, you should seek advice from a family solicitor to discuss your options.

GENUINE CONCERNS ABOUT YOUR EX NOT LOOKING AFTER THE CHILDREN

Don't confuse a differing parenting style with neglect.

What is your evidence for thinking your ex is not looking after the children?

Are the children happy, clean, fed?

Are they worried or stressed? Are they worried because you're worried?

Remember: if you have been the main carer and the non-resident parent has been only semi hands-on during your relationship, there will be a certain amount of 'learning' taking place. That doesn't mean there is neglect.

Adele Ballantyne

To parents: never make your child choose. El (17)

Drugs & alcohol

How do I leave my alcoholic partner?

Luke Chester-Master
MSc: counselling research, supervision, and training

Should I stay, or should I go? Anybody who has ever experienced this dilemma will know how difficult it can be to leave a partner whose drinking has become unmanageable. Being in a relationship with an alcoholic is painful, scary, and difficult to handle.

As dependence increases behaviour deteriorates and the ensuing anxiety can make it extremely difficult to know what to do. By the time leaving becomes the only sensible option most alternatives have been tried – sometimes repeatedly – and the merry go round goes on. Often the drinking partner is:

- Lying about or hiding alcohol use;
- Unable to stop or control their drinking;
- Neglecting responsibilities;
- Behaving erratically and sometimes aggressively – maybe in front of children;
- Manipulating people and situations;
- Promising to quit or regulate but unable to carry it out consistently;
- Unable in general, to sustain a healthy relationship.

The Process of Leaving
Stages

Leaving someone you've loved (and maybe still do) tends to take place in stages. Denial exists for you too. Your thoughts of moving out may have been triggered by a dramatic event (domestic abuse, child neglect, police intervention) or by an unpleasant atmosphere leading to frequent arguments, but this is the person that you have loved, supported, and encouraged for so long, and they have slipped into a lifestyle that you could not have imagined possible at the onset of your relationship: it's become your worst nightmare. After each alarming 'episode' contrition will be shown and in the ensuing inquest promises made. At the time these are agonisingly heart felt and you believe them because you want to: the alternatives are too much to bear. For a period of time positive changes might be made but after a while you get to understand that there will always be a next time. It's time to leave. The resolve is strong, but the process is frightening.

Pre-contemplation: 'this happens to other people'. A time when you would never contemplate leaving your partner.

Contemplation: 'it's happening and maybe I need to go'. The evidence begins to mount up and leaving becomes an option.

Decision: 'I may not know how I'm going to do it, but I need to need to go'. An event or an accumulation of events provides the evidence you need to make the decision to leave. It's overwhelming

114

Action: 'I'm leaving'. You make the break.

Maintenance: Making sure you stay 'gone'. Work on personal growth, self-worth and developing the skills necessary to protect yourself and your children. Starting afresh.

Sabotage, traps and tips

For some it's hard to stay away. The 'pull' might come from your remorseful spouse who knows how fragile your resolve can be. They may be skilled in the art of manipulation and know precisely which buttons to press. You, however, are just as likely to sabotage your new-found freedom. The monkey on your back will try everything to convince you to give it one more chance…

The children need us to stay together. Separating will destroy them. No, they are better off right now with you apart. They have been exposed to a toxic situation that they don't need or deserve. You have a wonderful opportunity to get stability back into their lives.

If I love them more, they'll stop drinking. Not true – their drinking behaviour is their responsibility not yours.

It's my fault that they're unhappy. No, it's not. You are not responsible for another's feelings.

What will our friends think? Your real friends won't judge you. They just want you to be happy.

How will my partner cope with me leaving? That's not your responsibility. You've given as much as you can. It's time to look after yourself.

How will I cope? By managing things, a day at a time and not projecting your worries too far into the future.

Co-dependency. If you have a tendency to rely on your partner for validation, happiness and self-worth, or struggle to express your needs within the relationship, you may be somewhere on the co-dependent spectrum. These patterns of behaviour are difficult to recognise and more so to acknowledge as they are likely to have their roots in childhood. They are typically associated with exposure to addiction, abuse and trauma. Co-dependents often struggle to leave unhealthy relationships and for this reason the subject is worthy of note. Much has been written about co-dependency and, if necessary, it can be revisited further down the road to recovery.

Asking for help and setting boundaries

Leaving is a major step but how you move forward will depend on the changes you make and their consolidation. Accessing your GP is a good place to start and breaks your secret: they will connect you to the appropriate local services who in turn will help you design a care plan. It will be imperative to set new and firm boundaries so that your children (whoever they are with) and your ex know exactly where they stand.

Alcohol Services will offer:

Ongoing Support: counselling and or family work.

Introduction to self-help groups: Alanon and Families Anonymous and link in with others who are going through the same as you. Friendship, identification, and discovering that you are not alone will be a huge relief. These groups are free.

A legal expert will offer:

Advice on your rights around the relationship, your children and access.

Mediation if deemed appropriate.

Conclusion

As a legal substance and our society's current drug of choice, alcohol tends to avoid the negative stigma so strongly associated with other substances. This is unfortunate as its misuse kills more people annually than heroin and all too often has a catastrophic effect on children and the wider family. Adult children of alcoholics are particularly

Drugs & alcohol

vulnerable to repeating their parent's patterns.

Extricating yourself from a relationship with an alcohol dependent partner is complex: the ties and traps are intricate and the temptation to go back might feel overwhelming. Denial, fear, guilt and shame will conspire to keep you in the mire and undermine your every step, but keep going because your other options are horribly limited. Making the break will be the foundation of your own recovery, and a chance to start afresh. After a while you will have a different perspective and increased energy to deal with the issues arising and in time you will decide whether to keep the door open or exit the relationship for good.

The realisation that your alcoholic partner is responsible for themselves allows you to concentrate on what's best for you and – if you have them with you – your children. Removing yourself from the toxicity of the relationship is your passport to freedom and in all likelihood the best move you will ever make.

> It takes both parents to be mature enough to be aware of their children, and how their decisions are going to impact their lives. Ellie (16)

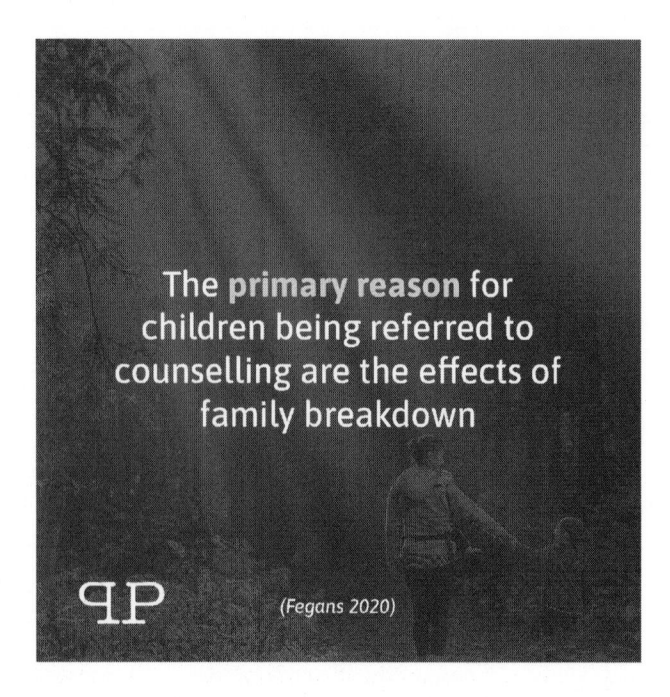

The primary reason for children being referred to counselling are the effects of family breakdown

(Fegans 2020)

Drugs & alcohol

I am sure my ex is taking drugs when looking after the kids. What should I do?

Carol-Anne Baker
Family Law Solicitor,
Bridge Law Solicitors Ltd

This is a statement heard commonly in children cases and can be a real issue, but further consideration needs to be given before the court or Children's Services will become involved. Whilst not condoning drug use, a parent may take certain drugs in a way that may not impact upon their parenting. The "looking after the kids" part of the statement is important as the issue is whether it is impacting on the welfare of the children. Be wary of comments from third parties who may have their own agenda.

When are drugs being taken?
Are the drugs being taken around the time spent with the children, being left around the house or causing serious lifestyle concerns?

The other parent may admit that they take certain drugs (commonly cannabis) but deny taking it when the children are in their care or say that they are getting help from substance misuse services. Other parents will deny any drug use. In more obvious examples, parents can appear to be under the influence of drugs to others regularly and may be involved in chaotic lifestyles linked with this usage, such as being homeless, constantly changing address, having damage to their home, having other adults spending extended periods at their home or being involved in crime.

If you are on speaking terms with your ex, you may wish to raise your concern with them initially. Try to do so in as non-confrontational way as possible. Explain why you have a concern and see what the response is. It may be that you feel reassured that either it is not happening or that it is not going to affect the well-being of the children.

Reporting substance abuse
If you are not reassured and are worried you could report this to Children's Services if you believe there is a risk of harm to the children. You could also decide to protect the children by stopping the other parent spending time with the children, limiting the time or insisting that the time is supervised perhaps by a family member you trust to ensure your ex is not under the influence of drugs around the children. Often it is difficult to communicate directly and be reassured or take protective steps without support. You may wish to see a solicitor for advice or you could make an application to court yourself for a Child Arrangements Order, mentioning that you do have concerns around drug abuse in the application.

Court involvement
The court will have to decide if drugs are being taken that impact upon the care of the children and if so what to do about it.

Drugs & alcohol

Sometimes, if a parent agrees for example to smoking cannabis, they could be asked to give an undertaking or promise to the court that they will not do so within a certain time before, or during time spent with the children.

The court may order drug testing to be carried out. This is expensive and with no legal aid generally, both parents will be expected to pay for it. This is usually carried out by way of hair strand testing, which can show a pattern of use over several months for most drugs rather than just at a single point in time, which is easier to manipulate. If the results are positive, a decision will be made as to whether this usage is likely to impact upon the parent's care of the children and if so steps will be taken to protect the children from harm. This could include the time spent with the children being stopped, reduced or supervised whilst the parent attends substance misuse services and further testing being carried out to review whether the issue is being addressed and if it is safe to change the arrangements.

In some circumstances, it may be the main carer for the children or both parents that are heavily involved with drugs. In those circumstances, Children's Services may become involved to determine whether it is safe for the children to be cared for by that parent or either parent. In some circumstances there could be a decision made that the children have been harmed or are at risk of harm from the drug related issues to the extent that it is felt necessary to seek a care order and remove the children from the care of the parent(s). The UK introduced a drug and alcohol court in 2008 and there are a number across the country as a way to try to help parents with such problems rather than remove children. They involve agencies such as the court, housing, social workers, psychiatrists and drugs workers working together to support families.

> Instead of hiding from my feelings I started helping my friends by telling them how I coped, and this really helped.
> Cerys (15)

Notes

DNA, hair drug & alcohol tests in families - what do you need to be aware of?

Dr Salah Breidi
Head of Forensic Toxicology, DNA Legal

Can a test show if my ex is still on drugs?

The misuse of both legal and illegal drugs can cause varying risks to your health and the welfare and safety of others around you. Drug testing is used to detect the presence of drugs in a person's sample, such as their hair, and can show a history of drug use over a period of time covering up to 12 months or more. All participants have the right to decline a blood and alcohol test, although this may have a consequence in cases that are ordered by the court.

When is a drug and alcohol test required?
A drug test might be required for several reasons, for example if an individual:

- is required to undergo pre-employment screening;

- is required to take part in a workplace testing programme
Is on probation for drug-related crimes;

- has been driving under the influence of drugs;

- has health problems that may be drug related;

- is pregnant and thought to be at risk for drug abuse;

- needs to rule out drug use for child custody cases.

What is hair alcohol testing?
A hair alcohol test is used to determine if a person has consumed alcohol over a certain period of time. The test works by examining the Ethyl Glucuronide (EtG) and Fatty Acid Ethyl Esters (FAEE) markers in your hair to establish alcohol consumption. Testing hair for alcohol is often used to determine alcohol abuse but it can also be required to show abstinence.

What is hair drug testing?
Hair drug testing can show up to 1 year of drug use, depending on the length of hair; 1cm of hair provides 1 month of drug history. A hair sample will be examined for the drugs analytes - the presence of the analytes in hair is a primary indicator of drug use within an allotted time frame.

The hair can also be segmented into monthly samples to allow a report to show a decreasing use of drugs over a period of time, rather than showing the whole test with a positive result.

What if you have no hair?
There are alternative tests available if your client has no hair. In some cases, if a person is required to undergo a hair alcohol or drug test, they may shave off

Drugs & alcohol

all their hair. In cases such as these, body hair, fingernail, urine or blood tests can be used.

How much will a hair test cost (prices will vary)?

A drug such as cocaine or cannabis test costs £55 per hair segment. Additional fees such as an expert witness report to interpret the results can be requested separately. The official legal aid rates are charged for any additional expert witnessing if needed (£108 per hour).

How much will a DNA test cost?

A home maternity or paternity testing kit is a simple peace of mind test, which includes everything you need to take a DNA sample in the comfort of your own home. It looks at an up to 68 DNA markers, and tests are run twice for 99% accuracy.

The test starts from £99 for a peace of mind test. The Legal DNA test is £299 which can be used for legal matters such as immigration and change of birth certificates. The chain of custody is preserved throughout the legal DNA test. The test includes the cost of the expert report.

What samples can be tested for drugs and alcohol?

Head hair, body hair, nails, urine, oral fluid and blood are all biological matrices that can be used regularly to carry out laboratory drug testing in humans. As a general rule, the detection time is longest for hair and nail samples, followed by urine, oral fluid, and blood.

Children testing

Children living in homes with drug-addicted parents are in a steady danger of poisoning and may suffer from neglect, maltreatment, and lagging behind in development. Hair analysis could be a suitable way to examine this endangering exposure to drugs. In general, hair from younger children contains higher concentrations than from their elder siblings.

If drug abuse is suspected in families where children are found, the family court can request drug testing for the children to confirm or deny the suspicion. Children drug assessments need to be done over a short period since a child's development is rapid within the first few years of life. Hair analysis can be employed to detect substances including opioids, benzodiazepines, barbiturates, amphetamines, cocaine, new psychoactive substances (NPS) and cannabis etc.

Professionals working in child protection often come under criticism which is why the Children Act 1989 requires proof of significant harm above a minimum threshold. Drug chemical analysis can form such an objective evidence to support their management. In the case reported here, the use of forensic science provided objective evidence within a matter of days. Similar to other forensic tests, the result of the children drug test has medico-legal consequences; therefore, hair or other types of sample analysis such as nails or urine analysis should not be used indiscriminately, and consent should be obtained. In child protection cases, the decision to obtain forensic samples should be based foremost on the child's best interests.

Can I DNA test to see if the child is mine and what consents are needed?

A paternal/maternal legal DNA test or peace of mind test can be conducted on a child to determine if he/she is related to the mother or father.

In order for the test to be undertaken, the birth certificate is required in cases where the instructing party is the father or the mother. If the child is under the local authority supervision/care, then an interim care order (ICO) can be made by the court to determine who has the parental consent. The ICO usually states the local authority or the named social worker to have the consent to instruct such a test.

Drugs & alcohol

Can I determine exposure from active use?

Passive exposure may have occurred from the use of the drug during a previous period, especially if the participant is exposed to the drug being in an environment that is contaminated with it. Environmental contamination through passive smoking or drug handling has been shown to contribute to the misinterpretation of results. Appropriate decontamination methods, detecting relevant metabolites and by placing threshold values can potentially minimize misinterpretation. The concern of passive contamination remains a problem. The diffusion of the drug deposits into hair reduces the ability to distinguish between passive exposure and willing ingestion.

Exposure, does not only include the consumption of small and/or infrequent amounts of the drug, but also in some cases different ways of passive exposure such as contamination of hair by the drug, ingestion through food or beverage, exposure through neglected/contaminated environment, passive smoking or drug handling and also previous ingestion before the tested period has shown to contribute to the misinterpretation of results.

The drug can still be traced in the hair when someone stops using the drug. This is due to the way hair grows and the different phases of hair growth - in this case, the hair resting phase, where hair stops growing for a period of time but still contains evidence of previous drug use. This inactive hair can last for several months and if any exposure had happened before the testing period, it is likely that it will be detectable at a later stage.

What are cut-offs and why are they used?

For drug testing, a cut-off is a drug concentration that is fixed to minimise the number of false positive results. The cut-off used by the Society of Hair Testing (SoHT) and The European Workplace Drug Testing Society (EWDTS) were found to determine active drug users in adults. In children tests, the cut-off level may vary. The SoHT and EWDTS did not publish cut-off levels for children. It is advisable to report any detected concentration of the tested children samples.

The main purpose of the cut-offs used in the drug hair analysis is:

- to minimise the detection of drugs used in previous periods of time instead of current use;
- to avoid the detection of drugs as a result of external contamination due to environmental exposure.

Crucial points to be aware of in children testing:

In children tests, the cut-off level may vary and therefore the level of the detected drugs were compared to the cut-off levels that are recommended by the SoHT, which determine adult drug abusers. It is important to take extra caution when interpreting a child toxicology result. The child is usually exposed to the mother's sweat, fluids and other sources, as well as external sources such as shared bedding and pillows or even direct contamination such as the tablet/drug powder being in contact with the hair etc.

That is why, when testing alcohol and drugs in children, it is recommended that paternal and maternal samples are to be tested to minimise and reduce the potential misinterpretations of the results. Moreover, it is advisable that any swabs are to be collected from the environments where the child is exposed to, such as bedrooms and living room.

Analysis of hair and nail washings

The analysis of washings can sometimes provide an indication of whether or not the drugs detected in the hair were as a result of active exposure and/or external contamination (either through sweat or

Drugs & alcohol

direct contamination such as the tablet/drug powder being in contact with the hair). This step will assist the toxicologist during the results interpretation to determine whether external contamination is likely or unlikely to be considered as the sole reason to explain the presence of the drug in the hair.

Conclusion

In conclusion, I recommend that drug and alcohol findings should not be used in isolation due to many variables and factors that may affect the results - they should be used in conjunction with other evidence from other tests and/or clinical assessments. In terms of DNA testing, it is always advisable to test more DNA markers especially when the test is not 99% conclusive.

> You are not alone,
> don't you worry my dear,
> remember, your family love you so don't shed a tear.
>
> A quote from a poem by Kat (15)

Notes

Mediation and non-court options

Before separating, you may never have heard of Mediation. This important process is demystified and explored in this chapter with articles clarifying what Mediation is, what happens in a Mediation Information and Assessment Meeting (MIAM) and how to write Parenting Plans. Mediation supports the key challenge in separation and divorce - communication, with one author describing mediation as putting "a break in the spiral of conflict". Having a third person can help couples to discuss difficult topics, to behave non-defensively and to think about the long-term.

Mediation & non-court options

What are the benefits of a mediated settlement?

Jo Edwards
Partner, Head of Family, Forsters LLP

I feel privileged when parents approach me about mediation and entrust me with helping them work through the children aspects of their separation. From run of the mill child arrangements cases with mild-mannered parents who have sadly fallen out of love, to highly conflicted parents arguing over whether one of them should be able to move abroad with the children, I have seen it all.

When speaking to parents in mediation, I tell them about the devastating impact of litigation. In certain cases, for example where there are parental alienation or domestic abuse issues, child welfare concerns or where one parent has an unrealistic view about what's in the children's best interests, court is inevitable and not to be demonised. But for the vast majority of separating parents, it is better for their children for them to make their own arrangements.

So, the question may be asked:

"What are the benefits of a mediated settlement?"

I highlight seven main themes:

Tailored outcomes

I have done many mediations where parents have wanted to think 'outside the box' and come up with creative solutions that a Judge may not. In one case the dad's holiday entitlement was so limited that he was prepared to let mum have the child for most of the holidays in return for having a more even sharing of term time than may otherwise have been the case (because he worked longer hours than she did).

I went to the mediation thinking that mum wouldn't agree, but eventually she did.

In another, dad wanted to move overseas with the two daughters, both of whom wanted to go, but mum was resisting in court. After three mediations, it became apparent that she did not oppose the move but wanted to defer it for a few months until she had found a job in the overseas country, so that she could move there also. Litigation is something of a blunt tool, with outcomes quite formulaic; who better than parents to come up with the best solutions for their kids?

Maintaining relationships

I say to parents in mediation:

"You may have fallen out of love with each other, but you have a lifelong relationship as parents".

There is nothing that ruins a parental relationship, sometimes irreparably, more than hard-fought litigation in which allegation after allegation has been made. I have parents I acted for in litigation 10+ years ago who contact me because they still cannot agree on anything, battle-wounded from the court experience. It is difficult to get parents back on the same page in parenting terms after litigation, even with family therapy.

In mediation, whilst parents may not always see eye to eye, I encourage them not to dwell on difficult memories from their relationship, but to look positively to the future - what can they each offer the children and how can the children benefit from all that they have to offer? That positive focus can reap rewards for future parenting.

Keeping control of the process

The most difficult cases I do, in litigation or mediation, are where parents are at different stages in the grief cycle. Where there are court proceedings, my experience of working with the left behind parent is that they are, at different points, in states of shock, denial, anger, bargaining, depression and (finally) acceptance.

How long each of those phases lasts will vary from person to person. The court timetable will not wait for them; their instructions can (understandably) be erratic and the process upsetting.

When working with a couple in mediation, it is easier to identify where they are in the grief cycle. Often I will encourage the person who is further on emotionally to give things time; to agree what the child arrangements are going to be for the next few weeks or months but not to push discussions around the longer-term arrangements until the other parent is ready.

I often also involve a therapist to help a parent who is struggling. By being able to control the pace, the parents are more likely to reach an agreement in the longer term interests of the children.

Longer lasting outcomes

The child arrangements which are most likely to stick are those agreed by the parents, rather than those imposed by the court.

I have had several instances of court-ordered arrangements breaking down. In some cases, one parent is unhappy with the outcome and will do everything they can to unsettle the arrangements or come back quickly for a second bite of the cherry.

In other cases, both parents are unhappy with the outcome and limp along with the arrangements before one of them applies back to court. Conversely, the whole point of a mediated settlement is that it has the parents' buy-in.

There is also an opportunity with a mediated arrangement to 'road test' any proposed child arrangements; I encourage couples to trial the agreed arrangements for a month or two and then come back to iron out any wrinkles (sometimes things as simple as, 'we had forgotten that Jamie's football lesson is at 4pm on a Thursday so handover at 4.30pm isn't practical'). All of this makes the arrangements much more likely to stick, and to evolve naturally as the children get older.

Hearing the voice of the child

Whilst there has been much discussion about bringing in greater opportunity for the voice of the child to be heard in the family courts, in practice this is still inconsistent across the country and often unsatisfactory.

In mediation, assuming that they are 10 or older, I will always discuss with the parents whether it would be appropriate to speak to the children. There is much more scope for planning this in mediation - the parents will agree the terms of a letter I may write to the children, the practicalities and agreed messages. For

> When talking to parents who ended up going through the court process they will tell you that they gave up on mediation too quickly. 'Stick at it' is our advice to parents.

Mediation & non-court options

children, it must feel like a less intimidating/stressful prospect to know that their views are being expressed to help mum and dad reach an agreement, rather than to inform an outcome imposed by a Judge.

Safe brainstorming space

Another benefit of the journey of arriving at a mediated settlement about child arrangements is that it affords a safe space to discuss ancillary issues. Many of the parents I see have solicitor negotiations or court proceedings on other issues in tandem. Sometimes one or both of them will turn up to mediation with reams of correspondence, complaining that it has cost them x thousand pounds to try to resolve, for example, an issue around the children's passports or the interim finances/living arrangements.

I tell parents that no topic is off bounds, provided they both agree it should be covered. Often with open, facilitated dialogue, an issue which may have become polarised is resolved.

Cost

A huge benefit of a mediated settlement is the saving in costs that will be made.

I saw a couple in mediation last year who had spent thousands and thousands of pounds trying unsuccessfully to reach an agreement. Over a series of sessions I helped them work towards an agreement. I couldn't help but think: imagine if they had come to see me two years earlier, they could have saved all that money.

Ultimately, it is far better for parents to preserve as much of their hard-earned money as possible by avoiding litigation and attending mediation. Parents will feel happier that money remains for the children, rather than a significant chunk having gone to lawyers.

The benefits of a mediated settlement, for parents and children, are hopefully clear. Whilst 90% of separating parents reach their own agreement over child arrangements, 10% don't. It has got to be our aim to reduce that 10% further, hopefully through mediation or other alternatives to court.

In child arrangements/contact cases I suggest the "wallpaper test". People don't like to be told what to do by their ex, so if you give them 3 different options as to times/dates etc which are acceptable to the resident parent and let the other one choose the option they want, that often results in agreement.

I used to do this with wallpaper with my husband. He wanted to choose it. So I would bring back 3 samples of wallpaper that I liked and he chose the one he wanted. He chose the wallpaper but I was happy with it!

Barbara Corbett, Corbett Le Quesne

Must read

Family Mediation Government Voucher Scheme for separated parents

Sushma Kotecha
Holistic Family Mediation & Coaching

Going through a separation or divorce can be emotionally challenging, especially when children are involved. To encourage separated parents in England & Wales to reach their own informed agreements efficiently and peacefully, the government launched the mediation voucher scheme in March 2021, initially in response to the Covid-19 crisis to support recovery in the family court and to encourage more people to consider mediation as a means of resolving their disputes, where appropriate.

The scheme has been extended twice since its launch because of the proven success in supporting parents to stay out of court and in control of their children's arrangements. The scheme is now available to families facing separation until April 2025. Here's what you need to know about the scheme.

What is the Family Mediation Voucher Scheme?

The family mediation voucher scheme is a government initiative that provides separated parents with a voucher worth up to £500 towards the cost of mediation services. Mediation is a process where an impartial mediator helps parents work together to reach mutually acceptable agreements on issues such as child arrangements, finances, and/or property.

Who is eligible?

The family mediation voucher scheme is for separated parents living in England & Wales who need help deciding arrangements for their children. It's available to all families and is not means-tested. But if the issues only relate to finances and/or property, you won't be eligible for the voucher.

How to apply for a voucher?

Only mediators who are authorised and registered by the Family Mediation Council (FMC) can apply for a voucher on behalf of their clients. If you want to use the scheme, it's important to find a mediator who is registered for it. So, when you're looking for a family mediator, ask if they are registered for the government family mediation voucher scheme.

Each parent will need to sign a consent form for a joint application to be submitted on their behalf by the chosen mediator. You will be requested to confirm that you have asked the mediator to apply for the voucher, have not already applied for another voucher as part of the same scheme, and have given consent to your mediator to give information to the FMC.

Where can I spend the voucher and what will it cover?

The mediation voucher can

127

Must read

be used towards the cost of joint mediation sessions once granted with the registered mediation service. It cannot be used towards any preparation work carried out in support of your mediation by the mediator or the cost of your initial separate mediation, information and assessment meeting, better known as a 'MIAM'. Dependent on the hourly rate of the mediator chosen, the voucher may cover the cost of a maximum of 2.5 hours of mediation based on an hourly rate of £200. If additional hours of mediation are required, parents can choose to pay for the service themselves or, if eligible, apply for legal aid mediation.

Conclusion

The family mediation voucher scheme is an invaluable resource for separated parents in England & Wales who need help agreeing on child arrangements. The government is providing financial assistance for mediation services to reduce the emotional and financial burden on separated families. If you qualify for the scheme, it's worth considering mediation as a first step.

Mediation lets you and your ex-partner stay in control of the decisions, without going to court. Your mediator will assess if mediation is safe and suitable for you, and the only initial cost is for the MIAM, which is usually around £100 to £150 each. If you're eligible for legal aid mediation, the cost of the MIAM will be covered. Mediation can save time, money, and stress for everyone involved. So, please take advantage of the scheme, if your case is assessed as safe and suitable.

Mediation can be a positive reassuring process that can help you both reach decisions about the practicalities of separation and more importantly decisions concerning your children.

However it is important that you are both in a position to agree in order for it to be successful.

Attending mediation when your partner is still at the 'car crash' stage of loss or has reached the angry stage will not always promote a conciliatory atmosphere. Counselling might help at this point.

Before you go to mediation ensure that you have thought about what you would like, especially where children matters are concerned.

Completing a Parenting Plan is a really good place to start.

Adele Ballantyne

How can I get the most out of mediation?

Sarah Hawkins
CEO National Family Mediation

Once you've decided that family mediation is the right service for you, you have a number of practical things to consider. But first and foremost, what you need most of all to underpin a successful mediation is the right attitude and an open frame of mind.

If you're completely consumed by anger and resentment towards your ex, the prospect of discussing and negotiating an agreement over vital day-to-day parenting, money and property arrangements will be nearly impossible.

But if your mindset is focused on moving things forward - not just for your own benefit but more importantly for children that are involved too - then mediation can work and be a great success.

So, assuming that as you've read this far you're interested in progressing with mediation, here are a few top tips to help ensure you get the most from the process.

Choose the right mediator

There are a number of factors you'll take into account in your choice, but number one must be quality assurance.

Get a mediator who's properly qualified. If you need a roofer or plumber you'll look for trade quality marks. The Family Mediation Council (FMC), the professional regulator, has an accreditation scheme: FMCA. Mediators holding this status have undergone relevant training and continuing professional development, working to high standards, and they follow the FMC Code of Practice. No FMCA? Rule them out of the equation.

Costs are always right there when choosing any professional. So look carefully at the fees you'll be charged for mediation - not just the initial Mediation Information and Assessment Meeting (MIAM) but for work that follows too. This will largely be shaped by the range of issues you want to mediate: this determines the number of sessions you will need and, therefore, the final cost. But do bear in mind that family mediation is almost certain to be considerably less expensive than pursuing matters through an acrimonious solicitor/family court

> When a close relationship ends, you have seen the best and worst of each other. You know what buttons to press!
>
> The analogy I use is you are co-workers/co-parents speaking to each other to get the best out of each other, like you would in the work place, to avoid a confrontation.
>
> *Tracy Allison, Allison Family Mediation Services*

Mediation & non-court options

route.

Your choice of mediator might also need to take account of child-inclusive mediation. If you feel your child would benefit from being included in the discussions (and it's not for everyone), do ensure from the start that the mediator is qualified to include children in the discussions.

Like any business relationship, personal qualities will play a part too. Does it feel like you can get on with the mediator, do business with them? What can you find out about their track record and their success rate in negotiating agreements?

What issues?

Consider all the areas of your future that you'll want to mediate over. Separation is going to affect just about everything in your lives. Some things will be easier to settle than others, but be clear about where potential disagreements may lie.

- Where will each of you live? Is that temporary, or for the foreseeable future?

- Where will the kids live, and how will both of you continue your parenting responsibilities?

- What about money issues, including too often overlooked debt and pension issues?

- What support payments will need to be made, when and by whom, in respect of the children?

- Who'll have the car?

- What happens to the dog?

Be as clear as you can at the outset which of these things you'll need to include in your discussions.

Prepare for compromise

Understand you're not paying for an expensive lawyer to 'hold your hand' and charge you lots of money every step of the way. Your mediator is shared with your ex. They aren't there to battle solely for you and win you a 'victory'.

Family mediation is not about telling your story to someone, outlining where things went wrong, how you hate him or her for it and your determination to settle those old scores.

Mediation is about the thoughtful construction of a future that works for everyone involved. Both people need to be ready to accept they won't get everything they want. It's that 'attitude' thing again. Put any remaining anger and hostility in a box and leave it behind. Shift your focus to the present and, more importantly, to the future - for your kids' sake, and for your own.

Think about the needs of everybody in the family. It's hard when your ex is one of them and you're feeling hurt and wounded.

But mediation is about compromise and negotiation, because at the end of the day those are things that will help you reach agreements that let you get on with your lives.

My parents' separation changed my whole world, not necessarily for the better, but I had no option but to go along with it. Cerys (15)

Top tips which may help you before your first joint mediation meeting

Sheena Adam
Family Mediator,
Children First Mediation

These are my 5 top tips which may help you before your first joint mediation meeting:

1. Try to focus on the future and solutions rather than the past and recriminations - consider what you want to achieve from mediation for yourself and your family. Blame is very tempting but does not usually help change anything and uses up a lot of your precious emotional energy. If there is a lot to sort out then it can also help to ask yourself

   "What is the one most important thing I wants to come away from today having achieved?"

2. Think "problem solving". Try to imagine this might be someone else's problem and what would you suggest. This is not to deny your strong feelings but to apply some of your positive rational side and to avoid the emotional aspects overwhelming you.

3. Mediation often talks about "Win/Win" outcomes. This means that we are aiming for outcomes which benefit everyone especially any children involved rather than one person feeling they have gained a lot and the other very little. That means thinking of compromises which you can both live with. If both of you approach mediation in terms of there being only your own preferred outcome, then you are locked in conflict "My way versus yours". However, if you can look wider at alternative solutions which might not be perfect but can work for both of you then these are more likely to be achievable. For example, if both of you really want the children to live with you, which is understandable as you both love them, then a shared care arrangement can work really well and help the children avoid the loss of either parent.

4. During the joint mediation session, you will be keen to say all that is important to you. The mediator should help ensure this happens for both of you, but it will also help if you can try to slow down and listen to your ex-partner rather than assume that he or she has nothing useful to say. You might be surprised and avoid missing perhaps a positive offer or willingness to meet you half way.

5. Towards the end of your joint mediation session make sure that you understand and are on board with what has been agreed. Again, the mediator should help clarify and summarise what you have agreed but it is really important that you do not:

   - agree to something which you know will not work

Mediation & non-court options

- feel awkward about asking questions to make sure you understand the outcome

You should then both receive identical written summaries of the outcome which reflect what you have agreed.

Notes

> You automatically think it's your fault or you had part in it, but it's not, it's between your mum and your dad. People fall out of love, people have arguments. It's how things go. Sammie (17)

Can I refuse to go to mediation?

Deborah Butterworth
Family Mediator, Mediation Dispute Solutions

People only ask the above question when they are convinced they should be going to court. They feel that a Mediation Information and Assessment Meeting (MIAM) is just another thing preventing them from getting what they want or they are the respondent who is being led unwittingly towards the court.

The answer of course, is yes - you can refuse. Mediation in the UK is still voluntary. A mediator cannot work with reluctant participants who are unwilling or unable to listen and engage with the other partner. However, the real question is:

> 'Should you refuse and what are the consequences if you do?'

Role of the mediator

Family mediators have two very different roles in the family law process. Their main function as a mediator is facilitating and working with separating couples to help them find a way to agree how to co-parent, separate their finances and assets and make sure they both have somewhere to live and the money to make those proposals work. People who engage in this process will work hard with a mediator to sort out their difficulties.

The other role for an Authorised Family Mediator is to see the prospective applicant (and invite and encourage the respondent) so they can hear more about their dispute resolution options before they make the court application. This can and, in my view should, be seen as an opportunity to put a break in the spiral of conflict which so often surrounds and takes over when couples separate. The mediator sits down separately with each client and tells them about all the different methods people use to decide what will happen to their assets and children. A mediator cannot force someone to mediate or sit in the same room with the other person and talk. The mediator informs each person about the process of mediation and where it fits in family law.

So often the history of conflict and the reasons why the relationship broke down makes everything too raw and too personal. The couple have seen each other as vulnerable, hurt, angry and scared. They also know about each other and will often accuse each other of lying, being vindictive or just out to hurt the other person. With that back-drop what is the point? Most people have probably never been in such a toxic relationship breakdown before. By trying mediation, a couple has nothing to lose and everything to gain, starting with their self-respect. If a couple can separate with dignity they give their children a good future and save money.

Mediation v court

To put the family court process and the requirement for a MIAM into perspective, only a very small number of family disputes end in a contested court hearing. How many of the potential cases are diverted from the court after the MIAM process is hard to tell because the best result is a consent order. The National Audit Office reported in 2014 that the average cost

133

Mediation & non-court options

and time of mediated outcomes was significantly less than using other methods - money and time which could be better spent re-building lives and moving forward.

If a court application is made without attending a MIAM a person may find their case is adjourned, pending a MIAM, causing a delay they did not want. Under section 10(1) of the Children and Families Act 2014, it is now a requirement for a person to attend a MIAM before making certain kinds of applications to obtain a court order. (A list of these applications is set out in Rule 3.6 and in paragraphs 12 and 13 [of the Act].) The person who would be the respondent to the application is also expected to attend the MIAM. The court has a general power to adjourn proceedings in order for non-court dispute resolution to be attempted, including attendance at a MIAM to consider family mediation and other options.

If the parties do not attend they are losing the opportunity to stay in control. Most family mediators can give couples a real insight in to what the court process is like. As soon as the application is received, the court takes over the case management and the couple's control over the outcome diminishes.

Going for a MIAM works because it gives the couple an opportunity to realise that they need to resolve the problem. They can do it with a mediator and they can get what they want: an end to the conflict, a fair financial settlement and a happy life for their children.

Remember it is easy to make a mistake when dividing assets if you don't fully understand the process or long term implications of your choices (legally and personally).

A good mediation service will step you both through the process and help you both consider options and outcomes that are safe for each of you.

Sarah England, Green Light Mediation

Notes

Mediation & non-court options

How do you expect me to mediate? My ex is a total nightmare

Paul Kemp
Principal Mediator, The Worcester Family Mediation Practice

The simple answer to such a question is: 'I don't expect you to'. There are many situations where family mediation is not the best option for an individual or a situation. This may be one – possibly.

But... If not family mediation, then what else can you do? Before I answer my own question, I should like to reflect on some of the issues that our title raises.

There are some occasions when mediation ought not to be attempted. Those cases will be identified by the careful screening carried out by family mediators before they agree to conduct a mediation. It may be because one partner is abusive or there may be mental health issues or other reasons why one party might be too vulnerable to try mediation.

But there are far more occasions when the difficulties presented by 'the Nightmare Ex' can be addressed within mediation by a skilled and experienced family mediator. It is part of what mediators are trained to do.

Nearly everyone who comes to family mediation has some negative feelings about their Ex. The breakdown of a relationship is a time of turmoil when individuals in and around a family have to find new ways of relating to each other. During that period, it is more than likely that the way individuals behave will make difficulties for those around them. And, whilst we might previously have seen the foibles of our Ex as minor irritations, they will now be experienced as major wrongdoings. (Psychologists call this 'negative sentiment override' and contrast it with the 'positive sentiment override' experienced by couples in the early stages of a relationship where the other partner can do no wrong.)

Add to that what the philosopher Bertrand Russell called 'emotive conjugations'* and all the ingredients are there for most separating individuals to see their Ex as a Nightmare.

However, what if your Ex really does deserve the title 'Total Nightmare'? If so, it may well be unrealistic for you to be expected to mediate.

Which is part of the reason why family mediation is strictly voluntary. You only enter family mediation if you choose to do so. What is more, if you change your mind, you are absolutely free to stop the mediation at any stage.

Choosing not to mediate

Of course, choosing not to mediate is not the end of the matter. You still have to find answers to the problems that come with the ending of a relationship. Questions like: 'What happens to our belongings?' 'How will the needs of the children be met?' and so on. Decisions about these issues will have to be made at some stage. And that almost always means that, sooner or later,

135

Mediation & non-court options

the two of you are likely to negotiate and reach agreement. So perhaps it might just be better if you could reach that agreement sooner and be done with it.

Choosing mediation

So what if you decided, after an Assessment Meeting with a Family Mediator, that it was worth trying family mediation? (an Assessment Meeting is known as a 'MIAM' which is usually compulsory if you wish to make an Application to the court for a Child Arrangement Order or Financial Relief Order).

Well, the 'Total Nightmare' will still be a total nightmare - but they won't be your responsibility. The Family Mediator will be responsible for managing the mediation process so that progress can be made. They will have various strategies and methods for managing the discussion. In the most difficult cases, they might even suggest that mediation takes place with you in separate rooms (though this does bring its own problems). Your only responsibility would be for yourself and your own behaviour in the mediation process.

What's more, if the 'Total Nightmare' proves unwilling or unable to behave reasonably, the Family Mediator can and will end the mediation process.

Assessment meeting

It may be worthwhile to reflect on what should happen at your Assessment Meeting. There are four elements to that meeting which is likely to last at least an hour:

1. A conversation about your situation - so that the Mediator understands what you are facing and the things you need to make choices about;

2. An explanation of the family mediation process – what it does, and what it doesn't do, how long it might take and what it is likely to cost – and other alternatives to court;

3. Importantly, a careful screening of the situation to check whether there are reasons why you should not mediate;

4. Thinking about your next steps.

Each part of this meeting is important to the decision whether family mediation is suitable: the issues that bring you to the meeting must be such that you are able to make choices; the process must offer you whatever you need so that you can then make informed decisions, there must not be factors that would make mediation unsuitable; and you must be free to make the final decision as to whether you want to try mediation or not. You will also know what other options there may be – including court – if you decide that family mediation is not for you.

If the Family Mediator has conducted the Assessment Meeting well, you should be fairly clear in your own mind whether, despite your Ex being a 'Total Nightmare', family mediation is worth trying.

But just a note of caution: if you don't feel that the mediator has listened to you carefully; if they haven't explained the process and satisfactorily answered your questions; if they haven't explored with you the things that might make mediation unsuitable; or if you feel that you are being pressurised into agreeing to mediate, then you should not mediate (or perhaps better, you

> **Think about what you want your life to be like post-separation and work out what is important to you and relay this to your lawyer. Try to focus on the bigger picture.**
>
> *Fiona Turner, Weightmans*

should not mediate with that mediator).

Remember that no-one has to mediate and if, having attended the Assessment Meeting, you decide that you don't want to mediate, then don't.

Alternatives

Which takes me back to my first question: 'If not mediation, then what else can you do?'

There are alternatives, and the mediator will explain them as part of the Assessment Meeting

You might feel more comfortable in Collaborative Family Law where you sit down with your solicitor, your Ex and his solicitor, with the two solicitors working together help you to negotiate. The fact that two solicitors are involved should tell you that it is a more expensive option, but it will be a better option for some, and there are two professionals to make sure your Ex behaves properly.

Or perhaps Family Arbitration with a private judge appointed to make decisions for you.

Or you might ask your solicitors to negotiate on your behalf with each other.

Or you might go to court.

The mediator will be able to explain all of these options to you and answer your questions, explaining what each is likely to cost you, and how long they are likely to take.

A final thought: When children hear their parents speaking ill of each other, it is toxic for them. So even if you think that your Ex is a 'Total Nightmare', if you have children, try your best to make sure that they don't hear you say it.

*Seeing your own behaviour as perfectly acceptable whilst regarding similar behaviour in others as terrible. It was memorably employed by the character Bernard Woolley in the 1980s BBC television series 'Yes, Prime Minister' who said: 'It's one of those irregular verbs, isn't it? I have an independent mind; you are eccentric; he is round the twist.'

Message to parents: support whatever the child wants to do, and don't influence their thinking. Jade (17)

'Ongoing family tensions' is one of the most common presenting issues in primary-age children who are referred for Place2Be's one-to-one counselling (67%)

(Source: Counselling and Psychotherapy Research Journal)

Mediation & non-court options

I have an abusive ex. Is mediation right for me?

Anna Vollans
Vollans Mediation

If you want to take your case to court, in most cases (unless you have made an allegation of domestic abuse and have specific evidence in support of the allegation) you will be expected to attend a Mediation Information and Assessment Meeting (MIAM). For anyone wanting to explore whether mediation is right for them, attending a MIAM is a really good place to start.

What is a MIAM?
The MIAM is an individual face-to-face meeting that will take place between you and the mediator. Your ex-partner will not be present at the first meeting. Sometimes people bring a friend or family member to the first meeting for support.

The mediator will not expect you to attend a joint mediation session. At the first meeting, the mediator will help you to consider whether mediation is right and safe for you and will identify when mediation will or will not be suitable. Where mediation is unsuitable the mediator will make sure you know the alternatives and will signpost you to appropriate sources of advice and support.

At the MIAM, the mediator will hear about your situation which will include asking about whether domestic abuse has occurred in the relationship. Domestic abuse is 'any incident or pattern of incidents, of controlling, coercive or threatening behaviour, violence or abuse (whether psychological, physical, sexual, financial or emotional) between individuals who have been intimate partners or family members regardless of gender or sexuality'.

What if you're at risk of harm?
Abuse covers a wide spectrum of behaviour including isolated incidents, on-going patterns of behaviour, threats of and actual physical violence. The mediator will discuss with you how the abusive behaviour and its impact might influence what happens in any joint mediation session.

If it emerges that you or your children are at immediate risk of harm, the mediator will help you to consider what action to take. Sometimes it might be necessary for the mediator to break their usual duty of confidentiality to ensure the safety of a child or an adult. In these circumstances, mediation would not be appropriate.

It is important that in the mediation setting, you not only feel safe but also comfortable and free to speak openly and honestly so that any discussions are balanced. If you would feel unsafe, fearful or intimidated by coming to a joint mediation session then it might not be suitable for you.

However, even where there has been domestic abuse, some people feel strongly that they want to mediate because of the possible benefits it offers. Mediation can still take place as long as all those involved are

Mediation & non-court options

willing to participate, and appropriate safety measures can be put in place.

Shuttle mediation

For example, mediation can take place on a 'shuttle' basis meaning that you and your ex-partner sit in separate rooms and the mediator moves between you. If you are fearful about coming into contact with the other person outside the joint session, you can arrive and leave at separate times and wait separately. In any mediation, the mediator will ensure that there are 'ground rules' to ensure that mediation is undertaken in a respectful and cooperative manner. If the ground rules are broken and the levels of conflict are excessive or harmful, the mediator will intervene and, if necessary, stop the session.

The key message for anyone who has experienced domestic abuse is that family mediation is a voluntary process and a joint session will only take place if you decide, with a mediator, that mediation is right and safe for you and where appropriate, the right safeguards are in place. Mediators are trained, skilled and experienced in working with families where there has been domestic abuse. Your safety, and the safety of your children will be any mediator's main concern.

> **"** We do **untold harm** for the sake of what we think is best for kids but also for our own egos. **"**
>
> *Dad.info survey*

Mediation & non-court options

How should I prepare for a MIAM?

Sarah England & Karen Shirn
Family mediators, Green Light Mediation

A MIAM is the first step whether you think you need to make an application to court, wish to mediate or even a combination of the two. You cannot make an application to court without attending a MIAM unless you are exempt (see page 129 for more information on exemptions).

What should I take to the MIAM?
If there are any relevant court orders make sure you take them with you. Otherwise, all you will need is a notepad to jot down any useful information you may hear.

There is absolutely nothing to be nervous about. The mediators are there to help you resolve matters so they will explain the process and principles of mediation. They will then ask you to sign an agreement to mediate. Don't worry - this does not commit you to anything other than to abide by the principles of mediation *if* you attend mediation. It ensures you both keep matters discussed confidential.

How to choose a mediator
If you are looking for a mediation service to provide a MIAM for you, top tips would be:

- Have a look at their website - is it helpful?

- Look at the costs of both the MIAM and the mediation session - if it goes well you will be paying for both.

- Check whether the mediator is accredited for children and family cases (this tells you your mediator has both experience and some successful outcomes).

- Ask whether the service is run on a sole mediator basis or co-mediation basis and, if the latter, whether they charge extra for this.

Co-mediation simply means you have the benefit of two mediators working for you to resolve the issue and, therefore, hopefully able to offer a higher success rate.

Most people choose to have their MIAM alone and that can be useful for both clients and mediators as it is a chance to calmly express your perspective regarding the dispute and understand how the process can help you.

A MIAM is an opportunity to meet and build rapport with your mediator and to ask any questions you might have so if you have a burning question write it down on your pad ahead so that you don't forget to ask.

How does child mediation work?

Angela Lake-Carroll
Consultant, Cambridge Family Law Practice

When you separate there may be so many things to think about that it can feel very overwhelming. As a parent, it is not unusual to be worried or concerned about how your children may be coping. Parents never want to cause their children hurt or upset and you may be concerned about how best to help them. Your family life will go on, but it will be arranged differently - sorting out how it is going to work best for you all is something that you can discuss together and arrange in mediation.

Mediators are trained and qualified to help you focus on how to help your children through the changes that are happening and to plan for the future. Your mediator will be concerned to get a sense of each of your children, what you think is important in any decisions you will make for them and to talk with you about what you think is important for each of the children. Depending on their age and understanding, each of your children will have different needs and your mediator will help you to think through what those needs and priorities might be. Mediators understand that it can often be difficult for you to be sure of your children's views or perspectives and that you may be worried about what you should say to them, how you can best talk with them and what they need to know about what has been happening and will happen in the future, especially before you have had the chance to think through the practical things to be sorted out.

Your mediator can help you to talk together about what is helpful for children, go through some of the things that can be damaging for children and discuss how best to start laying foundations to ensure your children's future security and well-being. Children often have questions to ask but can feel uncomfortable or be concerned about asking you, especially if they are aware that you are upset. So planning together how best to talk with them, to provide simple explanations and to encourage your children to ask any questions can be a very good way to help your children.

If you are concerned that your child or children may need additional help or support, your mediator can also help you think about who may be best to contact.

An increasing number of mediators are trained and qualified to talk directly with children and young people whose parents have chosen to mediate. Sometimes this can be a helpful way for parents to get a sense of how their children view things and what is important to them for their parents to know. It is important to say that trained and qualified mediators are not yet available in every locality but if a mediator is qualified to see children, that is included in the information available on the FMC Register (www.familymediationcouncil.org.uk/find-local-mediator).

If you think this might be helpful for your children, there are some things that are important to know and understand. First of all, both parents (and anyone who has parental responsibility for each child) must agree that their child or children

141

Mediation & non-court options

can be offered an opportunity to meet with a mediator. Usually, mediators invite children who are 10 or over and it is the child's choice as to whether they decide to come and talk with them. Some mediators prefer to arrange for a colleague co-mediator to invite and to talk with children. Where this is the case, your mediator will explain how they arrange this, including a meeting with you and their colleague to discuss and agree arrangements.

As their parents, you will be asked to sign an agreement about the arrangements for your child to be invited and to talk with a mediator. The agreement will ask you to consent to the practical arrangements and understand that in the same way as your meetings with your mediator are confidential, so would any meeting a mediator has with your child. Children can choose what, if any, information or messages they would like you to receive.

It is important that you also agree together that you won't try to influence what your child says or try to find out from them what they have said to the mediator in their meeting, and very importantly that you accept that any view the child agrees to share is their view and is respected. Any mediator who talks with children will explain all of these arrangements carefully to them in a way that they can understand and will check that they have fully understood things. Mediators also have a responsibility to ensure that a child knows that if they tell the mediator about any harm that has happened to them or the mediator has a concern about harm being caused to them that they would need to speak to a professional whose role it is to protect children and families from harm.

They will also explain that their parents are talking together with the help of their mediator to try and decide what is going to work best for everyone in the future and have agreed together that it would be helpful for them to know what is important for their children, whether there are things that their children would really like them to know and understand and what the children think might be working well, or is or would be difficult for them in their everyday life.

Your mediator will also talk with you at some length so that you can consider all of the things that are important about hearing what your child might choose to share, the effect that might have on you and how best to talk with your children afterwards, especially once you have reached some decisions together about the future.

It is unlikely to be helpful for your children to be offered the opportunity to talk with a mediator if there is a lot of conflict between you, especially if you have very fixed ideas about who your children should live with. A child is not coming to talk with a mediator to be asked who they want to live with, to give an opinion on either of their parents or to feel that they are being asked to make decisions. If your child is already being helped or supported by another professional, or if they already have been seen by a Cafcass officer, your mediator will want to discuss whether it is appropriate for them to be invited to talk to a mediator.

Your mediator will want to make sure that if your child is going to talk with a mediator, it will be helpful and reassuring for them and not make things worse or cause confusion or inappropriate upset for your children or for you. It may also be the case that having

> Mediation is not an easy process. It takes guts and commitment to see it through. But the benefits can be life changing.

Mediation & non-court options

talked with you about your child or children and the situation for you all, there may be other reasons why your mediator might feel mediation is inappropriate. If this is the case, the mediator will discuss with you the range of ways in which you might get a sense of what is important for your child/ren.

It is also important to know that mediators are not child counsellors or therapists and they do not and cannot provide any kind of report about their meeting with a child - just as in any mediation with parents, discussions are confidential. Their role in talking with children is to provide the child with a private space to talk about what is important to them, what they would like their parents to know and understand and to answer any general questions they may have about what is happening for their family.

> Children suffer when their confidence in their parents is fractured. Mary

Notes

Mediation & non-court options

Are arrangements made in mediation legally binding?

Rebekah Gershuny
Family mediator, Evolve Family Mediation

In most cases, working out your own arrangements in mediation following separation or divorce is the best way forward. This is because it is quicker, less expensive, and less stressful than court proceedings. Together with the mediator, you set the agenda, and you retain control of the outcome. To find a local mediator see familymediationcouncil.org.uk, nfm.org.uk or thefma.co.uk

Following separation, it can be difficult to make arrangements because there has been a breakdown in trust and communication. A family mediator, who acts as an entirely neutral impartial third party, can help to facilitate difficult conversations and assist you to structure arrangements that are unique to your own particular circumstances, whether these relate to financial matters, children or the future of your relationship. A family mediator will manage the process so that it is less overwhelming, and will help to reduce conflict and improve communication.

Where do mediations take place?

Most mediations take place with you and your ex in a room together with the mediator. However, if you have concerns about sitting in a room with your ex, you can discuss these in detail with the mediator in your initial meeting, and where appropriate, the mediator can arrange 'shuttle mediation'. This means that you and your ex will be in separate rooms, and the 'mediator' will shuttle between you. (For further information about domestic abuse see the National Domestic Violence Helpline website). The initial meetings that you and your ex have with the mediator are held with each of you separately, and are confidential. This gives you the opportunity to explain your circumstances, discuss your concerns and find out in detail about the mediation process.

Without prejudice discussions

The discussions that take place in mediation are 'without prejudice'. This means that they cannot be referred to in court, and the arrangements that you reach are not binding. At the end of the mediation process, your mediator will provide you with a document that will set out the proposals that you have reached. This is called a 'Memorandum of Understanding'. The mediator will also set out details of your

> Mediation cannot change what has happened in the past but it can help shape the future for you as individuals and your future co-parenting relationship.
>
> *Cressida Burnet,*
> *Cressida Burnet Mediation*

144

financial information in a document called an 'Open Financial Statement'. Unlike the Memorandum of Understanding, the Open Financial Statement can be referred to in future court proceedings if these become necessary because mediation breaks down.

How are mediation decisions made legally binding?

If you are getting divorced, the proposals that are recorded in the Memorandum of Understanding in respect of financial arrangements can be made legally binding by incorporating them into a 'consent order' which is submitted to the court for a Judge's approval.

If you have not been married, you can formalise the arrangements that you have reached in mediation in a 'separation agreement'.

It is a good idea for a specialist family solicitor to draw up the consent order or separation agreement to ensure that your proposals are properly implemented, and that if necessary you can enforce them in the future if your ex doesn't stick to what has been agreed.

Parenting plans

One of the major advantages of mediation is that you and your ex can draw up comprehensive arrangements for the future co-parenting of your children. These can be incorporated into a parenting plan which, in addition to covering the day-to-day living arrangements for your children, can also deal with broader issues relating to your children's health, religion and education.

Whilst it is not usually necessary, a court can make an order in respect of the arrangements if you do not think that your ex will stand by the child arrangements that you have reached in mediation. A family solicitor can advise you if this is necessary, and can draw up the court order for you.

OUR CHILDREN WANT TO LIVE IN DIFFERENT PLACES

As parents we want our children to be happy. This is never more important than when you separate. Obviously when children get older, they might want some input into decisions, but certainly for younger children it is imperative that the decision about where they are going to live lies with you, their mum and dad.

Asking a child who they want to live with puts them firmly in the middle of you both - how can they possibly choose when they love you both?

So, decide together and present it to them stating that the non-resident parent will see them regularly.

Sometimes teens pose a challenge when they are pushing against rules or boundaries. Try not to get into parent 'ping pong'. Be strong and back each other up. Emotionally it's much better for the child not to keep chopping and changing where they live.

Adele Ballantyne

Mediation & non-court options

(Almost) Anything But Family Court

Jo O'Sullivan
Founder & Principal, O'Sullivan Family Law

Most people don't realise that there are alternatives to court or the traditional letter writing service offered by most lawyers. I would urge you to take the three C's:

1. Consider all the other options throughout your breaking up journey.

2. Change the narrative around a break up and divorce. Do things have to be angry and acrimonious?

3. Consider where you are on the breaking up journey. The grief felt at the end of a relationship by couples, their children, friends and family is real. Grief is not linear so it's felt at different times. Do not mistake your difficult feelings with the need to have an acrimonious and difficult divorce. Instead, spend time working through the difficult emotions with a therapist, counsellor or family consultant. You may need to wait to get on with things until things calm down (but take legal advice to check).

As you can now jointly apply to the court for a divorce or dissolution of your marriage or civil partnership, there is no need to blame the other person. There is no need to state that there has been poor behaviour or adultery. No need to blame. The so called, 'no-fault' divorce is a new normal.

It's not an understatement to say that Judges do not want to see you in court. Judges only want to concern themselves with the most serious of situations. Most couples do not have a serious case. It will feel serious, of course, but it's very likely not a serious legal situation; it's just a normal case.

The courts are busy and so very overwhelmed that they are simply not the forum for the normal case. Delays and last-minute postponements are prevalent. Your privacy is not guaranteed with a push towards transparency in the family court. So, avoid it if you can. There are more than 10 ways of avoiding court. (Almost) Anything But Family Court (published by Onlymums/Onlydads) focusses on all the ways to sort things out without judicial involvement. They include:

- Mediation and Child Inclusive mediation

- Hybrid/assisted mediation

- One Lawyer: One Couple (Solicitor Neutral)

- Round table meetings

- Collaborative process with Arbitration

- Arbitration

- Arbitration with Mediation

- Private FDRs

- Early Neutral Evaluation

- Online help (e.g. Our Family Wizard)

Each process has advantages and disadvantages which are listed and discussed in the book. Assume that these processes can be used interchangeably, in a 'mix 'n match' kind of way. Your situation is unique - think

Mediation & non-court options

creatively about how these processes would suit you both.

There is a handy table which lists all the processes so you can cross compare them and choose which team members you might need.

POST-SEPARATION SUPPORT

Once you have separated the need for support can be vital. You can find support in many places and from different people. Below are some options:

- Family
- Trusted friends
- Relationship counsellors
- GPs
- Family solicitors
- Support groups - OnlyMums & Dads, Voices in the Middle, Gingerbread to name but a few
- Samaritans
- Citizens Advice

Adele Ballantyne

Notes

Mediation & non-court options

How to choose professional support

Claire Colbert & Rachael Oakes
Co-Founders, Family Mediation & Mentoring

So, if you are separating and possibly considering divorce, how do you choose the right professional support for you? First, you need to decide what type of support you need - but how do you do that when there are so many different options?

Here we try to summarise all the usual options and then we have set out some useful questions you can ask your chosen professional to help you make the right decision.

Ideally, you are looking for professionals who are going to support you to find amicable solutions so that you can avoid the stress, costs, and delay of court proceedings. Lawyers and barristers are trained to be able to take cases to court but what you would be best advised to consider, if you need a lawyer or barrister, is one who is also a good negotiator that has a proven track record of success at keeping appropriate cases out of court. Sometimes cases do have to go to court, but most do not.

What are the different types of professional support?

Lawyers

This is a generic term often now used to describe professionals who give legal advice. This can include solicitors, legal executives, and paralegals. Lawyers normally act for just one of you and your ex-partner has their own lawyer but some lawyers can now advise a separating couple together.

Some lawyers are also trained in a process called collaborative law where the lawyers for both parties will meet with their clients, together, in the same room, to discuss how to resolve a situation.

A good family lawyer will do everything they can to keep your case out of court and help you try and reach an agreement. They will give you advice but then follow your instructions about how you would like to resolve the issues that need to be addressed. This will involve them collating all the information and disclosure needed, advising you on practical solutions and what might happen in court. They will negotiate on your behalf by letters/emails or roundtable meetings. Lawyers can also draft the final documents that need to be prepared to achieve a binding and enforceable agreement.

Barristers

A barrister is someone who represents you in court and is an expert in the law. Barristers are normally instructed through lawyers to represent their clients at court hearings. Barristers can also be asked to provide written advice on the likely outcome of a case or about a specific legal issue which can help with negotiating a final agreement.

Some barristers will accept instructions directly from you. This is called direct access and can be used if you are representing yourself and would like to have a barrister to present your case to the Judge in court. You can also ask them to provide written advice about what a fair outcome in your case is likely to be.

Arbitrators

A separating couple can appoint a family arbitrator to determine a solution outside of court. You must agree with your ex-partner who the arbitrator will be. Arbitrators tend to be retired judges, senior barristers, or experienced lawyers. The arbitrator's job is to make a decision that will be final and binding about any financial and property disputes and they can also help with some child-related issues arising from family breakdown. Using an arbitrator is like going straight to a Judge you have hand-picked, in a timeframe you all agree on.

Mediators

The job of a mediator is to meet with couples to help them resolve disputes so that they do not have to go to court. This can be done face-to-face, online, with or without lawyers and some mediators are also qualified to meet with children to give them a voice in the process.

Whether meeting face-to-face or online you can be in the same room as your ex-partner or in separate rooms, separate virtual rooms if meeting online. Once proposals for reaching an agreement have been prepared a couple can get advice from their lawyer, if they want to, before a lawyer is then asked to draw up the formal court order that can be filed with the court for approval by a Judge. Mediation is a very flexible process: if you need advice between mediation meetings, then your lawyer can speak with you.

Therapists/Counsellors/Coaches

During your separation, you may experience, amongst other emotions, grief, anger, or depression. It is important to recognise the emotional side of separation and divorce and the impact it can have on you at a time when you are having to make important decisions. There are many different professionals who can support you including therapists, counsellors, coaches and specialist parenting experts who also run programs to help parents create a positive co-parenting relationship moving forward.

Other experts

Other experts like accountants, financial advisers and pension experts can help explain other issues that you will need to understand as part of your decision-making process where financial issues are involved. They can be asked to advise one of you or they can prepare a joint expert opinion or report if you and your ex-partner agree that you both need their advice.

The professionals that you choose will have an impact on the cost, timescale and way in which the legal issues you are dealing with are resolved. Often, it is helpful to think of some key questions when deciding which professional to appoint. Here are some key questions we would recommend you consider asking:

- What expertise and qualifications do they have, and are they accredited? Have a look on their website and read their profile because it will give you some information about them and the type of work they do.

- Check that they have specialist expertise in the area in which you need their support.

- Do they have any testimonials from people who have used their services and were they in a similar position to you?

Mediation & non-court options

- Do they offer a free initial call or meeting so that you can talk to them to decide if they are someone you would like to work with?

- If looking for a lawyer, ask them what their approach is. How do they negotiate and what percentage of their cases do they settle without having to go to court? How do they interact with other professionals and do they consider all of the dispute resolution options such as mediation and arbitration if that would be appropriate in your situation.

- How busy are they, are they going to have availability to deal with your situation?

- What hours do they work and what is their policy on how quickly they return calls and answer emails?

- Do they work virtually or live in the area local to you? Will you have to travel to see them?

- How do they charge, what do they charge and will you have to pay for anything upfront?

- How long do they think it will take to resolve things for you?

- Ask yourself, do you trust this person, do they make you feel comfortable and can you work with them? How able would you feel to ask them questions?

Helpful Links
You will find a list of key support organisations and professional bodies in the "Advice and Support" section towards the back of this book.

You do have a voice, speak up before no more can be said.
Ellie (16)

> **We both handled things badly and our child was the loser. If I could reach out to every parent making the same mistakes I would for the sake of the children.**
>
> *Dad.info survey*

Money

We need the security of knowing we are safe, have a roof over our head, and enough food and resources for the future. When we know this we can then channel all of our energies into feeling healthy and happy. This chapter explores the essential elements of security and safety - money, homes, pensions. Though these may be the last things you feel able to think about in the whirlwind of separation, discussing and planning housing and finance from the very start will smooth the transition into life post-divorce.

Money

My soon to be ex-husband has money all over the place. Where do I start?

Rachael Oakes
Co-Founder, Family Mediation & Mentoring

It isn't unusual for one person within a marriage, let us say the husband, to be in control of the parties' finances. This does, however, mean that the other party has little or sometimes no knowledge of their financial circumstances.

Duty of full & frank disclosure

If the financial matters that need to be resolved when going through a divorce are, or become, bitterly contested, there can be all sorts of allegations of non-disclosure or even fraud against an ex who does not disclose details of their financial circumstances or discloses income and assets that may be a lot less than what the other party expected.

There have even been cases where one party, again let us say the husband and in anticipation of getting divorced, may try and divest himself of assets so as to produce a more modest balance sheet, but a party who does this has to be very careful. A party going through a divorce cannot take any action that would deliberately minimise the other party's claim. To do so could, potentially, even amount to fraud. This could mean that any financial settlement reached during a divorce could be set aside and potentially, in the case of fraud, the guilty party might even be prosecuted for perjury.

To offer some sort of reassurance, each party going through a divorce has an ongoing duty to provide full and frank disclosure about their finances until a financial consent order is made. It is only on the making of such an order that the financial settlement the couple reach is legally binding on them both.

> The last mile in a settlement can be hardest. All anger/distress/sorrow is still there, but rather than resting upon a wide ranging dispute, it weighs HEAVILY on the issues which remain. The argument about the teapot is not about a chattel, but the last totemic lash of the tail.
>
> *Rhys Taylor, The 36 Group*

It is also important to remember that your instructing solicitor, if you use one, are officers of the court. This means that they cannot mislead the court; neither can they present a financial picture that does not represent the truth. Furthermore, solicitors cannot continue to act for a client who refuses to tell the truth.

Judges do not like a party who doesn't comply with the duty of full and frank disclosure. If one party refuses to disclose financial information or deliberately delays the court process it can lead to a Judge drawing an adverse inference from their behaviour, to their detriment.

Freezing assets

Depending on your concerns about the finances, it is possible to freeze the other party's assets if you are certain that the other party, again let us say the husband, is shortly about to sell or get rid of assets with the intention of preventing you from receiving some of that financial benefit. This is not just limited to assets in the UK - it can relate to assets worldwide.

So, on a practical level what can you do then if your ex has money all over the place?

Don't pry!

First, it is important to remember that you must not open your ex's post or log in to their email or accounts. Up until 2010, it was possible to do this and make copies of information found, a useful tool if one party thought their ex was trying to hide assets. However, a case now known as *Imerman* swept away those rules meaning you can no longer use information obtained in that manner. So, do not be tempted to do this but do make a note of any information about assets (e.g. a statement that is left, say, on the kitchen table or in a room that you both normally use, i.e. a joint study). This can then be cross-checked against the information your ex does provide when you exchange financial information in due course.

Secondly, make a list of what you do know the two of you have together as this will be a useful checklist. Your lawyer may also want to know about certain aspects of your relationship that might be indicative of your lifestyle during the marriage. With this in mind, also make a note of what holidays you took, where you travelled, how much they cost and how the trips were paid for. How often would you eat out?

Also, remember there are different ways that couples can reach a financial agreement and most processes will require exchange of financial information. Once that exchange has taken place, there is then the opportunity to ask questions on the other party's disclosure. It's at that stage that, if you think information is missing or has not been fully disclosed, questions can be raised in the hope that the other party will then provide full and frank disclosure.

Furthermore, whilst it is always a very last resort, there is always the ability to ask the court to deal with the financial matters. In that scenario and once the court timetable has been issued, if one party still does not comply then it is possible to take enforcement action at that stage.

Finally, whatever your circumstances, we would always recommend you obtain legal advice early on so that you fully understand your options.

Knowing where you stand from a legal perspective offers individuals peace of mind so they know the next steps involved and how they can best move things forward.

I just wanted to please my dad, because if I told them I wanted to go home he would be upset. Jade (17)

What is child maintenance?

Gingerbread

Gingerbread is a national charity that provides expert advice, practical support and campaigns for single mums and dads.

Child maintenance is when a parent who does not live with their children pays money towards their upkeep, including food, clothes, and other essentials. It helps to provide a stable home and is a way of making sure that children are brought up in the best circumstances possible.

Child maintenance usually works by the parent who does not live with the children most of the time paying money to the parent who does. It can also involve that parent spending money directly on their children as part of a family-based child maintenance arrangement.

Child maintenance has nothing to do with contact between parent and child. Legally a parent must pay maintenance even if they do not see their child. Equally a parent cannot be denied contact for not paying child maintenance.

Who has to pay child maintenance?

Child maintenance is a legal requirement, as all parents have a responsibility to look after their children financially. Any parent who has their child living with them for less than half of the time is expected to pay child maintenance. The amount of child maintenance that has to be paid will depend on how much time each parent has the children staying with them.

Child maintenance has to be paid for:

- all children under 16;
- children under 20 who are in full-time non-advanced education (A-levels or equivalent);
- children aged 16 or 17 who are not in full-time education but are registered to work or train with a careers service.

If you are not sure if your situation requires child maintenance you can always contact Gingerbread or Child Maintenance Options for advice (see below).

How to arrange child maintenance

There are three main ways of organising child maintenance:

- Family-based arrangement;
- Consent order;
- Child Maintenance Service.

If you and the other parent can reach an agreement then you can make either a family-based arrangement or a consent order. If you can't agree with the other parent then you can pay child maintenance through the Child Maintenance Service (CMS).

Family-based arrangement

A family-based arrangement is simply when parents agree among themselves how child maintenance is going to be paid. You can make any arrangement you like for child maintenance, as long as both parents agree. This could be regular payments of money, lump sums for certain items, or payments in kind such as buying school uniforms or nappies. It could be a combination of these things.

The Child Maintenance Options service can provide a form for you to write down what you agree. You can download it at www.cmoptions.org.

Family-based arrangements are the simplest option for child maintenance, as you can agree on whatever amount of child maintenance you want, in whatever form you want. Unlike other options they are free. It also helps to have an agreement in place to avoid potential arguments later on.

However, these arrangements are not legally binding - they're simply an agreement between both parents. If one parent changes their mind or stops paying there is no way to legally enforce it. If the arrangement does break down, you can still use the CMS.

Consent orders

If you reach an agreement with your child's other parent another option is to apply to the court to make the agreement legally binding. This is called a consent order. Both parents must agree to the terms of the order. A consent order is usually used when parents are divorcing and sorting out their finances, so it might include other agreements, such as who is going to pay the mortgage.

Consent orders can be enforced through the court if the child maintenance isn't paid. However, this option is more costly as there are court fees for making and enforcing the order. You should also get independent legal advice which you would have to pay for. You can't apply to the CMS for one year after a consent order is made, so you should be confident that it is going to last for the foreseeable future.

Using the CMS

If you can't reach an agreement with your child's other parent you can use the CMS to arrange child maintenance for you, even if you don't have contact with them.

Before you can apply to the CMS you must call Child Maintenance Options to discuss if you could make a family-based arrangement instead. If you have tried this and failed, or if such an arrangement wouldn't be possible, then Child Maintenance Options will give you a reference number that you can use to make your CMS application. There is a £20 application fee.

The CMS will work out the amount of child maintenance which they believe should be paid and notify both parents. They can take action against the paying parent if they don't pay the required amount. However, you can't control when and how the CMS takes enforcement action if the other parent doesn't pay.

Using the CMS is the best option to use if you have experienced domestic abuse. Gingerbread provides information about how to apply to the CMS if you have experienced domestic abuse.

How much should child maintenance be?

There is no definite answer to this. If you are using the CMS the amount is worked out using a standard formula that takes into account the paying parent's income and any other children that they are responsible for.

If you are making an arrangement with the other parent you can arrange any amount of child maintenance you like, as long as you both agree. Knowing how much to agree on can be difficult. The Child Maintenance Options leaflet 'Talking about Money' can help you look at your budget and what may be needed for children at different ages. The leaflet is available on their website and an online maintenance calculator can be found at www.gov.uk/calculate-your-child-maintenance.

What if the other parent lives abroad?

If your child's other parent lives outside the UK you won't be able to arrange child maintenance through the CMS. If you can't reach a family-based arrangement

Organisations

then you could apply for a court order that can be enforced in the country where the other parent lives. This is called a Reciprocal Enforcement of Maintenance Order (REMO). You can call Gingerbread for more information about this.

Where to find help
Gingerbread: www.gingerbread.org.uk; tel 0808 802 0925

Gingerbread provides lots of information about child maintenance and other issues affecting single parents on their website.

Child Maintenance Options: www.cmoptions.org; tel 0800 988 0988

Child Maintenance Options are the organisation you will have to contact before you can use the CMS and also provide free information and support on child maintenance.

Family Mediation Council: www.familymediationcouncil.org.uk

The Family Mediation Council can put you in touch with a local mediation service to help you come to an agreement with your child's other parent.

I support the **#ParentsPromise** helping parents make a positive commitment to their children today, in case of a relationship breakdown tomorrow

My partner owns the house but I have done all the improvements and upkeep. Where do I stand?

Emma Dewhurst
Solicitor, Hall Brown Solicitors

It is increasingly common for couples nowadays to put the idea of marriage on the backburner, instead prioritising setting up a home together. Some may not want to marry, being content to live together. Often one of the couple will move into a property already owned by the other, or they may buy a home in one of their names.

They may open a joint bank account, combine their finances, purchase furniture and undertake renovations to the property, often blissfully unaware that there is no such thing as a 'common law marriage,' or rights for cohabitees (see page 27 and the Must read article on page 23 for more information).

This means that if the property is owned in the sole name of one party, the other has no legal entitlement to a share of the property, even if they have spent considerable sums on improvements and upkeep.

This article will briefly explain the legal position arising out of this scenario, and then detail the practical measures you can take if you find yourself in this difficult situation.

The law

The law that applies in this scenario is general property law. There is no specific law which governs couples who live together.

It is set out in the Trusts of Land and Appointment of Trustees Act 1996 ('TOLATA') which creates legal principles based on the law of trusts. The question is who owns the beneficial interest in the property, and therefore an interest in the equity in the property?

The starting point is that the beneficial interest will follow the property title. Therefore, if a party is named on the title (they are named as the registered owner with the Land Registry), this constitutes an express trust and they will have the legal and beneficial interest.

The problem above arises when the property's title is held in one party's ('A') sole name, but another person ('B') has invested their own time and money into the property and view it as their home. The other party, B, will then have to establish a beneficial interest by way of a constructive trust, in order to establish an interest in the equity in the property.

To establish a constructive trust, B needs to show **all** of the following:

1. A common intention between the couple that B was to have an interest in the property, and not just that they would live there;

2. B acted to their detriment or altered their position in reliance

Money

on the common intention; and

3. It would be unconscionable for A to deny B's interest.

'Common intention' is usually expressed during conversation and it does not need to be a formal offer and acceptance. For example, if A says to B "what is mine is yours", or "you will always have an interest in this house", that would constitute an express intention. Sometimes behaviour in itself, such as opening a joint account and combining finances, may not in itself constitute common intention although it is still useful to refer to as it shows a pattern of behaviour.

'Detriment' is a concept subject to the discretion of the Judge if the dispute were to proceed to court. Improvements and upkeep to the property are likely to qualify, depending on the level of detriment incurred. Re-decoration or low cost general maintenance is less likely to qualify; however, financing a new kitchen or replacing a roof, for example, is more likely to be considered as detriment.

It must then be decided, taking into account all of the above, whether it would be unconscionable (i.e. unjust or unfair) to deny B's interest.

Practical steps
If you find yourself in this situation, how, you may wonder, do you go about meeting the three-stage test in practical terms?

Litigation in this area can be very expensive, especially because these claims are dealt with by the civil courts, rather than family courts. Claims are potentially 'high stakes' due to the risk of paying your ex's legal costs as well as your own because, in civil cases, the general rule is that the loser pays the winner's costs.

Unlike family courts, civil courts are less interested in the concept of 'fairness.' Their role is not to adjust interests in a property, but rather to determine and declare interests. The status of your relationship bears no weight however long you have been living together (unless you are engaged, which means you may benefit from protection under the Married Women's Property Act 1870).

TOLATA litigation is front-loaded, and as a claimant you would be required to set out your case fully at the outset, with as much supporting evidence as possible. Often these cases can seem like 'one word against the other,' so a paper trail or other corroboration is key.

To evidence common intention, any written correspondence such as text messages should be produced. Was there a conversation before any improvement work took place on the property? Was there an understanding that if you paid for the improvements, that was your 'contribution' to the property? What discussions took place when the house was purchased or when you moved in? Were promises made in the presence of, or were they repeated to, third parties? Consider the reasons why you were not on the legal title if there was a common intention you would have a share. Was it intended that you would be added to the legal title at some point in the future, but you simply never got round to it?

To evidence that you have incurred detriment by paying for improvements and upkeep for example, you should produce the relevant bank statements and invoices.

An alternative
As people are becoming more conscious of the expense and risks of starting formal court proceedings, they are increasingly open to attempting mediation as a much cheaper and more conciliatory option. Indeed, the courts will expect you to have tried mediation before starting proceedings. Rather than being subject to the decision of a Judge, bound by the strict statutory

Money

framework and inability to adjust interests, it is often preferable to discuss matters directly with your former partner with the assistance of an independent third party. This can be beneficial, especially where there are children of the relationship.

> When completing the financial disclosure forms, print off the form and have a pad and pencil with you.
>
> Cross out the pages that are not applicable to you and make a list of information that you need to obtain - breaking the task down helps to make it feel more achievable.
>
> *Cressida Burnet, Cressida Burnet Mediation*

Notes

Money

What should I do if I am going through a divorce and one party has cryptoassets?

Victoria Clarke
Head of Family, Elite Law

When you are going through a divorce, part of the process will involve financial disclosure so that you can reach an informed decision about the split of your marital assets. There are other questions in this book that go into further detail about what that process looks like, but this addresses what you should think about if one or both of you have cryptoassets, such as Bitcoin or an NFT, as part of your disclosure exercise.

What if I have cryptoassets?

Firstly, the key to a successful disclosure exercise is to be clear and open with your assets. When it comes to cryptoassets, this involves a clear breakdown of the assets that you own. You will need to download 12 months of transactions from any trading platform or exchange website that you are currently using or have used within the last 12 months. Each wallet that you own should also be disclosed by way of a 12 month transaction history for each wallet, showing what has entered and left your wallet in the last 12 months.

If you hold wallets, you will be familiar with the concept of your Public Key and Private Key. You should not provide anyone with the Private Key of your wallets, even in legal proceedings. If a solicitor asks for your Private Key, you should take time to explain that this key gives anyone control over your wallet and so this is why you will not be providing this information. There is a chance that someone may see this as reluctance to provide disclosure but if you ensure that everything else you provide is clear, then you should be fine.

You may want to consider whether you want to provide your Public Key, as this gives someone permanent access to your wallet even after proceedings. It would also show movement from that wallet to anywhere else should you wish to transfer assets to a new wallet, as each transaction is on the public ledger. You may feel this is more information than you are willing to provide. It is reasonable to request a Public Key in order to keep track of what is happening with a wallet, so the other party may have more justification for requesting this information. If you feel uncomfortable providing this information then discuss it with the other party first to explain your concerns and see if a compromise can be found.

For any NFT cryptoassets that you hold, you should ensure that any documentary evidence of your purchase of the NFT, and the market value of the same, is provided. Do not worry if your NFT is worth a lot less than what you purchased it for - this is common with NFTs as at the time of writing and some may grow in value again or others will remain at their lower value due to the initial excitement of the market in 2020-2021.

Finally, you should ensure that you have fully investigated your tax liability for your cryptoassets. HMRC guidance states that any trade, even token to token, is a taxable event. It is therefore not the case that transfers to fiat (centralised money) are the only taxable event. You must calculate your tax to avoid a scenario where you are having to transfer cryptoassets to your ex-partner and you are left with the tax bill as well.

With the financial settlement, be cautious about relying too heavily on retaining your cryptoassets. They may have a high value but they are volatile and can leave you out of pocket very quickly. You should try to ensure you have a mixed portfolio of cryptoassets and less volatile assets such as property or liquid capital. Clear and informed legal advice is key in reaching that decision.

What if my ex has cryptoassests?

It is natural to worry that an ex-spouse may be trying to hide assets, especially if you do not understand them very well. Cryptoassets can be quite complicated for people who are not comfortable with technology or investing money, and having a spouse own cryptoassets can require a lot of trust from the other party.

However, you should not automatically worry that just because your spouse has cryptoassets, they are doing something untrustworthy. The first thing to do is try to give your spouse the benefit of the doubt that their interest in cryptoassets is not because they are trying to hide their assets but because this is something they are just genuinely interested in, even if you cannot see the appeal yourself!

If you decide to be legally represented, explain to your solicitor that you believe your spouse has cryptoassets. Ensure that your representative understands these assets because it is risky to dismiss the importance of them as they can have a high value. You must allow your spouse to provide their own version of disclosure for these assets before you start asking for further information, but there are certain things that you should expect to receive in the first instance.

Wallets are the form in which people can store their cryptoassets. You have a different type of wallet for each type of cryptoasset, so if your spouse holds Bitcoin, Ethereum, and Litecoin, they would have three wallets, one for each. They can also have a trading account on an exchange platform, where people sell and trade cryptoassets. They can have one account which holds all the different types of cryptoasset, as the trading platform manages the different wallets from behind the scenes.

Wallets have a public address, called a Public Key, that enables anyone to view the contents of the wallet and the movement of the contents in and out. If someone sends tokens to the wallet they use the Public Key. Wallets also have a control code, called a Private Key. This enables the user to move assets out of the wallet. You should not expect your spouse to give you the Private Key to their wallets, but you may request the Public Key if you do not trust the transaction breakdown that they give you.

You should expect to receive 12 months of transaction history for any trading platform that your spouse has used, and 12 months of history for every wallet that they own.

Your spouse may say that they do not want to give you their Public Key, because they are uncomfortable with you watching the movement of cryptoassets within the wallet itself. It is understandable that someone will not want another individual to have the ability to watch their wallet indefinitely and so you can consider whether

Money

the evidence they have given so far is sufficient to illustrate what assets they hold. Your spouse would also be expected to provide updated disclosure if you are going through the court process and so you would receive an updated transaction history in case you have concerns that any assets would be dissipated.

With the inevitable financial settlement, you should consider carefully whether you want to receive a share of their cryptoassets. It depends on how many cryptoassets there are and whether they make up a large portion of the marital pot. They are volatile assets, and the value could increase or decrease significantly from the point you receive them in a settlement. If you feel confident that you can manage them then a transfer can take place, but if you do not want to be heavily involved with investment or a fast moving and high-value market, it may be better to offset your interest in those assets against other matrimonial assets. You should ensure you receive clear and informed legal advice before making your final decision.

Expect a big change in your lifestyle.

Your life is going to change dramatically - it is the surprise of this that can often lead to resentment and breed conflict.

Your partner's life will be changing too and they will be having the same problems, adjusting as you are.

Yes, really.

Peter Martin, OGR Stock Denton

What if we are separating and have a joint business?

Natalie Sutherland
Partner, Burgess Mee Family Law

Just as every family is different, every business is different and when it comes to divorce, how to deal with a jointly owned business can be complex.

Business assets in divorce cases come in all shapes and sizes. They could be:

- businesses jointly owned and run by both spouses set up during the marriage where one or both spouses wants to continue running the business without the other;

- inherited businesses created by previous generations now being run by one or both spouses where a spouse could argue that the business is non-matrimonial and should be left out of the divorce calculation altogether;

- businesses owned solely by one spouse which is the family's main source of income and which has no actual value without them;

- businesses owned by one spouse with other third parties where only that minority shareholding is relevant to the divorce.

Documentation

In each case it is important to first consider the business documentation such as the Shareholders Agreement or Partnership Agreement to establish the ownership and respective contributions to the business. Pre-Nuptial Agreements may set out what should happen to the business in the event of a divorce. Whilst not legally binding, they document what the spouses wanted to happen in the event of a divorce, agreed at a time when everything was amicable and, provided they were properly entered into, they will likely be followed by a court.

In the absence of these documents the family court's starting position will be that the entirety of the business value will fall into the "matrimonial pot" for division. When considering how to divide the pot, the court will consider what is fair. The starting point will be an equal division of the assets unless a spouse is able to justify why that equal division would be unfair in all the circumstances of the case. The business will likely be one of many assets in the "pot" and there are many ways in which that pot can be divided to achieve fairness.

What should happen to the business?

It will be important for the spouses to consider what it is they want to achieve with that business asset following the divorce, when taking legal advice. Questions to consider will be:

- Should the business be sold?

- Can the shares be sold or transferred?

- Should one spouse buy out the other?

- Should restrictive covenants (such as non-compete and

Money

non-poaching clauses) be negotiated to protect the business from a departing spouse?

- Can spouses who want to continue running and owning the business together continue to do so?

Running a business together as well as going through a divorce could potentially be disastrous for the business itself. Prior to a final decision being made the parties must continue working together and practical business decisions will need to be made.

Underhand dealings

If trust has broken down, getting early advice from a specialist family solicitor is crucial, especially if you are the spouse without the control of the business. Your solicitor and forensic accountant (if one is necessary) will be able to scrutinise the accounts to ensure that no underhand dealings have been going on. Whilst relationship breakdown often comes as a surprise to one party, the other may have been financially planning for it for many months. For example, the liquidity and valuation of the business may have been reduced in anticipation of the divorce by the gift or sale of a valuable business asset at a lower price, perhaps to a friend, with the intention of buying back that asset after the divorce, or delaying account preparation in order to frustrate the financial disclosure process.

Identifying these tactics is key. If underhand dealings are discovered the court has the power to reverse these transactions or include the value back into the matrimonial pot for division between the parties so that no real loss is suffered.

Covid-19

Covid-19 and the subsequent economic fallout has decimated many businesses with the consequence that the value of an important family asset has been all but wiped out. The ability to sell the business may also now be impossible.

For those couples who have not yet started the divorce process, you will need to consider whether now is the right time to divorce. If the business was the main asset and you are the financially weaker party, you may want to wait to see if the business will bounce back after the crisis has ended. Conversely, if you are the business owner, you may now want to press on with the divorce whilst the assets in the pot are minimal, also in the hope that better times will come.

For those couples who have just finalised their divorce which involved a business asset, you should seek legal advice as to whether that settlement is now fair in light of the economic crisis caused by the coronavirus.

I was never going to be able to control what my parents did, I could never have changed it because they're their own person just as I am mine. Kay (16)

Can you advise me on pension sharing?

Mary Shaw
Consultant, David Gray Solicitors

KISS - the phrase 'Keep It Simple Stupid'- whilst rather forthright, can be a reminder not to over-think some things when getting divorced: for example, painstakingly trying to value all of your house contents is probably a waste of time.

But not so for pensions because pensions are complex and can be a much more valuable asset than you may realise. Only married people and civil partners can share their pensions on dissolution of their relationship. The court is tasked with considering whether the pension in those circumstances should be shared.

Two of the most important decisions that you will make about your divorce will be about timing and process: pushing on with a divorce when your spouse is reeling from the news could backfire very badly; and deciding how to sort your separation/divorce business out can be a critical decision determining what state your relationship with your ex will be in at the end. This is key if you have children or if you have warm relationships with your in-laws. Talking-round-a-table processes such as mediation and collaborative practice lend themselves very well to discussing how to sort out pensions

Your spouse or civil partner's pension is likely to be a matrimonial asset which can be shared. Clients will often say 'He (or she) worked for it and earned it and I don't want any of it'. The court looks at contributions and whilst your partner was earning their pension you were quite possibly bringing income into the relationship or keeping house and raising children: in other words your marriage was a joint effort.

Before you make any decisions about whether you want to share or have a share of a pension it is important to get its 'cash equivalent value' (CEV). This is easily obtained and you are entitled to a minimum of one a year at no cost to you (Providing the pension is not in payment; if it is in payment you may pay a fee for the CEV).

The cash equivalent value of a pension is not a pound for pound accurate measure of the pension's value - this is where things get complex and 'apples and pears' becomes a good way of

---

Remember that whatever happens, the two parents will be that child's two parents forever.

One day that child may graduate from university or get married, and those two parents will have to face one another at those special events.

Laura Martin-Read, Family Law Group

Money

explaining why: a personal pension could be considered an 'apple' whilst many occupational pensions (in particular public sector and 'uniformed' pensions) are 'pears'. This is because £10,000 of capital value of a police pension will buy you a whole lot more than £10,000 of a personal pension with, say, Scottish Widows or Standard Life. If there is a choice of pensions to share, and you share the wrong one, both parties may end up worse off than if the right pension were shared.

If you and your partner want to come to an arrangement where one of you keeps their entire pension and the other one gets more of the savings or the house, a pound of pension cannot be treated like a pound of savings or a pound of equity in your home so understanding the 'offset' value of your pension will be important. This is a highly technical area.

The particular rules of different schemes can inform how you should share pensions to *both* get maximum income from them. So doing a quick calculation on the back of an envelope risks you losing out on income for the rest of your life at a time in your life when you could need it most - unless you can successfully sue your solicitor for negligence.

Whether you are recently separated or been apart for a while, the threat and the restrictions imposed due to Covid-19 will create feelings of anxiety, frustration and stress. As humans we are not particularly well designed for change. While we can all adapt over time, there is a transition phase during which the uncertainty and instability of life can lead to significant tension and fatigue.

While your children look to you for comfort and reassurance, you may find yourself with no one to lean on, making it harder for you to be the kind of parent you want to be. That's when information and advice from trusted, knowledgeable professionals is even more important for our continued well-being. At times of uncertainty, we look for certainty. The articles in this book, written by leading professionals are a series of helping hands, supporting you through this uncertain time.

We are all going to emerge out of this period a little bit changed. We may have had time to review our priorities. If we're lucky we will have had an opportunity to reconnect with one another; if we're less lucky we will have felt imprisoned in an already very difficult family situation. The importance of working together to create the best kind of childhood for our children is a parent's number one priority. Sometimes we can all lose sight of this fact, especially at times like this. By using the shared wisdom of the experts in this book, you will find your way back to what is important – your children.

Dr Angharad Rudkin

How can people deal with debts when they divorce or separate?

Hasan Hadi
Managing Director, Southgate Solicitors

When married couples divorce or cohabiting partners separate their first concerns will probably be about child arrangements or how to divide their assets.

Before long, however, they may have to tackle an equally difficult issue: how to settle their debts, some of which might be in joint names. Who is liable to pay? Could you end up being held responsible for your partner's debts, even if you knew nothing about them?

The law can be complex and to make things even more difficult, different rules may apply for married and cohabiting couples.

Debts in one person's name

As you might expect, you will be liable for debts that are in your name only, but not for those in your partner's name only. However, for married couples, debts in one person's name that were used for the benefit of the family may be subject to division or sharing between the spouses or civil partners.

It is generally more difficult for cohabiting couples to seek the other partner to share debts in sole names, unless there is a legal agreement between them.

Debts in joint names

Things get a little more complicated for debts in both your names. You will be held jointly responsible and separately liable for these debts - this means that the creditor can either seek for both to settle the debt, or pursue only one of you to settle it.

What can the court do?

It is not unusual for couples to disagree about responsibility for debts and they may have to take legal action to determine liability. In these circumstances, the court will look at the debt and consider how it arose, whether the partners benefited jointly or individually and then decide who should bear the burden of repayment.

For example, if the debt was used to pay for school fees or a family holiday then it's likely that the court would rule that both partners are jointly liable.

However, if one partner incurred the debt largely for his or her individual benefit then the court may decide that they should bear most or all of the liability. This could apply in cases where one partner has spent lavishly on a hobby, bought an expensive car for their own use or run up gambling debts.

The courts are more likely to order that liability should be

> "The grass always seems greener, but it isn't. You can soak in long hot baths, watch whatever you want on the telly, get a cat and wear orange."
>
> *Patricia, Mum*

Money

shared for debts incurred during the marriage than before the relationship began, although this might not apply in exceptional circumstances, such as in a very long marriage.

Deciding responsibility for debts can be complex whether you are married or cohabiting and it is always advisable to seek advice from your solicitor before incurring any debts.

CHILDREN SAYING ONE THING TO ONE PARENT AND ANOTHER THING TO THE OTHER

Children do this in families where parents are still together. They are even more likely to do this when parents are living apart.

When parents don't 'get on' or have poor communication, this can cause many problems.

Some tips for when this happens:

- If your child comes home following a contact and says, for example "Mum says I can have that new bike", before you react with fury, upset, and anxiety, check it out.

- Calmly and without emotion ask your child if that statement is correct.

- Mention that you're probably going to check with mum that she has indeed said that.

- Often if the child is playing one parent against the other they may confess at this point.

- At a convenient time contact mum and explain the situation in an enquiring and non accusing way, for example: "Matt came home today and said that you had agreed that he can have a new bike. I am just calling to ask what, if anything had been discussed?"

- If you can agree in the early days of separation how to handle this kind of situation then calls like this will become familiar.

Adele Ballantyne

My parents' separation changed my whole world, not necessarily for the better, but I had no option but to go along with it. Cerys (15)

How can I move from a 2-income to a 1-income household?

Tom Farrell
Tom Farrell Financial & Mediation

Divorce or separation can mean radical financial change. You may not have much experience of dealing with certain aspects of your finances and that can cause anxiety.

Add the stresses of change and the emotional context of your situation to the mix and you have the perfect excuse to put things off. Although this might be a natural response, it's not a sensible one.

If you get yourself organised and work in a methodical way, you will be able to get to grips with everything and I promise you that you will feel better once you've done it. Taking control and having a sense of future is worth the effort.

Cash flow

Cash flow is money in, versus money out. Without an understanding of this, you won't be able to plan, identify problems or make sensible changes.

Money In

This could be from:

- earned income or pension, after tax;
- maintenance that is paid (maintenance is tax free);
- benefits received (some are taxable, some are not);
- interest or income from savings and investments (again, some are taxable, some are not).

Money out

Have your bank statements to hand, or access your accounts online, and make a note of everything you spend your money on, like:

- rent or mortgage payments;
- credit cards and loans;
- household bills;
- weekly shopping;
- insurance costs;
- car and transport costs;
- children's clubs and activities;
- school costs;
- nights out and entertainment;
- cash withdrawals (try to think about what these are usually for).

If more is coming in than going out, then great. That means you have scope to save and to plan for other things, like holidays and bigger expenses.

If it's the other way around, then don't panic. With a little analysis, you can work out the shortfall and try to do something about it. Look again at your expenditure and find ways to economise.

Tips

- Try to put your cashflow into a format that you can keep track of and update over time. You could put it into a spreadsheet or write it out. Doing this will cement the

Money

information in your mind and help you understand it. Alternatively, use one of the online tools provided by charities and other organisations.

- Don't be afraid to ask for help. If you can afford to pay for advice, then find a good independent financial planner. If not, then talk to trusted family and friends who may be able to help you. You could also book an appointment with Citizen's Advice, or access some of the free online resources available.

- Don't ignore things on your statements that you can't identify. You may be paying for something that you don't need!

- Try to categorise your expenditure, between the essentials and the things that you could do without if you had to.

Debt
Mortgages

You may have an existing mortgage. If so, take the time to understand it:

- how long is it for?
- how much do you still owe?
- is it a repayment mortgage, or interest only?
- if it's interest only, how are you planning to repay it?
- are there penalties if you change your mortgage or repay early?
- do you have Life Insurance to cover your mortgage?

If your financial circumstances have changed, your ability to borrow money will have changed too. Mortgage lenders are far stricter than they used to be about lending. They will want a detailed assessment of your income and expenditure, to asses 'affordability', before making a decision.

If you receive maintenance, it can count towards income for some lenders, but usually only once it has been in payment for six months or a year and only if it is subject to a court order.

There are new mortgage products coming to the market all the time and some of them will allow your family to offer security or to borrow on your behalf.

If your mortgage deal has come to an end, you could see your payments go up, or down. It might be a good time to look at a new deal with your existing lender or move to a new one.

Credit cards, store cards, overdrafts and loans

It is frightening how easily people can access borrowing and how quickly it can get out of control. You need to know:

- what is the balance owing?
- what interest rate you are paying?
- are your payments just covering the interest or paying the debt off too?
- are you near your borrowing limit?

Tips

- Consolidating debts can save money, or reduce monthly payments, but be careful about the overall costs and how long you will be paying things off.

- Seek proper independent advice before making mortgage decisions, it could make the difference between getting a mortgage or not and could save you a lot of money.

- If you are struggling to make your mortgage or debt repayments, don't ignore it. Seek debt counselling advice and open up a dialogue with the people you owe money to.

Benefits

You may be entitled to benefits now that you didn't qualify for before. Child benefit, free childcare,

Universal Credit; the list is long and the rules can be very complicated. Taking the time to find out what you are entitled to could be life-changing though, so put in the work.

Tips
- Access the many free online resources provided by government and charities, they will give you the best start in identifying what you might be able to claim.
- Make an appointment with Citizen's Advice or a charity that offers advice.

Resources
Money Advice Service: https://www.moneyadvice-service.org.uk

A huge resource for all aspects of managing your finances. Register on their site and you can save your work as you go. Excellent budget planner and good signposting to all manner of advice.

Citizens Advice: https://www.citizensadvice.org.uk

An excellent website with lots of information and good advice. You can make an appointment for face to face advice and telephone them too.

I often tell the financially stronger party: "there is no weakness in generosity".

So often people are told by friends not to be taken advantage of when in fact they want to provide for their family, but just don't want to be seen to be being rolled over.

Barbara Corbett, Corbett Le Quesne

Notes

Are assets split equally on divorce?

Andrew Meehan
Managing Director and Solicitor, Harrogate Family Law

It is not uncommon for one party to have left dealing with money during the marriage to their other half. One party may have been the breadwinner and the other the homemaker. English and Welsh law recognises that the contribution made by the person who has not been the breadwinner can be equally as valuable as one made by the person whose job it was to provide financially for the family. Neither party is supposed to be discriminated against because of the roles they adopted in the marriage.

This means that, when a marriage comes to an end, you are entitled to ask for a share of the assets built up during it. This is the case even if the assets are not held in your name. They will form part of the financial resources that will be divided between you.

Each of you can claim for financial provision to be made for you from the property and assets. For example, the law gives the court the power to order that property should be transferred to one of you, or that it should be sold and the proceeds paid out in whatever way is fair. It also has the power to split pensions and to require one party to pay maintenance to the other, amongst other powers.

However, every marriage is different. This means that there is no fixed formula for deciding who gets what on divorce. It is normally a question of negotiation. A financial settlement on a divorce must be "fair" in the eyes of the court. To decide what is fair, various factors must be weighed into the balance, such as:

- the welfare of any children under 18;
- what assets you each have, can access or may have in the foreseeable future (whether they are in sole or joint names);
- what you both earn and could earn;
- what your expenditure is;
- how old you both are;
- your state of health;
- how long you have been married;
- what you each need to house yourself and pay for everything you need to;
- whether you had a pre-nup and, if so, what it said and whether it was fair.

The starting point is that the assets you have built up during the marriage, as well as the house you occupied as the family home, should be shared equally. This starting point is, however, often departed from and an unequal share of the assets happens. This is because simply dividing the assets built up in the marriage might produce an unfair outcome to one party. The priority tends to be to ensure that the parties and their children have a roof over their head and enough money to live on, as far as is possible.

Assets that are not built up during your marriage might be treated differently. This is because they have come from an external source, not

Money

by your joint efforts. For example, an inheritance, or a gift, or some other asset that a party owned before the marriage might not be shared.

The starting point for these types of assets is that they should be put to one side and not taken account of in the split of assets. However, very often these assets do need to be looked at to ensure that the settlement is fair. If they have increased in value during the marriage, this increase in value can be shared even if the underlying assets aren't.

The source of these assets and how they have been used might be very relevant to how they are treated. If they have been paid into a joint account and used in some way for example, then this might also affect the starting point.

Deciding what is a fair outcome is an art not a science because of the lack of a fixed formula. Divorce tends to be a once in a lifetime event, so people tend to have little to no experience of what a fair outcome is likely to be. For this reason, it is vital that you get legal advice from a specialist solicitor. They can check that your spouse's financial resources are fully investigated.

One party might also try to hide assets or use them so that there are fewer assets to divide between you. In addition, there can be different ways to value assets which can produce markedly different results. A specialist solicitor can check that the assets have been valued fairly and that your position is protected against them being hidden or used.

Most importantly, an expert solicitor will have far more experience than you of divorce cases. They will be able to advise you what they think a fair outcome is likely to be. This will ensure that you do not make any mistakes which could otherwise cost you a lot of stress and money.

I always remind parents who are arguing on silly things that their job is to make this process as easy as possible for their children; that they ultimately win if in 20 years time their children have no negative effects from the divorce or separation and are able to form happy healthy relationships for themselves.

That is the true win - not managing to keep a bit of furniture etc.

Charlotte Harper, HF Legal

The worst thing I remember was being sat on the floor between my mum and dad and being told to choose who I wanted to live with. Kaitlyn

Notes

Going through the family court

Welfare Checklist, SPIP, C100, CAO. These terms serve as a reminder of how the previously emotional based commitment of marriage/partnership is now moving into the realms of law. Just as the language changes to reflect this move, the way you think needs to change too. Dealing with the legal aspects of a divorce requires reason, logic and cool-headed thinking. These processes use different parts of the brain, moving from the emotional decision-making of most days (e.g. "I feel furious, I'm going to text them right now") to rational-decision making (e.g. "I feel furious, but I will write down my thoughts on a piece of paper and wait until tomorrow to decide whether to send it or not). When our brains are flooded with stress hormones and fizzing with anxiety, our decision making processes change. This chapter points you in the direction of all the support and guidance available out there to help you make clear decisions which have your child's best interests at heart.

The Children Act paradox

Kathryn McTaggart
Professional Support Lawyer, Woolley & Co

> You set out to be a parent and that role hasn't changed through separating. Be the best you can, regardless of the circumstances.
>
> Suzanna, Mum

Writing about whether Family Court decisions are always in the best interests of children requires a gargantuan effort to separate the objective from the subjective. There is a 'best interests' criteria courts must follow and, if they do not do so, then the decisions are plainly wrong and can and must be appealed. That, however, ignores the vast human evidence that evaluates Family Court decisions and finds them wanting, unsatisfactory and sometimes unfathomable.

From my perspective as a family solicitor I cannot really recall any real shockers of decisions that stand out for their sheer ignorance or neglect of the best interests of the children involved. Perhaps that is because most of the children cases I deal with settle after hard work and compromise, or I usually end up with a court decision that I consider to be in the children's 'best interests' myself. This is not to imply that I have an unusually successful children law practice but rather, that I take the slightly unfashionable view that our antiquated and imperfect system, bolstered by the under resourced but battling Cafcass officers, mostly has Judges who are committed, intelligent and sensible human beings who are determined, despite the challenges of the system, to make sound decisions in the best interests of children.

The premise is really that in most cases 'a relationship' between children and both parents is in those children's best interests.

Delay, emergency applications and actual emergencies

Unfortunately the system sets itself up for a fall. The Children Act makes it clear that delay is likely to prejudice the interests of any child. But when is a groaning court system, relying on at least four busy legal professionals, the reports of overstretched Cafcass and Social Services and, occasionally, at least one obstructive parent, going to be able to make speedy and lawful decisions in the best interests of children?

Some of the worst decisions I have seen have been made swiftly without notice to the other parent on an emergency basis. The Judge has one sided information from a parent who considers the stakes are so high that to present misleading or even fabricated evidence is a reasonable thing to do in the 'best interests' of his or her children. The damage done, even on a short-term basis, is often not at all in the best interests of the child as time progresses. Better to get things done right than done quickly.

And it is also a case of priorities. Objectively, the fact that your week's summer holiday with your children in Spain may be at stake because the ex isn't

Going through the family court

playing ball can't really compete for court time with an application to stop a child being abducted to Yemen. However, that is not going to be of much comfort to the parent who has to explain to some very disappointed children that there is no holiday this year.

Multiple Judges, multiple breaches, no changes

The need to secure a court hearing in a not untimely fashion means that the same Judge will not always be available. This is extremely demoralising for those parents whose time with their children is constantly frustrated by the other parent when a different Judge treats each occasion as a 'one off' blip rather than a systematic denial of a relationship between parent and child.

Enforcement of existing child arrangements orders remains problematic. New legislation and various carrots and sticks arise to deal with failing to allow children to spend time with their other parent and Judges try hard not be so namby pamby, but really hands are tied. When is it ever going to be in the best interests of children to reduce a mother's (and in the vast majority of cases it is mothers) income with a fine or remove her from her children for a short sharp prison shock? But that is cold comfort for fathers proceeding on the principle that a relationship with both parents is in the best interests of a child.

Parents oppose children spending time with the other parent for lots of reasons. Sometimes they have convinced themselves that no parent is better than one who does not measure up (in their eyes). Sometimes, personal feelings of rejection and hurt make it impossible to see the value of a relationship between the child and the other parent and it is too painful to have even limited contact at handover. Sometimes withholding a child is the most effective punishment for wrongs inflicted and, in any case, bad partner = bad parent. On occasion it boils down to suspicion, dislike of a new partner or simply control. For some it is the loneliness and fear of not having a precious child with them at all times. Whatever the reason, these feelings are formidable and some parents will go to extreme lengths to protect their child or, in reality, themselves.

False allegations

Accusations of abuse, physical or sexual, are always horribly difficult to confront. The court has no choice but to suspend, curtail or supervise time with that parent (in the best interests of the child) until appropriate investigations have been made. As a result the child in question suffers months of messed about time with that parent in artificial environments, is questioned (however appropriately and skilfully) and, in some cases, subject to physical examination. In the child's best interests? I think not.

But the risk of harm cannot be ignored either. More parents than you would think consider that the end justifies the means. In some cases, parents' bad behaviour seems to actually be rewarded by the court who assess that to continue to enforce child arrangements will expose the children to emotional damage at the hands of the hostile primary carer and it is therefore in the best interests of the child to let the relationship with the other parent fall by the wayside.

When twice weekly arrangements become twice annually arrangements

Often the cases with the highest stakes are those in which one parent seeks to relocate to another country either with their new family or to return to their home country. These cases are enormously complex and hinge on a multitude of factors individual to each family but, in very simplistic terms, the effect on the primary carer (and new family) of being forced to stay in a desperate practical, emotional or financial situation is balanced against

177

Going through the family court

the effect on the child of a reduction in time with the other parent.

When is reducing time with a much loved parent in the best interests of a child? But I suppose, neither is living with a carer who is in dire straits. The courts are less ready to give permission to go than previously but still these difficult decisions are made, apparently in the best interests of the children concerned.

Missing out

Sometimes the court is faced with two parents whose hostility is such that only the most detailed and rigid order will suffice. So, if a best friend's birthday party falls on dad's weekend, too bad - the child misses out. If dad's ski chalet is only available in mum's week, the child does not go. Flexibility is almost always in the best interests of children but sometimes it is impossible and the court must do its best to ensure relationships between parents and children survive animosity.

Making it all 'equal'

In the days of shared care and 'hands on' dads the shared care order is king. Equal time is the new holy grail and some people really do make it work for themselves and, most importantly, for their children.

I cannot help but sigh inwardly when I am presented with a schedule by parents who have divvied up their children's days between them so it is all 'equal' and 'fair' and have not noticed that their little ones will sleep in a different bed every night of the week. Does this sound like it is in a child's best interests? I am not convinced.

The court and Cafcass continue to have concerns about this type of arrangement, particularly for school age children but many parents believe 'equal time' is in the best interests of their children.

The imperfect parent

We continue to expect perfect decisions in less than ideal situations in an imperfect world. Not many of us would choose to have our children in the care of a cannabis user or with someone who has beaten his wife or who will have the children in the same bed in the morning with each new boyfriend. But if that is who the child's parent is then that is what the court has to work with.

A relationship with both parents will be in the best interests of the child unless there are serious and pressing concerns about the harm this would cause to the child. Sometimes that leads to what are considered surprisingly lax decisions in the eyes of the other parent.

Beating the paradox

So when are court decisions in the best interests of children? The answer is always and, sometimes, never. It is the paradox of the Children Act. The objective and the subjective. A Judge is not of your family although he or she may well do their level best to educate his or herself about what that means. A decision will be made in the best interests of the children as identified and assessed by an unknown third party.

If parents want a decision that is truly in the best interests of THEIR children, then they must make that decision themselves, jointly with their co parent. Anything else will undoubtedly be in the children's best interests but, at the same time, probably not so.

How should I prepare for court?

James Belderbos
Specialist Family Lawyer,
Belderbos Solicitors

The thought of attending court for those who haven't been before can be harrowing but being properly prepared and informed will reduce a lot of that stress. The more you put in, the less stressful you will find the process.

Whilst this short article is prepared to assist you in preparing for court it is worth repeating here that applications to the court should be considered as a last resort.

Reasons why you should avoid seeking answers and solutions through the court process include other people making decisions about your family, you not being in control of the process, greater costs and the inadequacies of the court system with overburdened staff, lack of accommodation and delay. A court order is a blunt instrument for resolving unique issues for you and your children.

You may have no choice but to attend court if other solutions including mediation and the collaborative process have failed or you are responding to an application made by a former partner.

Whatever type of hearing you are facing, it is vital that you are prepared for what may happen at court and at home whilst you are there.

Representation

To be fully informed and prepared, representation by a solicitor or a barrister is best. They will lift a considerable burden from you. Some solicitors will offer fixed fees or you could instruct a barrister on a direct access basis. Most solicitors offer a reduced fixed fee for an initial consultation during which you can make an informed decision over what is right for you. If you can't afford legal fees, publicly funded representation or legal aid may be available if you can fulfil strict criteria. Always consider who the right representative is for you. You need an expert, preferably accredited by Resolution and someone you feel comfortable with.

If you are represented, simply ask the solicitor or barrister what will happen at court and what you will need to do. That overview should give you the peace of mind that you require to approach the case constructively.

As a solicitor I always discuss with my client, as soon as I have a hearing date, what will happen on the day so that I can address any fears and dispel any myths that may be clouding my client's view on what they can achieve for their family.

You may be surprised to hear that your first attendance may be the first of three or four hearings, possibly more. In the majority of cases there is the opportunity to settle a case so always ask your solicitor what can be done to avoid further hearings and costs.

Take along a friend or relative

Whilst they won't be allowed into the court room you will find it beneficial to have them with you. Think about the right friend or relative. If you have a new partner they are unlikely to be the right person to take along. Always consider what your former

Going through the family court

partner will feel if they see you accompanied by someone. Will the person you choose to support you assist or aggravate an already difficult situation?

Keep the day free for you

You must ensure that you have the date marked clearly in your diary and, as far as is possible, booked off from work and other responsibilities. This means ensuring that someone is available not only to look after the children in the event of illness but there to pick them up from school and give them their tea.

Whilst a hearing may be listed for 9am with a time estimate of one hour it is best to set aside the whole day. Courts will often list many cases at one time and it is rare for hearings to start at the published times or time estimates adhered to. The last thing you want is to be concerned that you are not going to be at work for the afternoon if you've just taken the morning off.

If a hearing finishes early, you deserve a rest or the opportunity to catch up with all the other things that you haven't been able to do. Frequently negotiations take a considerable amount of time and can cause delay. This can, however, be advantageous if they result in a settlement, especially where this was never considered a possibility.

Make sure you know where the court is

On the day itself you will find your mind preoccupied with what is going to happen at court. If your solicitor has not told you where the court is, ask them and find out where the best place to park is. Find out the cost of parking and have the right change with you. If taking a friend then make sure they know when to nip out and top up the meter. Better still, choose a car park with payment on exit or one which offers internet payment.

Documents

If you haven't done so already, ensure that your lever arch file with your papers is in good order. If represented, your solicitor should have prepared a bundle of core documents for the hearing. Ask for a copy of that from your solicitor. Try to avoid bringing large amounts of documents to court but if you do bring new ones ensure that you have sufficient copies for your representative and your former partner or representative.

Communicate

Talk through any of those fears. Be honest and clear about your concerns with the other parent. It is likely that they will share those fears in any event.

Be flexible

Discuss options, be willing to compromise, get creative in making alternative arrangements.

Make the right decisions for now

Many parents will be worried about agreeing something else for fear it might set a precedent for the future, but they need to work together on what's best now. Deal with what is in their best interests after the pandemic, after the pandemic.

Karen Holden

A City Law Firm

On starting your case, open an email folder in your inbox specifically for letters and correspondence relating to the matter and a separate folder to include your own documents and those received.

You may prefer to have hard copies of all the documents and so it is always worthwhile having a lever arch file or box file in which to hold all your documents. It is vital that if you wish to hold hard copies of documents that you are sent that this file is as organised as possible so that you can easily find what you are looking for.

Whilst technology at courts is improving, keeping everything on your laptop isn't always helpful - wifi at courts isn't as good as you might expect.

Make sure your laptop and/or phone are charged and both turned to silent.

Bring your diary and dates that you need to avoid, like holidays, medical appointments or other events, for the next hearing. Dates can be changed but doing so isn't easy and may necessitate another hearing and further costs.

Security

A trip to court is no holiday but the security is similar to that experienced boarding a flight. Umbrellas are best avoided and if you bring one it will be left at security along with drinks and a whole host of other items. Drinks even in sealed containers will be checked by court staff. Avoid bringing anything you don't need that will set off metal detectors as you are scanned on arrival. Security officers are told to confiscate anything that could be used as a weapon, even stiletto heels!

Court hearings are not enjoyable for parties and you will undoubtedly find them difficult, but being nervous is normal. The more you can do to prepare and the more open minded you are the more likely that you will get what you want from the day. You will be tense but you must remember that each court hearing can be another hurdle conquered bringing you closer to what you want to achieve. This moment like all will pass.

Primary carer/Main parent – THINK

Regardless of what the arrangements were before separation, it is often inflammatory and unhelpful for either parent to claim that they played a more important role as parent. When most families separate children will usually spend some time with each parent even if that time is not divided equally. Only when one parent takes on the vast majority of the care for a child would it be appropriate to classify them as the primary or main parent but this can still cause conflict. How would you feel if you were referred to as a 'secondary' parent to your child?

Going through the family court

Top tips on the day of court

WESTGATE CHAMBERS

Nicola Sully & Scott Sharp
Pupils at Westgate Chambers

Attending court can be daunting. The idea of representing yourself in court for any reason could be terrifying. In the family courts, this is further compounded by the very subject matter being emotionally important to its participants.

None of the professionals involved in the family court want to cause you distress. You should always keep this in mind. No matter who you are speaking to, even if you feel overwhelmed and emotional, everyone is just trying to do their job. If you are courteous, others will be courteous in return.

Below, we have compiled our top tips to best represent yourself in the family court.

- The family courts are largely investigative, not confrontational. The court wants the relevant information to make a balanced decision on the issues. Therefore, any submission you make should not be about 'scoring points' against the other side. The court is not there to teach adults how to deal with each other nicely; it is there to ensure the best decisions are made for the welfare of the child.

- Generally, attend at least an hour before your listed hearing. In the family court, parties are expected to discuss matters prior to entering the court room. An hour sounds like a long time but it is comparatively little when discussing family arrangements that need to last until the children are into adulthood.

- Speak to the usher prior to the hearing, to register your attendance, and to confirm if you have any special requirements such as to be accompanied into the hearing by a McKenzie Friend (that is a helper that can take notes for you, help organise documents and make question suggestions that you can ask).

- All family proceedings are private so whilst it is only the parties that are allowed into the hearing, you are allowed someone to accompany you in the waiting area; think about asking someone along who can support you, keep you calm and encourage you to focus on the important issues.

- During the hearing, speak clearly and concisely. As a litigant in person the court may ask questions to assist you. When asked a question, answer directly and try not to wander into other information which may lose sight of the key issues.

> Everyone enters mediation with doubts and worries and concerns.
>
> The important thing is to tell the mediator what these are. No point keeping them to yourself.

182

Going through the family court

- A good technique to control nerves in the court room is to pause and think about what you want to say before you say it. Slow down your speaking pace - it will give your brain time to think as you do but it also allows time for the judge to write down what you have said.

- Be confident in your position but open to flexibility. It is rare any party walks into a court room and walks out with everything they are seeking. In child arrangement disputes it is the child's welfare, not your own, that is the centre of discussions.

- In court each party has an opportunity to speak. Whilst you will not agree with some information, every party has a right to be heard so refrain from interrupting. Instead, have a note pad and pen with you, jot down key words to remind yourself that you need to mention your view or evidence on that point when it is your turn to speak.

In the end, you must walk away understanding the consequences of the court's decision and what is required of you. Professionals will assist you, and will not take advantage of your lack of legal knowledge. Do not be afraid to ask questions. In our view, closure often comes from understanding the outcome.

Message to parents - Don't guilt trip us! Meg (17)

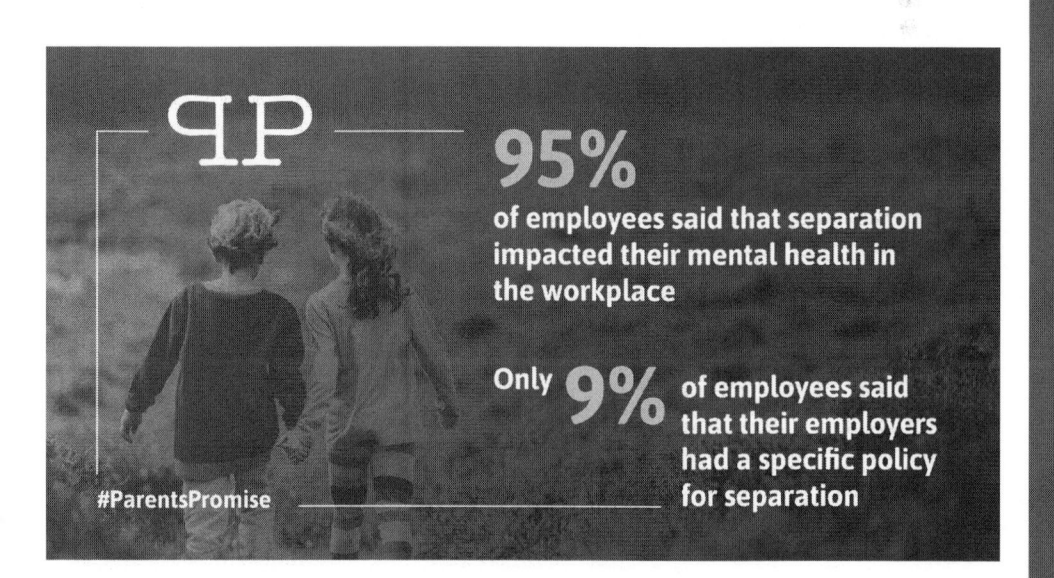

#ParentsPromise

95% of employees said that separation impacted their mental health in the workplace

Only **9%** of employees said that their employers had a specific policy for separation

183

Going through the family court

Should I appoint a barrister?

Lucy Reed KC
Barrister, St John's Chambers

Not a lot of people know this, but since 2010 it's been possible to instruct a barrister to advise or represent you without going through a solicitor (this is called 'public access'). To understand whether or not that's something you need to know or care about, you need to understand what the difference is between a barrister and a solicitor.

They are all lawyers. Barristers are not senior to solicitors, and you do not graduate from solicitor to barrister. But the two types of lawyers do perform different roles. In a nutshell the difference is this:

A barrister is a specialist advocate - they will also be a specialist in their field. Their work will be exclusively in-court advocacy and negotiation and advising their clients. Barristers are self-employed and out and about. This means their infrastructure and administrative support is slender, but their overheads are lower, making them cost effective in the right circumstances.

A solicitor will handle the paperwork - they will issue the applications, deal with the correspondence and send documents to the right person. They too will advise their clients. They may also do some or all of their own advocacy but, because of their additional responsibilities and the different business set up, few solicitors will be in court as frequently as barristers, or will deal with as many complex trials as barristers.

A solicitor will usually instruct a barrister to represent their client in court for two reasons:

- their commitments to their other clients mean they can't attend court on that day; or
- they feel that the case requires a specialist advocate or expert guidance.

Having said that, the legal sector is in the process of

> Google research is not equal to expert legal advice.
>
> *Hasan Hadi, Southgate Solicitors*

deregulation and the ways that lawyers organise themselves are changing and are likely to change even more. Public access instruction of a barrister is just one example of those changes.

When should I consider instructing a barrister directly?

You might particularly consider instructing a barrister directly in the following circumstances:

- You are not involved in a court case but think that you might be, or that you might need to start a court case. A barrister could give you some advice so that you can understand where you stand and what application you should make.

- You are unlikely to be able to afford to pay lawyers to represent you continuously through a court case but need some one-off advice.

- You would like some advice before you decide whether to pay for representation at a hearing.

When direct access might not be appropriate

If you need urgent advice, if you need to issue an application very quickly, or if you want to be represented at a hearing in the immediate future you should seek advice from a solicitor. This is because a barrister is likely to be in court much of the working week and may be unable to respond to urgent enquiries in the same way that a solicitor's office can. A solicitor will be part of a larger firm and will be able to rely on administrative staff and other solicitors to deal with urgent matters, but a barrister's business model cannot allow this. They can instruct a barrister to represent you if needs be - and if necessary should be able to locate one who is available at short notice on your behalf.

If your case is likely to require significant amounts of correspondence, the gathering of lots of evidence (for example obtaining police records) and preparation of witness statements, or the instruction of experts your case might be better dealt with by a solicitor.

Assessment for public access

Before a barrister can agree to advise you or represent you they have to assess whether or not it would be better for you to be represented through a solicitor. If you are struggling to manage your paperwork or to organise your thoughts, or if you are going to have real difficulty in managing the administrative part of your case a barrister will probably have to refuse your case as a public access case and suggest that you contact a solicitor (you could still instruct a solicitor and ask them to instruct a particular barrister for you).

If you would like to get some advice directly from a barrister the best way to ensure that your case is suitable for public access is to follow the guidance below:

Leave plenty of time: The commonest reason that barristers decline public access instructions is that things have been left too late. Remember that a barrister's diary will be full up in advance with court bookings. You need to leave enough time for them to consider the papers and to advise you. If everything is up to the wire you will probably be better off going to a solicitor first - they can access a pool of barristers and will usually be able to find someone who can make the date of your hearing. If you want to instruct a particular barrister you are entitled to ask them to do this for you.

Organise your paperwork: Before a barrister can take a case on they have to be confident you can manage the administrative side of the case that a solicitor might otherwise handle. Keep your papers in order: file orders and applications, statements, correspondence and other material separately and in chronological order. Generally a barrister will need to see all the papers in the court bundle even if you think they are not relevant. If you are asked for a particular document send that document - let the barrister decide what is and is not relevant.

Formulate your questions: Know what you want the barrister to do. Do you want general advice about how strong your case is? Do you want a specific technical question answered? Do you want practical advice about what application to make or what to do next? Or do you want advice about how to maximise your chances of getting the best possible outcome?

Be frank and balanced: Your barrister will need to know not just how you see the case but also how the other party sees the case. It is pointless asking for advice about the case when you

Going through the family court

have only given half the story. Explain the issues being raised by the other party even if you don't agree with them. Be honest with yourself and your barrister about the weaknesses in your case.

Legal aid is not available to pay for the costs of instructing a barrister through public access, so if you are likely to be eligible for free legal advice/representation it is likely you will be advised to instruct a solicitor in order to benefit.

> I blamed myself and I let my anger take control. Kay (16)

Acronyms– THINK

Family lawyers love shortening terms and use acronyms to describe almost anything! The Children Act 1989 could be CA89. Court hearings are abbreviated such as a PTR (a pre-trial review) or a FHDRA (a First Hearing Dispute Resolution Appointment in children proceedings. FHDRA is also sometimes pronounced fehe-drah. The parties in proceedings could be described as M, F, H, W, A or R (that's Mother, Father, Husband, Wife, Applicant or Respondent). A paternal grandmother could be a PGM. If you do not understand something then do not be afraid to ask. The system is there for families and it is important that they understand what is going on.

Going through the family court

What does it mean to 'instruct' a solicitor?

Melanie Bataillard-Samuel
Family Law Solicitor, MBS Family Law

Separating from your partner will inevitably mean going through some changes in your life which will often become more complicated when children are involved. Where will you both live? Who will the children live with? What about money? The list can feel endless - where do you start?

Do you need a solicitor - first steps?
A good first step is to consider whether you can discuss things with your ex. Being clear about what you each want and are expecting the other to do will go a long way to making moving on easier. If you feel you need a little support at this stage, then consider mediation. You and your ex would still be in charge of the negotiations, but with the added help of a neutral third party who would facilitate these negotiations.

It is highly recommended that you take steps to understand your specific legal position before entering into discussions. This will help you to be clear on your issues regarding children (if you have them), finances and other matters. It will also help with reaching an agreement you and your ex are both happy with. Speaking to a solicitor and obtaining legal advice when you first start considering a separation can often provide reassurance which in turn may help to smooth out the stress of the situation. It's never too early to seek legal advice. And, of course, if discussions or mediation are simply not a possibility then a solicitor will help with the court process should you need it.

First meeting?
The first meeting with your solicitor is important - you should leave their office with enough options and information to allow you to make decisions. The more prepared you are for the first meeting the more you will get out of it. It is therefore not a bad idea to turn up with the following:-

- An idea of what is it you want out of the situation - financial settlement, care of the children, etc. If your solicitor has an idea of what you are considering they can advise on that or propose other options for you.

- A short summary of your

Court waiting rooms are dreadful places. Your ex may well be there.

If you don't have a professional advisor with you it is perfectly in order to take a friend along to sit with you.

You are also free to ask the court usher if you might be able to sit alone in one of the ante-rooms. These are often occupied however.

Going through the family court

situation to include some details about you and your family with dates. This will provide your solicitor with a quick overview of the situation and allow more time in the meeting to discuss your legal position and options.

- Any previous letters/emails/texts exchanged with your ex/their solicitors or any documents you might want your solicitor to look over (such as an offer or an application made to the court). Although your solicitor may not have sufficient time or the information necessary during that meeting to fully advise you on these documents, they can consider everything in outline and give you an idea of what to look out for or what now needs to be done.

- Make a list of questions you want to ask - it'll help to keep the meeting focused on what you want to know and will help the solicitor tailor their advice to you. Of course, your solicitor will probably think of a few extra things to discuss that are not on your list!

- A friend/family member to accompany you. This is a stressful time and you will have a lot to think about - someone taking notes of the discussion for you to consider later on may remove the pressure of remembering everything your solicitor says. Some solicitors do provide a written note of the meeting so you may want to ask about that when you book the meeting.

- ID - both photographic and a proof of your address.

Going through a separation is a stressful situation where emotions can run high. Listen to what your solicitor is saying - they will let you know if you're being unrealistic and propose other options they think will benefit you. Use this meeting to identify the important issues that need to be addressed first.

Don't be afraid to ask questions if you don't understand or if you're worried - there are no silly questions.

To instruct or not to instruct

Once you've had that first meeting you should be in a position to decide whether you want to 'instruct' (or hire) your solicitor to act for you. This may not always be the case - perhaps you only wanted to understand your legal position before discussing things with your ex, or you've decided to represent yourself and just wanted to know where you stand.

If you want to hire a solicitor to act for you pick one you trust and feel comfortable with - personalities play an important part in choosing a solicitor and don't be afraid to specify if you would rather instruct a male or female solicitor. If the first solicitor you meet does not suit you, you should look for another one. Shop around!

He walked out of the door and it felt like my life had been demolished before my eyes. Mia (12)

Can I get the Judge to speak directly with my children?

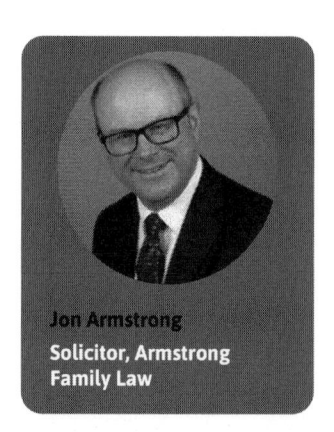

Jon Armstrong
Solicitor, Armstrong Family Law

Parents in cases involving disputes about children will often feel that it is important that the children's views are taken into account, rather than have their views ignored by the grown-ups. The law recognises this. It says that children's views will be taken into account in light of their age and understanding. Therefore, a child aged, say, 5 years old, is not likely to have any weight attached to his or her views, whereas a child of, say 13, will find that the court will take into account their views, albeit that these views will not be the only factor that the court will take into account.

Older children may find that their views are the determining factor. It is relatively rare to see disputes about children aged between 14 and 16 being dealt with at court, as the court will often take the view that it cannot make a child of that age do something which they do not wish to do. (The court cannot usually make orders about children aged 16 or above).

Will the Judge speak to the child?

Judges will often be very reluctant to speak directly to a child. They generally prefer to leave that to people who are better trained to do so - the Cafcass Officers.

At an early stage in any application to the court (usually at the First Hearing Dispute Resolution Appointment or FHDRA), the court will consider whether or not it should order a section 7 report to be prepared to provide the court with independent recommendations about what it might be ordered. These reports (which grizzled older solicitors and barristers sometimes still refer to as Court Welfare Reports) are usually prepared by the Cafcass Officer.

Sometimes the only thing that the Cafcass Officer has to address in their report is the child's wishes and feelings. The Cafcass Officer will not simply parrot what the child says. The Officer will speak to the children about what they want and will also bear in mind that it is common for children who are at the centre of disputes to be telling each parent what they want to hear, rather than what the child actually wants. Experienced Cafcass Officers can be very good at getting to what the child actually wants.

In a small number of cases a Judge has talked directly to the child in a case. One Judge, Mr Justice Peter Jackson was praised in 2017 by family lawyers for the sensitive and intelligent way in which he wrote a letter to a child in order to explain his decision to the child.

Mr Justice Jackson has even used emojis in such letters to help communicate with children about their case. However, he is somewhat unusual in his approach. Most Judges prefer not to speak to the children directly and instead rely on parents to explain the court's decisions to their children.

Going through the family court

The children's guardian and children's solicitor

Sarra Gravestock
Director and Head of Children & Social Services, Biscoes Solicitors

> "Every bit of damage inflicted on either partner is damage inflicted on the kids, so treat your ex like you treat your kids."
>
> *Paul, Dad*

Who are Children's Guardians?

The name "Children's Guardian" is a confusing one. It is often confused as a foster carer or some other form of alternative carer. This could not be further from the truth. A Children's Guardian is employed by CAFCASS (Children and Family Court Advisory and Support Service). They are specialist Social Workers who help families in court proceedings.

What does a Children's Guardian do?

When the adults in a child's life cannot agree with whom a child should live and how often the child should see their other parent, it often falls to the court to make that decision. Whilst in the majority of cases this can be resolved through mediation, as a last resort a judge will make a decision if either parent, or other adult, applies to the court for an order pursuant to section 8 Children Act 1989. These are now known as Child Arrangements Orders, setting out where a child lives and the way in which they spend time with other people. These used to be called Residence and Contact Orders.

During court proceedings the court will often direct a welfare report, also known as a section 7 report. Unless your family is, or has been, known to Social Services, a Children's Guardian will undertake that report. They will report to the court not only on the parents views, but also the wishes and feelings of the child and they will, importantly, make a recommendation to the court as to what they think is in the best interests of the child.

There are occasions when the court considers that the appointment of a Children's Guardian under Rule 16.4 Family Procedure Rules 2010 would be of assistance, usually where the facts have become complex and serious and there is no resolution or compromise in sight; or when an older child is opposed to the recommendations being made by the Children's Guardian. This requires the court to make the children parties to the proceedings. The Children's Guardian will also appoint a solicitor to represent the child.

The appointment of a Children's Guardian means that the child will have an independent voice in court. The Children's Guardian will want to meet the child, often away from the adults to allow the child to speak freely. The Children's Guardian will make recommendations to the court as to what he or she thinks is in the best interests of the child; sometimes this is not always in accordance with

Going through the family court

the child's wishes and feelings as that is just one factor that the court must take into account when making decisions about children. When the Children's Guardian makes a recommendation to the court, and when the court makes a decision, the welfare of the child will be paramount and they will be applying the welfare checklist set out in section 1 Children Act 1989 when reaching those conclusions.

Who is the Children's Solicitor?

When a child is made a party to Court proceedings and a Children's Guardian is appointed, the Children's Guardian will go on to appoint the child a solicitor. That solicitor will be a member of the Children Panel and experienced in representing children through their Children's Guardian.

The solicitor's fees will usually be covered by legal aid.

The solicitor's role is to represent the child in court. The solicitor will take their instructions from the Children's Guardian and not from the parents.

It may be appropriate for the solicitor to meet the child, but this will depend on the age of the child and whether the child has expressed a wish to meet the solicitor.

In some circumstances it may be appropriate for the child to meet the judge who is going to be making the decisions to express their wishes and feelings. The child's solicitor will arrange this and accompany them. Whatever the child says to the judge is not considered to be evidence. The judge will also make sure that the child understands that what is said is not a secret - the parties will be made aware of what the child has said. The child will also have an opportunity to ask the judge questions.

What if the child does not agree with the Children's Guardian?

Sometimes what the Children's Guardian is recommending to the court is not in accordance with the child's expressed wishes and feelings. When this happens the child's solicitor will need to assess that child's competency and

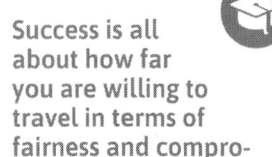

> Success is all about how far you are willing to travel in terms of fairness and compromise.
>
> *Nav Mirza, Dads Unlimited*

understanding of the proceedings to decide whether the child can instruct a solicitor independently of the Children's Guardian. Age is an important factor when making this decision but is not the overriding factor - emotional intelligence and maturity is also considered. If the solicitor concludes that the child is competent, he or she will take instructions from the child directly. The Children's Guardian will continue to play a role and will continue to make recommendations to the court either directly themselves or through another solicitor.

My parents might not be together but I have all the support I'll ever need from family and friends. Anonymous (16)

What is the Welfare Checklist and do I need to know about it?

David Starkey
Solicitor, John Hodge Solicitors

If you are contemplating divorce or separation from your partner, your first concern will probably be about where your children will live and how they will spend time with both parents. As parents, you know your children best, so you will be best able to consider the effects of your break-up on them and, hopefully, together devise the most suitable living arrangements for your children. Family mediation services, together with Resolution mediators and solicitors, can help you to achieve this outcome.

If you can't agree upon the arrangements, you can ask the courts to decide the matter by making an application for a Child Arrangements Order. Prior to making any application to the court, it is necessary for the parties to attempt mediation.

Welfare checklist

The Children Act 1989 is the main piece of legislation dealing with family disputes about children. The Children Act states that the child's welfare is the paramount consideration when the court considers any question in relation to the upbringing of a child. Therefore, the court will apply what is known as the 'welfare checklist' to help it make its decision.

The welfare checklist looks at:

The wishes and feelings of the child (considered in the light of their age and level of understanding)

This will normally be determined by Cafcass or Social Services, and reported to the court. The court will take into consideration whether or not a child's wishes and feelings are their own, or whether outside factors may have influenced their decision. The court will balance the views of the parties concerned, including the views of a child who is of an understanding age (normally 9 years of age) and mature enough to form their own opinions.

Their physical, emotional and educational needs

A child's emotional needs can be quite difficult to deal with, and the court will consider who is best able to provide for the emotional needs of the child, both

> I always tell separating couples to remember that they are parents and regardless of their relationship having failed, they must not fail their children. I stress that there will be many occasions where their children will want them both there, their children must not be forced to choose or be in an awkward position but rather see their parents putting on a united front for THEM.
>
> *Amanda Adeola, BHP Law*

short term and long term.

The likely effect of any change in their circumstances

The potential impact of changes to the child's life will be considered. The courts will aim to make an order that causes the least disruption to a child's life - however, this will be balanced against the other factors to be considered.

Their age, sex, background and any characteristics which the court considers relevant

The court will consider specific issues such as race, religion and culture when making a decision about a child. They may also take into consideration the parents' hobbies and lifestyle choices if they feel it will impact on the child's life, now or in the future.

Any harm which they have suffered or are at risk of suffering

The courts will look at the risk of harm to the child. This will be immediate risk of harm as well as the risk of harm in the future. 'Harm' includes physical, emotional and mental harm. The courts will decide upon the potential risk of harm to the child in the future and make an order as they feel is appropriate. An order may include safety measures to protect the child.

How capable each parent is of meeting their needs

The courts will consider how able each parent is to care for the child and to meet their particular needs. This will be subjective and depend upon the facts and circumstances of each case, the needs of the child and the abilities of the parents concerned.

The range of powers available to the court

The court must weigh up all of the factors under the welfare checklist, and consider all available orders within their discretion. It will then make the best order available that is in the best interests of the child.

The welfare checklist is therefore extremely important when considering where a child should live and how much time they should spend with each parent. It is the framework by which the courts use in order to reach their decision. As a result, it is important to know and understand the welfare checklist prior to making any application to the court regarding your child.

Shared care – GOOD/THINK

Many families will end up with a shared care arrangement following a separation even if they don't realise it. Shared care does not mean that children spend an equal amount of time with each parent (although this can sometimes be the case). It simply means that both parents play an active and meaningful role in raising the children of the family. Even an arrangement where a child spends every other weekend with one parent could be considered shared care. Recognising this could help to diffuse parental conflict.

Advocate

About Advocate

Advocate is a charity which helps to find pro bono (free) legal assistance from volunteer barristers.

Who are we?
Many people struggling with family legal issues are unable to afford legal representation and do not qualify for legal aid. We are a free service that matches those in need of legal help who can't afford representation or get legal aid with volunteer barristers who kindly donate their time and expertise.

Since we were founded by Lord Goldsmith as the Bar Pro Bono Unit in 1996, we have helped thousands of individuals and small organisations to get expert free legal help. We became Advocate in October 2018, with a renewed focus on modernising our service so that we can help provide the right legal help to as many people as possible across England and Wales.

Our vision
Our vision is to be able to match everyone needing legal help quickly and easily to the right expert barrister.

We can assist with:

- Specialist legal advice, drafting and representation;

- Cases in all areas of law;

- Cases in all tribunals and courts in England and Wales.

On average, we hear from 50 new people every week facing a legal problem alone. Each year, we receive more family cases than cases in any other area of law. Our applicants might be struggling to see their children, attempting to gain a custody order or going through a difficult separation.

Barristers can:

- Give legal advice in a meeting or in writing;

- Draft documents such as skeleton arguments;

- Represent in any court or tribunal.

Barristers cannot:

- Prepare a case and paperwork for the court or tribunal;

- Lodge papers at the court or tribunal on your behalf;

- Provide administrative support;

- Write letters on another's behalf.

Advocate ensures that in each case the barrister providing assistance has the same expertise and experience as would be expected in a paying case. We may be able to help if:

- An individual or organization cannot get legal aid, pay privately, or get legal help elsewhere;

- The matter involves the law of England and Wales;

- The case is appropriate for assistance on a pro bono basis;

- The help needed will take 3 days or less (exceptions may apply);

- The case needs a

barrister who can act if necessary without a solicitor.

How to apply to Advocate for help:

- All applications must be made through a referring agency such as a solicitor or advice agency (e.g. a Citizens Advice Bureau, a Legal Advice Clinic or Law Centre).

- An application may also be referred by your MP.

- The application form is available on our website or we can send out hard copies on request.

- Once completed, the application form needs to be returned to us in hard copy along with copies of any case documents.

The referrer:

- helps make the initial application to Advocate and can identify the supporting documents required.

- can, if they wish, act as a point of contact throughout the process.

Eligibility

- If you can pay privately or are eligible for public funding (legal aid) for your case, we will not be able to help.

- We cannot help in cases unless we receive the completed application and all the relevant documents at least three weeks before the hearing or deadline, unless there are exceptional circumstances; i.e. your child would be taken into care.

Assistance

Assistance cannot be guaranteed as we rely on the services of volunteer barristers.

We are not a frontline agency and do not have barristers in our office to give legal advice directly. We are an application-based service that focuses the Bar's pro bono resources where they are most needed.

Case study

Daniel is the father of three young children. He applied to Advocate for legal assistance in seeking a residence order against his children's unstable mother. Advocate was able to match Daniel with a volunteer barrister who represented him in court. The case was successful and the residence order was granted, offering Daniel and his children more stability and hope for the future. Daniel spoke about his experience with the Advocate:

"I cannot thank the Advocate enough for the incredible help and support you provided for a desperate father. The barrister you supplied came into my world yesterday and completely changed the landscape of myself and my children's future. Without her work and the work of yourselves, my life would be in a terrible state; instead I look forward to a future with my children."

To find out more about us and the work that we do to help people like Daniel, please visit our website: https://weareadvocate.org.uk.

When your children are upset (as they will often be during the period after parents separate) it is better to respond to their feelings and not their behaviour - you can best help by showing understanding and respect for your child's feelings.

Paul Kemp, The Worcester Family Mediation Practice

Going through the family court

Can I change my Cafcass Officer?

Mark Leeson
Partner and Head of Family, Brachers Solicitors

In a word: no. The following article explains a bit more about Cafcass and what they do.

Who are Cafcass?
Cafcass stands for Children and Family Court Advisory and Support Service. Cafcass is separate from the court service itself but provides expertise to the court when required. When a children application is made to the court Cafcass will initially undertake a safeguarding check on the parents which includes a criminal records check. They will usually try and speak to both parents and then provide a short report to the court on any issues which arise.

At the First Hearing a Cafcass Officer (who will have a social work background) will meet with both parents and make recommendations to the court as to next steps. If no issues emerge which create a concern about the children's welfare then it is likely that Cafcass will have no ongoing involvement in the proceedings before the court.

Section 7 report
If however issues do arise which affect the welfare of the children then the court can order that Cafcass prepare a report (called a 'section 7' report) on the issues and make recommendations to the court about the most appropriate arrangements for the children. These recommendations will have a significant influence on the eventual outcome of the application.

Cafcass Officer
The Cafcass Officer is appointed by the court. It is not possible to change the Cafcass Officer because you do not agree with the conclusions they have reached. If you do not agree with the recommendations that the Cafcass Officer has made it is possible to challenge their conclusions in the court.

If you have a concern about a Cafcass Officer's performance or conduct whilst undertaking their duties Cafcass have a complaints procedure and there is a useful fact sheet on their website at cafcass.co.uk. However, it will still be the decision of Cafcass or of the court as to whether a Cafcass Officer's performance or conduct is such that they should be removed from the case.

In some cases where the issues are complicated and the Cafcass Officer has been unhelpful it may be possible to ask the court to make the children a party to the proceedings. If that order is made the court will appoint a guardian who also comes from Cafcass. However, the guardian's role is to represent the children's position and can therefore provide an alternative view to that of the Cafcass Officer.

Have you any tips for dealing with an abusive partner at a court hearing?

Claire Fitzgerald
Partner, Barrett & Thomson

Sue Scott
Senior solicitor, Barrett & Thomson

If you can afford legal representation (i.e. have someone speak on your behalf) it is likely to be easier for you to face your ex-partner. Unfortunately solicitors and barristers can be expensive and not everyone can afford to pay their fees. However, many solicitor's firms are very understanding and may be able to help you in a number of different ways such as:

- Offering a discounted rate if you are on low income;
- Acting on a fixed fee basis (this will need to be agreed in advance);
- Helping you with a specific piece of work, such as preparing a statement or completing an application form (this option is known as "unbundled services".

Instructing a solicitor

It's wise to shop around before instructing any solicitor. You need to find one who not only specialises in family law but more especially in domestic abuse cases.

Accredited Resolution specialists in domestic abuse can be found on the Resolution website http://www.resolution.org.uk/domesticabuse. The "Find a solicitor" section of the Law Society website http://solicitors.lawsociety.org.uk is also useful to help you find a solicitor in your area, and it will give details of whether they undertake Legal Aid work plus their specialisms registered with the Law Society e.g. family panel or child panel.

Instructing a barrister

Some barristers will accept direct instructions from a client (this is called Direct Access) rather than the usual method of through a solicitor. So if you just want representation at a hearing this is something to consider but remember that barristers will not help you prepare any paperwork needed beforehand. Make sure you find a set of barristers' chambers that specialises in family law.

You may qualify for Legal Aid if you are the victim of domestic abuse. If you do qualify, you will be able to get representation at a hearing. You can check your eligibility on the LAA website https://www.gov.uk/legal-aid .

McKenzie Friends

If you cannot afford a solicitor or barrister then you may consider a McKenzie Friend to offer support and assistance in court. There are different types of McKenzie Friends, including:

- family members, or friends;
- voluntary helpers attached to institutions or charities especially domestic abuse agencies, who generally do not charge for their help;
- fee-charging McKenzie Friends. Their charges can sometimes be quite high and you may be better off instructing a solicitor. So please do your research beforehand and if possible use someone who has been recommended.

McKenzie Friends can help by, providing moral support, taking notes in court, helping with paperwork but they are not allowed to speak in court unless the Judge gives permission.

Who is representing the perpetrator?

If the perpetrator has a solicitor or a barrister then they should be easier to deal with - they may try and negotiate with you before you go into court to narrow down the issues. They may question you in court but they have to follow certain rules.

If both parties have legal representation the court hearing will be easier to handle as any discussion will take place between the representatives.

If neither of you have representation the Judge will lead the conduct of the case.

Making applications

Things to consider when making an application to the court are:

- **Confidentiality**. If your address is confidential and is not known to the perpetrator you can request the court's permission not to disclose it to them on any documents. This is done on a C8 form which is available on the court website https://assets.publishing.service.gov.uk/government/uploads/system/uploads/attachment_data/file/687801/c8-eng.pdf. Once granted permission by the court you can leave your address off any documents that they will be sent.

- **Finances**. If dealing with finances then ensure you blank out any details which may reveal your whereabouts before they are disclosed to the court, for example cash withdrawals or debit or credit card expenditure in your local area.

- **Children**. If dealing with Children Act matters you should complete a form C1A (see https://www.familylaw.co.uk/system/uploads/attachments/0006/9033/C1A.pdf). On this form you will give the court details of the abuse you and/or the children have suffered and it will ask if you need any "special measures" (see below).

Waiting at court

Before going to court you need to let the court know in advance that you will need what is known as "special measures" to be put in place for you to attend safely. This can include separate entrances from the perpetrator, separate waiting rooms or a screen in court so you don't have to face them. You should contact the court manager in plenty of time before the hearing to discuss the special measures you require. Be aware that every court has different facilities available and some have none at all! Get them to confirm in writing if possible.

On arrival at court make yourself known to the security staff and if necessary show them any written confirmation you have that special measures are to be put in place. It is usually a good idea to call the court a day or two before the hearing to check that they have made the necessary arrangements.

Security at court is very similar to that at airports so don't worry about the perpetrator bringing in any weapons.

In addition to any legal representation or McKenzie

Going through the family court

Friend, always take someone with you (a good friend or family member) to support you while you wait to go into court. Be warned: you may have to wait a long time before you go into the courtroom. It's therefore useful to have someone there to talk to and take your mind off things as well as run errands, for example getting a drink or speaking to the usher to find out what is happening. They will not be able to come into court with you, so they may want to take a magazine or newspaper to read while they wait.

Refreshment facilities differ from court to court. Some have a café and some vending machines, all of which vary in quality. So go prepared. Security will ask you to sample any drinks on the way in.

In court

If no screen is given then **do not look at the perpetrator,** just look at the Judge. The perpetrator or their representative may ask you questions in court but the Judge is the person who needs to hear the answer.

Be prepared for the perpetrator to make false allegations against you, particularly if they are acting in person. They may accuse you of being a drug addict, violent or seen as an unfit parent, etc. Remember that just because they are making accusations it doesn't mean that they will be believed. Judges are used to hearing false allegations so bear that in mind when you go in.

Answering questions

Look at the Judge. If you are not sure how to answer the question you can ask for it to be repeated - this will give you more time to think.

The perpetrator may try and intimidate you in court, often by staring. They may know how to wind you up or to make you more nervous so just try and ignore that. The Judge is likely to notice their attempts to intimidate you and intervene. The Judge will also stop any questioning that is irrelevant, argumentative or abusive.

If you are representing yourself you may like to provide a Position Statement setting out your position prior to the hearing which can be given to the Judge. It is not a statement of your evidence but is, as its name suggests, your position on the matters the court is being asked to deal with at this hearing. Use bullet points or numbered paragraphs to help keep your position statement succinct. You could instruct a solicitor (on an unbundled services basis) to help you prepare this, if necessary.

A lot of people worry that their ex-partner will not agree to a fair settlement, particularly in financial proceedings. You need to be aware that the Judge can impose an order on the other party and therefore you don't have to back down or to be bullied into agreeing to something that you are unhappy with or you think is unfair.

Cafcass

If the court proceedings relate to children, Cafcass (https://www.cafcass.gov.uk) are likely to be involved at some point in the proceedings. They usually have to do a "safeguarding check" before the hearing and will send a letter confirming the outcome to the Judge. You will usually have the opportunity to speak to Cafcass before the hearing. Make sure that you list the allegations, or make Cafcass aware of the allegations, that you are making against your former partner. Cafcass should check police records and check with social services to see if there have been any incidents in the past. Details of any incidents will be included in the letter to the court.

What is a C100?

Rajan Thandi
Associate Family Law Solicitor, Southgate Solicitors

The C100 is the title of the application form many people will need when applying to the court for a Specific Issue Order, Prohibited Steps Order or a Child Arrangements Order. When seeking any of these types of orders you may be told by people or even solicitors that you need to apply or put in an application. The C100 is that form.

Although it sounds very technical, the form is fairly straightforward. However, if you are completing or preparing an application yourself make sure that you double check that everything which is relevant to your case is completed, otherwise the court may send the application back which will only cause delays.

Most solicitors (if you have one) will have access to the forms through various software packages. If you are completing it yourself then the Gov.uk website is the main source for court forms and should be used over any other website. You can find the C100 form on the Gov.uk website under the Parenting, childcare and children's services section.

Types of orders

Specific Issue Order: Where there is a dispute between (usually) parents about a specific issue such as schooling or perhaps medical treatment, then a Specific Issue Order is the order you will be asking the court to make.

Prohibited Steps Order: If you want to stop the other parent doing something or from taking a course of action you will be seeking a Prohibited Steps Order, for example if one parent is talking about going abroad and you are worried they may not return with the child.

Child Arrangements Order: Finally, if you cannot agree on arrangements between yourselves as to who your child lives with or spends time with then you will be seeking a Child Arrangements Order.

Completing the C100

On the front page of the form where it asks if there are concerns about risk of harm, you need to tick the relevant boxes and then provide further information on Form C1A. Again, the Gov.uk website is best for this - just type in C1A into the search box on the main website to access the form.

When completing the form, it is important to put in as much information as you

---

At the start of a separation, think of a statement which sets out your hopes and aspirations for your children after the process has ended. If negotiations or discussions become difficult, you can go back to your statement and remind yourself of what is most important. This may help you to unblock an impasse.

Rachel Duke, Aletta Shaw

can, especially when it comes to details of the other party - the court will need this to be able to send a copy of the application to them so that they are aware of the proceedings.

There is a requirement to provide your address details as well. However, if you do not wish to disclose these because you are worried about the other party having your address then a C8 form (again, search for this on the Gov.uk website) will need to be filled out - this is a very simple form which asks you to list any details that the court is to keep confidential.

When completing the form, it is helpful to put as much detail as you can about the orders you are seeking. You do not need to put the history of the case in lots of detail as that can be explored later but the court needs to know what you are seeking and why.

If you are seeking a Specific Issue Order or a Prohibited Steps Order then try to be as specific as possible since these are usually for singular issues and the court needs to know why there is a dispute.

For a Child Arrangements Order it is helpful to have an idea of the type of contact you are seeking or if you want your child to live with you - the more detail you can give the better.

When filling out a C100 you will see that the front page and pages 4 to 9 talk about a Mediation Information and Assessment Meeting (MIAM). It is now a legal requirement that, before applying to the court for an order, the applicant (i.e. the person seeking the order) has to have attended a MIAM unless an exemption applies. The idea is to encourage people to resolve issues outside of court between themselves.

Sometimes this is not possible or appropriate, for example in cases of domestic abuse or child abuse - in these sorts of cases you do not have to attend a MIAM. The C100 lists the evidence that the court will accept as proof of domestic abuse or child abuse and you will need to attach that to your form. There are other exceptions such as urgency; insufficient contact details for the respondent or that you have previously attended a MIAM.

If your case does not fit into any of these exceptions then you will need to attend a MIAM and you can use Resolution's handy search tool to find a trained and accredited mediator in your area (see resolution.org.uk).

Urgent applications

An important point to note when completing a C100 is that the usual time frame for the court to deal with these applications is 4 to 6 weeks.

There are times, however, where you cannot afford to wait that long and need an urgent order. In that case you can tick the box on page 1 of the C100 setting out that an urgent order is needed. You will then need to complete pages 11 and 12 setting out why the application is considered urgent and whether:

- you are asking for a 'without notice' hearing i.e. you need a hearing immediately and the other person isn't told about the first hearing, being only asked to attend a later return hearing; or

- 'abridged notice' is required i.e. there is a deadline (e.g. with a school application) and an issue needs resolving quickly but doesn't need a without notice hearing.

In those circumstances you need as much detail as possible to show the court why no or shortened notice is needed.

The C100 looks much more complicated than it is. Take your time filling it out, be specific and make sure that any other forms such as the C1A, C8 or domestic abuse/child abuse evidence/MIAM form are attached.

Representing yourself in court

Olivia Piercy
Partner, Hunters

Navigating the Family Court without representation can feel daunting. This article aims to demystify the process and give you some useful pointers to help you to represent yourself at court.

Who's who?
If you are representing yourself in court proceedings you are called a 'litigant in person'. The litigants in a case are known as 'the parties'.

The party who made the application to court is called 'the applicant' and the other party is called 'the respondent'.

Sometimes there is more than one respondent and it can get confusing when more than one person makes an application. You might find it easier to refer to yourself and the other party as 'the father' or 'the mother' or just by your actual names.

Your case may be heard by magistrates or by a judge.

The court may appoint a Cafcass officer to investigate your case and report back to the court.

What to call the judge
If your case is heard by a district judge or by magistrates, call them 'Sir' or 'Madam'.

If your case is heard by a judge with the title 'His/Her Honour Judge X', call them 'Your Honour'.

If your case is heard by a judge with the title 'Lord/Lady Justice X', call them 'Your Lordship/Ladyship'.

Making an application
If you want to make an application to court, you need to use the correct court form for the application that you are making. You can ask your local family court which is the correct form to use. The most common forms are:

- Form C100 - to make applications in relation to your children.

- Form DIV1 - to apply for a divorce.

- Form A - to start financial remedy proceedings in relation to divorce.

- Form FL401 - to apply for protection from domestic abuse.

You can make your application by posting it or handing it in to the court. You may need to pay a fee so check with the court how much that will be. If you cannot afford to pay the court fee, you may be eligible for a fee remission, if you complete Form EX160. The court will 'issue' your application and will send a copy to you and a copy to the other party. If appropriate the court will arrange a court hearing.

TIPS
- It is a good idea to read the guidance on the back of court forms, which sets out how to complete the form.

- You can find all of the court forms on the Form Finder page of the HMCTS website.

- If you do not hear back from the court, telephone them to make sure they have received your application, as paperwork does sometimes go astray.

- Provide the court with

three copies of your application form and three copies of any other documents you file - one for you, one for the other party and one for the court file.

- Read any paperwork you receive from the court very carefully.

- Any documentation that you provide to the court will be sent to the other party. If you don't want the other party to know your address, do not put it on the application form. Instead, include your address on a Form C8 and do not put it on any other documentation. The court will keep the Form C8 with your confidential address on the court file.

How to prepare for a court hearing

Letters from the court: carefully read all of the documents from the court and the other party as soon as you receive them. They may include important information such as the date and the venue for the next court hearing. They may also set out important directions including documents you need to provide by certain dates.

The bundle: at a court hearing, the judge and parties will usually have a file of the relevant documents, called the 'bundle'. If the other party is represented, their solicitor will prepare a court bundle. They should agree the contents of the bundle with you in advance and they should also provide you with a copy of the bundle. If both parties are unrepresented, the court will prepare the bundle, but you should still bring all relevant documents to court with you.

Cafcass: a Cafcass officer may telephone you before the first court hearing to ask you if you have any safeguarding concerns about your child or the other parent. Try to be as helpful and honest as possible with the Cafcass officer.

Position statements: before each hearing, you should also prepare a position statement. This is different from a statement of evidence. A position statement includes a summary of what has happened so far and sets out your position for the hearing, including what you would like the court to order. Your position statement should be typed if possible. It should not be more than four A4 sides long. You should email it to the court and to the other party the day before the hearing. You should bring a few copies to court.

Special assistance at court: if you will need arrangements to be made due to a disability, or the assistance of an interpreter, make sure you contact the court well in advance to put in a request. If you are afraid of the other party, you can ask the court to find a separate waiting room for you and a separate entrance to the court. You may even be able to have a screen in the court room so you can't see the other party, or to join the hearing via a video link. Ask the court how they can assist you. You should chase this up with them more than once to make sure they have put the special measures in place.

Representing yourself at the court hearing

There are different kinds of hearings depending on what application has been made and the stage of the proceedings. Usually the first court hearing is used to see whether the parties can agree. If they can't agree, the court will direct what evidence each party needs to provide so that the court has all the information it needs in order to make a decision. The following tips may be helpful whatever kind of court hearing it is:

- You should get to court an hour before the hearing if possible.

- If you are representing yourself you can bring a friend or family member with you. They are called a 'McKenzie Friend'. Tell the court and the other party that you have brought a McKenzie Friend. Your McKenzie

Going through the family court

Friend can sit next to you, take a note and help you to organise your papers. They cannot speak on your behalf unless the court gives them permission.

- When you arrive at court, check the notice board to see which court you are in. Find the court room and hand your position statement to the court clerk. Explain who you are and ask them to hand it to the judge or the magistrates so that they can read it before he court hearing.

- Sign in at the front desk. You may see that the other party has already signed in. They may wish to negotiate with you before the hearing. You can try to agree matters if you wish, but you don't need to. It may be that some issues are agreed and others are not. Remember to give them a copy of your position statement as well.

- When you are in the court room you should take a note of everything that the judge says. Check that the judge has had a chance to read your position statement. If not, give them another copy.

- You may feel angry or upset in the court room. It's OK to cry, but it's important not to lose your temper with the judge or with the other party. If you do not feel you have had an opportunity to express yourself clearly, make sure the judge is aware that you still have more to say. It's important to put all of your most important points in your position statement in case you get nervous in court and forget to say them.

- After each hearing a court order will be drafted. If the other party is represented, their lawyer will prepare the order. If not, the court will prepare the order. Make sure that you have exchanged email addresses with the other party's lawyer and with the judge's clerk, so that you can check the order and so that you are copied into any correspondence with the court.

- Make sure you know and that you write down (1) when the next hearing is, (2) whether you have to file any documents and if so, by what dates, and (3) whether the other party has to file any documents and if so, by what dates.

Representing yourself in the Family Court can feel overwhelming, especially when the case is about your children. Court proceedings follow a process and are usually broken up into stages. So long as you have read everything from the court very carefully and you have followed the directions that the court has given you, you can't go too far wrong.

The most helpful thing you can do to make sure you are really prepared is to draft a position statement in advance of every hearing and bring along a lot of copies. Don't be shy to ask your friends and family for support. It can be really hard to take in and remember everything that was said during a court hearing or during a negotiation with another party, so it can be a great help to have someone else there to take a note. If you don't feel you have anyone to ask, you can contact the Personal Support Unit ('PSU'). The PSU is a charity which operates in many family courts around the country. It can often make someone available to support you at court and even during your court hearing.

Above all, remember that the Cafcass officers and the judges are all very overworked and busy. However, their main priority is to make decisions in the best interests of your children. Try to present your case clearly so that the right decisions are easier to make.

204

Going through the family court

Going to court is rarely the answer when sorting out the financial issues that need to be addressed as part of a divorce or separation.

Most cases settle before any final hearing because Judges encourage and support discussions and negotiations but by then a lot of money will have been spent on the litigation process.

Where possible you can avoid costly litigation by negotiating and preparing at the outset a list of what you really want and what you would be prepared to negotiate on.

You will then have a very clear focus and an idea of what your negotiation parameters are.

Rachael Oakes, Freeths

Parents, don't bad mouth the other parent to your child.
Josie (15)

Going through the family court

How should I prepare for a meeting with a professional to save time and money?

Ursula Rice
Managing Director
& Solicitor Advocate,
Family First Solicitors

So, you took the plunge and made the call. You have an appointment with a solicitor. How should you prepare?

Remember you are paying money one way or another to meet with this person. Even if the meeting is free there is every chance that you have taken holiday, paid or unpaid, from work, to make the meeting.

Below is a list of the pre-meeting things to find. Of course you can mix and match them according to your circumstances...

If you have divorce and financial issues

- Make a list of your assets. Define those in your name, your ex's name and anything owned jointly. Try and get some broadbrush figures together.

- Date list: when were you married, roughly the length of time you were you together before marriage and how long you were cohabiting if applicable.

- I assume you remember your children's birthdays and full names! Now's the time to check you do!

- Bring any court paperwork if there is any.

If you have domestic violence issues

- If you kept a diary, take it with you.

- Police URN numbers are helpful and any police letters (PIN letters).

- Harassing messages, printed or on your phone are helpful so your solicitor can assess your evidence.

- Any paperwork from social services.

- Any court paperwork if there is any.

If you have Children Act issues

- If your son or daughter was born in late 2003 and you never married the other parent then bring the birth certificate with you (this is to check the situation over Parental Responsibility).

- Bring a selection of emails. No one wants War and Peace, but an indication of the recent communication styles and immediate issue sis helpful.

- Previous or current court paperwork if any.

Trust of Land issues (cohabitation financial issues)

- If there is one, the deed of trust.

- Any paperwork saying or indicating you and your ex were intending to share the property.

- The Land Registry official copy of the property in question.
- Try and remember or dig out some paperwork from the solicitors who dealt with the house.

Generally...

Before you go, arrange flexible child care. Don't be in a rush. Try to leave your children with someone. Kids are awesome, but they shouldn't be privy to the conversation - they will get bored and you might cry. So bringing your kids is not cool, plus you will only take in half of what is said.

Look up parking and the address before you go.

Have a think about what you want to achieve at the meeting. A basic sense of the law? Something specific answered? A plan of action going forward?

Bring a friend if you can. It's so supportive and helps to have someone to debrief with.

A note book and pen is helpful. Write down those legal nuggets!

Prepare a list of questions before you arrive. What is vexing you or confusing you?

Remember to make a note of costs and don't be afraid to press for a ballpark figure of overall costs.

Immediately afterwards, try and make a note of how you felt about the meeting. This is really helpful if you have lined up a few solicitors to talk to, as you may forget who is who!

Follow the above and you will be more prepared than most to extract maximum value from the meeting.

More often that not, once a couple have reached an agreement over the financial division of assets, their relationship improves and they can parent more collaboratively.

Uncertainty fosters mistrust and unpleasantness and once their financial future is more certain, they can concentrate on working together for the sake of their children.

Tessa Bray, Simons Muirhead & Burton

It was strange to begin with living with my dad, I'd never had that much to do with him before. But we both knew that if we were going to get through this, we had to do it together. Sally (16)

Going through the family court

What are directions orders?

Norman Hartnell
Joint Managing Director, The Family Law Company by Hartnell Chanot

Family law and family life is complicated, or at least it can be.

Courts are there to apply family law to help find solutions to problems which spouses, partners or parents (collectively called 'parties to the proceedings') can't find themselves by negotiation. Courts approach their problem-solving role in a clear and methodical way by making 'directions orders' to gather together all relevant information to equip the Judge to make the best decision possible. These directions orders specify what steps are to happen to gather all the evidence.

Whether a problem relates to children, money or the relationship itself every court application starts with a set application form giving all basic information, but that is far from a complete picture. There are always two perspectives (at least) and sometimes there are other people who know and can contribute information for the court. In financial cases, these may include property valuers, or pension experts; in children cases, Cafcass Officers and sometimes experts such as psychologists.

Directions hearings

In some cases, as soon as court proceedings start, the court issues standard (the usual) directions. This happens, for example, in every financial case when a timetable is set, and those starting or on the receiving end of proceedings are told what documents they need to file (send to the court) or serve (send to their opponent) and by what timescale. In other cases, there may be one or more 'directions hearings'; that is a hearing when the Judge will make orders as to how and when missing information is to be gathered.

Courts have tried to standardise this process as much as possible, so that the norms of how problems are to be solved are known from the outset, and as much preparation as possible can be carried out in advance. Once the court has set a timetable, it will expect it to be followed to avoid unnecessary delay.

Enforcement

The court does not automatically keep an eye on the progress of the case so, if orders are not obeyed, the court will expect someone to alert them to what is happening. In those cases an enforcement order can be sought, in which case the person who has not complied with the previous directions order may be

> If you think you will need someone to represent you at a court hearing, talk to one of the OnlyMums/Dads Panel Members (www.thefamilylawpanel.org).
>
> They will talk you through your options and if they think you need a Barrister they will have all the local names and contact details. Professional diaries are busy though and the earlier you sort things out the more chance you have of being represented by the professional best placed to help on the day itself.

ordered to carry out a task by a certain date or face imprisonment. This is the court's main sanction, by means of what the court calls a 'penal notice' - a formal notice warning of the consequences of not obeying a court order.

Apart from the gathering of evidence, the court has to consider setting a hearing date which could be a date when the court will check on progress or a final hearing date when the decision will be made.

Tips

So, if you are attending a directions hearing:

1. Always think about what information the court will need to make its decision.

2. Go to court prepared with solutions, not problems, for the Judge.

3. If you think that you will need an expert of some description go on the internet and read FPR Practice Direction 25. You'll see how much advance thought has to be given to such matters. If your case involves any allegation of harm in a children case, read Practice Direction 12J. In all children cases, it's Practice Direction 12B; in financial cases, 9A. There are practice directions covering every conceivable situation.

4. Get advice. These are complicated matters. The directions hearing sets the whole direction of the case. If you start off taking the wrong fork in the road it can take an enormous effort to get the case back on track. Sometimes that is not possible as once a track is set it is extremely hard to go back if a mistake is made.

Family law solicitors and barristers live and breathe these matters day by day and are well placed to help, even if they are limited to giving you guidance to enable you to do as much of the work yourself to save legal costs.

Family Judges have been known to end their judgment by stating if both parties leave court today equally as unhappy with my decision then I've done my job.

I will often use this phrase to focus clients on achieving resolutions and avoiding the court process.

Laura Clapton, Consilia Legal

For 15 years I've wanted a voice. At 18, I'm ready to talk about what my parents, and their divorce, have done to me. Kaitlyn (18)

What happens at a fact-finding hearing?

Fiona O'Sullivan
Consultant Solicitor,
Weightmans LLP

In cases concerning arrangements for children, it is very common for factual disputes between the parties to arise. The court must be very careful to distinguish between allegations, which if true, would impact on the welfare of the child or children concerned.

The court exercise great caution and consider the relevance of allegations to the issue to be determined. If, for example, serious allegations are made against one of the parents, but the incidents occurred before the child was born, or when the child was much younger, then the court is unlikely to investigate those historical allegations, as they will not directly impact on the time that parent will spend with the child [see the case of Re V (A child) [2015] EWCA CIV 274].

Where the court is satisfied that the allegations, if true, will impact on the welfare of the child, then the court will order a separate hearing to consider the evidence about the allegations. Having considered the evidence the court will make findings in writing. The hearing is known as a fact-finding hearing.

A fact-finding hearing may be necessary if the following allegations have been made:

1. Alcohol or drug abuse;
2. Physical or sexual abuse;
3. Verbal or emotional abuse;
4. Repeated non-compliance with previous court orders.

The decision to direct a fact-finding hearing is a judicial decision, not one for the Cafcass officer or for the parties. However, in considering whether to direct a fact-finding hearing, the court will consider the views of the parties and of

---

This can be a nerve racking experience for mums and dads.

It is never too late to settle any disputes prior to hearings and decisions made together are always preferable to ones made on your behalf.

Try to keep calm. It's an unfamiliar environment so nerves are inevitable.

Keep to the point, so only talk about the presenting issues.

Try to keep emotions at bay, not easy but they can overwhelm and cloud your thinking.

Listen to your legal team, they know what they're doing.

If you get angry try to negotiate a 'time out' so that you can calm down.

Listen fully and if there is something you do not understand, ask.

Adele Ballantyne

Cafcass, It will also consider whether the party facing the allegations has made admissions, which could provide a sufficient basis on which to proceed, or whether there is other available evidence which provides a sufficient basis on which to proceed.

Although a fact-finding hearing may delay the case and mean that additional time is spent at court (in some cases many additional days), the early resolution of whether relevant allegations are found to be true by the court enables the substantive hearing to proceed more quickly, and enables the court to focus on the child's welfare with greater clarity.

Having reached the conclusion that a fact-finding hearing is necessary, the court will then give detailed directions as to how the fact-finding hearing is to proceed. These directions will include specifying the written evidence from the parties and considering whether documents are required from third parties, such as the police or health services.

To assist the court and the parties, the court usually directs the party making the allegations to prepare a template (called a Scott Schedule) itemising the specific factual issues to be decided by the court. The template is set out in such a way that the responding party is able to comment briefly by stating whether the allegation is agreed or denied, and a separate column is included to record the findings of the court having considered all the evidence. This template enables the court, when subsequently adjudicating on the substantive issue, to have a clear summary of the findings of fact. The party making the allegations should draft them in such a way that the court can give a yes or no answer on the Scott Schedule.

The aim of the fact-finding hearing is to ensure that the allegations are put and responded to. Both parties have an opportunity to give oral evidence and to cross examine the other party. The burden of proof is on the person making the allegations. The court determines the matter on the balance of probabilities, not on the higher, criminal, standard of beyond reasonable doubt.

Having considered the evidence, the court will make findings of fact. The court will then give directions as to the future conduct of the substantive hearing. This may include directing a report from Cafcass.

Once a fact-finding hearing has taken place, the court must consider the child arrangements in light of their decision. If no findings are made, the court must proceed on the basis that the allegations did not happen. If some findings are made, then the court must consider the child arrangements in the light of those findings, and must consider how any risk to the child can be managed.

Fact finding hearings will not therefore be ordered in every case, but can be a very useful tool to provide a template for the court in taking into account proven serious allegations which are likely to impact on the welfare of the child.

Stay out of the arguments, don't take sides and just explain how you are feeling. Jade (17)

What is a Child Arrangements Order?

Shanika Varga-Haynes
Team Leader, Partner, Stowe Family Law

> Don't expect the other parent to behave how you behave. Understand that it's difficult and different from both sides.
>
> *Mandy, Mum*

A Child Arrangements Order is a court order which regulates where a child lives and/or how much time a child spends with the other party. A Child Arrangements Order can also say that a child lives with both parties and it can provide for other types of contact such as through phone calls, video calls, cards and letters etc.

Unfortunately, these orders are not always complied with or situations change and they are no longer considered to be the best arrangements for the child. There can be a number of reasons for an order not working including (but not limited to):

- One party breaching the order by withholding time with the child from the other party;

- The party's circumstances change meaning they can no longer comply;

- The needs of the child have changed;

- There is a concern that the child is at risk of harm.

What can you do if your ex-partner breaches a Child Arrangements Order?

Unless an agreement has been reached between the parties to informally vary the order, one party will be in breach of the order if they do not comply with it.

If it is possible, the parties should try to discuss the breach of the order and resolve the matter between them. However, if this is not possible then an application will need to be made to the court to either enforce the order or vary it. The court charges a fee for this which is currently £215.

Since 2008, all orders dealing with arrangements for children have a warning notice attached to them which states that if you do not comply with the order, you may be sent to prison and/ or fined, made to do unpaid work (community service) or pay financial compensation. Orders that were made before 2008 do not contain these warnings and so before you can enforce them, you have to apply to the court to have the warning notice added to the order. Once it has been added, you can then apply to enforce the order.

What power do the courts have?

Failure to comply with the order can result in the defaulting party being found in contempt of court. This does not necessarily mean that it will lead to a term of imprisonment. The court will have a number of options which will depend on the nature and frequency of the

Going through the family court

breaches. The court could:

- Make a referral for the party in breach to attend a Separated Parents Information Programme - a course which helps parents understand separation from a child's point of view and learn the fundamental principles of how to manage and reduce the impact of conflict on their children.

- Vary the Child Arrangements Order - to make it clearer or alternatively in serious cases, change who the child lives with to the other party.

- Make an Enforcement Order or Suspended Enforcement Order - An Enforcement Order imposes unpaid work up to a maximum of 200 hours.

- Make an order for financial loss - for example, for the cost of a holiday which may have been lost due to the breach.

- Committal to prison - generally the last resort and will usually be suspended (put on hold).

- A fine - again, this is generally a last resort.

If it becomes apparent that the party has a reasonable excuse for breaching the order, then the court will not enforce it. It may instead consider whether it is necessary to vary the order.

If a party finds that they are not able to comply with the order and an agreement cannot be reached to change it then they should make an application to vary the order before it is breached so that the court can consider why the order is not working and if necessary, change the arrangements so that they are considered in the best interests of the child.

If the party who is in breach of the order is the one who is supposed to be spending time with the child and they are not then it becomes more difficult to deal with. The court will have the power to enforce the order but it may not consider that it is in the best interests of the child to force someone to spend time with them when that person does not want to or make any effort to. It can be quite emotionally harmful to a child to be put in this situation as it may make the child feel more unwanted than if the contact just stopped. In such circumstances, the court could consider discharging the order if an application is made, meaning that the order would no longer exist.

What can you do if the order no longer works for you or your child?

It is quite common for parties to reach the stage where the Child Arrangements Order is no longer working for the child or for the parties themselves. Before an application is made to the court, all other methods of negotiating should be explored. Solicitors can be instructed to negotiate on a party's behalf or the parties can, for example, attend mediation. In some cases where there are older children involved, they too can engage in the mediation to tell the mediator what it is that they want. Arbitration is also another possibility in children matters.

At any point, until the child reaches the age of 16, either party can apply to the court for the Child Arrangements Order to be varied. Once a child is 16, it will only be in exceptional circumstances that the court will be able to deal with the case.

The primary concern for the parties and for any court is the welfare of the child. Where possible, trying to resolve any issues related to a Child Arrangements Order is a more preferable route to going back to Court. Clear legal advice is important in all cases to support and guide you through the process and get the best result for you and the child.

What is a Parenting Co-ordinator?

Claire Webb
Mediator, Family Law Specialist, Collaborative Lawyer & Arbitrator, Mediation Now

As a Parenting Co-ordinator (PC) I am appointed by a couple and provide **education** about the long term effects to a family of high conflict, **mediation** where there may be an issue to be resolved and **binding decisions** in certain circumstances, when mediation has not been successful.

PC is the new kid on the block in non court resolution. It is widely used in the USA, Canada and South Africa where it is considered to be the "norm". It works for those who have an ongoing pattern of conflict regarding arrangements for their children and are unable to agree.

I can only work with parents or carers who have a Parenting Agreement or a Court Order.

What does Parenting Co-ordination cover?

The underlying principle of a parenting coordinator is to keep a focus on the children's best interests and to assist the parents in making the best decisions they can for their children.

Where decisions for children's arrangements are required, and the parents are unable to plan without anger, it can have a serious impact on the children's developmental and psychological needs. The PC's intervention will reduce the amount of damaging conflict between parents to which the children are exposed. Divorce and separation in themselves need not harm children; what causes them harm and possible ongoing problems throughout their lives is being in the middle of conflict between their parents

PC can improve the family's immediate, but especially long-term narrative. It can identify strategies that can affect even small adjustments in functioning that will help set a separated family on an improved track. It can show positive role modelling for children's management of future relationships and identify triggers and calm rather than stoking the fire.

It takes an educational role, recognising the positives and building from there to ensure children can flourish as best they are able.

The approach

The PC process is a forwarding looking process - it tries to draw a line in the sand. The emphasis is on recognising that a parenting relationship is a new type of relationship and helping that relationship become a problem-solving relationship.

Most PC agreements last for about two years, participants can tailor make their agreement to what they both want.

PC allows parents and carers to move away from continuous court applications to vary or enforce and work together to be the best parents they can be.

What does PC cover?

- Conflicts in the arrangements for the children's day to day care;

- Difficulties related to the children's transitions between their parents, including codes of conduct and transportation;

- Developing any necessary clarifying provisions that were not anticipated when the parenting plan or order was developed;

- Assisting parents to communicate more effectively where appropriate;

- Assisting parents with the exchange of information about the children (i.e. health, welfare, education, religion, routines, day-to-day matters, etc);

- Addressing temporary changes to the usual holiday child arrangements, to accommodate special events and circumstances for the children and/or the parents;

- Resolving conflicts concerning the children's participation in recreational, enrichment or extracurricular activities, lessons, and programs;

- Addressing movement of the children's clothing, equipment, toys and personal possessions between households;

- Addressing matters relating to the children's travel with one parent;

- Resolving conflicts concerning day to day health care, education, and activities; and

- Resolving conflicts about any other parenting function, issue or decision as may be agreed between the parents (with some exceptions).

> Sometimes mums and dads can be accused of terrible things regarding their children. Some may be true, that occurred when they were still together. Others may be 'news to them'.
>
> Sometimes accusations can be made as a form of 'punishment' to either partner. This can occur if either mum or dad are at the angry stage of loss. It is not unusual for past behaviour to be seen through a different lens when angry or upset.
>
> Respond by being honest and try not to involve the children by asking them what they think.
>
> *Adele Ballantyne*

What does PC not cover?

- Requests for a permanent change to the child arrangements that would substantially change the children's time with one parent;

- A request by one parent to move the children's place of residence;

- A request by one parent to remove the children from the jurisdiction of England and Wales, whether temporarily or permanently;

- Decisions regarding life-changing or life-threatening medical treatment;

- Decisions regarding the choice of full-time school, college or other educational establishment to be attended by the child;

- Any case where a parent lacks capacity under the Mental Capacity Act 2005;

- Any case where a person with parental responsibility for the child is a minor; or

- Any other decision which the PC considers, at their discretion, goes beyond the implementation of an existing parenting plan or order and requires determination of a substantive welfare issue relating to the arrangements for the care of the child.

Going through the family court

How to appoint a Parenting Coordinator

Appointment of a PC takes place after both participants have had an initial conversation with their prospective PC, to make sure they feel comfortable with that person. Clients are then sent the PC agreement and must take legal advice about the implications and impacts of the documents to ensure they understand the process, and the kind of decisions that can be made that may affect the family. Each person's solicitor will also need to sign to confirm they have given legal advice.

Qualifications, memberships and experience to look for

Parenting Coordinators are highly experienced family practitioners, often specialising in non-court resolutions. They usually have three years post-qualification mediation experience and will be accredited with the Family Mediation Council. PCs come from various legal and therapeutic backgrounds.

Top Tips

1. Speak to your solicitor, if you have one, to obtain your child arrangements order.

2. Attend a Mediation Information and Assessment Meeting, where an accredited mediator will be able to explain all non-court resolution processes to you, and will be able to point you in the right direction.

3. You should start to be able to paint a picture in your area as the same names may come up. Then have a look at the Parenting Coordinators website https://parentingcoordinators.co.uk/ where you can see the biographies of the PCs.

4. Arrange to have a short chat with a couple of PCs, and see who you feel comfortable with, so that you can move to the next stage of the process.

I learnt that there was no need to choose sides. Isaac (15)

Access, Contact & Residence – STOP

These words are outdated and no longer form part of the law in England & Wales. They encourage parents to view disagreements about their children in terms of what they are entitled to. The correct legal term is 'child arrangements' which can be adapted to fit in with many types of schedules and can help to diffuse conflict. This child focused language needs to be supported by wider language that focuses on promoting and maintaining a relationship with both parents whenever possible.

Do courts automatically think kids are better off with mum?

Gillian Bishop
Consultant, Family Law in Partnership

> Kids are not weapons or bargaining chips - they are innocent bystanders. The relationship didn't work, so try to make the separation work.
>
> *Kevin, Dad*

My first reaction to being asked to write an article on this topic was that I had drawn the short straw. "Can I pick again?" I wondered.

The reason for my reaction I think is obvious to most family lawyers and those people who have had the misfortune to have to take disputes concerning their children to court. Ask this question to a group of them and 9 out of 10 would immediately answer "yes" and ask what the next question is.

I am acutely aware, too, of how emotive the whole issue of a separated father's role in a child's life has become. There are any number of dads out there who feel very badly let down by the system in the face of parental alienation and often with very good reason. There are other fathers who have become quite militant and, regrettably, given their cause a bad name.

What is undeniable is that the ideal situation for a child is for them to have a good relationship with both parents and for their parents to have a good enough working relationship as co-parents. And I believe that Cafcass and Judges start from that view point.

We live in a society which still has the mum, dad and two kids ideal at heart (although more diverse family units are becoming increasingly common). And within that ideal mum, as the child bearer, is regarded as the primary carer if the idyll is broken and mum and dad separate. Since our Judges and Cafcass are drawn from our society it is unsurprising that most of them will also start from that idealistic view point.

In any event, there is no getting away from the fact that in the majority of cases before the courts the mothers are the child bearers and as a result will have had a very different and, at least to start with, closer bond with their children. I know an eminent child psychiatrist who says that a child under 7 should not, in an ideal world, spend more than 7 to 10 days apart from their mother at a stretch.

So I decided that there was not much point talking in generalities when it came to trying to answer the question. Everyone knows the generalised answer. I decided to draw on my own experience and to ask my colleagues what their experience was.

Pro-father cases

Some of the instances that were described to me were:

- A District Judge telling a mother at the outset of a case that he expected her

217

Going through the family court

to agree to mid-week contact even though she had been opposing it;

- A Judge ordering shared residence notwithstanding the finding that the father was a bully to both the mother and the three children;

- A Judge finding against a mother who wished to return to her native European country because the father enjoyed an equal time split, even though when the child was at his father's house he actually spent more time with his paternal grandparents than with his father.

For each of these apparently 'pro-father' cases there were ones where it seemed societal norms prevailed.

Pro-mother cases

- An order for shared residence with a time split slightly in favour of the mother, despite Cafcass reporting that the children had a closer bond with their father who had been their primary carer;

- No changed residence order despite the mother making dreadful and unfounded allegations of child abuse against the father. This in a case where the mother retracted the allegations and agreed to work with the relevant services to enable contact to re-establish;

- Any number of leave to remove cases where the mother has been able to return 'home'.

Parental alienation

When you get litigation over children you get stressed children who, mostly, will tell Cafcass what the parent they feel most bonded to wants, as if that is their wish too. In a vastly overstretched and underfunded service it is no surprise if Cafcass take these 'ascertainable wishes and feelings' as gospel.

But there is no doubt that times are changing and changing quite fast. Leave to remove applications are not the 'shoo in' for mothers they once were. Cafcass has launched a pilot scheme to crack down on parental alienation and there is significant interest in parenting coordination as a means of supporting families stuck in a high conflict situation.

There is a greater realisation among all involved in family justice, and some father's groups like Families Need Fathers, that the answer lies not in the amount of time a child spends with either parent but in the ability of the parents to work co-operatively together as separated parents.

This is borne out by the recent increase in workshops and courses being run for separated parents. There is the in-court Separated Parenting Information Programme (see page 219) and the Parenting After Parting workshops run by my firm to name but two. The requirement that all parents wishing to bring Children Act applications will have to be assessed for mediation is, at least in part, an indication that the bigger picture is understood by a wider spectrum of society.

Society is changing, and it needs to change more, but with that change will gradually come a different answer to the question. Eventually, it won't be necessary to ask the question any more.

Be the bigger person. Even if your nearly ex is trying to play dirty, don't rise to the bait. It is easier said than done, but I often hear from people who years later regret that they allowed themselves to get lowered to that level.

Peter Martin, OGR Stock Denton

Going through the family court

How will the court decide on where the children will live?

Ruth Hawkins
Partner, Solicitor, BH&O LLP

When families split up, it is often extremely stressful and emotions can run high. When parents are separating and/or divorcing, and cannot agree on arrangements for their children, this adds to the pressure.

There are a number of ways to resolve issues such as where the children will live, and when and how they see their other parent.

If parents are able to reach their own agreement, then the courts do not need to intervene. This is known as the 'no order principle', contained in the Children Act 1989, which states that where parents are able to reach their own arrangements the court will not become involved.

Parents can reach their own agreements directly with one another, or by using a family mediator. Cafcass ("Children and Family Court Advisory and Support Service") have produced lots of helpful guides, including a Parenting Plan to assist with this.

A family mediator would meet with both parents, preferably in the same room (but it can be separate - called 'shuttle mediation'). The advantages to this way of resolving issues include an often speedier and more targeted or personal approach; the parents are in control of this process, whereas if they are using the court process, the court is in control; it can often be a cheaper process; and legally aided mediation is available for those who qualify (provided there is a legal aid provider in the area!). It is also possible to arrange for child inclusive mediation with a qualified mediator, which can be a really good way of exploring the child's wishes and feelings.

But not everyone is able to reach an agreement, and it takes both parents to agree. Sometimes only one person is willing to try mediation, sometimes neither are or there may be good reasons why it is simply not safe or appropriate.

In those instances, a parent may need to make an application for a Child Arrangements Order ("CAO") to the court.

The courts no longer deal with 'custody' or 'access', or 'residence' or 'contact' and instead deal with the child's arrangements. This change in terminology was brought in in 2014.

> Imagine you are listening to your child/children at 18 talking to their friends about how they experienced mum and dad separating; you would want to hear: "it was ok - I was fine - knew I was loved by both and free to love each of them", not: "it was a nightmare..."
>
> *Debbie Wahle, Norfolk Family Mediation*

Going through the family court

If the court is considering an application, it will usually be about where the child is going to live, or when they will spend time with the other parent, although other issues such as which school they attend, or medical treatment and other specific issues, can also be considered by the court, where appropriate.

The court's main consideration when deciding such matters, is the child's welfare. This is set out in Section 1 of the Children Act 1989 which states that "...the child's welfare shall be the court's paramount consideration".

The court is required to go through a 'welfare checklist':

- The ascertainable wishes and feelings of the child concerned (considered in the light of their age and understanding);
- Their physical, emotional and educational needs;
- The likely effect on them of any change in their circumstances;
- Their age, sex, background and any characteristics of theirs which the court considers relevant;
- Any harm which they have suffered or are at risk of suffering;
- How capable each of their parents, and any other person in relation to whom the court considers the question to be relevant, is of meeting their needs;
- The range of powers available to the court under this Act in the proceedings in questionnaire.

This all looks straightforward, but *how* does the court ascertain all of this?

A short safeguarding report or letter will be filed with the court and served on the parents before the first hearing from Cafcass, confirming whether there are any safeguarding concerns from the police or social services perspectives.

Where there are safeguarding issues raised, the court can order a report from Cafcass, to look into these aspects. This report is often referred to as a 'section 7 report'.

In families where there has been social services involvement, the court will generally ask the social worker who has been dealing with the family to prepare the section 7 report, instead of Cafcass.

The Cafcass officer, or social worker, will speak to each parent, and will usually speak to the child, usually in their offices, or sometimes at school, or occasionally at home. Once they have done so, they will prepare their report, file it with the court, and also serve it with each parent and/or their solicitors if they have them.

The court will generally have timetabled a short DRA Hearing (Dispute Resolution Appointment) shortly after the report is due, to consider whether the parents can reach agreement or not. If they can't, then the court will generally order a contested hearing to be listed for maybe a day or so, depending on how great the issues are, and potentially how many witnesses may need to give evidence. In most cases, the witnesses the court will want to hear from will be limited to each parent and the Cafcass officer or social worker, but occasionally other witnesses, including a new partner or family member, may be allowed too.

During these final hearings, the court will hear the evidence and then hear 'submissions' from the parents or their lawyers, and then the Judge or Magistrates will make a decision.

My ex is threatening to take our children abroad. What should I do?

Emine Mehmet
Director & Solicitor,
Duncan Lewis Solicitors

This area of law is complex so if you are concerned that your child is going to be abducted then you should consult a solicitor immediately.

What is child abduction?

Child abduction is essentially taking a child under 16 away without the consent of the person who usually cares for them (the resident parent) and has parental responsibility (PR) for them.

International child abduction occurs when a person (such as parents, guardians, or anyone with PR for a child) takes a child, or keeps a child, out of the country the child normally lives in without either:

- permission from everyone else who has PR for the child; or
- an order of the court.

This means that if both parents have PR and there are no court orders in place, neither of the parents can take the child out of the UK without the written permission of the other parent.

However, if a Child Arrangements Order has been made by the court stating that the child will live with one of the parents, that parent can take a child abroad for 28 days without getting permission from the other parent, unless a court order says they can't or the holiday coincides with time the child would normally have spent with the other parent.

International child abduction is a criminal offence and anyone found guilty of this offence can be sent to prison or fined or both.

What if I think my former partner is going to take the children away from me?

There are a number of reasons why you may have concerns that your children will be removed from the jurisdiction and practically, if you have these concerns, you should not allow your former partner to remove your children from your care at all. Neither must you provide your former partner with the children's passports until you have had legal advice or have made an application to the court.

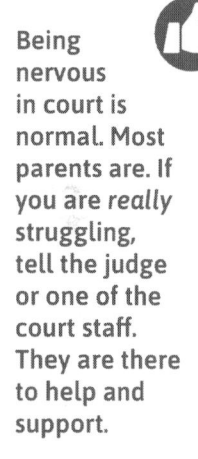

If you have these concerns, you can apply to the family court for a Prohibited Steps Order (PSO). A PSO can stop someone removing children from your care or from the jurisdiction without your permission.

> Being nervous in court is normal. Most parents are. If you are *really* struggling, tell the judge or one of the court staff. They are there to help and support.

221

Going through the family court

Without notice applications

You can make this application without telling your former partner (called a 'without notice' application) if you fear that they may remove the children if they learn of your application before it is determined. Your former partner will be informed of the application only after the first hearing, and there will be a further hearing which you both attend for the court to decide whether the PSO, ordered at the first hearing should continue.

If you are making the application on a without notice basis, you will need to explain your reasons for doing so. In an emergency situation, the court can make other directions when a PSO is made such as a port alert to prevent the children from leaving the country. This means that the police will flag the child's name at all UK airports and points of departure.

The court can also issue an order requiring a UK passport to be surrendered which can prevent the Passport Service from issuing a passport or travel document. However, these actions usually require proof that the children are likely to be removed from the UK within the next 24 or 48 hours.

Remember that the court's paramount consideration will be the child's welfare and they will usually allow a child to leave the UK with one of the parents unless there is evidence to suggest the child might not be returned.

90% of employees said that separation affected their ability to work

Only **9%** of employees said that their employers had a specific policy for separation

#ParentsPromise

What is a Leave to Remove application?

Fiona Turner
Partner, Weightmans LLP

Lottie Tyler
Associate, Weightmans LLP

For separated parents, the possibility of a move abroad is fraught with complexity. If a child's parents end up living in two different countries, it is going to have a substantial impact on their upbringing. This article looks at the considerations for the international relocation of children.

If a parent is looking to move overseas and intending that the children move with them, they will need the other parent's agreement to make the move, or alternatively an order from the court. A court application is for what is termed 'leave to remove' i.e. permission to take a child out of the jurisdiction of England and Wales.

Trying to reach a collaborative or mediated agreement is preferable to court. Such an approach would give the other parent time to adjust to the idea and the opportunity to contribute to a plan. Through either of these processes it would properly be a joint decision and one therefore most likely to benefit the children moving forward.

The law and the guidance

A court approaching an application for international child relocation should note:

- The welfare of the child is the court's paramount concern.

- There is no presumption in favour of either parent.

- There is a distinction between 'principle' and 'guidance'. Regard can be given to guidance in previous cases, provided that overall that particular case is decided on what is in that child's best interests.

- The welfare principle is key; the court's enquiry is the same whether there is a primary carer and or if there is a shared care arrangement. It is not about the labels given to child arrangements.

- The court should reach its decision by undertaking a global, holistic evaluation of the options. This requires it to:

> Separation and divorce is scary for children. One of the best things you can do to help is to reassure them that no matter what happens, they still have two parents who love them.
>
> *Vikki Martin, Wolferstans Solicitors*

- conduct a welfare analysis of each realistic option for the welfare of the child on its own merits and in the context of what the child has to say;

- conduct a comparative evaluation of each party's plans; and

- if appropriate, scrutinise and evaluate each parent's plan by reference to the proportionality of the same; (considering the proportionality of the parents' respective plans is necessary to ensure that the decision reached is not open to challenge under article 8 of the European Convention of Human Rights).

What this means when preparing a case

Within the context of the evaluative approach, it is clear that the success of an international relocation case is heavily dependent upon the facts of each case.

In preparing a case, the following (non-exhaustive) list of points should be considered in conjunction with the welfare checklist set out in s1 Children Act 1989. The list is in no particular order:

- the nationality, domicile and habitual residence of the parties;

- the child's cultural background and ties, including the history of where they have lived and the frequency and quality of time spent in other countries and the languages that they speak;

- the child's personality and interests;

- significant people in the child's life other than their parents;

- the connection of each member of the family to the place of the intended relocation;

- the reason for the application including an assessment, where appropriate, of whether there is a motivation behind the application that undermines the reason;

- the 'infrastructure' in place in the UK and in the proposed new country in terms of income, accommodation and practical support;

- the intentions and feasibility/practicality of promotion of time spent with the other parent and how it will be facilitated;

- the other parent's ability to relocate and whether there is any question that the 'staying parent' may not remain in the UK in the foreseeable future;

- what the child wants;

- the impact on the child's education, whether this is the right time for the move and whether this is a good moment to transition between schools/educational systems;

- the impact on the child of a potential reduction in contact; and

- the impact on both parents, to the extent it could impact on the child.

If you think you will need someone to represent you at a court hearing, talk to one of the OnlyMums/Dads Panel Members (www.thefamilylawpanel.org). They will talk you through your options and if they think you need a barrister they will have all the local names and contact details. Professional diaries are busy though and the earlier you sort things out the more chance you have of being represented by the professional best placed to help on the day itself.

Going through the family court

Advice from abroad should be sought

Unless a family law practitioner is dual-qualified in both the UK and the country the parent wishes to relocate to, their advice alone will be insufficient. The parent should also consult a lawyer in the destination country for advice on immigration/visa requirements; the extent to which any English order will be recognised; and the merits of obtaining a 'mirror order' (this is an order made in one country which reflects the original order made in another country).

This advice is an important part of strengthening a case, enabling parents to understand as early as possible any potential difficulties in enforcement. An overall understanding of the legal position may also help to allay the fears of the other parent.

What should I do?

Advice to anyone contemplating such a move who anticipates resistance from the other parent should research the resources available for the children in the new location and start building up a picture of what their life would be like. In advance of any discussions with the other parent, information should be gathered and detailed consideration given to how it is presented to the other parent. It will also provide the other parent with the opportunity to do their own research into schools, nurseries and neighbourhoods.

Conversely, a parent who thinks their former partner is making decisions about their children's future without seeking agreement, or without providing full information about the arrangements, can consider making an application to the court for a prohibited steps order to prevent the children being taken out of the country, either at all or just until proper arrangements have been put in place. These arrangements will include when that parent will see the children if they were to relocate, and, until they have had an opportunity to take advice, what steps can be taken in the courts of the other country to ensure that that court would enforce an order made in England or Wales. Alternatively they could consider whether a 'mirror' court order should be made in the country where it is proposed that the children are to live.

Expert advice from a family law solicitor should be sought at an early stage of the planning/discussion.

DO I HAVE TO TELL THE COURT EVERYTHING - I FIND IT HARD TO TALK ABOUT THINGS?

I assume you've made a full statement, which will be a court document. Your ex's representative will probably ask you about it, and it would be a good idea if you prepared calming strategies (e.g. mindfulness exercises), ask for time to answer, do it at your pace, and point out to your rep and the judge if you feel upset with the questions, or how they're being asked.

Mike Flinn

I've been ordered to attend a SPIP by the court. What should I expect?

Laura Beech
EMDR, Integrative and Relational, Trauma Therapist, MBACP (Accredited)

The Separated Parents Information Programme (SPIP) was devised for Cafcass as part of an ongoing process to enable better co-parenting and to help parents understand separation from the child's point of view. It is not a parenting course and will not teach you how to be a good parent - you already know how to do that. SPIP focusses on your emotions and practical aspects of parenting - it does not cover the legal or financial aspects of being a separated parent.

Parents are either 'directed' by the court to attend a SPIP or they can choose to attend the course themselves independently. If the court orders parents to attend, the course is free.

What happens at a SPIP?

Each parent will attend separately - you will not be expected to attend the same course as your ex. It is hoped that, by attending, you will become clearer about what your children need most from you as children of separated parents, and that you learn and understand the fundamental principles of good communication and how to manage conflict and difficulties between you and the other parent using positive behaviours.

You will be introduced to the 'loss cycle' theory and be asked to reflect on your own emotional journey and responses to the relationship breakup or situation and to realise that your children will also experience loss, even subconsciously, and how that might affect them.

The total length of the course is 4 hours and can be delivered in two, 2 hour sessions or one, 4 hour session with a break in the middle depending on your provider. It is important that you turn up on time or even early as there is a cut-off time which is generally 15 minutes or so from the start time. If you are in a small group of four people or fewer it will be delivered by one trainer; if the group is bigger it will be delivered by two trainers.

It is natural to feel anxious if you have been ordered to attend a SPIP as no one likes to be told what to do and this can make participants' feel defensive or hostile to begin with.

Don't feel alarmed if the course feels very dry to begin with - the trainer has a lot of information that they are required to give to you. It is important that the trainer does not stray from the script to ensure that every parent receives the same message wherever they take the course.

There are exercises throughout the day and 2 videos to watch. You will be expected

> *If I could turn back time, I would push harder for my ex and his family to keep in contact. It is their choice not to be but I wonder if I could have done more.*
>
> Lisa, Mum

Going through the family court

to participate in the exercises and feedback sections of the course; however, if you are struggling with any part, especially if it has triggered strong feelings, you can ask to pass on those parts. If you continue to struggle with your emotions on the day, talk to one of the trainers as they may be able to help you. One of the things they may suggest is that you come on another day when you feel more able to cope.

You will be given a handbook to keep which has all the information covered on the course plus some other useful hints and tips. This handbook can be shared with your friends, family or whoever supports you with your parenting and anyone else who would also benefit from the material.

You are not expected to be experts at the end of the course. You should try to see SPIP as an ongoing process, to improve your communication skills and to realise that the effect of conflict is very damaging to your child's development. It is not the separation that causes the most harm to the children but the level of conflict they experience as a child of separated parents. SPIP invites you to think from other peoples' perspectives so that even if you disagree, you can appreciate someone else's point of view and perhaps understand it.

After the SPIP

You will be given a certificate at the end as proof that you attended - some attendees are required to prove this to the court. Feedback forms will also be given during the session and it is important for your voice to be heard, so, if you have any changes to recommend or experiences you would like to share that you think will be useful, please make sure you do this. The feedback forms are taken seriously and help to modify future courses.

If you have been ordered by the court to attend the SPIP, the trainers will only report to Cafcass that you attended unless you have displayed disruptive behaviour or did not participate in any way. They will not report back on your responses.

Most attendees get

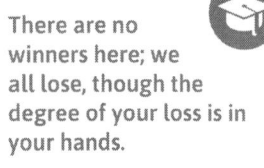

> There are no winners here; we all lose, though the degree of your loss is in your hands.
>
> *Nav Mirza, Dads Unlimited*

something useful from the day. Some have said that they felt less alone once they attended the course as they met others in a similar situation. Others have said they can understand different points of view better, and they can identify their strengths as a parent that they already had but had forgotten. Other parents feel better just being able to talk to other separated parents. So, although it can feel daunting attending a SPIP course, go with an open mind and a positive attitude. As the day progresses most people find that they relax and may even enjoy the day!

> *My parents separated when I was 3. I was made to believe at such a young age that it was my fault. That guilt stayed with me for years. Ellie (16)*

Broken court orders: what are my options?

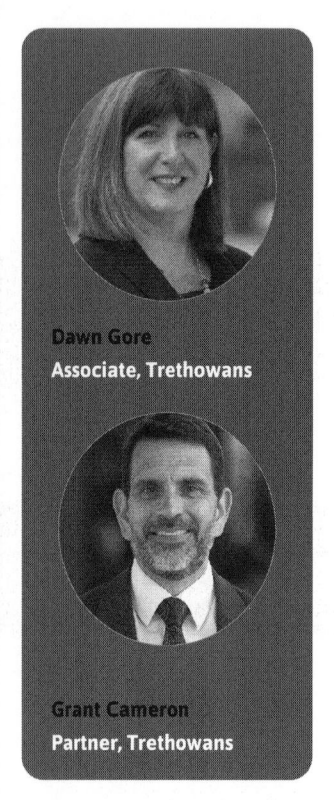

Dawn Gore
Associate, Trethowans

Grant Cameron
Partner, Trethowans

> Keep in mind a more peaceful resolution. Whatever option, it has to be the one that grants peace for both parents.
>
> *Craig, Dad*

A court order is legally binding and is expected to be adhered to and complied with. However, there may be occasions when a court order is broken or 'breached'. This could be for a variety of reasons and it is important therefore to attempt to establish why that is the case.

Why was the order not complied with?
It may be that the child was ill or there was some extreme circumstance beyond the control of the parties which meant that an order could not be complied with. It may even be that an issue has arisen which has led to a concern for the child's welfare such that complying with the terms of the order may place the child at risk of harm.

If you are the parent who is unable to comply with the terms of the order, it is important that you obtain urgent advice from solicitors or the Local Authority Children's Services. It may be necessary for you to make an application to court to vary or suspend the terms of the existing order.

Communicate with the other parenT
Although this may not always be possible especially as tensions are likely to be heightened due to a broken order, trying to keep lines of communication open will help and may avoid the situation escalating.

Sometimes couples need a helping hand to get talking. Family mediation is an important aspect of family law and can be particularly useful when focusing on the arrangements for children, as well as various other areas in dispute.

Mediation will be led by an impartial mediator whose key aim is to help the parties reach acceptable solutions. However, family mediation cannot go ahead unless both parties give their consent and is completely confidential. Mediators do not make judgements and will listen to both points of view. Mediators cannot advise either party but can provide information in relation to the law to help the couple to make informed decisions. Mediation takes place in a neutral setting to put the couple at ease.

A mediator will strive to work with the couple to reach long-term solutions which will alleviate stress and hopefully improve communication moving forwards. It also helps the

Going through the family court

children by helping their parents to work together to plan and adapt for their future.

As an alternative, the couple may wish to consider adopting the collaborative law approach. It is recognised that the best solutions are those that the couple have worked out for themselves together. With the collaborative law approach the couple each instruct their own separately trained collaborative law solicitors to represent them.

Discussions take place in a series of face-to-face meetings consisting of the couple and their own legal representative. The couple remain in control but with collaborative law, solicitors present to provide guidance and advice. Sometimes it may be suggested that the couple bring in other professionals such as a family consultant who can provide invaluable support focusing on the emotional aspects, to help the couple find a workable solution.

Application to court

In the event that a satisfactory reason has not been given for the alleged breach of an order, consideration may need to be given to an application to court for enforcement. The court has the ability to enforce the order in a number of ways.

A child arrangements order will have a warning notice attached which sets out the consequences of failing to comply with its terms. The range of powers available to the court include an enforcement order, an order for financial compensation or, where the court is satisfied that a breach amounts to a contempt, imprisonment, fine or the seizure of assets.

When an application is made to court for enforcement, the court will list a hearing at which it will hear evidence from the person alleged to have breached the order and it will be for that person to satisfy the court, on the balance of probabilities, that they had a reasonable excuse for not complying with the order. If the court is not satisfied that this is the case, it must then be satisfied beyond all reasonable doubt that the order has not been complied with before then determining how the order is to be enforced.

> **When mediation fails do try again and if that fails, try again.**

Unfortunately, there can be significant delays within the court process. The couple may want to consider family arbitration which may prove a more attractive option. They choose an arbitrator, usually with the help of a solicitor. The arbitrator can make a decision about issues affecting the children.

The process is designed to enable the couple to address the dispute more quickly and cheaply, adopting a less formal and more flexible approach. The process also allows the couple to deal with a specific aspect of the dispute as well as a broader range of issues and is therefore very focused on the couple and their family.

The best thing to do while your parents are splitting up is talk to your parents about how you're feeling, don't leave it all trapped in. Molly (15)

Organisations

Cafcass

About the author
Sophie Vessey, Policy and Communications Manager at Cafcass.

> Only tell children what they need to know. Keep it simple, be honest, they don't need details.
>
> Bridie, Mum

Cafcass represents the best interests of children in family court cases, acting independently of other parties. We help to ensure that any risk to a child is identified and assessed at the earliest stage, and that from the outset the child's welfare and best interests are at the forefront of the parties' and Judge's minds.

This includes 'private law' (divorce and separation) cases, where parents can't agree on arrangements for their children, such as who the child will live with or who they will spend time with. We also represent children in care proceedings (when a local authority has serious concerns about a child's welfare) and in adoption applications (these are 'public law' proceedings).

We become involved in cases only at the request of the court. In private law, when a parent or carer makes an application to the court, the court will usually refer the case to Cafcass. We received over 42,000 private law applications in 2017-2018. The Cafcass person who becomes involved in private law cases is called a Family Court Advisor (FCA).

There is a lot happening when parents separate - it can be an emotional time with risk of conflict between separating parents. Children may feel caught between their parents, picking up on emotions and feelings. Our role is to provide the court with the information needed for a safe and sustainable decision to be made for the children, which may include assisting the adults to reach a safe agreement.

There are three stages of private law work:

Before the first hearing at court
An FCA undertakes safeguarding checks with the police and local authority to determine whether there are any risks to the children. This is followed, where possible, by separate telephone interviews with the parents where any concerns regarding safeguarding can be discussed. A safeguarding letter reporting the findings from this work will be provided to court at least three days before the first hearing. If the telephone interviews do not take place, the FCA at court will try to speak to the parents before the hearing and provide a verbal update to the court.

At the first hearing
If no safeguarding concerns are identified ahead of the hearing, the FCA will work with the parents to support an agreement to be made without further court proceedings, usually through a parenting plan. This allows the parents to set out any practical difficulties surrounding child arrangements following their separation.

If agreement is possible, a consent order can be made

by the court, which makes this agreement binding and ends the court proceedings.

If no agreement can be made or the FCA has concerns about the safety of the child, the court can refer the parties to a range of support services such as mediation to assist in reaching an agreement, or ask us to undertake further work. Most of our cases close at the first hearing with a safe agreement reached by the parents.

After the first hearing

The court orders further work from us in around a third of cases, usually in the form of a 'section 7' report. The FCA will decide what information they need for the report based on what the court has asked them to look into. This may include talking to children about their wishes and feelings, speaking with the parents, and making enquiries with other people such as family members, teachers or health workers. The report will be provided to court for the following court hearing and will help the Judge make a safe decision for the child.

We recognise that some cases can be safely resolved outside of court proceedings if parents are supported to come to an arrangement that works for their child. We also recognise that, for those cases where our involvement continues past the first hearing, this needs to be tailored to the specific issues in the case.

We are looking at a range of options to continue to improve our services to children in private law. This includes initiatives designed to provide parents with a safe alternative dispute resolution pathway, supporting parents after the first hearing to focus on the needs of the children, and improving the information available for families going through separation.

More information on the role of Cafcass in the family justice system can be found on the Cafcass website, Cafcass.gov.uk.

> Don't believe everything your partner tells you about your rights or lack of them.
>
> *Carol-Anne Baker, Bridge Law Solicitors Limited*

WILL MY FORMER PARTNER BE IN COURT?

It would be best if you prepare as though they will be. Sometimes partners say they're going to attend and don't, just to wind the other up, but if you prepare calming strategies (e.g. mindfulness exercises) and ask for a recess if you feel too upset then you will be managing your feelings. If you are represented then make sure your rep knows how you feel, as they can petition the court for some protection from the ex, e.g. not allowing them to intimidate.

Mike Flinn

What records can I keep and can I make secret recordings?

Shivi Rajput
Associate Solicitor,
Charles Russell Speechlys

A frequent cause of frustration within family proceedings is that many disputes take place in private within the confines of the family home, so there is rarely an independent third party present to corroborate your version of events. As a result, it is often your word against your former partner's and it is left to who the Judge or the Magistrates believe. This can be very unsettling.

Without independent witnesses, how does a parent prove that the other is being abusive during handovers, or is inappropriately influencing the children behind closed doors? Often the children themselves are unable to recognise that any manipulation is occurring and even if they do, they may be too young for their account to be given proper consideration by the court.

The temptation can therefore arise for parents to make records, including covert recordings, to gather evidence in support of their concerns. This temptation is heightened by the ever-increasing sophistication of modern recording equipment and the ease with which this equipment is accessible to the public. Almost every parent now owns a smart phone which can easily be used to video incidents. Whilst the desire to collect evidence is understandable, parents should exercise caution when making secret recordings which they later attempt to rely on within children proceedings.

Contrary to popular belief, taking secret recordings for personal or family use is not illegal, but any person who seeks to rely on such recordings in court must first obtain the court's permission to do so, and this is not necessarily an easy task.

Secret recordings of children

In the recent case of *M v F (Covert Recording of Children)* [2016], the father and his current partner had placed recording devices on the child without her knowledge for the purposes of gathering evidence. The father had sewn 'bugs' into the child's clothing, which enabled secret recordings to be made over a number of years.

The Judge stated that it is "almost always wrong" for a recording device to be placed on a child for the purposes of gathering evidence within family proceedings, whether the child knows of its presence or not. In this case, the Judge made a final order for the child to live with the mother, stating that the father's actions in making the covert recordings demonstrated a lack of understanding by him as to the child's best interests and created a secret which was likely to cause the child emotional harm and adversely affect her relationship with adults in general when she came to learn of it.

This is clearly an extreme example; in other cases, the court has allowed covert recordings into the proceedings as evidence and has relied upon them as a useful

Going through the family court

corroboration of one party's version of events, but the position remains very case specific.

Secret recordings of handovers

Caution should also be exercised when making secret recordings of the other parent during handovers. In a recent case, the Court of Appeal concluded that video recording handovers amounted to intimidation and could be used in support of an application for a non-molestation injunction.

Secret recordings of professionals

The issues faced may be with professionals involved in the case, such as the Cafcass officer or social worker, who you believe is inaccurately reporting matters to the court. Whilst Cafcass have stated that they should have nothing to fear in being covertly recorded and therefore should not object, it is best practice to inform the professional before any recordings are made. Secretly recording anyone is rarely likely to be considered appropriate.

As can be seen above, whilst it is lawful to make covert recordings for personal and private use, there are risks involved, and even if they are allowed into the court proceedings to be used as evidence, the court may consider that the recordings are harmful to your case. The court may conclude that secret recordings, especially of a child, have led to inappropriate questioning for the purpose of gathering evidence, which can amount to emotional abuse. Secret recording is often regarded as a breach of privacy, regardless of legal principles.

What records can and should be kept?

It is advisable to keep a diary and a handover log, where you contemporaneously note down any issues with handovers, or any other problems, as and when they occur. An up-to-date diary is typically considered to be good evidence, as the entries are made at the time of the incident or shortly thereafter, so the recollection of events is likely to be accurate and detailed, and therefore reliable.

If contact is taking place in a contact centre, you may be able to obtain notes from the contact centre staff, confirming what happened during the contact sessions and if there were any issues or concerns.

> If you're writing something to the other person that you wouldn't want your child to read when they're older, don't write it.
>
> *Matthew Richardson, Coram Chambers*

> *Don't keep it bottled up to yourself. I'm not saying everyone must know; they don't need to, but seek advice in another person, it helps! Tyla (15)*

Going through the family court

Can my ex withhold our child's passport?

Caroline Young
Chartered Legal Executive, Senior Associate, Clarke Wilmott

Most parents would generally agree that it is in their child's best interests to be able to have the opportunity to enjoy a holiday abroad. However, when parents separate and emotions are running high, people often act out of character and place their own needs before that of the child.

Taking a child abroad

What if your ex-partner has booked a holiday without consulting you and is planning to travel abroad without your permission?

Firstly, it is a criminal offence to take a child out of the UK without the consent of everybody who has parental responsibility unless the court has given permission. However, if an order has been made that a child is to live with a person, that person may take that child out of the UK for up to a month at a time without obtaining permission.

If there are no orders in place or you are the one who has the order, your permission must be sought. If you do not consent to the holiday your ex-partner is entitled to make an application to the court for what is known as a 'Specific Issue Order' to request permission to travel. Unless there is a safeguarding concern or a risk that your ex-partner will not return with the child it is likely that such an application would be granted. It is important, therefore, that you consider fully the reasons why you are not willing to consent.

Passport disputes

What can you do if your ex-partner is holding your child's passport and is refusing to hand it over to enable you to book a holiday or even to attend a holiday that has already been booked?

If you do not have a 'lives with' order (previously known as a Residence Order) in your favour, then you would need your ex-partner's permission to remove the child out of the UK for a holiday. As stated above you would be able to make an application to the court for permission to take the child on holiday and for the passport to be released.

If the holiday has already been booked and your ex-partner is refusing to

> Focus on working together. It's easier said than done but you will still need to talk to each other long after this is over. Any issue you can resolve with each other, builds a foundation for your future (and is something you're not having to pay your lawyers to sort for you).
>
> *David Lillywhite, Burgess Mee Family Law*

hand the passport over then you would have to make an urgent application for the release of the passport. Provided you can show that there is no reason why the child should not be able to accompany you on the holiday and that you plan to return to the country after the holiday, there should not be any issue with securing the order in your favour.

Often in these situations the problem relates to trust, with the party wishing to go on the holiday being reluctant to divulge their plans in any detail and the person holding the passport refusing to release it without having a full itinerary.

People should be encouraged to put aside their differences and provide full details of their travel plans to include flight numbers, dates and times and the contact details of the hotel or other accommodation. Arrangements should also be made for facetime/telephone contact during the holiday to provide reassurance that all is well.

If you are concerned that this is going to be a recurring problem, then it is possible for there to be an order that the passport is held by solicitors and released only for the purpose of a holiday after which it is returned.

If there is a genuine concern that the child will not be returned after the holiday and you are the parent holding the passport it is important that you notify the passport office that the passport has not been lost. There have been cases where, sadly, a parent has indicated that a passport has been lost and obtained a new one enabling them to travel. Once a child has left the UK it can be extremely difficult to secure their return, depending on where they have travelled to.

See page 76 for more help on securing your child's return if they have been removed from the UK.

> I went years not speaking to anyone about what happened because I thought nobody would ever understand. Emily (16)

Warring parents – STOP

Many parents come to a family lawyer already expecting a confrontation because this is the way society and the media portray family breakdown. It does not have to be like that. If you have children with someone then you need to learn to co-parent in a way that is child focused. Language like this is unhelpful and creates conflict which we know to be damaging to children.

Must read

What is the law in Scotland?

Rachael Noble
Brodies Solicitors

There are many issues which separating parents need to bear in mind under Scots' Law. This article will address some of the most common queries.

Who has parental rights and responsibilities in respect of a child?

A child's mother automatically has parental rights and responsibilities (PRR) in respect of a child, regardless of whether or not she has at any time been married to the child's father. The father of the child will automatically obtain PRR if he was married to the child's mother at the date of conception or at any time thereafter.

The father will also obtain these rights if he is registered as the child's father on the birth certificate.

Where a woman is married to, or in a civil partnership with, the child's mother then she will also automatically have PRR in respect of the child.

An application can be made to the court to obtain PRR in respect of a child by any person with an 'interest'. A genetic or emotional tie to the child would be sufficient to constitute an 'interest'. Any person with an 'interest' in the welfare of the child can also make an application.

What are parental rights and responsibilities?

Those with PRR are responsible for promoting the child's health development and welfare and to provide guidance to the child. Parents must decide where the child is to live and to ensure that contact is maintained with the non-resident parent. They can also act as the child's legal representative. It is important that the child's parents consult with one another in relation to all major decisions affecting the child.

What if there is a dispute in relation to the exercise of parental rights and responsibilities?

Separating parents will often find themselves in dispute in relation to decisions affecting the child. They may, for instance, disagree with each other as to where, and with whom the child should live, how often they see the other parent, and which school they should go to. Although court is generally seen as the last resort, in those circumstances, it may be necessary for a parent to apply to the court to ask the sheriff or Judge to determine the dispute.

In considering whether or not to make an order, the court has to exercise its discretion. The paramount consideration is the welfare of the child and the court ought not to make any order unless it considers that it is necessary and it would be better for the child that the order be made than that none should be made at all. The test is ultimately what is in the best interests of the child.

The court will allow a child to express a view in relation to the matter in dispute. The court must, however, take account of the child's age and maturity in determining how much weight to give to that view. A child aged 12 or over is presumed to be of sufficient age and maturity to form a view, but consideration can be given to the views of a younger child if the sheriff or Judge is persuaded that they are sufficiently mature. The law in this area will be changing by virtue of the Children (Scotland) Act 2020. Under the new sections 1 to 3 of that Act (not yet in force) the legal presumption that a child aged 12 or over is considered mature enough to give their view will be removed and children of all ages will be presumed capable of forming a view and should be given the opportunity to do so.

Courts will generally encourage parents to make decisions about their children. They know their children best after all. If agreement can be reached, this can be documented in a 'contract' signed by both parties. Mediation is also often encouraged.

What happens if one parent wishes to move to another country with the child of the relationship?

It is not uncommon for separating parents to disagree about whether a child should be permitted to relocate with the other parent. In those circumstances, it may be necessary for an application to be made to the court for a 'specific issue order' permitting such a move in the absence of consent from the other parent.

It is unlawful for a parent to remove a child who lives in Scotland outside of the UK unless there is consent from the other parent or an order from the court. Even if a parent wishes to move to another territorial unit of the UK, it is clear from Scottish case law (see the case of *GB or L v JC* [2017] CSOH 60) that the appropriate course of action in that situation is for the parent seeking to relocate to seek an order from the court to do so if the other parent will not provide the necessary consent. The matter will require to be litigated in the country where the child is habitually resident, even if the child has already been removed from that country without the other parent's consent.

In considering whether or not to allow a parent to relocate with a child, the court will have regard to a range of factors, including the arrangements in place for the child at the new location, schooling, accommodation, child care, how contact with the other parent will operate, the family ties that the child is leaving behind and the reasons for the move. The child's views may also be considered. The court will ultimately need to consider whether the move is in the child's best interests.

An 'interdict' (an order preventing a course of action) can be obtained to prevent a child being removed from Scotland if a parent is concerned that this may take place without their consent.

What if I want to take my child on holiday abroad?

The consent of both parents is required to take a child on holiday abroad. Details ought to be provided of the proposed trip and if consent is not forthcoming, an application can be made to the court for a 'specific issue order' regulating this.

Who requires to pay maintenance in respect of a child?

Both parents ought to support their child financially. For the purposes of child maintenance, a 'child' means a person under the age of 18 years or a young adult between the age of 18 to 25 who is in full time education. Therefore, the obligation to maintain a child continues if for instance, they attend university. It is therefore open to an individual who is engaged in further advanced education to raise an action against a parent if they do not consider that they are receiving adequate financial assistance.

Where an individual is under the age of 16, or under the age of 20 (if they satisfy certain conditions, for instance if they remain at school or college) then the Child Maintenance Service can regulate maintenance in the absence of agreement. In calculating maintenance,

Must read

the Child Maintenance Service will take into account the number of nights that a child stays with the non-resident parent. In certain circumstances, it may be possible to apply to the court for a 'top up' of maintenance.

If you require further advice in relation to this, or any other family law issues in Scotland, you should contact a family law solicitor specialising in Scots' Law.

> Put your role as a parent first and communicate with each other openly about all issues involving or affecting the children. It may be difficult but it is essential. Showing a united front and providing reassurance to your children is crucial. Make sure they know that, although their parents may no longer be together, they each love them and will continue to be there for them.
>
> *Shivi Rajput, Eric Robinson*

Notes

Parental alienation

Parental alienation is a term generally used to describe complex circumstances where one parent undermines and interferes with a child's relationship with his or her other parent, to the point where the child may reject the other parent. While there is not one single definition, this can take the form of limiting the time the child spends with the other parent and their extended family, and bad-mouthing and belittling the other parent. This section explores the various definitions and descriptions of parental alienating behaviours in more depth and offers guidance on action you and the courts can take to overcome parental alienation.

What is parental alienation?

Dr Sue Whitcombe
Psychologist & Family Consultant, DCounPsych CPsychol AFBPsS HCPC

All children are affected by family breakdown. In most families, both parents work together to help their children adjust to a new way of being, and to minimise the negative emotional impact. In a minority of families, this does not happen. Adjustment to a healthy post separation life can be difficult where there was prior domestic violence, abuse or inadequate parenting. Parental alienation is a particular type of adjustment difficulty where there was no prior exposure to domestic violence, abuse or significantly poor parenting. Other labels which have been applied to this concept include Hostile Aggressive Parenting (HAP), Implacable Hostility, Attachment Based Parental Alienation (AB-PA), Parental Alienation Syndrome (PAS) and the Resist/Refuse Dynamic.

Parental alienation refers to a situation where a child appears resistant to an ongoing relationship with a parent despite having had a "good-enough", loving relationship prior to the family breakdown. Their resistance is a disproportionate response when the entirety of their experience is considered. This is the child's coping strategy. When one loving, caring parent tells a child that mum or dad is dangerous, nasty or doesn't love them - this causes a psychological tension in the child. This is not their experience. This doesn't make sense - but their parent wouldn't lie to them would they? These conflicting messages are difficult to process for a young child whose brain development is not yet complete. Children quickly become aware that the less often they see their parent, the less often they feel anxious or upset. This is not usually a conscious process, particularly in younger children. A child will develop a narrative that gives a plausible explanation for not wanting to spend time with their mum or dad. This narrative is created with input - information, stories, non-verbal communication - from the present parent.

Children's brains are wired at birth to ensure they attach to their parents. This attachment is necessary for survival; it ensures that a child has its basic needs met. A child attaches to a caregiver regardless of the quality of care received, even if the caregiver is abusive and neglectful. When a child states they do not wish to see a parent - or they hate them - this is a clear indication that something is amiss. Is this child rejecting an abusive parent? This is known as estrangement and is an adaptive coping mechanism for the child to protect themselves. Or are they rejecting a loving parent due to the alienation process? This would be a maladaptive strategy. When alienated, children may appear to function well. However, continued use of this maladaptive strategy over

> The children need both of you to be their parents, especially after you've separated.
>
> *Juliet Thomas, Shanahans-Law*

time means they are likely to have an impaired ability to sustain effective, healthy relationships throughout their life, as well as an increased incidence of mental health and psychiatric disorders and substance misuse.

Both estrangement and alienation are signs of underlying psychological distress. If we do not understand why a child is resistant to a relationship with one of their parents, we risk the child remaining in a harmful, psychologically abusive environment. Fortunately, with a good understanding of abuse, parental alienation and normal and abnormal child development, it is possible to differentiate between estrangement and alienation.

Children, particularly young children, who experience what is usually considered abuse - physical, sexual, emotional maltreatment - or neglect, rarely reject their parent. In fact, these children crave an ongoing relationship with an abusive parent. They are torn. They are ambivalent. A lack of ambivalence, psychological splitting, where the child idealises one parent and devalues the other, has been shown to differentiate between alienation and estrangement. An alienated child will have an overly close relationship with one parent, while rejecting the other. Often this polarisation extends to the wider family.

Alongside their rejection, a child may appear fearful or overly anxious. They may be verbally or physically abusive, while not demonstrating any remorse or guilt for their behaviour. Children will often suggest trivial reasons for not wanting to see their parent, insisting that their "decision" is their own, not otherwise influenced. Alienated children may speak with adult language, sometimes with a rehearsed or coached quality. They may talk about matters which should not be in their awareness, such as the financial matters or incidents prior to their birth or cognitive awareness. These symptomatic behaviours and the underlying psychological processes in alienation have been independently identified since the 1980s by researchers and practitioners in social work, law and psychology.

In the alienation process one parent engages in behaviours which foster the fracturing of the child's relationship with the other. These behaviours have also been the subject of much research. Typical behaviours include bad-mouthing a parent, suggesting they are dangerous or have abandoned the child. These messages are reinforced by the removal of photographs and other signs of the absent parent from the home, with no positive dialogue about the parent or their relationship with the child. Children pick up on these messages; they are attuned to the behaviour and body language of their parents. Parents may withhold affection, exhibit excessive anxiety or distress; all contribute to a child's internalised representation of a 'bad' other parent or a needy, vulnerable aligned parent.

Active alienating behaviours include preventing or frustrating direct and indirect parenting time and communication between the child and parent. There may be overt pressure forcing a child to choose between its parents. Parents may be angry with a child or criticise them if they express love or enjoyment of time with their other parent. False or unsubstantiated allegations of abuse, neglect or domestic violence are common.

In assessing a child's rejection of a parent, a full consideration of the historical and current social context of child, alongside their developmental history, behaviour and that of their parents, is necessary. This will enable an understanding of the child's rejection - whether estrangement, alienation, or a combination of both - and inform the most appropriate intervention.

Parental alienation

How do I recognise and deal with the first stages of alienating behaviour?

Alison Bushell
Independent Social Worker, Child & Family Solutions

When parents separate or divorce, the process can produce very extreme emotions; grief, fear and anger are usually around and if there is also trauma in the birth family of one or both of the parents this complicates matters further as can any mental health or psychological issues.

What I have learned throughout particularly my recent social work practice with separating and separated families is that even the best parents can use some pretty appalling tactics when separating and that previously responsible people will behave in quite dreadful ways when arguably they are needing to be at their most level headed and altruistic.

Children are frequently caught up in hostile communication and care arrangements fraught with stress. This is not good for children and in the long term can cause real damage. Having both loving parents in their life-however flawed one or both of those parents are, by virtue of being human and fallible-is what is proven to be best for children and to maximise their optimal healthy development in all spheres.

Having a parent 'written out' of their life damages their life chances and there is now a wealth of research evidence to support this. It has a seriously detrimental effect on their adult relationships and can lead to substance abuse and self harm.

Parental alienation is now accepted by the UK Court system including Cafcass as serious emotional abuse of children and thus needs to be remedied in their best interests.

> Any order made by a court is a blunt instrument - you are far more likely to have something that works for you if you can negotiate a settlement which can be as detailed as you want it to be, yet still endorsed by the court if necessary.
>
> *Keri Tayler, No5 Barristers Chambers*

So, whilst almost 90% of couples manage to make arrangements for the children with no court intervention, an increasing number who thought things were sorted out before the decree nisi even came through find that they are encountering issues such as their children resisting spending time with them and behaving in ways that appear hostile or hard to fathom.

Parental alienation

There are therapists and certainly social workers who will say this is 'just because the child is caught in the middle of you both' and there are certainly plenty of cases where that holds true. However, those children, if they get good support from their parents, learn to adapt to the situation and things usually resolve in time.

This is not always the case however, and parents can find a child will continue to be distant and hostile and at worst refuse to see them at all. This is perplexing and distressing and parents frequently struggle to manage their feelings and get advice - who do you go to? If you are not in court, having sorted out the care arrangements with a mediator or on your own, then where do you focus your concerns - who do you talk to?

Most parents have no idea how to tackle such difficult or rejecting behaviour and if left unaddressed this can escalate and lead to a breakdown of the relationship between the child and the parent who is not the main carer.

As freelance social workers and family support workers, myself and my team are actively supporting parents on social media, one runs an online support group for parents who are struggling to see their children post separation, one runs a local group for dads and our consultants do assessments when those cases are in court as well as undertaking mediation and therapy, frequently reuniting children with estranged and alienated parents.

We are quite literally involved right at the beginning as well as when things have got so bad that court is the only option. We therefore have a good idea of the 'warning signs' of what is known as parental alienation.

Early intervention is key

Some of the child behaviours that parents come to us with which can be the early signs of parental alienation are what we call rejecting behaviours, such as;

- Your child asking you not to attend a school play or an important match.

- Your child's sudden rejection of previously loved family members on your side of the family, including grandparents.

- Your child saying they don't want to see you, see you as much or have staying contact.

- Your child repeating or making allegations against you such as inappropriate chastisement/neglect.

- Your child starting to call you by your name rather than 'daddy' or 'mummy'.

- Your child blaming you for any difficulties in the resident parent's home such as lack of money.

- Your child having too much/age inappropriate knowledge of financial issues or court proceedings.

- Your child ignoring your behaviour boundaries and authority and refusing to comply when they would previously have done so.

- Your child becoming withdrawn, reluctant to talk or distrustful of your ability to keep them safe.

- Your child seeming to 'rewrite history' in their newly negative recollections of happy family events.

Some of the difficulties with co-parenting with your ex which might indicate that alienation is present include:

- Difficulties or increasing demands over child support and insistence on having 'their time" even if they are working and won't be spending time with the child themselves.

- A tendency to try to draw other agencies in without telling you, for example going to the school alone

Parental alienation

to talk about the child's issues. This can set you up as the problem or as disinterested.

- You might feel undermined/unsupported in terms of setting boundaries regarding screen time, bed times etc.

- You might begin to feel undermined, criticised or completely bypassed in medical or educational decisions, unilateral decisions being taken in these areas by the other parent.

- The other parent might pick up on a perceived weakness in your parenting, your relationship with your child or your home situation and exaggerate its significance to the child, other agencies and the parent.

- This can lead you to defend yourself. You might then send an angry text which is then shared by the alienating parent with others without context to make you seem unstable or unsafe. (Sadly your child might then also get drawn into this narrative and be encouraged to support accusations against you).

- In this sense, parental alienation is a form of gas lighting, with the alienating parent seeking to use the child/ren to support them in making the alienated parent seem unsafe or a poor parent, to the point where you as the alienated parent will begin to believe this yourself and lose confidence in setting boundaries etc.

Any of these signs in either area are a cause for concern and if you can identify several in one or both areas you certainly need to get advice and help.

Parental alienation doesn't get better if these issues and this behaviour isn't dealt with quickly. Unhealthy patterns can develop and you can be reactive or respond as a parent in a way that actually fuels a child's rejecting behaviour.

There are frequently 'triggers' for your child behaving in these ways - we find that this is frequently the arrival of a new partner in one of the parents lives. It can, however, also be a life event in one of the parents lives such as the loss of a parent.

What to do?

If you suspect that your child is being alienated from you or is showing the early signs of this you should try to speak to them about how you are experiencing their behaviour. With pre-teens or teenagers this can be reasonably straightforward but with a young child it can be tricky and it is usually best to try to get professional advice. Saying the wrong thing or making the child feel that they are being told off can make things worse.

Parental Alienation – THINK

Parental alienation is defined by CAFCASS as "the unjustified resistance or hostility from a child towards one parent as a result of psychological manipulation by the other parent." When a family separates there will always be a period of adjustment for everyone but especially for children. Allegations of alienation between parents are common in these situations but often do not meet the level of psychological manipulation required to come within what is a complex and serious issue. Understanding the term correctly is important to ensure that it is not misused as well as discouraging parents from finding reasons to blame the other parent when a more collaborative approach may ultimately lead to a better outcome for the family.

Parental alienation

Do this in a non-blaming way. Explore possibilities, ask them how they are feeling. Reassure them of your love and support.

Never criticise the other parent to them.

Approach the school or nursery yourself, explain your position. The SENCO or head teacher are the best people to speak to.

Make sure you are 'visible' and involved where your children spend their non-parenting time.

There are sometimes justifiable reasons why a child is resisting contact and this could be linked to feeling, for instance, frightened by something or unsupported by you at a difficult time or being angry due to an ongoing issue. Maybe you have disciplined them or said no to something they wanted or even broken a promise?

Have you had a sudden change in your life such as a new partner moving in or meeting your child? My practice experience would indicate that children can find it very hard to come to terms with suddenly not having you to themselves and they can also fear the new partner is trying to replace their other parent. This can cause real difficulties for some children and can create complex feelings of resentment and even guilt (if they like your new partner) and disloyalty to mum or dad.

Whilst it might also be the case that the other parent might also be failing to support you or even undermining your parenting decisions or lifestyle choices, it remains the fact that these issues can cause or contribute to contact resistance and it cannot therefore ALWAYS be assumed that it is the negative influence of the other parent.

In trying to resolve this, as well as considering the above, try to speak to the other parent calmly and with a non-blaming approach and if it's too difficult one-to-one, involve a third person, like a godparent or mutual friend.

Seek an appointment with a mediator if this doesn't work. Make sure they specialise in family mediation.

Get support from online resources, there is so much support and information out there.

Don't worry about feeling that you might need to involve the court - its best to act quickly if mediation isn't successful, as it can take a while to get a hearing.

If you can afford a solicitor find one who from is a 'Children's Panel' firm or who are members of Resolution. Ask for a breakdown of likely costs. Don't overcommit yourself as this can become an additional stress.

If you can't afford legal representation and wish to represent yourself there are some very good paralegals and McKenzie Friends out there. Make sure they have references or a checkable online profile or are qualified. Be prepared to pay around a quarter of what you would pay for a lawyer BUT you'll have to speak in court. This can seem daunting but it gets easier...and again there are many resources to help you.

Finally...ask for support, seek counselling if you feel you can't cope, attend a local support group, join an online forum. There are many parents in your situation and there is a lot of help out there.

Stuck in the middle. Not a good place to be. El (13)

Parental alienation

My children don't want to see their dad. What should I do?

Anthony Jones
Director, O'Donnell Solicitors

This is clearly a difficult question to answer as it depends on the reasons as to why the children do not want to see their dad. Children should be encouraged by their mum to see their dad if it is a safe and loving environment.

The starting point is that children should grow up knowing both their parents. If there is an issue as to why they do not wish to go to see their dad then that needs to be explored and resolved. Sometimes it has to be resolved using professionals, whether that be medical or legal professionals.

It is important that children are not ignored. When children reach a certain age and understanding their wishes and feelings will be taken into account. The legislation that deals with children matters is the Children Act 1989 and the court's paramount consideration is always the child's welfare. The court also considers the welfare checklist (a set list of factors) in deciding what is best for the child (see page 192 for more).

You should try and resolve any dispute regarding contact with each other first. You could use mediation to assist you in doing this which could include the children if they are old enough and understand the situation.

If you cannot resolve the matters, then court proceedings may have to be issued but this should only be seen as a last resort. Many people believe that going to court will resolve their problems but in my experience, whilst the court can make orders in respect of arrangements for children, those issues still need to be resolved so that they do not occur again.

If you are a dad whose children are indicating that they do not wish to see you, it is important to act quickly as any delay is likely to be prejudicial to you. If court proceedings have to be issued then those proceedings will not be resolved overnight - they can take months to resolve and important time will be lost if you do not take action.

There are many solicitors out there that will be able to assist dads in this situation usually by offering a free initial appointment. My advice is to look for a Resolution Member as they adhere to a code of conduct so that your matter can be dealt with constructively and in a non-confrontational way. This will assist in avoiding the situation getting worse.

The best thing about a break up can be the introduction of whole new extended families to their children's lives, because the more people that love their children and think they are amazing the better.

Julie Hobson, Gullands Solicitors

Parental alienation

How does the court deal with parental alienation?

Jeremy Ford
Partner, Cambridge Family Law Practice LLP

A child being alienated from one parent by another parent is not a new concept. It has had different guises over the years - whether that be intractable contact or hostility to contact. The term parental alienation is the current and perhaps the most apt description.

It is important for parents not to focus too much on the label but rather to identify the behaviours which are impacting on the relationship between child and parent.

The court, when considering arrangements for children must:

- base any decision on the welfare of the child which is the court's paramount consideration as set out in s1 Children Act 1989 and the welfare checklist in s1(3). The most likely relevant parts of this checklist when considering alienation are:

  - the child's ascertainable wishes and feelings based upon their age and understanding;
  - any harm which the child has suffered or is at risk of suffering;
  - how capable each parent is of meeting the needs of the child;

- consider s2A as inserted by the Children and Families Act (CFA) 2014 s.11 that the court is

  "to presume, unless the contrary is shown, that involvement of that parent in the life of the child concerned will further the child's welfare."

- consider the child's Article 8 right to family life pursuant to the European Convention on Human Rights

- consider Practice Direction 12J, with the obligation to consider when any allegations of harm are raised, whether those allegations will impact upon the ultimate welfare determination the court has to make and if so make a finding as to those allegations.

If a child is refusing to see one parent, the court will have to consider *why* that child is refusing to see that parent. A child is likely to be refusing to see one parent either because of 1) their lived experience of that parent, or 2) their perception of that parent which may be wholly unjustified. If their perception of a parent is wholly unjustified it is important for the court to consider why the child holds such a distorted perception - it may or may not be because of the covert or overt actions (or inactions) of the resident parent.

So rather than run with the phrase 'parental alienation' it is going to be far more helpful to the court to consider the evidence as to *why* a child is exhibiting such negative behaviours towards one parent. If the court finds that these

247

Parental alienation

behaviours are a result of the actions of one parent, the court will then need to consider whether those actions are emotionally harmful to the child.

A common misstep in proceedings is for only the child's wishes and feelings to be recorded. The statute is clear that it is the child's *ascertainable* wishes and feelings which are relevant. The question is - why are they saying what they are saying? It may be because of their lived experience of a parent or a narrative they have come to adopt due to parental influence caused overtly or covertly.

Where one parent suspects that the other parent is alienating a child from the other, it is important that the court identifies the issues and makes findings swiftly so that it may then make a decision based upon the child's welfare. Delay is the biggest problem in these types of cases because the longer the children are permitted to believe a false or distorted narrative, the harder it is to rectify those beliefs.

Cafcass has recently published its Child Impact Assessment Framework with the aim of promoting a consistent approach to how Cafcass officers identify what is happening in a child's life and whether a child is being alienated or is rejecting a parent due to inappropriate or harmful behaviour. It has a particularly helpful tool on the types of behaviour exhibited by alienated children. This will not eradicate alienation but is a step in the right direction to ensure that there is a consistent approach across the family justice system.

The role of Cafcass is to report to the court. Cafcass is not there to offer therapy, counselling or work with families. It is therefore important for parents to arm themselves with details of experts who are able to assist children and the family members who have been subjected to alienating behaviours for family life away from the court.

The following are examples of what children may say in circumstances where they are being alienated by one parent against the other:

- They hate their parent but can't give any reason or the reasons are trivial;

- The reasons the children give may seem rehearsed;

- They see one parent as completely good and the other as completely bad;

- The child is quick to point out that these are their own feelings and the other parent has not influenced them;

When parents separate and there is conflict around the arrangements for their children, I try to impress upon them that one day their children will be adults and will look back at what took place.

This helps parents to think about how their behaviour and choices are perceived objectively, rather than being caught up in the moment. It also keeps the focus on resolution rather than accusation or blame.

What is important are the memories that are being built for the children, and that the parents and the children themselves can experience a positive future.

Matthew Delaney, Hepburn Delaney

Parental alienation

- The child displays an apparent absence of guilt for their behaviour and attitudes towards the non-resident parent yet in all other respects has a good circle of friends, is performing well at school, and has no problems entering new scenarios;

- The child uses phrases or examples that are very similar to the resident parent or recalls incidents where they would have been far too young to recall them;

- The rejection often spreads to the rejected parent's wider family;

- They start referring to the parent by their first name;

- The child, whilst enjoying contact at a contact centre, refuses to take presents home;

- They become extremely panic stricken over the prospect of visiting their other parent - wide eyed, screaming, sobbing.

The following are examples of what the resident parent may say or do:

- They are encouraging their children to see their parent but are in fact taking no proactive steps for that to happen;

- It is the decision of the children and they respect that decision;

- They will not force a child to do something they don't want to do;

- Remove children from public school events;

- Use disguised language or behaviour which makes clear to the child that emotional permission is not given for the child to see the other parent;

- Engage the child with a therapist/counsellor with the professional only hearing one side of the story;

- Speaking about the other parent in a derogatory manner in front of the children;

- Refuse to collect the children from the house of the other parent;

- Despite a child enjoying contact at a contact centre will say that the child was distressed following contact;

- Make handovers difficult by either hanging around or being too involved.

It has to be said that on the other side of the equation is the parent who alleges alienation when actually the problem lies at their door but they lack the insight to accept the impact of their behaviour on their child. So parents, practitioners and the court must be alive to the fact that the allegation of alienation may be raised by a parent who is unable to accept the role they have had to play in the presentation of their children.

When parental alienation is raised as an issue it is deeply distressing for the parents and the children as it calls into question what the children are saying. The court deals with evidence and it is important that whichever side of the argument you are on that the court is provided with legitimate examples so that it can make a decision in the best interests of the child.

The splitting up taught me that happiness can be found with more than one person. Bryony (16)

Notes

Co-operative parenting

Co-operative parenting is one of those phrases that is easier said than done. The challenges separated parents face are emotional, numerous, complex. The pages that follow address some of the main stumbling blocks to co-operative parenting head on and offer advice and tips for working through them.

What makes a successful handover?

Ashley Palmer
Family Consultant, Accredited Child Inclusive Family Mediator, Psychotherapist, A Palmer & Associates

Families all over the world separate and for children *one* home becomes *two*. Do we underestimate the importance of a successful handover?

To see each parent, children now take part in a transition between two homes. This transition can say one of two things: my parents care more about their conflict than me or my parents care more about my wellbeing than anything else and they are happy for me to enjoy time with each of them. The latter will set them up to be well adjusted and happy adults one day.

Children will be dealing with how they feel about the family separation: they're faced with 'what is not there anymore' – the absence of what was the 'familiar family'. Establishing a secure base in a two-home family (whatever form that is in the beginning) will help to bring about a new normal, and build strategies and processes where everyone knows what is happening.

The transitions of moving between homes can either be filled with uncertainty, anger, hostility, conflict, heavy silence, a big empty space where the children are made to walk the transition alone or they can be smooth, amiable and concern free. Parents are in charge of the children's experience: the calm steps of moving between two homes.

The handovers

When both parents approach the transition with the intention and commitment to make this experience calm and smooth for the children, it brings about a positive mindset and offers structure: a framework of good intention, focus and goodwill. If it's a 'roleplay' of

> "Build a strong support network of friends and family, for the times when parenting becomes difficult or loneliness is overwhelming.
>
> *Mandy, Mum*"

goodwill in the beginning, then so be it. Children will appreciate that parents are making a huge effort for them.

Practicalities - kids belongings

If the children have important belongings (their special blanket or toy) that they want to take to each home, let them take them. It's much easier for the children if parents can agree beforehand which items will move back and forth, until they are either redistributed, duplicated or added to. Packing and unpacking basics like toiletries, PJ's and other daily items can make them feel like a visitor so the sooner these items are in both homes the better. Over time the children will have different things in different homes and will enjoy the variety.

The all-important bag

The luggage industry is enormous - people care about the bags they use for holidays, work, sports and weekend trips. Children care too: having the right handover bags can make all the difference. A bag too small means they have to leave something important behind; having a big suitcase can make it a big ordeal. Depending on the age, let them have some input. What does it look like? Does it have wheels? Is it a funky backpack? It just needs to be something big enough to hold books, games, trainers, trunks and a few favourites. In the beginning it might be a good idea to pop a checklist into a clear plastic sleeve taped to the inside: helpful when re-packing.

It's a given that in the first year items are likely to be forgotten. Accepting this rather than blaming the other parent or the child will keep the goodwill going. Keep focusing on learning and getting better at it. When things are important to the children, they tend to get better at reminding the parents.

Who packs the bag?

Children might resist packing/preparing for the handover just as they once resisted brushing their teeth, getting ready for bed or indeed getting up out of bed. Why wouldn't they? It can be a drag and for some it can feel like they constantly have one foot out the door. Try creating a workable routine and if parents need to do it for them or help, why not? Be patient, practical and persevere. If it's not being done right, they will soon want to do it themselves.

Arriving at each home

When they arrive home, maybe create an atmosphere of simply being at home. Keeping it low-key and maybe having some down time together will allow them time to adjust. If they want a little space, maybe do something nearby and in a short while, things will get back to normal.

Children thrive on routine, so parents could try to establish some kind of routine when they come home: maybe a certain meal, a game or something you know they enjoy. It can really help with the transition.

Conflict at handovers

Parental conflict is a challenge for many separating families. We cannot pretend there is a magic wand and bingo, separated and the conflict is gone - no. For some families it's more helpful to initially use a neutral environment for handovers: dropping off or picking children up from nursery, school, a mutual friend or family member can shelter them from on-going conflict. Everything else above can be done to offer the children the freedom to move between two homes with emotional permission of both parents.

Finally, if there are adult relationship issues getting in the way of having a robust co-parenting alliance parents can look into working together with a family mediator to get there.

Know that children will be proud of their parents for showing them how to navigate through difficult times and that as kids, they were free to be just that - kids.

If you go to court you will be asking the judge who doesn't know you, doesn't know or love your child or probably ever meet your child to tell you what your future arrangements are going to be for your child. Is this what you want?

Helen Pittard, 174 Law

Co-operative parenting

Do I have to do all the driving?

Chris Fairhurst
Partner, Family Law & Divorce Solicitor, Simpson Millar

When I'm asked this question, I'm reminded of a case I dealt with some years ago where the couple were trying to divide up the equity in the matrimonial home and other assets of the marriage. It wasn't a huge case and the assets were modest but both appeared sensible individuals and had their own jobs which meant there was going to be a clean break on making of a final order. Incidentally, there were no children so it was more straightforward than it could have been, or so I thought.

Although the couple didn't see completely eye to eye, negotiations took place between solicitors and after a bit of toing in froing a comprehensive agreement was reached in respect to sharing the proceeds of sale and other capital assets and a draft consent order drawn up for submission to court. And then, without any prior notice in any of the prior exchanges, the curveball came: a demand from the other party's solicitor that the whole deal was off unless she could keep the picture over the fireplace. It's value was in the hundreds of pounds when the other assets were in the tens if not hundreds of thousands.

And the deal very nearly collapsed as a result: my client on principle demanding to keep it, as it was one of a pair and therefore there were two to share, the former partner happy to walk away despite the costs incurred to date getting an agreement. It was a case of who would blink first. My advice to my client was to leave it and buy another with the money he would save on my fees for arguing about it. Reluctantly, but eventually, the advice was accepted but not without criticism of me from my client that I hadn't secured the picture and the other lawyer had. I had offered the opportunity of applying to court and letting a judge decide but my client made the sensible decision that the costs of doing so were disproportionate to the value of the picture and there was the uncertainty in any event of what a judge, a stranger to both parties, would decide.

So, what's this got to do with travel and seeing my children, I hear you ask? Well, the issue of who collects and returns the children after time with a parent is the 'picture over the fireplace' equivalent in child arrangements cases. It is sadly an issue that rears its head more often than it should between parents who don't love each other anymore but clearly love their children and in their own way want the same for their children, that they be happy, even if they have different views about how that might be achieved.

My advice is to follow the course of least resistance.

On many occasions, sometimes at the court door, protracted discussions and agreements can be brought crashing down by an insistence that one parent or another 'do all the travelling if s/he wants to see them' or 'I don't see why I should do it all, s/he has a car as well'. Does it sound familiar?

Faced with that predicament, everything else agreed, what's a court to do? Unfortunately, it's a question of a contested hearing with

Co-operative parenting

evidence and submissions from both sides about why the court should favour one parent or another. And yes, if pushed, the court could decide that the travel is shared, or not! You pay your money, you take your chance.

There is no hard and fast rule about any arrangements for children. The family court strives to achieve an order which it believes is in the best interests of any children of the family by applying the welfare checklist which appears in the Children Act 1989 (see page 192).

However, the law is discretionary and the reality is that no two families and therefore no two cases are alike. Each will turn on its own facts and when dealing with travel arrangements, there is no presumption in favour of one parent or another, nor is the court obliged to share the travel because that is the fair thing to do.

All things being equal of course, 2 parents earning the same, with the same working hours and similar access to transport, or family members to assist, you would hope that arrangements to share the travelling could be agreed without the need of a third party deciding which might not actually satisfy anyone, particularly the children. And it is widely recognised that a child will benefit emotionally from seeing both parents co-operate and 'be happy', being able to enjoy being taken by one parent to the other and vice versa.

However, real life isn't like that. Parents increasingly work different shift patterns; one parent may earn a lot more or have a car when the other might not.

The starting point must be, however difficult, to try and put yourself in the other parent's shoes. Can arrangements be made that make travel arrangements easier for one or both? Is there someone in the family or close friends that you both trust that can help you out?

But consider this - is sharing the travel necessary to ensure that the children continue to have a relationship with you, and by the other parent not doing so would that equate to them failing to facilitate the relationship, or is it just a point of principle?

If the former, then if matters cannot be agreed it is something you may want to consider getting legal advice about if mediation, whether formally or with trusted others, cannot assist and as a last resort make an application for a Family Court to decide based upon the circumstances as they apply to you and your family.

If the latter, then you really need to consider the financial and emotional cost of making an issue out of it where all else is agreed. I'm sure it's happened, although I've never dealt with an application, where the family court is asked to simply deal with the sharing of travel and you'll likely have to attend at least 2, if not 3, hearings before a court would even decide one way or another. An expensive exercise if you're paying good money for a lawyer to represent you.

My advice, a bit like to the client with the picture, is to follow the course of least resistance. Do it if you can - if you can make a concession to help the situation then you may find it helps discussions about something else that can't be agreed now or further down the line. If a parent simply says, 'I'm not doing it' you can show you've done everything possible if the need arises.

> The only thing I had to keep me calm was my sport. Bryony (16)

Co-operative parenting

Co-parenting with your ex-partner

Marcie Shaoul
Director, Rolling Stone Coaching, The Co-Parent Way

> Get legal advice, however "amicable" things are at the moment.
>
> *Colin, Dad*

You're splitting up and you have children. You might not want to be connected to your ex any more, but the fact is, you will be. You might be ending your relationship, but you are still a parent. And there are still two of you. And this is the point at which you realise that you are going to be intertwined with this person for a long time. Right around now, you might be hearing lots of different and well-intentioned advice from people about what to do. And that can be confusing. So, we've written this article to help you try and see the wood from the trees and to make decisions about your co-parenting and how you want it to look.

What is co-parenting?

Co-parenting is not necessarily equal time between houses. Rather, co-parenting is about sharing decisions and information about your children and making them feel as though they have two parents who can parent them effectively and together. It's about communicating with your ex about your children in a positive and practical way.

Your children aren't choosing to divorce you, they want both of you. They love you both. Parents need to be parents, and make fair and strong decisions that mean that their children can be children.

Why should I do it?

When you're getting divorced or are separating it can be easy to lose sight of what's happening for your children and what they are experiencing.

Much of the time when we're splitting up with someone, we are going to be managing big emotions. And when we're feeling full of emotions it can be hard to see things clearly and it can be hard to see how we're needed as parents, by our children.

Sometimes we can end up using our children as bargaining collateral, withholding access, wanting to feel as though our children are on 'my side'. These can feel like victories in the moment.

But these aren't victories. These actually create a really negative experience for your child. And the impact of these actions, even if they are for a relatively short time period, can last a lifetime. They can impact on how your children form their own relationships, how they show up in society, their anger management, their confidence and so much more.

Learning how to parent together massively reduces the negative impact and helps your child grow up in a whole and functional way.

Parents who work together to keep their child safe, will see their child held and ok. Acknowledging to your kids that it's not easy going from house to house where rules and the relationship system differ goes a long way to making your child feel heard. If your child feels heard and ok to say when things aren't working or when things are hard, then you are succeeding in your co-parent relationship.

How do I co-parent?

If you've just come out of a difficult break-up, the idea of co-parenting can be really tricky. So the first thing you need to do is take a breath and try to focus on the bigger picture. Try to think ahead to when your children are adults. What do you want them to say about their childhood and their upbringing? How do you want them to be as human beings? The chances are you'll want them to be fundamentally together people who can deal with challenges as well as form loving and healthy relationships. If you can keep that in mind, even when things are tough, then you'll have a good basis for co-parenting.

More practically, the most important step you can take in co-parenting is the sharing of information about your child. So, emails that focus on what the children have done recently is always helpful. Avoid talking about yourself, avoid asking your ex questions about their personal life. Keep it business like, and neutral. Listen to what your co-parent has to say. Listen and pause and respond. Ask for opinions about a child related decision. And hold your intention and your co-parents intention of having the welfare of your child front and centre.

What are some top tips to co-parent well?

Have regular meetings. Once a month or twice a year, whatever you need, but schedule them in to talk and catch up with each other about the children. Set an agenda, meet somewhere neutral and have a defined time limit. This keeps the boundaries in place and allows you to just talk about your children.

Set holiday allocations for the twelve months ahead. This way you can plan, your co-parent can plan and your child knows where they will be and when. This is really important for children as stability and structure are key for their resilience.

Don't question your children about what's going on in their other house. If you have a functioning co-parenting relationship you should know the key points to talk to your kids about. So by all means discuss the trampoline park they went to with daddy, but don't question them about things that might make them feel uncomfortable.

What do we do if it gets difficult?

Remember that it won't be perfect and it will be difficult. Don't kid yourself, there will absolutely be bumps on this road. But how you respond to them is key. Try to always be respectful and dignified. It's not easy, but your children will benefit.

From the outset if you can agree together how you will show up to your co-parenting relationship then this can be helpful. At **The Co-Parent Way**, when we work with parents, we help unpack their intentions for co-parenting with each other and we come up with a charter to help parents remember about how they want to be with each other, even when things are tough. Time and again, parents call me up to say how useful this reminder was during a disagreement.

And finally, your children aren't choosing to divorce you, they want both of you. They love you both. Parents need to be parents and make fair and strong decisions that mean that their children can be children.

Co-operative parenting

What should I do about an unreliable ex?

Louisa Dickson
Mediator, Child Consultant and Family Coach at Southern Family Mediation

They don't show up, or show up late almost every time, leaving your child standing at the window, coat on, asking "how much longer?". They promise to call or Skype the children...and then don't. They frequently "forget" to share important information....your daughter had a temperature of 102 degrees over the weekend, or your son scored the first goal of his life. Leaving you seething, and at the same time breaking each time you see them crushed and disappointed by the other parent.

Unreliable parents often don't seem to realise that their behaviour not only makes it almost impossible to co-parent with them, but also seem oblivious to the damage they are doing to their child.

A child's relationship with their parents

Children develop their sense of self-worth and their knowledge of the world through their relationship with their parents. A child's self-esteem is built on the unconscious thought, "I matter and am worthy to the extent to which my parents take an interest in me." Children operate in quite a binary way - it's fair/not fair, right/wrong, with the ability to understand the shades of grey that make up life not being developed until towards the end of their teens.

When a parent is unreliable or flits in and out of a child's life, the child may be emotionally wounded, feeling unworthy and unloved. Their take-away from this experience is the belief that people can't be trusted, which will have profound effects on their emotional development and will make it hard for them to form secure attachments later on. They downgrade their expectation of love, questioning its value. They're filled with anxiety, guilt or shame, they struggle to trust.

Some may even demonstrate these feelings of unworthiness through disruptive and/or destructive behaviour. They turn inward with depression - or act out in anger, fear or despair. Long term this can result in the inability to form close relationships, dependence on alcohol or drugs, and depression.

But there **are** things you can do to ease the pain for your children, ameliorate the damage and actually use it as a positive learning experience for your children.

Communicating with your ex

Tell the other parent that their relationship to the children is important. They may feel that you don't value their relationship with your children, and therefore not see their behaviour as being that much of an issue.

Remain calm. Do not reveal your anger or frustration to your children as this will only increase their bad feelings and guilt. However, do talk with your children about their feelings. Reassure them that you love them. It is OK to explain that their parent's actions are a reflection on difficulties they are having and not a reflection on the children. Do not disparage the other parent. When you bad-mouth the other parent, you bad-mouth your children because they know they are 50% of each of you.

You may wonder why your child still loves or even idolises a parent who is unreliable, and this will in turn feel hurtful to you when you are the one that is always there. As I said above; your ex, no matter how terrible, is still "half" of your child. So to your child if that parent is "bad" then this means that they must be "bad" as well. In order for them to feel good about themselves, they may need to ignore their other parent's bad qualities and focus on the good ones. Be the adult and don't make them feel guilty for adoring your ex. Give them permission to love their other parent. As they get older, your child will acquire a more balanced view. Be the bigger parent. Remember that you love your children more than you may dislike (or even hate) your ex, and so you do it for **them**.

Acknowledge how their other parent's behaviour makes them feel. Tell them "this has nothing to do with you, but I know it hurts your feelings. I'm sorry." Use this as a great learning opportunity and talk to your children about what they can't control (other people) and what they can control (their own actions and thoughts).

Always have a back-up plan. Make sure that your children are not left with nothing to do, allowing them to focus on their upset and get disruptive due to bad feelings. Direct their focus and energies into a positive activity that will make them feel good about themselves.

Be an open door for their feelings. Let your child know that they can come to you with their feelings and questions. And let them know it's also OK not to talk, if they don't want to.

Children have different ways of dealing with painful feelings; often coming out in bad behaviour or anger. It may be too overwhelming right now for your child to speak about the other parent. Bring up the subject from time to time, but don't pressure your child to have a conversation if they don't want to talk. You just want them to get the message that you are always available to listen and that whatever feelings they have are OK and they are entitled to them.

Disappointment is a part of life, and we shouldn't insulate them from it. The key though is to keep them from seeing the disappointment as a reflection of their worth. Use this as a powerful learning experience. Help them understand the situation and make sure their time remains full. This will ease the impact of the situation and teach them the life skills of managing their emotions and how to deal with other disappointments that they will face in life; without going into the default thought of "it must be me".

How you deal with separation can affect your children for years to come. Your relationship as a couple may have ended, but your relationship as co-parents endures for the whole of your lives. Remember: your children love both of you and if you hurt their Mother/Father in words or actions, you indirectly hurt your children.

Amanda Holland, Sydney Mitchell Solicitors

Practical strategies to help children cope with two homes

Kate Daley
Divorce Specialist, Co-Founder Amicable

The transition from one family home to two homes is a big change for the whole family. So how do you make it work, stay organised and on the same page with your ex? Here's what we've learnt from the couples we've helped to transition from parents to co-parents and from one home to two.

Be practical

Work out the practicalities together as parents first before involving the children. Factor in where you will both live, where your children will go to school or nursery and the distance between this triangle. Too much to-ing and fro-ing, and spending hours in the car for pick-ups and drop-offs will take a toll on all of you. If you are forced to live a long distance apart, pick a home that will be the children's base. Think about what is best for them, not what feels 'fair' or 'equal' to you. A great relationship with your children is not predicated on whether they stay at your house half the time - its built on love... and it's the little things that count.

If you aren't on good terms with your ex, then try not to worry if things aren't consistent right at the start - sometimes things take a bit of time to bed in.

Once you've made the decision, tell your children

You might not know where you are all going to live when you first tell the children you are separating but saying nothing is rarely the best option. It's ok not to have all the answers but keeping the children in the dark can be frightening or frustrating depending on how old they are. Tell them what you know... for example that they will be

> If you agree to an arrangement with the children then stick to it - disappointment is hard for the children and for the parent having to try to comfort or explain the situation to them.
>
> *Natalie Wiles, Langleys*

Co-parenting – GOOD

There is no specific definition of co-parenting but it is usually used to refer to parents working together to make decisions in relation to their children and to facilitate child arrangements. It is a good term to use as it does not presume that either parent is more important than the other which can create conflict.

staying in the same school. Ask them what will help make the new house a home. (Prepare for the answer to be a 'puppy' and know what you are going to say!). Avoid taking them to first viewings, create a short list or screen properties with a friend or family member before showing the children especially if they are young as this can be unsettling. If you are feeling really amicable, you can involve your ex in looking for your new home.

Get them involved in the house move
This depends on the age of your children, but it can be effective to let the children stay with the parent who's moving out/getting a new property for the first few days in their new place. That way they are there to help unpack, discover the house, cook the first meal/get a takeaway, go through the experience together. Try and make the first night under a new roof exciting for both you and the children. This will make it feel more like a home for all of you from the off as they will feel more involved in it.

Keep some consistency
One or potentially two new homes will be a big enough change. Keep as much as possible 'normal' so your children can ease in and adjust slowly. Sharing bedtimes, homework routines or tech time limits can help establish a new house feeling like home quickly. Things like a teddy or favourite toy that your child gets comfort from or sleeps with can travel between homes. You can always buy spares of 'special toys' just in case something is left in the wrong home or lost in transit! If you aren't on good terms with your ex, then try not to worry if things aren't consistent right at the start - sometimes things take a bit of time to bed in.

Be organised
Have things that they need in each house (toothbrush etc). When packing bags for them to have at the other house, keep a list yourself (or get them organised to do it independently if old enough) so you know what needs to go. It's very stressful for the kids if you forget to pack the football boots/right kit etc, so best to be organised. If you can afford to duplicate common items in both homes, then do so … it will feel easier on the children. Start with school uniform as this is usually the thing that causes most stress if you get it wrong.

Talk positively about having two homes
Help children see the positives of a new home. Involve them in the design of their bedroom, picking a colour scheme or items of furniture. Help them explore new things that might be on their doorstep. Be practical too and practice things like walking to the nearest shop, bus stops or the walk to school before they have to do these things for real and under time pressure.

Create a parenting plan
Setting expectations, creating boundaries and pre-empting what might crop up is a transformational exercise. The more you think about things before they are an issue, the easier the transition will be for all of you. Plan ahead.

No matter what you think of the other parent please don't influence your child to think the same way that you do about them. Jade (17)

Notes

Grandparents

The ripple effects of a separation can be felt far more broadly than the immediate family. Grandparents, uncles, aunts, cousins who were all closely involved with the family pre-separation can find themselves removed and excluded, a casualty of the separation. This can feel very hurtful for the family members, and the removal of this layer of family contact will also be keenly felt by the children. This chapter explores ways that Grandparents and other family members can still keep their ties to children during and after the emotionally sensitive time of a separation. It is common for grandparents to take sides, to favour their own child, but keeping a balanced view and responding to the needs of the family, will help in maintaining positive relationships.

Grandparents

The importance of the grandparents' relationship with children

Jane Jackson
Founder of the Bristol Grandparents Support Group

It is a privilege to be a grandparent, it is a totally unique relationship.

There is something extraordinary when your child gives birth to their own child.

I remember when our first granddaughter was born, holding this tiny precious person in my arms was almost overwhelming and I can only describe it as falling in love all over again.

It was a truly magical experience, and those same enveloping emotions have happened with the other three grandchildren as they came into the world.

We must remember that we are a supporting role, available when help is required, and not to fall into the trap of telling our adult children and partners how to bring up their children.

As parents we all made mistakes - it goes with the job description - and we must allow our adult children to also make mistakes and learn from them as we did.

Grandparents have lived a life and have learnt along the way. We have stories to tell, have knowledge of family history and hopefully a little wisdom.

We can teach our grandchildren about traditions in our family and keep them connected to the past. Learning about the past within our families helps with their identity.

Often grandchildren will talk to their grandparents about things that they feel they can't talk to their parents about; we all have a good listening ear and can be non-judgemental.

We are able to give the most precious thing of all, our time.

Parents are busy, time is often short, as they are working hard to keep their families safe and happy.

Spending time with our grandchildren is treasured time, time spent memory building.

> We can teach our grandchildren about traditions in our family and keep them connected to the past. Learning about the past within our families helps with their identity.
>
> *Jane Jackson, Bristol Grandparents Support Group*

Grandparents

We can become a trusted person for the grandchildren.

Grandchildren keep us on our toes, always keen to bring us up to date with the latest technologies etc. A close bond is mutually beneficial.

I know if I am feeling a bit low, just a smile, hug or giggle with my grandchildren just makes the sun shine and brings such joy.

Within this unique relationship we can also have fun, I personally enjoy my role of being a 'silly' grandparent, many a time their eyes just roll when I say something daft. Which is probably far too often!

"Oh Gran," can be heard at most visits.

Above anything else, just show your grandchildren how much you love them, and remember it is OK to be an OK grandparent - you don't have to be a Superhero!

For 15 years I've wanted a voice. At 18, I'm ready to talk about what my parents, and their divorce, have done to me.
Kaitlyn (18)

Notes

Grandparents

How can I retain contact with my grandchildren after their parents have separated?

Alun Jones
Director, Alun Jones Family Law

It goes without saying that most grandparents make a positive impact on their grandchildren's lives. They can ultimately help to shape and help to define a grandchild by taking the time to teach, mentor and pass on some of life's most valuable lessons which only come from experience. The time spent together is therefore often treasured on both sides.

Sometimes, however, life can get in the way of this important relationship and the precious tie can sometimes be destroyed. Whether the separation occurs because of a divorce that's ripped the family apart or because of a disagreement that's simply got out of hand, there often needs to be a resolution sought.

This article centres on how contact can potentially be resumed between grandparents and their grandchildren.

Assuming that direct contact has failed at this stage you may now be looking at your other options in order to find a peaceful resolution.

Family mediation

Family mediation can help to resolve differences of opinion and to also potentially find a lasting resolution. Family mediation, however, is often only as effective as the mediator that is involved in the process, so do make your choice wisely. Take your time, speak to your mediator face-to-face and get a sense of whether they are the right person to mediate across both sides. Mediation can be effective at bringing both sides together and working through differences of opinion that are held. It's also worth keeping in mind that family mediation is only effective if both sides enter the process with a willingness to mediate. It is not uncommon at all for one side to not want to participate within the process and dig their heels in from the outset.

What happens if mediation doesn't work?

There are alternate dispute resolution methods available to you. For example, collaborative law can also be attempted. Family mediation and collaborative law are indeed different, but both work on the same principle that both parties want to reach an agreement outside of court. Sometimes, however, one or both sides of the disagreement have no intention of settling matters outside of court amicably. This therefore renders both methods of dispute resolution simply unviable. Therefore, the only option is to involve the family courts in certain circumstances.

It is at this stage where it may come as a surprise to some grandparents that they have no automatic right for the courts to intervene and help them regain contact, unless the circumstances are

Grandparents

exceptional. Grandparents or their appointed family lawyers will have to apply for permission first in order for the courts to review the case. This does, therefore, add an extra layer of complexity before the case is even accepted or rejected. Grandparents or their appointed advisors must therefore apply to the courts stipulating what they are actually applying for in terms of the type of order that they would like to achieve.

The most common arrangements that are requested are set out below.

Child Arrangements Orders: 'lives with' and 'spends time'

A Child Arrangements Order sets out with whom the children shall live (sometimes referred to as a 'lives with' order) and with whom the children spend time (sometimes referred to as a 'spends time' order). It should be noted that the distinction between a 'lives with' and 'spends time' order can sometimes be so subtle it is almost indistinct.

Like the previous (and now unused) Residence and Contact Orders, no order will be made setting out with whom the children shall live or spend time unless it is necessary to make such an order.

In both instances the court will ask the grandparents to set out what it is that they seek and why they feel it is appropriate.

On some occasions the court may ask a member of Cafcass to assist by preparing a report. The grandparents' views supported by the report will then be considered by the court.

Special Guardianship Orders

When grandparents want their grandchildren to live with them it is sometimes necessary to consider an alternative type of order that provides greater parenting powers. This is called a Special Guardianship Order. Cases of this nature can be procedurally complicated and emotionally challenging and it is vital that the proper procedure is followed.

To apply for either a Child Arrangements Order or a Special Guardianship Order professional advice should be obtained first, ensuring that you are clear on how to proceed. A family law practice will then be able to pursue the matter on behalf of the grandparents. Applications to court can be frightening - however, when there is no other option but to go to court, most grandparents will agree it's certainly a cause well worth fighting for.

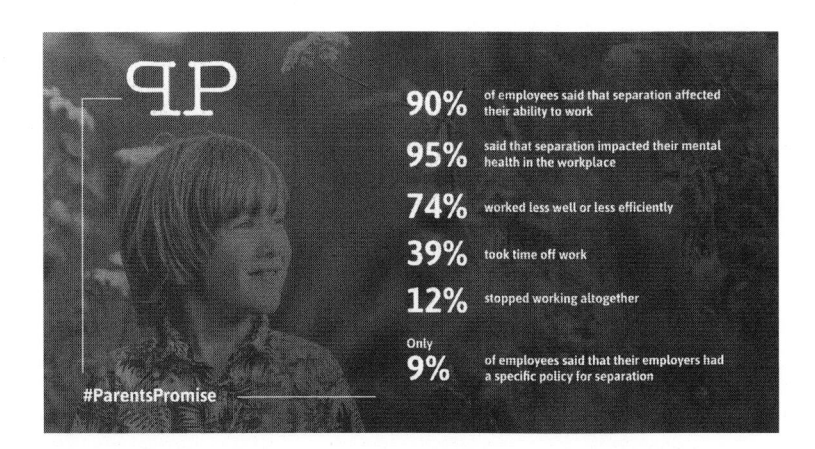

#ParentsPromise

90% of employees said that separation affected their ability to work

95% said that separation impacted their mental health in the workplace

74% worked less well or less efficiently

39% took time off work

12% stopped working altogether

Only **9%** of employees said that their employers had a specific policy for separation

Grandparents

I don't see my grandchildren. What rights do I have?

David Kendall
Partner, Wollens Solicitors

If your relationship with your grandchildren is ended unilaterally then thankfully you don't have to sit there and bear it. There are steps that you can take.

Usually it's not your fault and can happen for many reasons; perhaps where the parents have separated when 'sides' can be chosen, or for some lesser reason or even sometimes when parents feel like their toes are being stepped on.

Making lawful decisions about the children usually requires a concept known as Parental Responsibility (PR). Parents usually get this when their children are born but courts can agree or order this subsequently if it is right for the children. Grandparents can acquire it. Unless you have parental responsibility for the child, you have no automatic rights of access to them. Essentially, this means that as a grandparent, without parental responsibility, you cannot start proceedings for contact through a Child Arrangements Order without first obtaining the courts permission.

However, the law recognises that in certain situations it is in the child's best interests for contact to take place. Grandparents are often seen as not only great babysitters but are fundamental in helping children develop an understanding of their family roots. Grandparents can be and usually are a very valuable and important relationship for children.

To avoid problems with the issue of not having parental responsibility you would need to ask the court for permission to seek an order or 'leave'. The court will always consider what is in the best interests for the child first and foremost and each matter is decided on the merits of the case but it will be necessary to prove that you have or at least did have a stable and positive relationship with your grandchild; and that a risk of any family fallout or tensions in future (that may be witnessed by the child) is outweighed by the positives a relationship with you will have.

Since you are already at a stage where access has been halted by those with parental responsibility, it is likely that they will contest or oppose any application you make seeking a contact order. Whilst this may prolong the proceedings the court will ensure that there are no unnecessary delays.

Before any application is made you will need to consider or undertake some mediation to try and resolve any issues between you and the parents. If mediation is successful it will mean a more streamlined and less costly way forward.

Sadly, legal aid will almost certainly not be available to fund these applications as they involve private law matters and therefore will need to be funded privately.

Grandparents

My grandchildren are telling us worrying things and it sounds like neglect. What should we do?

Kimberley Bailey
Divorce & Family Solicitor, Woolley & Co Solicitors

Children say such weird and wonderful things sometimes, don't they? But sometimes they say something which causes real concern and it's then tricky to decide what to do about it, if you should do anything at all. Did they mean what they said? Did you misconstrue it? Should you ask them again for more details?

As a grandparent you've already been there, done that and got the T-shirt parenting your own child. Whether it's occasional visits or whether you now help regularly with childcare for your grandchildren you have a role to play in their life, shaping their understanding of the world around them. You also have a role in keeping them safe, but you don't want to upset their parents who may take your concern as personal criticism, or risk your concern impacting on your relationship.

Abuse isn't just physical harm. It can be verbal, causing emotional harm and impacting on the child's mental health and well-being. Neglect is the ongoing failure to meet a child's basic needs and is the most common form of child abuse. If the children are saying things which mean you think they may be subject to neglect and/or abuse you have to act.

As a rule of thumb, perhaps try to detach yourself emotionally from this being YOUR grandchild and start with health and safety - do you feel that they are being put in danger, even unintentionally? If so, it is time for

> Children of separated families can flourish. What can cause harm is unresolved disputes between mum and dad. If your children were here now, what would they say they wanted?
>
> *Debbie Wahle, Norfolk Family Mediation*

> We must remember that we are a supporting role, available when help is required, and not to fall into the trap of telling our adult children and partners how to bring up their children.
>
> *Jane Jackson, Bristol Grandparents Support Group*

Grandparents

you to act, however difficult that may be. You can:

- Contact the NSPCC for confidential support and advice.

- Call your local Children's or Social Services department and notify them, either anonymously or by confirming your identity and relationship to the child.

- Call the police and report your concerns.

Your concerns will then be investigated by the appropriate public bodies and action can be taken, as necessary, to safeguard the children.

If you are concerned that this isn't a matter for the police or social services (or perhaps their enquiries determine that the problem isn't sufficiently serious for them to become involved) and want to do more but you aren't able to discuss it directly with the parents, you can make an application at court to define your involvement with your grandchildren.

There are various court applications which grandparents can make (see page 266 onwards for more information).

It's worrying to take the steps to report neglect, particularly when you are no doubt worried about the impact on your family relationships and the possibility of a false flag, but remember that neglect shouldn't be ignored and your grandchild depends on you for love, support and safety.

To parents: never make your child choose. To my fellow voices in the middle: you are never to blame for their separation. El (17)

Notes

We have ended up as parents to our grandchildren. Can we make it official?

Camilla Fusco
Partner, Anthony Gold Solicitors

Grandparents often play an integral role in their grandchildren's lives providing valuable support. However, in some cases, for example where the parents are unable to look after a child, a grandparent might assume a parental role by caring for the child full time. In such a situation a grandparent would need to have the legal status to be able to make important decisions involved in the child's upbringing. This is called having 'parental responsibility' (PR).

Acquiring PR
A grandparent can obtain PR for a grandchild through the court granting them a Child Arrangements Order (CAO) or by being appointed Special Guardian of their grandchild. Other ways of acquiring PR as grandparents are by obtaining an adoption order or by becoming the child's testamentary guardian. In care proceedings a grandparent who acquires an Emergency Protection Order will be granted limited PR for as long as the order remains in force.

The two main legal options for grandparents raising grandchildren and wishing to formalise the arrangements are:

Applying to the court for a Child Arrangements Order
This is an order made under section 8 of the Children Act 1989 regulating with whom a child will live, spend time or otherwise have contact.

Generally, grandparents do not have an automatic entitlement to apply for a Child Arrangements Order and they must obtain permission from the court before they can apply. There are some exceptions to this such as:

> Collate as much financial disclosure as early as you can and put it in chronological order. It will save your lawyer a lot of time and you a lot of money!
>
> *Fiona Turner, Weightmans*

- If the grandchild has lived with them for a minimum of one year immediately before the application (in cases where the grandparent seeks a CAO naming them as a person the child shall live with).

- If the grandparent has the consent of every person who has PR or who is named in a CAO as a person with whom the child lives.

- If the child is in the care of a local authority and the local authority consents.

Grandparents

- If the grandparent is already named as a person in a CAO as someone with whom the child is to spend time.

Otherwise the grandparent must apply for permission. In deciding whether to grant permission the courts consider:

- The nature of the application;
- The applicant's connection with the child;
- Any risk that the proposed application might disrupt the child's life;
- The local authority's plans for the child's future and the wishes and feelings of the child's parents (in cases where the child is under the care of the local authority).

Even where permission is given this does not necessarily mean that the court will make a CAO providing for the child to live with the grandparent(s). This will depend on what the court considers are the best interests of the child determined in accordance with the Welfare checklist at section 1 of the Children Act 1989 (see page 192). The court will also bear in mind the need to avoid any delay in reaching a decision.

If the court makes a CAO naming a grandparent as a person with whom their grandchild is to live they will have PR while the order is in force. The order will usually last until the child is 16.

Applying to the court for a Special Guardianship Order

A Special Guardianship Order (SGO) confers PR for the child on the Special Guardian until the child is 18. An SGO is often made where children are being cared for long-term by members of their extended family but adoption is not suitable and the child cannot be cared for by the parents.

The SGO provides the Special Guardian with more secure legal status than being named under a CAO partly because the parent(s) cannot apply to the court to discharge it unless they have permission to do so. Also, whilst the parents retain PR for the child, their ability to exercise it is limited. In the 2006 case of *S v B and Newport City Council; Re K*, the Judge stated that Special Guardianship allows "familial carers, who are not parents, to have all the practical authority and standing of parents, while leaving intact real and readily comprehensible relationships within the family".

The following people can apply for an SGO:

- A person named in a CAO as a person the child shall live with;
- A person with whom the child has lived for 3 of the last 5 years and within the preceding 3 months;
- A person who has the consent of all those with PR for the child;
- Any person with permission to make the application;
- Foster parents with whom the child has lived for 1 year before the application.

Notice of intention to apply for an SGO must be given to the Local Authority and the applicant will undergo an

---

Often grandparents will talk to their grandparents about things that they feel they can't talk to their parents about; we all have a good listening ear and can be non-judgemental.

Jane Jackson, Bristol Grandparents Support Group

Grandparents

assessment (similar to a foster carer assessment) so the court can be satisfied that making a SGO will be in the child's best interests. As with a CAO the child's welfare is paramount.

Local authorities are required under the Children Act to make arrangements to provide support for Special Guardians. This may be counselling, advice and information or other services including financial support.

There is a discretionary Special Guardianship Allowance which is means-tested and the Special Guardian can also claim child benefit. This is often a crucial factor for grandparents in deciding whether or not to apply for an SGO, or agreeing to be appointed as an SGO in any care proceedings as a 'Kinship Carer'.

Before applying for an SGO or CAO a grandparent will usually need to attend a Mediation, Information and Assessment Meeting (MIAM) to investigate whether mediation may be appropriate.

Whilst it is possible for a grandparent to apply to adopt their grandchild this would not usually be considered the best option as the adoption would sever links with the birth parents.

Talk to your parents individually and explain how you're feeling. Sophie (16)

Thanks to the companies already signed up, the Parents Promise HR initiative is making a difference to over

600,000
employees

#ParentsPromise

Notes

Profiles

Divorce or separating with children may mean coming into contact with family justice sector and/or therapeutic professionals. The profiles in this section offer an insight into the sort of work they do and the different approaches they take in best supporting their clients. Each profile ends with 'tips' on how to get the most out of their professional skills and experience and we would encourage you to take note of all the points raised.

Profiles

The family solicitor

Paul Linsell
Partner, Mediator, Head of Family, Boyes Turner

What I do

Good family lawyers are great problem solvers and will look to find ways to help resolve your issues in a prompt and cost-effective manner that preserves familial relationships.

The primary role of a family solicitor is to provide expert advice on what the law is, how it can help you and what legal obligations you have. They can help you understand the realities of your circumstances, find creative solutions, and guide you on what you can do to achieve your aims.

Most of the work done by family solicitors is in assisting people in resolving issues concerning children or finances during or after a relationship breakdown. However, they can also help in happier times with cohabitation agreements or pre/post nuptial agreements that can help if difficulties arise later.

As well as giving legal advice, a family solicitor can correspond on your behalf if that is difficult, assist with any negotiations, prepare necessary legal documents and, where necessary, represent you at court or in other dispute resolution processes.

Traditionally a family solicitor would act only for one party, but this has changed and some solicitors will now assist both sides of the separating couple.

What I don't do

Experienced family solicitors often have a breadth of knowledge that means they can offer valuable and practical insight that reaches far beyond the law. However, the following are things we don't do:

- There are strict rules about who can provide financial advice and most solicitors will be unable to do so for this reason. A separate accountant or financial adviser is usually needed for financial advice.

- While family solicitors can likely offer some emotional support, it is usually better, and more cost-effective, to seek emotional support from someone other than your family solicitor. Specialist counselling or coaching support is likely to be best.

- A family solicitor cannot make decisions for you or your family. They are there to guide you and help you understand any pros and cons, so that you can make informed choices.

- A good family solicitor will not just do whatever you ask, and they should refuse to take steps that they consider to be destructive or unhelpful. They are not a 'hired gun' to be used to help you take revenge on an ex-partner or to abuse a dominant position.

- There is a common myth that involving a family solicitor may make things harder or that they may deliberately stir up animosity to increase the work required and their fees. While there may be some family solicitors out there where this approach creeps in, for the vast majority this could not be further from the truth. Most family solicitors care deeply about the work they do, the families they try to help and will do everything they can to minimise conflict. All solicitors are duty bound to act in the best interests of their client and are regulated by the Solicitors Regulation Authority.

Qualifications, memberships and experience to look for

Finding a good family solicitor can be vital in achieving the best outcomes for you and your family. When looking for one:

- Get personal recommendations wherever possible by asking around your networks. Try to get a range of names and ask why they are recommended but be mindful that your circumstances may be different.

- Look for a specialist family solicitor, i.e. someone who only practices in family law, rather than someone who dabbles in it alongside other legal services. Check the Law Society find a solicitor website for their details.

- Consider solicitors that offer alternative methods of dispute resolution such as mediation or other joint service approaches. Often these solicitors have been trained with additional skills that can help ensure a holistic, child-focused approach is adopted. You can search for accredited mediators on the website of the Family Mediation Council.

- Check that the solicitor is a member of Resolution, meaning they should abide by a set code of practice. If you have a complex issue then consider whether a Resolution Accredited Specialist is needed, meaning they have demonstrated particular skill in certain areas.

- Do some homework online. Do the messages they put out online come across as offering the right style for you and your family?

- Consider the level of experience (usually years practicing in family law) the solicitor has and whether they have others in their team with more experience supervising them.

- Do not pay much attention to any self-proclaimed awards or rankings; many of these are a result of self-nomination.

- Remember offers of 'free advice' or 'free initial meetings' are a marketing ploy to draw work in. Understanding overall pricing structures and what the solicitor will do to help keep costs down are better indicators of good value, but ultimately you get what you pay for.

Top tips for getting the most out of my profession.

- Invest in early advice, when more options and potential solutions are available, even if you then pause before taking further action.

- Take responsibility for what you need to do to progress matters, whether it be gathering information or documents, making decisions, or responding to questions. Doing your bit in a timely fashion will ensure that you stay on track.

- Use a solicitor as part of a wider team of support.

Profiles

The family barrister

Stephanie Heidjra
Family barrister at Clerksroom

What I do

As a family barrister, my primary role is to represent individuals in legal proceedings related to family law matters. This includes divorce, financial remedy, where the child lives and what the contact arrangements should be, domestic violence, non-molestation and other issues that affect family relationships and dynamics. I work closely with my clients to understand their specific needs and goals and use my knowledge of the law and legal system to advocate for their rights and interests. In my role as a family barrister, I mostly work in court, presenting arguments and evidence to support my clients' positions. I may also negotiate with opposing counsel or litigants in person to try to reach a settlement or resolution outside of court. In addition to my legal work, I also provide guidance and support to my clients as they navigate the often complex and emotional legal process.

What I don't do

As a barrister I do not conduct litigation which means that generally I would not file legal documents and paperwork with the court, prior to the hearing interview witnesses and gather evidence to support your case. Traditionally, this type of work falls under the remit of solicitors who tend to deal with the entire process with the exception of court representation.

While my primary focus is on family law, there are certain areas of law that I do not handle as a family barrister. For example, I do not practice criminal law or tax law. If a client comes to me with a legal issue outside of my area of expertise, I may refer them to a lawyer or firm that specialises in that particular area of law.

Qualifications, memberships, and experience to look for

Your barrister must hold a valid practising certificate. In addition to basic legal qualifications, it is also important to look for a family barrister who has experience handling cases similar to your own. It can also be helpful to look for a family barrister who is a member of professional organizations, such as the Family Law Bar Association (FLBA) or the International Academy of Family Lawyers. These memberships can be

---

Technical terms - THINK

Whilst efforts have been made in recent years to make the language of family law easier to understand there are still plenty of technical terms that are needed. For example, parental responsibility, prohibited steps order, non-resident parent, special guardian and child arrangements all have a technical legal meaning. Even the term 'child' is defined by the law. If you do not understand something then do not be afraid to ask. The system is there for families and it is important that they understand what is going on.

an indication of a barrister's commitment to staying up-to-date on the latest developments in the field and maintaining the highest standards of professionalism. Barristers nowadays will also have reviews online either in the form of testimonials on their chambers' website or on well known review sites. The star-rating and frequency of their reviews can be an indication of their recent activity in their field as well their regard for client satisfaction.

Top tips for getting the most out of my profession

If you are seeking legal representation from a family barrister, there are a few key steps you can take to get the most out of the process:

- Be upfront and honest with your barrister about your situation. This will help them better understand your needs and goals, and provide you with more accurate advice and guidance.

- Be prepared to be patient. Legal proceedings can be time-consuming and may involve several hearings. It is important to stay patient and trust that your barrister is working hard to achieve the best possible outcome for you.

- Communicate openly with your barrister. Keep them updated on any changes in your circumstances or relevant information that may impact your case.

- Follow your barrister's advice. While you are ultimately the one making the decisions in your case, it is important to trust your barrister's expertise and follow their recommendations.

- Don't be afraid to ask questions. If you have any concerns or are unclear about anything related to your case, don't hesitate to ask your barrister for clarification. It is their job to help you understand the legal process and ensure that you feel informed and supported during the hearing.

There were no arguments in front of us, no tears, no slamming doors. I know they did this to protect us. The downside of That Silence though was that it was a complete shock to us. Abigail (16)

Notes

Profiles

The solicitor neutral

David Lister
Head of Family, Ward Hadaway LLP

Believe it or not, there is such a thing as a good divorce. If you and your partner want to separate well, consider using the same solicitor, sometimes called a Solicitor Neutral.

What I do
I will meet with you both separately to assess whether using the same solicitor is a suitable option for you. If I'm satisfied it is, I'll then ask you to make a commitment to each other, using a Participation Agreement, which makes clear that you'll each come to the table with your cards facing up, provide full financial disclosure, and remain respectful of each other's views.

During our first joint meeting, I'll tell you both about the process, the law, the costs and the likely timescales. You'll be able to ask me questions, share what you're most worried about and what's most important to you. We'll agree some core aims; you'll want each other to be housed adequately, to be able to have control over a budget that enables you to move forward without financial anxiety and to make the most of your assets. I'll then give you a list of documents to gather, and we'll set a date for our second joint meeting.

Before the second meeting, I'll prepare a schedule of income, assets and liabilities, to give you both clarity. During our second meeting, we'll work through the schedule together, highlighting any issues as we do, such as the need for formal valuations.

Once the financial picture is complete, we'll have another meeting to discuss the parameters for settlement. I'll set out for you what types of decisions a Judge might make, and we'll discuss a range of settlement options, including the net effect of those options. Providing illustrations of what the outcome could look like will give you a chance to think "Would I be happy with that?", "Can I live with that much money?" and "Does that feel fair?"

My function will be to assist you in:

- Understanding the extent of the matrimonial assets, through sharing information.

A legal fight – STOP

Family law is about helping people to reach amicable agreements whenever possible. One of the first things a family lawyer will do is explain all of the ways in which you can reach an agreement without needing to go anywhere near a judge or a courtroom. These include mediation, child inclusive mediation, arbitration, collaborative law as well as solicitor negotiations. If a family lawyer tells you to expect a fight or writes aggressive correspondence then they may be doing more harm to your case and your family than good.

- Understanding the parameters within which a Judge might make a Financial Order, in the event you can't agree matters.

- Discussions with one another, that lead to a final agreement being reached.

- Having that agreement formalised by way of a Court Order being made by mutual consent.

What I don't do

I screen every case to see if there has been abuse of any sort, hence an initial separate assessment meeting, to allow you to speak freely. Cases involving allegations of domestic abuse won't be suitable.

A solicitor has a duty to act in the best interests of their client(s). I can't act for both parties where there is the possibility of one party being placed under duress or where there might be an imbalance of power.

Another duty solicitors have is to maintain confidentiality, but in this process, you'll both need to agree that all communication exchanged is open and transparent, meaning you'll both be copied in on all emails and all calls. I can't keep your secrets from each other.

I'll record in clear terms how much airtime each person has had during joint meetings, to ensure fairness. I will not take sides.

Qualifications, memberships and experience to look for

Only a handful of lawyers in the country, at this stage, offer couples the option of using the same solicitor.

Resolution has launched a training course to help lawyers who want to offer this service. They call the method of resolving disputes Resolution Together. The first training took place in December 2022, with more lawyers signed up to train.

The process may be very different to being a table-thumping solicitor in a court room, but it isn't for the faint-hearted. You'll need an experienced solicitor who knows the law, has the confidence to express their views on the likely outcomes, and one who can control the discussions that will take place, in a fair and balanced way. Trained mediators and collaborative practitioners undergo extensive training around working with multiple interested parties. They'll already have a solid grounding from which to propel the same solicitor model.

Top tips for getting the most out of my profession

Ask for a fixed price. There are few cases that can't be properly costed at the outset. Fixed pricing is not the same as low pricing. Your solicitor is an expert and, like anything in life, you get what you pay for. Certainty on costs means you'll have one less thing to worry about. You'll know exactly what to budget for. It will also keep your solicitor focussed.

Set your objectives at an early stage. Think about what you want and tell your lawyer. It's far easier to hit a target once you know where to point your arrow.

Ask about alternatives to court. I appreciate the idea of using the same solicitor is new. From years of experience operating in the Family Court, the outcomes I've seen for the couples opting to do things differently are faster, more pleasant, and cost a lot less.

Profiles

The chartered legal executive

Emma Taylor
Partner, Mediator, Goodlaw Solicitors

When I started working in family law, now over 15 years ago, the title Chartered Legal Executive was uncommon and often (and incorrectly) viewed as meaning less qualified than a solicitor. However, more and more we are seeing Chartered Legal Executives not only in family law but across the board in all legal fields. So, what is a Chartered Legal Executive and what does it mean?

A Chartered Legal Executive is a qualified lawyer who specialises in a particular area of law. It is a qualification obtained via vocational training, which means that, upon qualifying, a Chartered Legal Executive will likely have years of experience in their given field already and be able to hit the ground running with case work.

What I do
In my role, I undertake all of the work that a solicitor would. I have full conduct of my cases, provide legal advice, attend court, am responsible for supervising other members of staff within the department (solicitors/cilex/paralegals) and have become my firm's first CILEX Partner (CILEX stands for Chartered Institute of Legal Executives). Chartered Legal Executives are able to obtain additional practice rights should they choose to do so in their specialist area, which gives them additional skills, such as higher rights of audience. A Chartered Legal Executive is able to be a Judge, a partner, set up their own firm and, really, has the same opportunities and skillset as a solicitor.

What I don't do
There is very little that I don't do as a Chartered Legal Executive. There has been a massive shift over the last ten years for there to be parity between the recognised and regulated legal professions and a Chartered Legal Executive now has the same opportunities as any other legal routes to qualify as a lawyer. If anything, when I'm employing new people to join my team, I am always encouraged when they mention CILEX as an option for them because I know, as an employer, I will end up with a vocationally trained lawyer with a real specialism and interest in the area that they practice that has developed over a number of years.

Qualifications, memberships and experience to look for
A Chartered Legal Executive will be a specialist in their practice area, having committed to it during their vocational training and have years of "pre-qualification" experience. Therefore, a key thing to look for when identifying a lawyer for your case when they are a Chartered Legal Executive is not necessarily when they qualified but how long they have worked in that area for. To qualify, the Chartered Legal Executive will have needed to undertake legal work already and therefore, it could be that they only formally qualified a short time ago but that they have been working in the area for many years.

It is always worth considering what other memberships a lawyer has. In Family Law, a key membership that I would recommend is that the lawyer is a member of Resolution. Resolution members sign up to the Resolution Code of Conduct and are committed to approach cases in a non-confrontational and constructive way to achieve the best for the families that they work with.

I am also a member of the Association of Lawyers for Children, which supports my development with regular training so you should keep an eye out for any other memberships held as this can be a good indicator of that lawyer's areas of interests, specialism and their commitment to ongoing professional development.

Top tips for getting the most out of my profession

As the Chartered Legal Executive qualification is vocational, lawyers will have started at a paralegal/support level and worked their way up. They will therefore likely be really up to speed on administrative issues and IT and this can really benefit and speed up cases. The key to working with a Chartered Legal Executive and getting the most out of your lawyer is regular and clear communication and usually this happens by email or phone. If you have an expectation, set it out and be clear from the outset about what you expect your lawyer to do for you. This applies to everyone really, not just Chartered Legal Executives. It is then the lawyer's job to properly assess and manage your expectations so that you are properly advised and understand what is a realistic expectation and how your preferred outcome can be achieved.

Another tip is to look into testimonials and reviews of any Chartered Legal Executive you are thinking about working with and also perhaps have an initial conversation with them to see whether you think you will work together well. As with all professions, different people are suited to different types of lawyers and there can be a benefit to considering your options before you settle on instructing someone. You might end up having to have your lawyer in your life for a number of years and it is important you work with someone you trust and have faith in.

Without the support of my nan and my boyfriend of now 10 months, I wouldn't have been able to do what I have. Amy (15)

Profiles

The arbitrator

Claire Webb
Mediator, Family Law Specialist, Collaborative Lawyer & Arbitrator, Mediation Now

What I do
As an arbitrator I am appointed by a couple and make decisions that are be final and binding on both participants. Arbitration can be used for financial and property disputes and for some child-related issues arising from family relationships.

This enables couples going through family breakdown to resolve differences more quickly, confidentially and in a more flexible and less formal setting than a courtroom. It is also usually much cheaper than a court application.

The same arbitrator can deal with everything, or the couple may wish for different arbitrators to consider the child or financial arrangements. Equally, arbitration can be used to settle specific disagreements; it doesn't have to be used to settle the whole case, making it a good option for couples who get 'stuck' on a particular issue.

Together with their arbitrator, the couple can choose their venue, whether to meet face-to-face or through writing only, and the specific points they wish the arbitrator to deal with.

In the UK, arbitration is run by the Institute of Family Law Arbitrators (IFLA), and regulated by the Chartered Institute of Arbitrators (CIArb). If a couple cannot agree on the appointment of an arbitrator, but wish to use the scheme, they can ask IFLA to choose on their behalf.

What areas does the IFLA Financial Scheme cover?
Any financial and property disputes arising from family relationships including (but not limited to) disputes under:

- Matrimonial Causes Act 1973
- Inheritance (Provision for Family and Dependants) Act 1975
- Part III Matrimonial Finance and Property Act 1984
- Sch. 1 Children Act 1989
- Trusts of Land and Appointment of Trustees Act 1996
- Civil Partnership Act 2004
- Married Women's Property Act 1882

What areas are not covered by the IFLA Financial Scheme?
- The liberty of individuals
- The status of individuals or of their relationship
- Any arrangements regarding children except for financial arrangements
- Bankruptcy or insolvency
- Welfare benefits
- Jurisdiction or stay cases
- Issues over recognition of a foreign marriage or divorce
- Decisions from Sharia councils and other similar bodies

What areas does the IFLA Children Arbitration Scheme cover?

- Generally, any issue between parents or other persons holding parental responsibility or a sufficient interest in a child's present or future welfare

- Where a child should live including shared living arrangements

- Visiting arrangements including holiday time to be spent with a non-residential parent

- Education

- Disputes concerning routine and non-life threatening medical treatment

What areas are not covered by the IFLA Children Arbitration Scheme cover?

- Applications to have a child returned to England and Wales from another country

- Applications to remove a child from England and Wales, whether permanently or for a temporary period (e.g. for a holiday) to another country

- Disputes involving the powers of a court outside of England and Wales

- Disputes concerning the authorisation or management of life-changing or life-threatening medical treatment

- Any dispute where a person under 18 years of age has parental responsibility for the child

- Any case where a party to the proposed arbitration lacks capacity under the Mental Capacity Act 2005

How to appoint an arbitrator

Step one. Whether you choose an arbitrator or ask IFLA to nominate one, the first step is to complete an application form ARB1. The Financial Scheme and Children Schemes each have their own forms.

Step two. It is recommended that you seek legal advice about the nature of the agreement you are entering into and the implications of an arbitral award being made upon you. It is crucial that you understand what effect the outcome will have on you and your family.

Step three. The application is sent to IFLA.

Step four. You will work with the arbitrator to find a suitable date and time for a hearing, either in person or online. At the preliminary meeting you will decide with the arbitrator what documents you will produce and when. You will agree the timescale and venue. You will confirm if you are being represented by solicitors or barristers.

Step five. If you have chosen to have a meeting/hearing, this will take place and you will each set out your cases, give evidence (whether it is your own or expert evidence) and the arbitrator will decide whether any further evidence or hearings are needed.

Step six. You will receive a written determination and/or award.

Qualifications, memberships and experience to look for

Arbitrators are very experienced family law professionals who are usually:

- a practising barrister,

- a practising solicitor,

- a part time fee paid judge,

- a practising Fellow of the Chartered Institute of Legal Executives; or

- a recently retired member of the above.

They have to have at least 10 years' experience in family law and be supported by two referees, many of whom are judges or current arbitrators. Often, arbitrators are also specialists in other non-court resolution models,

Profiles

such as mediation and collaborative family law.

Top Tips

Speak to someone who can recommend an Arbitrator.

Attend a Mediation Information and Assessment Meeting, where an accredited mediator will be able to explain all non-court resolution processes to you, and will be able to point you in the right direction.

Take legal advice and ask your solicitor for a recommendation.

You should start to be able to paint a picture in your area as the same names may come up. Then have a look at the IFLA website https://ifla.org.uk/search-for-an-arbitrator/, where you can see the biographies of the arbitrators.

Arrange to have a short chat with a couple of arbitrators, and see who you feel comfortable with, so that you can move to the next stage of the process.

> When my parents split up it broke me, but now I'm independent and I look back on it as a lesson in life. Ivy (19)

Notes

Profiles

The family mediator

Jo O'Sullivan
Founder & Principal,
O'Sullivan Family Law

What I do
I can help you sort out all issues to do with breaking up (although some mediators will only do children OR finances. Those that help with both children and finances are called 'all issues' mediators.

I help you resolve all financial aspects of your separation.

I help you sort out the caring arrangements for the children - creating a parenting plan together is the ideal.

I help with the finances and how to care for your children. I will help you see that any plan is an organic one and will change according to your child(ren)'s and your own needs.

I can work with you online as well as in person.

I will openly discuss domestic abuse with you and we will decide if mediation is suitable.

I give you legal information. Mediation takes place in the 'shadow of the law'. So, I can give you an idea of what a court might order (this falls short of legal advice) so you won't agree something that is legally naive.

I will make sure you consider everything you need to consider.

I will help you create a flexible agenda to keep you on track with your discussions.

I will keep you 'safe' in the mediation space (online or in person).

I can help improve the communications between you and your ex.

I will help you work out what other expertise you need. I can work with those experts or simply refer you to them e.g. tax advice, valuers, pension on divorce expert (PODE) or a child inclusive mediator.

As our work is not legally binding, it is possible to 'fine tune' and try things out e.g. arrangements for the children.

I can convert your proposals into legally binding documentation (or a consent order).

I provide one of the cheapest ways to create solutions that suit your family.

If I am experienced and accredited, I have a high success rate (upwards of 70%).

I can let you know if mediation is not working for you and recommend how to move forward and avoid court.

I must report you if the Proceeds of Crime Act applies.

I must report you if I have concerns about the safety of your children or either of you (although I will encourage you to report yourself if appropriate).

What I don't do
I can't compel you to come to or continue with mediation.

Usually, our work together is not legally binding.

I will not (usually) keep secrets or confidences and will I circulate any emails

Profiles

you send.

I will not give legal advice (this is different to legal information).

I will not tell you what to do.

I will not take sides because I am neutral and I want to help you both.

Qqualifications, memberships and experience to look for

All family mediators must have attended and passed a recognised and approved family foundation mediation course. Only the National Family Mediation Council can approve a course provider. Those who currently provide such approved courses can be found at:

https://www.familymediationcouncil.org.uk/approved-foundation-training-courses/

After a mediator has enough experience, they can apply to be an accredited mediator. It's best to use an accredited family mediator as they have reached a certain standard of experience and expertise to be accredited.

https://www.familymediationcouncil.org.uk/find-local-mediator/

Top tips for getting the most out of my profession.

Read everything that is sent to you, more than once.

Do all the homework set and meet the deadlines agreed; if you don't think you can then let everyone know in good time.

Ask questions. Ask lots of questions. If you don't understand something then ask; it's likely that clarity is needed for everyone. Don't worry about asking the same question again - mediators are used to it and welcome these questions.

Attend all sessions as agreed. If you can't then give everyone lots of notice to re-arrange.

Work with family consultants, therapists and counsellors to help your emotional well-being. It's a very difficult time so anything you do to improve your mental health the more able you will be to deal with mediation.

Try to explain how you feel about things, what's worrying you and ask the mediator to help address your concerns.

Don't keep secrets about your current life or your future intentions. All information is crucial and can be dealt with appropriately.

Don't' try and 'second guess' an outcome. Be willing to consider all options and ideas. That way they can all be discussed and checked to see if they will suit you both (and your children).

Keep going! It's hard work but worth it when you have a solution that works for your family.

Notes

The child inclusive mediator

Louisa Whitney
Founder, LKW Mediation

What I do
Child Inclusive Mediators (CIMs) meet with children whose parents are in mediation so that the children can share their thoughts and worries. It's a confidential process and a safe space for them to offload to an impartial person. This is generally for older children who are aged 10 and above but it's not a fixed rule; for example, if you have more than one child then it would be unfair if one child got to talk to the mediator and one didn't so all children in a family should be offered the chance to talk to the mediator if one is 10 or over. It can be a helpful thing to offer children to see if they'd like to talk to someone who isn't connected to the situation, even if they decide not to meet with the mediator. Children often worry about saying things to their mum and dad because they love you and they don't want to upset or hurt you. They are often very tuned into you as their parents and know far more about the situation than their parents think!

Following their conversation with the child a CIM then agrees with the children what messages they want fed back to their parents. There might be a particular worry they want their parents to know about, or they might have creative solutions for their parents to try. Children naturally bring a child's perspective whereas adults tend to focus on the problem from an adult perspective. This process gives children a voice in what happens next for them as part of their parents' separation and enables parents to factor their children's views into arrangements that they're making, and how they approach supporting their children.

What I don't do
We don't meet with children with a list of questions or an agenda to go through. It's an informal chat that starts with talking about things they're interested in to break the ice. Then it flows from what they want to share.

CIMs don't prepare a report for parents. After meeting a child the mediator meets with parents to share the messages they wanted their parents to hear. This usually happens very soon after meeting the children. Nothing is written down and we don't interpret or add to what children have said. **It's their words only**. It's different to children meeting with CAFCASS because their views do not form part of a report and it isn't fed into a court process.

CIM is not about giving children any responsibility for decision making. It is purely about giving them a voice in what's happening. All the decision making responsibility continues to rest with you as their parents.

Qualifications, memberships and experience to look for
Any mediator offering CIM should be a member of the Family Mediation Council. They should have undertaken CIM training and continue to have updating training. They should also be insured to speak to children.

As with selecting any mediator talk to them and get a feel for them and their approach. Most parents worry about how their children will cope with their

Profiles

separation. You naturally want to protect them from being hurt or upset. It can therefore be worrying thinking about them meeting with someone who will be a stranger to them. It helps a lot if you both trust in the mediator and the mediation process so spending some time finding the right mediator for you at the outset will be really useful here. Most mediators work online and in person but if you think your children would prefer to see the mediator in person then you will need to ensure you find someone geographically close to you.

Top tips for getting the most out of my profession

If you think this might be a useful way forward for you then pick a mediator that is CIM trained, or who is able to offer this service (some mediators bring in another professional to talk to children). You can find a CIM via the Family Mediation Council's website.

If you decide to get the ball rolling with CIM then talk to the mediator about how to approach this with your child or children. It helps if you can talk to them together with an agreed approach.

Approach the idea of CIM with an open mind. Your children may welcome a safe space to offload even if they're nervous about it.

The mediator will ask you both to agree not to coach your children and tell them what to say, or ask them afterwards about what they said. Many parents worry about this happening so it can be reassuring that you will both agree to these rules.

Advice to other young people: don't get caught in the middle. Olli (17)

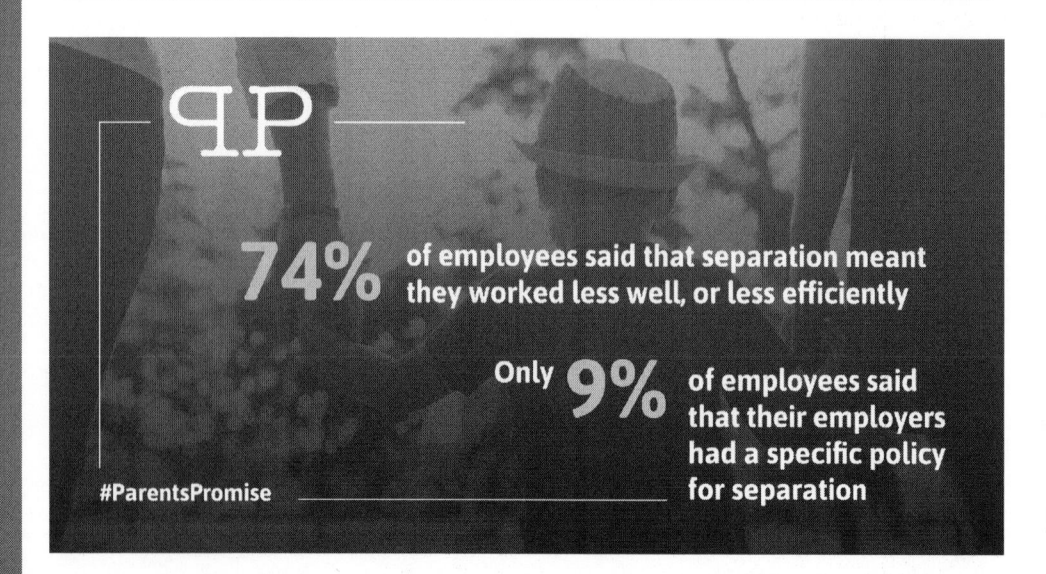

74% of employees said that separation meant they worked less well, or less efficiently

Only **9%** of employees said that their employers had a specific policy for separation

#ParentsPromise

The divorce specialist financial planner

Tamsin Caine
Chartered Family Planner, Smart Divorce

What I do

I work with both individuals on an advisory basis or couples on an information basis.

For individuals, we start helping right at the beginning of the process. The first step is to collate your financial information so that you can exchange your financial information with your ex. This is known as financial disclosure and usually means completing a "Form E" with all your financial information, confirmed by evidence, such as bank statements, pension information and mortgage redemption statements, etc. At this stage, we will also help you to understand what your lifestyle costs now and may cost in the future, so that we can see how any settlement may work for you.

Many of our clients need to better understand their finances, during and post divorce. We help by providing financial education to understand pensions, investments and spending plans.

Once your financial disclosure is complete, it is common for one party to make an offer to the other. We can help you to understand what an offer means to you in the context of your lifestyle (either one your lawyer suggests or one you receive from your ex). It may be that there are some small changes that might be appropriate to make to the offer to make it acceptable to you. We find that this part of the process can help to resolve the financial settlement without the need for court, although there is no guarantee of this as it depends on your ex as well as you.

Divorce Specialist Financial Planners are experts in pensions. We are often brought into the process by a lawyer to provide information on the pensions or to help to understand the actuarial report and advise on how the recommendations impact you. We can also discuss the options available from pensions on divorce.

Once you have reached your financial settlement and the orders have been sealed by the court, we can implement the pension sharing orders if you need to transfer your share externally. This means either setting up a new pension, or using one you already have, to transfer the benefits into.

In some cases, a lump sum will be ordered to be paid. It may be that this money will provide income for you instead of spousal maintenance or a pension. We can help you to invest this for income, or grow to be available in the future.

> "Don't put the other parent down or argue in front of the kids. It is easy to do - I know, I've been there, done that.
>
> In the long run it is better for the kids if you are civil in front of them.
>
> *Sarra, Mum*"

Profiles

After your divorce is completed, you will want to begin to plan for your future. We work with you to understand what your plan currently looks like and the steps you need to take to rebuild your wealth and achieve the lifestyle that you want. There may be personal aspirations that you have, perhaps to live abroad, retire early, or just travel more. We can help you to work out how to make this happen.

For couples, we work slightly differently, as we only provide information, to avoid conflicts of interest. Our work is as a "financial neutral". We provide information on financial products, so that both parties hear the information from the same source. We explain the pension benefits that you each have and then explain the options for these pensions. We can also explain the information provided in your actuarial report

What I don't do
I don't provide capital gains tax calculations. These would need to be provided by a Tax Adviser.

I don't provide actuarial reports. These are written by an actuary. There has been some confusion around Pension On Divorce Experts, or PODEs since the seminal PAG report was released in July 2019. Financial Planners can be PODEs but can still not write an actuarial report.

I don't provide legal advice. I am not a lawyer and so strongly advise that you seek this from a family lawyer or solicitor.

I don't provide counselling or therapy. Although many financial planners are great listeners, we are not trained to provide you with the emotional support that most people going through divorce will need. There are some excellent divorce coaches and therapists, who should form part of your divorce team.

Qualifications, memberships and experience to look for
You should always look for a divorce specialist, preferably one who holds the Resolution Accreditation as they will have been tested on the areas that are most important for those going through divorce. You should also look for Chartered or Certified Financial Planners, who will additionally hold advanced level exams.

Top tips for getting the most out of my profession
Remember it is a partnership and so there will be information that you need to provide.

Be honest and open, as this will help us to help you to live the life that you desire.

Allow us to speak to your lawyer, even if there is a cost involved as the team work will save you money in the long run.

> Focus on the choices you have and the things you can do, because focusing on the other person's reasoning and actions is wasting energy on things you can't know and can't control.
>
> *Matthew Richardson, Coram Chambers*

The Pensions on Divorce Expert (PODE)

Ian Hawkins
Chartered Financial Planner, Oculus Wealth Management

The term Pensions on Divorce Expert (PODE) is wide-ranging and encompasses those who write expert witness reports and those that don't. For the purpose of this section I will focus on The PODEs that provide expert witness reports.

Pensions can often be a significant proportion of family wealth and need to be shared in the same way as non pension assets as part of a divorce. There are many different types of pensions and it is therefore not as simple as adding them up and then halving as this solution will inevitably not provide equality in retirement. For additional information with regard to the treatment of pensions in divorce I would refer you to 'A survival guide to pensions on divorce' which is available at www.advicenow.org.uk.

What I do

The report writing PODE effectively crunches the numbers in order to provide a report that assists divorcing parties to reach an agreement from an informed position. This analysis is typically, but not exclusively, aimed at calculating the pension sharing order(s) required for the parties to receive a similar income in retirement based on benefits that have accrued to date.

It is sometimes the case that one party will wish to retain their pension whereas the other may wish to receive a greater proportion of the non pension assets, say equity within a property. The pension on divorce expert will also calculate the non pension assets that should be transferred should a pension sharing order not be implemented. As with most things this is not necessarily an all or nothing calculation and a solution may be part pension share part offset - these figures would also be provided.

> Never give up contact and regular visits, no matter how many miles away the children have been moved. They won't ever forget. I did it for 11 years.
>
> Jon, Dad

Where there are court proceedings the report is provided jointly to the parties as part of the court process.

The PODE can be engaged outside of the court process whether this be within mediation or collaborative law and in these scenarios is able to explain the report to the parties jointly if this is deemed beneficial.

What I don't do

The report writing PODE does not provide advice or recommend any particular solution to the parties. The duty is typically to the court and advice is provided to the court with regard to the solutions as opposed to individual advice to one or both of the parties.

If personalised advice is required this can sometimes be provided by the none

Profiles

report writing PODE and is typically provided on an individual basis to one party.

Qualifications, memberships and experience to look for

PODE's come from a range of professional backgrounds. Typically these will be either actuaries, financial advisers, financial planners or former financial planners.

There is currently no professional qualification or regulatory system for PODEs, nor is there a database or list of PODEs. The best route to a PODE is via a referral - solicitors, mediators and the courts should be able to provide details for a number of PODEs. From there you should then do your own research with regard to fees and the experience of the PODE, which will be available from a Fee Quote and a CV.

Top tips for getting the most out of my profession

Be as precise as you can with what you are asking the PODE to do and try to limit the number of calculations (e.g. use the retirement age that is most likely as asking for figures at multiple ages will increase the complexity of a report and also the cost).

Be clear about what you are seeking to achieve and make this clear to the PODE. Whilst the PODE will not provide advice they will try to provide you with the information you require with which to reach an agreement.

Read 'A survival guide to pensions on divorce' in order to gain an understanding of the types of pensions and the options available prior to instructing a PODE.

HOW CAN I REBUILD A CHILD RELATIONSHIP AFTER YEARS APART?

Apologise!

Admit your mistakes.

Tell them you love them, and miss them.

Don't blame anyone else, unless you have proof you tried and were blocked, in which case show what you did but don't blame.

Get ready to deal with their anger. They'll defend the custodial parent. You went once, so you are at risk of going again in their eyes, whatever the circumstances.

Very gently begin to fill them in with your life as it is now. Respond to their questions honestly and age appropriately.

Mike Flinn

IT ISN'T YOUR FAULT. It's very easy to believe that your parents unhappiness is because of you, it isn't (I promise).
Brianna (16)

The family consultant

Kim Crewe
Director of Client Wellbeing, Family Law Partners

What I do

As a Family Consultant I work with both individuals and couples to help them navigate their way through the separation and divorce process, which includes supporting them emotionally and practically. The emotional side of the divorce starts well before clients contact a solicitor and continues for a long time after the legal side is resolved.

My approach as a Family Consultant is solution-focussed and forward-thinking. In the initial sessions, we discuss family and relationship histories, not to try to resolve past issues but rather to support clients as they develop their own resourcefulness and start to set goals for the future.

My aim is to enable my clients to feel heard and understood, without any judgement. If I am working with a couple, we may discuss communication patterns between the partners so that communication between them stays as healthy as possible throughout the separation process and beyond. The task here is to help couples move from their couple relationship towards a healthy future and, if they have children, a strong co-parenting relationship.

It is very easy to get caught up in thinking only from one's own point of view, so encouraging clients to think about their situation not only from their own perspective but also from their partner's is a key aspect of my Family Consultant role.

At Family Law Partners I play an integral role in the one-couple, one lawyer model, known as 'Agreeable'. This model is designed for couples who are seeking legal advice together and want to find solutions that will work for them and for their family. Before they begin their work with the lawyer, I will talk with them about their priorities, the outcomes they are looking for, what most worries them, and what their children might need. We create a safe, creative space where the couple can play with ideas and leave with a 'roadmap' they can follow.

This might be the first time in a long while that the couple have really listened to one another, without interruption. It is my role as a Family Consultant to be able to tolerate and hold difficult feelings and to encourage the couple to talk more openly about them. One partner is usually further behind in their readiness for separation, and this time to talk to one another allows that person to catch up, and for their feelings to be heard. This is a key part of the foundation-building process for a better post-separation relationship.

If the couple have children we will discuss how, when and what to tell the children about the separation. We will then work together on a parenting plan that will enable the children to feel secure and have a sense of stability.

Some of the clients I work with are preparing for the mediation or the collaborative law process. My role is to help them feel more confident, so that they can work out the questions they may want to ask. In my experience, clients feel

Profiles

reassured by knowing there is a team around them, each member of the team attending to different aspects of the separation or divorce process.

I aim to support them to become more accepting of their situation, and thus more able to think about the future, and imagine a new life.

What I don't do
I am a qualified counsellor, and this is important because it helps me to be sensitive to the rawness of the feelings clients can bring. But my role as a Family Consultant is not to be a therapist. I adopt a more coaching and solution-focussed approach.

I don't generally work with clients long-term. Most of my work is short-term, but with follow-up review appointments available.

I don't offer legal advice. But I can bring to our discussions my long experience of working in a legal context with couples facing separation or divorce.

Qualifications, memberships and experience to look for
Family Consultants generally have a broad range of different experiences and backgrounds. They must be educated to degree level and have a recognised qualification relating to couple and family work. It is important to look for someone one who understands the legal processes for divorce, so that they can explain to clients the different options available.

Some Family Consultants, like me, have a therapeutic background, in counselling or psychotherapy. The minimum qualification to look for in a counsellor is a Diploma in Counselling. Family Consultants may also have a Psychotherapy or a Systemic Family Therapy qualification, or a qualification in Mediation, Coaching or Social Work. In all cases, check that they are members of a professional body, with a code of ethics.

Family Consultants often have extensive parenting experience of their own and may in addition have a qualification in child development or art therapy with children. Those who are working with children or young people will also have had an enhanced-level police clearance check.

All recognised Resolution Family Consultants will have completed the approved familiarisation training.

Top tips for getting the most out of my profession
It can really help if lawyers refer clients to a Family Consultant right at the start of the separation or divorce process. We can support clients through emotional turmoil, work on unhelpful communications, and help plan the separation.

Potential clients - do pick up the phone and talk to us. We are happy to talk your situation through with you, to see if we can help or else signpost you to other useful services.

If both parents drive or have access to a car, could you negotiate one picks up and the other drops off? Or alternate trips? If the ex won't negotiate then it's better that the children see you trying to be reasonable, and just doing the driving. Children almost invariably understand what's happening, and when they are able will voice their views. They will also learn from your actions to be reasonable in the face of unreasonable behaviour. Don't criticise the other parent to them, just try to rise above it all.

Mike Flinn

The counsellor

Lesley Edelstein
Counselling Psychotherapist

What I do
As a Counsellor I offer compassionate, non-judgemental, and confidential assistance for individuals going through the divorce/separation process. Psychological support is essential to navigate the emotional turmoil that effects not only the way we understand and approach feelings and thoughts but also the outcome of the break-up.

What I don't do
I do not encourage or support blame. I do not discuss anything that is disclosed in the therapy space with solicitors, confidentiality is upheld, and boundaries are firmly promoted. I do not advise on legal matters.

Qualifications, memberships, and experience to look for
It is vitally important that you seek a practitioner who is qualified and a member of a governing body such as the NCS, BACP, BPS, FMC.

You are putting your state of mind into the hands of someone who has to be equipped to hold you in both emotional and psychological safety. The most essential aspect of this type of support is the therapeutic relationship - do you trust them? Can you challenge what is said without fear of rupturing the relationship?

Your chosen practitioner has to be qualified, an accredited member of a reputable governing body and insured but most importantly develops a relationship with you where you can safely divulge everything without fear of judgement.

Top tips for getting the most out of my profession
To prepare for your sessions it helps to keep a journal. When our minds are flooded with the chaos that divorce/separation brings, we often only remember events according to how we felt at the time, clouding our judgement and the way we think/talk about events later.

Be prepared to explore your own role in what has taken place. This can be difficult when we are focused on who is wrong and who is right.

Was it a blessing or a curse?
That Silence.
Did it mask the cracks or make them worse?
That Silence.
Abigail (16)

Profiles

The divorce consultant

Rhiannon Ford
Divorce Consultant

What I do

A divorce consultant can serve many different purposes, but the focus is to provide support and guidance with both the personal and legal challenges of the client's family breakdown.

My work complements that of the family law solicitor, and I can assist with non-legal issues as well as the client's questions that do not require formal legal advice. This helps them to save on legal costs as they are not using their solicitor unnecessarily.

Like me, many divorce consultants have previously worked as a family law solicitor. This allows me to ensure my clients understand what to expect in the legal process, and help prepare them for meetings, mediation sessions and/or court hearings. Practical help is also available to assist them with paperwork, e.g. the financial forms and documents, as well as help to effectively communicate their wishes with the other parties involved in their case.

As a trained coach, I support my clients with the mental and emotional issues that can come up as they navigate through this challenging time in their life.

What I don't do

Divorce consultants cannot provide legal advice and I cannot speak/write to the client's ex-partner or represent the client in their legal case. That is for their solicitor. I also only work with one of the parties and not the couple together. It is worth remembering that divorce consultants are not qualified counsellors, and should the client require this additional type of help, I can provide details of appropriate counsellors for them.

Qualifications, memberships and experience to look for

I recommend choosing someone who is an ex-family law professional and who is also a member of Resolution. Knowledge and experience in family law will help ensure the client receives accurate guidance. It would also be helpful if the divorce consultant had undertaken some coaching training as well, so they can provide the client with emotional support and not just legal guidance. I suggest avoiding choosing someone who doesn't have these credentials but has simply been through a divorce themselves, as they will be an expert in their own divorce, not the individual client's.

Top tips for getting the most out of my profession

Working with a divorce consultant can save the client time, money and stress. To get the most out of working with a divorce consultant, I recommend:

- preparing for the calls/meetings by writing a list of questions and issues the client wants to discuss. This helps focus the client on what they want to get out of the conversation.

- taking notes during the calls/meetings so the client can look back on them afterwards. They then don't have to worry about remembering everything and can also ask follow up questions if clarification is needed.

Profiles

- contacting the divorce consultant before contacting a solicitor. The divorce consultant will direct the client to a solicitor if the help needed is outside their remit but if they can help, it could save the client quite a bit of money with their solicitor.

> I really want them to get back together and it work out, but it is not that simple. Emily (9)

Notes

Notes

Epilogue

*L*ast words from Angela Lake-Carroll and Claire Molyneux.

How to be successful separated parents

Angela Lake-Carroll
Consultant, Cambridge Family Law Practice

Very many families today live in situations where children go between their parents rather than living with both - or just one. Being a successful separated parent takes work - and compromise. Listed below are some hints and tips that you may find useful as you plan or begin your changed role as a parent.

Put your child or children first

Whatever has happened that has resulted in your separation as adults is secondary to meeting the needs of your child or children and ensuring their continued and future happiness. Muddling your anger or hurt about the ending of your relationship with what needs to happen to ensure your children's continuing security is dangerous. Ending your relationship is adult business. Raising secure, happy children is your responsibility as their parents.

Continuing conflict between parents causes emotional harm to children that may affect their whole lives

Children caught in conflicts are more likely to have significant problems as they grow up, to under-achieve and to find making adult relationship difficult.

Don't make your child or children take sides

They don't want to. They love you as their parents, it is hurtful and damaging for them to feel that they have to make choices between the two people they love most in the world.

Finding it difficult to be civil to each other?

Think of yourself as partners in a family business - just as sometimes happens in work situations, you may not get on or even like each other, but you have an investment in your children and a task to complete in raising them to adulthood. Keep your communication as parents going - even if it is in a business like way, it will help your children to understand that you remain, as their parents, together and united in your concern for them.

Don't assume that your child or children can't manage living between you

The practicalities that are our responsibility as parents don't affect children and young people in the same way. They can be much more flexible and adapt to sharing their time between you if you provide a secure framework for them.

Think about how you can ensure that neither of you becomes either the 'guest' parent, or the 'hard slog' parent

Children don't differentiate - you are both their parents. They expect you to be in their life, responsible for their day-to-day living, their discipline and to be able to spend time with them. It's important for children to know that their parents agree about them.

Don't think of the time your child spends with you as 'your time' but rather *their* time.
Remember too that older children and especially teenagers need to form their own social circles and grow towards being an independent adult - with your help. Giving them 'permission' to spend time with their friends is an important part of them understanding that you recognise their growing independence.

Think about the language that you use to help your children and you to be reminded that you both remain parents.
Start sentences with 'we speak' e.g.

> 'Dad/Mum and I hope that', 'have decided that', 'think that'.

Make sure that if you're not sure what the other parent thinks or has said, simply say that you need to check it out with them. 'Hope' is a great word - don't make promises that you may not be able to keep, instead tell your children what you hope might happen.

Think about how it felt for you when your child misbehaved in public
And then think about how it would feel to your child or children if you and their other parent did so at a public event important to them - school plays, sports day, parents' evenings. Your being there at significant events is important to them - as is your civil behaviour together. If you really, really can't manage to attend together, alternate your attendance at significant events.

Happy Birthdays
To a child, a birthday is an exciting occasion - they deserve to have happy birthdays free from worries about an atmosphere between their parents and free to enjoy their day. They would prefer to spend it with both of you (where it is possible for you to do so) - try to ensure that they will have some contact with both of you, by phone or for a short time at least.

Making their Christmas
Or other significant dates in the calendar means thinking through how you can each compromise to ensure that your child or children can look back at those occasions in their childhood with good memories. Try to think ahead and plan for these events ahead of time - don't make assumptions and don't plan or book things without talking to their other parent, and remember older children and teenagers need to be part of any planning because they too may have things they want to do at significant times of year.

Think about other significant things that happen as children grow up
Typical events could include change or choice of school, medical treatment, problems at school and everyday things such as bedtimes and discipline. Try to think through how you need to ensure that each and both of you know what will happen if and when there are decisions to be made or action to be taken. If you can't do that without help, think about using a mediator to help you set out a framework for all the important areas of your children's growing up.

Children need families
Don't forget that your children have other family members to keep in touch with - Grand-parents, Aunts and Uncles and family friends. A sense of family and of belonging aids children's feelings of security so ensure that they can continue to spend time with all the family members whom they have previously known and loved.

New partners and friends
Face it - if you haven't already, there's a strong likelihood that you will have a new partner or friend. Just because they are significant to you, do not assume that they will be immediately significant to your child. If they are going to be part of your life for the future, there

Last words

is plenty of time for them to become involved in your children's lives - don't rush it, children need time to adjust to new arrangements and new people, and your new partner will not thank you for dumping them into a wicked step-parent role!

How would you like to be treated when you have a new partner?
And how would you expect your new partner to treat your children? Whatever that is, apply that to your ex and their new partner.

Help friends and family to know how you want them to help
Friends and family need your guidance to know how they should behave and react. People who love you often want to protect you from hurt or show loyalty. Occasionally and sadly, friends may be acting out their own agendas about past hurts of their own. Be clear with them that you and your ex are trying to work things out together and that is important to you and for your children. Be clear that you want them to support your children - and both of you, no matter what their view about what might have happened.

Remember:
Children learn what they live

Growing up in a situation where things are dealt with through conflict or anger and where there is little or no communication between their parents means that you shouldn't be surprised if your children deal with their relationships with you, their friends and the wider world in the same way - it will be how they think adults behave. Growing up knowing that their parents love and care for them and want them to share their time with each of their parents is a fundamental life lesson for children about relationships, sharing and caring.

Stay confident
When a relationship ends it is easier to feel failure than gain. Remember, however, that no relationship that has produced children is a failure. Try to stay proud of your achievements as parents - and don't lose confidence in your ability to continue to parent well and successfully.

I sat waiting at the window for hours on end every day waiting for him to turn up but he didn't... Sophie (17)

Notes

Final reflections

Claire Molyneux
Mediator, Accredited Divorce Coach, Mills & Reeve

This publication is packed full of advice and guidance from many highly respected professionals who are passionate about supporting families through separation. As well as providing informative chapters that cover many of the administrative aspects of a separation, it recognises with equal importance the need to invest in looking after the wellbeing of each family member. Every contributor has provided tools and guidance to support you through your family's unique separation journey, and they have done so with a keen wish to ensure you take care of yourselves and your children, placing access to the right types of holistic professional support at the top of your priority list.

Research has demonstrated that the old adage of staying together for the sake of the children is not correct. It also informs us that it isn't the separation itself that is ultimately most challenging for children, but instead any ongoing parental conflict that lasts well beyond the period of separation. Taking this into account, the priority for families, where safe and appropriate, is to manage separation in a way that enables everyone to come out the other side positively.

Recently, and soon after a series of adverse events in my own life, I attended a course in which the delegates were asked to draw a timeline to represent their life from birth to date. We did so on a piece of A4 paper (landscape) and the line moved up for a good event and down for something that was more challenging. I was not expecting this type of exercise to form part of the course, and initially felt quite reluctant. However, as delegates, we saw clearly that we all had peaks and troughs in our lives, with periods of middle ground in-between. We agreed it had been a great exercise for stepping back, surveying the course of a lifetime and accepting the inevitable peaks and troughs, including events that may have challenged the core of our value systems.

Separation requires an untangling on many levels. A great deal of time and energy is required to achieve this reasonably well during a period when one's time is generally stretched and their energy reserves low. If you are separating, and you are feeling vulnerable or slightly overwhelmed, there are certain initial steps you can follow that will help you manage the process, rather than feeling as though the process is managing you. It is helpful to think of traffic lights, with an initial stop, amber and then go.

STOP. At the top of the list is putting your own safety mask on first - your wellbeing matters and it is really important not to minimise it or set it to one side in pursuit of putting others first. If you are feeling overwhelmed, you will not be in a position to make reflective and informed decisions. Attuning to the needs of your children, which is key through your separation, will also be more challenging if you are not taking care of yourself. Set aside dedicated slots of time when you can process how you are feeling and identify what can help.

STOP. At the outset, consider

Last words

your immediate needs, but it's important also to reflect on your medium and longer-term needs. Consider where you want to get to in one year, five years and ten years' time. Reflect on your core values and boundaries and feel confident to stick to them; on the journey of separation, you can manage your own behaviour and approach, even if you can't manage others'. Consider what is best for your children, knowing that unless there are issues of safety or domestic abuse, children benefit from having a close relationship with both parents. Put these ideas together as a mission statement of sorts and share them with any professionals with whom you choose to work.

AMBER. Work out a broad plan. As is usual in many areas of life, investing time at the beginning to work out what options are available means you will move through the next stages with more purpose, confidence and with less potential for overwhelm. Although within the media and our local communities the court process is perhaps the most well-known starting point, we know that court should only be relied upon if other support processes are not appropriate.

To give one example about achieving healthy longer-term and sustainable outcomes for families, I often think of a longitudinal study by Dr Robert Emery. In the study, he worked with parents who had applied to court to help with living arrangements for their children. On receipt of their court application, he allocated the parents completely randomly either to continue into the court process, or to come and have approximately six hours of mediation as their starting point. He kept in touch with the families for the next twelve years, periodically collecting data about which parents the children were seeing, how often and - importantly for children's wellbeing - how each rated the other as a parent. He was interested to discover that the results became more marked the longer time went on. After twelve years, those parents who had been into mediation but did not live primarily with their children were seeing and speaking with their children more often. The mediation group parents also rated one another more highly as parents than those who been through court.

Since you are reading this publication, you have access to many resources to help you prepare and plan, and you are already well ahead in this respect and ready to move to GO!

GO. Select professionals with whom you can build a good rapport, who share and support your values and objectives and from whom you can take advice. If you've moved through **STOP** and **AMBER**, you'll be well on your way to being able to communicate your thoughts, to consider and reflect on advice and guidance and to chart a positive course through the steps needed to separate.

Think about engaging support that helps not only with the administrative aspects of your separation but support that protects you and your family's wellbeing - we refer to this as holistic support.

Separation is hard: emotionally, psychologically, for children, financially, in terms of time and in many other ways. What professionals wish for your family is that you work towards achieving a safe and reasonable separation. For the majority, it will inevitably form a trough on your own life timeline, but with the right support and planning we hope the trough won't dip so far down that the clambering back spans too far along the page. If approached with consideration, you and your children can be resilient and emerge positively. Children who have lived through some adversity, provided it is role modelled reasonably well (none of us being perfect!) will take that forward and use it constructively for the rest of their lives.

Advice & support

Action for Happiness
A movement of people taking action to create a happier and kinder world.
https://actionforhappiness.org

Adfam
Information and support for the families of drug and alcohol users.
www.adfam.org.uk

Advice Now
Plain English information on a website run by a group of organisations including the Citizens Advice Bureau.
www.advicenow.org.uk

Advocate
A Charity which finds free legal help from barristers.
www.weareadvocate.org.uk

Alcoholics Anonymous
www.alcoholics-anonymous.org.uk

AMIS
Amis is Scotland's leading male domestic abuse charity that supports victims. It operates a dedicated helpline, digital information services and in-person support for male victims.
https://abusedmeninscotland.org/

Asian Single Parents Network
A network for Asian single parents whether widowed, divorced or single by choice.
https://aspnetwork.org.uk

Australian CSA
Information about payments and services for separated parents providing financial support to children.
www.servicesaustralia.gov.au/individuals/separated-parents

Barnardos
Charity supporting vulnerable children and young people in the UK.
www.barnardos.org.uk

Black Mums Upfront
London-based collective of supportive black mums tackling inequality and disproportionality. Run a very popular podcast.
www.blackmumsupfront.com/

Bristol Grandparents Support Group
Support grandparents all over the UK especially those unable to see their grandchildren.
https://bristolgrandparentssupportgroup.co.uk/help-and-support/

Child Maintenance Calculator
Free child maintenance calculator is for use in the UK.
www.familylawpartners.co.uk/what-we-do/child-maintenance-calculator

Child Maintenance Service
The Child Maintenance Service is for parents who have not been able to make a private arrangement about how their child's living costs will be paid.
www.gov.uk/making-child-maintenance-arrangement

Child Poverty Action Group (CPAG)
Information about welfare benefits and tax credits.
www.cpag.org.uk

Child Protection Resource
Help for anyone involved in the Child Protection (or Child In Need) process.
www.childprotectionresource.org.uk

Childline
Confidential help and advice for children.
www.childline.org.uk

Children's Legal Centre
Experts in all areas of children's rights.
www.childrenslegalcentre.com

Advice & support

Citizen's Advice Bureau
Public access to advice at branches throughout the country.
www.adviceguide.org.uk

Civil Legal Advice
Get free and confidential legal advice in England and Wales if you're eligible for legal aid.
www.gov.uk/civil-legal-advice

Countries where you can enforce child maintenance decisions
List of countries where parents can apply to enforce or change a child maintenance decision made in UK courts.
www.gov.uk/government/publications/countries-where-you-can-enforce-child-maintenance-decisions

Dad Info
Service providing separated parents with suggestions about the most successful way to communicate, negotiate and solve problems after family breakdown.
http://dadinfo.splittingup-putkidsfirst.org.uk/home

Dads Unlimited
Charity offering unbiased and independent advice.
www.dadsunltd.org.uk

Families Need Fathers
Charity concerned with maintaining a child's relationship with both parents during and after family breakdown.
www.fnf.org.uk

Family Lives
A national family support charity providing help and support in all aspects of family life.
www.familylives.org.uk

Family Mediation Council (FMC)
The Family Mediation Council is made up of 5 national family mediation organisations in England and Wales.
www.familymediationcouncil.org.uk

Family Rights Group
Advises parents and other family members whose children are involved with or require children's social care services because of welfare needs or concerns.
www.frg.org.uk

Fegans
(Now Spurgeons Children's Charity) provides therapeutic support to children and their families.
www.fegans.org.uk

First Light
First Light is a charity supporting people in Cornwall, Devon and Wiltshire who have been affected by domestic abuse and sexual violence.
www.fristlight.org.uk

FLAG DV
Flag DV is based in Newbury, but covering the whole Thames Valley area. It provides weekly legal advice clinics to those suffering Domestic Abuse.
www.flagdv.org.uk

FLOWS
Flows is a legal support service for women survivors of domestic abuse. It can help women access injunctions from the court.
www.flows.org.uk

Frolo
Have a mission to connect, support and empower single parents.
www.frolo.com

Galop
LGBT & anti-violence charity.
www.galop.org.uk

Gamblers Anonymous
www.gamblersanonymous.org.uk/

Gingerbread
National charity supporting single parent families to live secure, happy and fulfilling lives.
www.gingerbread.org.uk

Grandparents Plus (now called Kinship)
National charity working for grandparents and kinship carers.
www.grandparentsplus.org.uk

Advice & support

Happy Steps
The UK's only research-based stepfamily resource centre.
https://happysteps.co.uk

Kids Come First
Kids Come First offers specialist support for parents seeing to help their children through the separation process.
www.kidscomefirstuk.co.uk

LawWorks
Solicitors Pro Bono Group.
www.lawworks.org.uk

Legal Aid Finder
Directory of legal advisers and family mediators who do legal aid work.
https://find-legal-advice.justice.gov.uk

ManKind
Confidential helpline for men suffering from domestic abuse.
www.mankind.org.uk

Match
Charity offering support and information to mothers apart from their children.
www.matchmothers.org/

Men's Advice Line
Help and support for men experience domestic violence and abuse.
www.mensadviceline.org.uk

MIND
For better mental health.
www.mind.org.uk

Money Advice Service
Information about financial issues, including sections on divorce and separation.
www.moneyadviceservice.org.uk

Narcotics Anonymous
hppt://ukna.org

National Association For Child Support Action (NACSA)
Nacsa provides expert advice and guidance to parents who encounter problems with Child Maintenance Service decisions
www.nacasa.co.uk

National Association of Child Contact Centres (NACCC)
Search facility for contact centres by location and type of service. Range of information for families. Helpline: 0800 4500 280 (9.00 - 1.00 Mon-Fri).
www.naccc.org.uk

National Children's Day
The aim of National Children's Day UK is to create events and activities that highlight the importance of healthy happy children.
www.nationalchildrensdayuk.com

National Debtline
A national debt advice charity.
www.nationaldebtline.org

National Domestic Abuse Helpline
The 24 hour National Domestic Abuse Helpline, run by Refuge is for women experiencing domestic abuse, their family, friends and others calling on their behalf.
www.nationaldahelpline.org.uk

National Family Mediation
NFM is a network of LSC contracted and accredited family mediation services countrywide that offer practical and emotional support to those affected by separation or divorce.
www.nfm.org.uk

National Youth Advocacy Service (NYAS)
Provide information and advice to children. Act as children's guardians in difficult contact or residence cases.
www.nyas.net/

NHS Choices
Advice to help you make the best choices about your health and wellbeing.
www.nhs.uk

No Family Lawyer
Website supporting Lucy Reed's book 'The Family Court Without A Lawyer'.
www.nofamilylawyer.co.uk

NSPCC
UK's leading children charity preventing abuse.
www.nspcc.org.uk

Advice & support

OnePlusOne
Supports parents through separation and co parenting difficulties. It can also be used by parents who are just worried about their relationship.
www.oneplusone.space/the-parent-connection/

Our Family Wizard
The Our Family Wizard website and mobile apps offer divorced or separated parents an array of tools to easily track child arrangements, share important family information, manage expenses, and create an accurate, clear log of co-parenting communication.
www.ourfamilywizard.co.uk

Parenting Apart Programme
This organisation specialises in providing supervision of contact in a safe welcoming environment where children and families can be brought together.
www.parentingapart-programme.co.uk

Pink Tape
Lucy Reed's family law blog.
www.pinktape.co.uk/

Place2Be
Children's mental health charity working with pupils, families, and staff in UK Schools
www.place2be.org.uk/

Refuge
Support and information about domestic violence.
www.refuge.org.uk

Relate
Counselling services and relationship advice.
www.relate.org.uk

REMO Unit
Government advice relating to child maintenance if a parent lives abroad.
www.gov.uk/child-maintenance-if-one-parent-lives-abroad/other-partner-lives-abroad

Respect
Domestic Violence Perpetrator Programmes.
www.respect.uk.net

Rethink
Advice and helplines for people with issues relating to mental illness.
www.rethink.org

Reunite International
UK charity specialising in international parental child abduction (click on "resources" for a list of signatories to the Hague Convention).
www.reunite.org/

Rights of Women
A women's charity working in a number of ways to help women through the law. Their site has some really useful free guides to the law.
http://rightsofwomen.org.uk/get-information/legal-information/

Royal Courts of Justice Advice Bureau
Citizen's Advice Bureau providing free advice to litigants in person, including family law. Able to refer to Bar Pro Bono Unit where appropriate. Appointments line: 0844 856 3534 (or 0300 456 8341 from mobiles).
www.rcjadvice.org.uk

Safe Lives
Safe Lives are the UK-wide charity dedicated to ending domestic abuse, for everyone and for good.
www.safelives.org.uk

Samaritans
Confidential non-judgemental emotional support for people experiencing feelings of distress or despair.
www.samaritans.org

Shared Parenting Scotland
Shared Parenting Scotland (formerly FNF Scotland) supports individuals who are struggling to achieve meaningful parenting time with their children after separation or divorce, including grandparents and extended family members.
www.sharedparenting.scot

Shelter
The housing and homelessness charity.
www.shelter.org.uk

SingleParents
Connecting, supporting and empowering single parents across the UK.
www.singleparents.org.uk

Advice & support

Southall Black Sisters
Empowering BME women to escape domestic violence.
www.southallblacksisters.org.uk

SPLITZ Support Service (South West)
Splitz Support Service is a registered charity delivering support services to adults and young people experiencing the trauma of domestic abuse and sexual violence. Splitz delivers services across South-West England. The Devon Helpdesk for Splitz can be contacted on: 0345 1551074.
www.splitz.org

StepChange
National debt advice charity.
www.stepchange.org

Stonewall
Campaigns for the equality of lesbian, gay, bi and trans people across the UK.
www.stonewall.org.uk

Support Through Court (previously Personal Support Unit)
Voluntary service helping litigants in person.
www.supportthroughcourt.org

Talk To Frank
Confidential drugs advice.
www.talktofrank.com

Tavistock Relationships
Provide a range of affordable services to help people with relationship difficulties, sexual problems, and parenting challenges.
https://tavistockrelationships.org

The Transparency Project
Explains and discusses family law and family courts in England & Wales, and signposts to useful resources to help people understand the system and the law better.
www.transparencyproject.org.uk/

Two Wishes
An international non-profit organisation dedicated to the wellbeing of children and families.
https://twowishesfoundation.org.uk/#about

Victim Support
Specialist practical and emotional support to victims and witnesses of crime.
www.victimsupport.org.uk

Voices In The Middle
A dedicated place for young people to find help and support.
www.voicesinthemiddle.com

Wikivorce
Advice and support on divorce.
www.wikivorce.com

Women's Aid
Support and information about domestic violence.
www.womensaid.org.uk

Your Rights
Liberty guide to human rights. Tells you how a conviction becomes spent.
www.yourrights.org.uk/

Glossary

Access
This term is no longer used as it focusses on the parent's rights. We now have "child arrangement orders" which can include with whom, or when a child spends time with or otherwise has contact with a parent.

Acknowledgment of service
A standard form (sent by the court with the divorce petition/matrimonial order application) that the respondent must sign and return to the court to confirm that they have received the petition/matrimonial order application.

Adjournment
In a family law context, this generally means a hearing is postponed to a later date.

Adultery
This used to be one of the five facts or bases for getting a divorce, i.e. sexual intercourse that takes place during the marriage between a spouse and someone of the opposite sex who is not their husband or wife. The requirement to rely on facts has since been abolished and will only be relevant for divorces started prior to April 2022.

Ancillary relief
This is now called financial proceedings or financial remedy application.

Answer
This is the formal defence to a divorce petition/matrimonial order application, rebutting the evidence. Since April 2022 you can no longer object to a divorce based on evidence unless there are issues of jurisdiction. It is very rare for divorces to be defended.

Appeal
The process of asking a higher court to change the decision of a lower one.

Applicant
The person applying to court for an order.

Arbitration
An alternative to a judge deciding the case introduced in early 2012. The parties can choose an arbitrator to rule on all or just some of the issues in dispute. The arbitrator's decision (called an award) is then made into a binding court order.

Arbitrator
An arbitrator is a third party who reviews the evidence in the case (or a discrete issue within the case) and provides a decision that is legally binding on both sides and enforceable in the courts.

Barrister
This is a lawyer who spends the majority of his or her time arguing cases in court. Barristers also use that advocacy experience to work with solicitors in advising on possible outcomes. Also referred to as counsel.

Cafcass
This is the Children and Family Court Advisory and Support Service. A Cafcass officer assists the court with matters relating to children and, in disputed cases of contact or residence for example, may be asked to prepare a report for the court on what orders or action would be in the children's best interests.

CEV
A cash equivalent value (CEV) is the value of the rights accrued within a pension scheme (previously called cash equivalent transfer value).

Charge on property
This is sometimes used as a means of security if one spouse is awaiting payment of a cash lump sum on a delayed sale of a home. It works like an additional mortgage, but without interest being paid, and is usually expressed as a percentage of the value of the property. It gives the holder of the charge security because they know that they will be paid out of the proceeds of the eventual sale.

Chattels
Legal term for personal effects, usually house contents or personal possessions.

Child abduction
The wrongful removal or wrongful retention of a child from his or her place of normal, day-to-day residence without permission from the other parent.

Child arrangements order
This order regulates arrangements relating to with whom a child is to live, spend time or otherwise have contact. It also relates to when a child is to live, spend time or otherwise have a contact with any person. It replaces contact and residence orders and brings together arrangements for both in one order. If you already have a contact or residence order, from April 2014, you will be treated as having a child arrangements order.

Child maintenance
An amount that one parent pays to the other parent in order to support the child.

Child Maintenance Service (CMS)
Replaced the Child Support Agency in November 2013. Its role is to make sure that parents living apart from their children contribute financially to their upkeep by paying child maintenance. It is intended to be used by only those parents who cannot come to an agreement themselves over child maintenance. All new applications for child maintenance made after November 2013 are dealt with by the CMS. There is a child support calculator on the Child Maintenance Options website.

Child Support Agency (CSA)
Replaced by the Child Maintenance Service in November 2013. It continues to administer all applications made before November 2013.

Circuit judge
In the family law context, this is a senior judge who deals with the more complicated cases in the Family Court. Appeals from magistrate's or a district judge's decision are heard by a circuit judge.

Civil partnership
The Civil Partnership Act 2004 came into operation on 5 December 2005 and enables a same sex couple to register as civil partners. Being civil partners enables the couple to have equal treatment to a heterosexual married couple in a wide range of legal matters, including on the breakdown of the relationship.

Clean break
An order of the court barring any further financial claims between the divorcing couple. A clean break settlement cannot include spousal periodical payments/maintenance (it can include child maintenance though). A clean break is only effective if the financial agreement is confirmed within a court order. The court has a duty in all financial proceedings to consider whether a clean break is possible.

Co-respondent
A person with whom the respondent is alleged to have committed adultery. Co-respondents cannot make financial claims against each other in the same way that married couples can and have to rely on the law of property.

Glossary

Cohabiting/cohabitation
An arrangement in which an unmarried couple lives together in a committed personal relationship. Cohabitants cannot make financial claims against each other in the same way that married couples can and have to rely on the law of property.

Collaborative law
An approach to dealing with family law issues such as finances on divorce and children arrangements built on mutual problem solving where the couple and their lawyers pledge to work together to negotiate an agreement without going to court.

Committal to prison
Sending a person to prison for breaching a court order.

Common law husband and wife
This is a common misconception; there is no such thing as a common law marriage. The rights and responsibilities of a couple who live together but are not married differ greatly to those of a married couple.

Conditional order
The interim order of divorce indicating that the court is satisfied that the marriage has broken down irretrievably. This can be applied for by the applicant after 20 weeks have passed from the date the divorce application was issued. Six weeks and one day after the conditional order has been made, the applicant can apply to the court for a final order which will terminate the marriage.

Consent order
A court order made by a court giving effect to the settlement terms that have been agreed between a husband and wife.

Contact
Contact can form part of a child arrangements order or can be by agreement between the parents. Indirect contact means the exchange of letters, telephone calls or presents. Contact arrangements within a child arrangements order can also be made in favour of others, such as grandparents.

Contact orders
As from April 2014, contact orders no longer exist. They have been replaced with "child arrangements orders". See also Child arrangements orders and Contact.

Counsel
Another name for a barrister.

Counselling
Specialist counsellors, with the right background, are able to help adults or children who are going through a separation. Other help can be provided by psychologists, therapists and family mediators with specialised training in working with adults or children within the family context. These professionals can be referred to as family consultants.

Family consultants can be brought into the collaborative law process to help spouses work out and articulate what they want, and to help and advise on ways to improve communication. Further support can help reduce conflict, help develop coping strategies for dealing with the emotional issues that may affect the family now and in the future and help everyone to move on with their lives following the divorce. Family consultants may also work with children, seeing them separately in appropriate cases, helping them to voice their thoughts, feelings, needs and concerns.

Glossary

Court
The courts handle all types of family law disputes. From April 2014, there are only two types of court that deal with family law disputes. The Family Court will hear most cases and, depending upon the complexity of the case, the judge might be a magistrate (also called a lay justice), district judge, circuit judge or a High Court judge. Mostly, you will find your local Family Court based at your local County Court. Very few specific types of family disputes will be heard in the High Court.

Court fees
These are the fixed administrative costs paid to the court when making an application. Fees vary depending upon the type of application. If you are in receipt of public funding (legal aid), then the court fees are generally exempt.

Custody
This term was removed from the law in 1991 because it was focused on the rights of parents and caused conflict between the parents. We now use child arrangements orders which can be balanced in favour of both parents. See also Child arrangements order.

Decree absolute
The final order of the court, which terminates the marriage. This is now called a final order. Decree absolute will only be granted in divorces commenced prior to 31 March 2022. See also Final Order.

Decree nisi
The interim decree or order of divorce indicating that the court is satisfied that the marriage has broken down irretrievably. Six weeks and one day after decree nisi has been made, the applicant can apply to the court to make the decree nisi absolute (decree absolute) and the marriage is then terminated. Decree nisi now only applies to divorces commenced prior to 31 March 2022. This is now called a conditional order. See also Conditional order and Final order.

Directions order
A court order directing how the case will proceed (e.g. what evidence needs to be filed and what the timetable to trial is going to be).

Disclosure
This is the process of providing complete financial details about a person's capital, income, assets and liabilities. This is either done voluntarily or the court can order it. It is a necessary first step in any discussions about finance, even in mediation or in collaborative law. This is usually done by filling in a Form E.

District judge
A judge who sits in the Family Court. Most family disputes that end up in court are dealt with by a district judge.

Divorce
This is the process which leads to the termination of a marriage. There are two orders: conditional order and final order.

Divorce application
Formerly a divorce petition. This is the application that is made to start divorce proceedings. Since April 2022 it can be made by one spouse as a sole application or by both spouses as a joint application.

Divorce, Dissolution & Separation Act 2020
The legislation which removed the requirement to establish facts and allocate blame in order to be able to obtain a divorce.

Divorce.co.uk
The most comprehensive free resource on the web, provided by the family lawyers at top 50 UK law firm Mills & Reeve. The information provided on the site aims to help families manage their way through relationship breakdown. Find out more at www.divorce.co.uk.

315

Glossary

Domestic violence/abuse
This has many forms including threats of and actual physical aggression, sexual abuse, emotional abuse, controlling or domineering behaviour, intimidation, stalking or passive/covert abuse such as neglect.

Duxbury calculation
Duxbury calculations are made to assist the decision as to whether or not a clean break is possible. The calculation produces a figure of what level of lump sum payment the recipient needs in order to spend the rest of their life at a certain amount of expenditure each year.

Equity
Refers to the net value of a property after mortgages or other charges are paid off.

Ex parte
This is now called without notice. It most commonly refers to emergency hearings that are conducted with only the applicant present at court. If the court makes an order without notice hearing, the judge will ensure that another hearing can be held quickly afterwards in order to hear the respondent's case and then make a final order. Often without notice hearings are used to deal with injunctions i.e. to prevent the other party from doing something.

Family proceedings court
The name given to the division of the magistrates' court that dealt with family law matters. It was abolished on 22 April 2014.

FDA
First directions appointment, sometimes called a first appointment of FA: this is the first court appointment in financial cases and tends to be mainly administrative (family lawyers sometimes refer to it as a "housekeeping" hearing). The judge will consider what information is needed from both sides in order to progress the case. If the couple is able to agree the directions prior to the FDA then it may be possible to treat it as a financial dispute resolution (FDR).

FDR
Financial dispute resolution appointment/hearing: the second court appointment under the standard procedure in financial proceedings. This is an opportunity for the parties to negotiate on a without prejudice basis and with the assistance and guidance of a judge. Importantly, the judge who deals with the FDR cannot take any further part in the case if it does not settle at that hearing, other than to give directions for progressing the case to a final hearing. The FDR can, in more simple cases, sometimes be combined with the first appointment (FDA) to save costs and speed up progress.

FHDRA
A first hearing dispute resolution appointment: the first court appointment in a private law children application.

Final hearing
The trial and the final court appearance in all proceedings. A judge will hear the parties and any experts give evidence and will make a binding court order as a result. In limited situations there are grounds for appeal.

Final order
The final order terminates the marriage. An applicant can apply for a final order after six weeks have passed from the date of the conditional order being granted.

Financial proceedings
See Financial remedy application. These are generally the court proceedings following a divorce to reallocate the income and capital of a family.

Glossary

Financial remedy application
This used to be called ancillary relief. This is the application to the court for financial orders following a divorce. The court can make a variety of orders about the finances of a divorcing couple. These are lump sum orders, property adjustment orders, property transfer orders, variation of trusts orders, periodical payments/maintenance and pension sharing orders.

Five-year separation
This used to be one of the five facts or bases for getting a divorce, i.e. the couple has lived apart for five years (no consent needed). The requirement to rely on facts has since been abolished and will only be relevant for divorces started prior to April 2022.

Form A
The application form sent to the court that begins the process of dealing with the financial claims on a divorce. It puts in place a court led timetable for financial disclosure and also sets a court date, which will either be an FDA or an FDR depending upon how much can be done beforehand.

Form E
This is the court form setting out a person's financial circumstances (called financial disclosure) as well as details about what orders are sought. It is about the same size - and as much fun - as a tax return. It is obligatory to complete and confirm the truth of this form in court led proceedings. It is often also used as a checklist for voluntary financial disclosure and in those cases where the parties are able to come to a financial agreement without needing the help of the court, directly or through mediation or collaborative law.

Form G
This is a simple form sent to the court before the FDA confirming whether or not it is possible to combine the FDA and the FDR hearing.

Forms H and H1
These are forms filed before each court hearing, which provide details of each party's costs and what has been paid towards them.

Former matrimonial home
The house in which the divorcing couple were living together before they separated. If it is owner occupied, it is often one of the biggest assets that has to be dealt with on divorce.

Get
A document made in a Beth Din (a court of Jewish law) dissolving a Jewish marriage following proceedings under Jewish law. It is handed over by a husband to a wife.

HMCTS
His Majesty's Courts & Tribunals Services, or HMCTS, is the formal name for the Court system in England & Wales.

Injunction
An order of the court preventing or requiring action, usually made in an emergency.

Interim maintenance
See maintenance pending suit.

Joint lives order
An order for maintenance that does not have a specific term i.e. it will continue until one party dies or the Court makes a further order. It is rare to see such orders and they are usually made only when it is not yet possible to ascertain when maintenance should stop or if there is no prospect of the receiving party attaining financial independence.

Joint tenancy
A form of joint ownership of land in which both parties share the whole title to the property. If one party dies, the survivor will own the entire property (the "right of survivorship").

Glossary

Judicial separation
A formal separation sanctioned by the court, which enables the court to make orders about money and property but does not actually terminate the marriage.

Leave to remove
An application to the court for permission to remove a child permanently from England and Wales. This is now called permission to remove.

Legal Aid Agency (LAA)
Provides both civil and criminal legal aid and advice to those people who qualify for it. Due to government cuts in the legal aid budget, there are very few family cases which benefit from legal aid. However, you may be able to get legal aid if you have been the victim of domestic violence or if you are using mediation to resolve your dispute.

Legal Services Commission (LSC)
Now called the Legal Aid Agency.

Litigant in person
A person acting on their own behalf without assistance from a solicitor.

Lump sum order
A fixed sum of money paid by one person to another. It may be payable in one go or in instalments. This is one of the financial orders open to the court to make when deciding a financial settlement on divorce.

Maintenance
A regular payment of money by one spouse to another under a court order or following an agreement. Spousal maintenance refers to maintenance paid from one spouse to another. It is possible to capitalise spousal maintenance by the payment of a lump sum to achieve a clean break. Maintenance can be secured on the assets of the paying party if there is a risk that the order may be breached. Those assets can then be sold to ensure the recipient's claim is satisfied. Those orders are rare. See also Child maintenance.

Maintenance pending suit
In financial proceedings, a person can apply for interim periodical payments/maintenance, which is payable on a temporary basis while the proceedings are ongoing and before they are concluded. It is sometimes called interim maintenance or MPS. This is particularly useful if the financial proceedings are going to take some time to conclude.

Matrimonial order application
This used to be called a divorce petition. This is the document that starts the divorce proceedings. See also Divorce application and Dissolution application.

McKenzie friend
An individual who assists a litigant in person in the courtroom.

Mediation
The process through which independent mediators try to help a couple reach agreement about the arrangements to be made for children and/or finances following their decision to divorce or separate. It is sometimes wrongly thought to be a discussion about the relationship and whether a reconciliation is possible.

Mediation information & assessment meeting (MIAM)
Before court proceedings can be issued - either about children or about finance - you will usually be required to attend a meeting about mediation to ensure you have information about the process. This is called a mediation information and assessment meeting (MIAM). This meeting can be a useful way of finding out more about mediation, although it is better to have explored the option of mediation before you decide that you want to start court proceedings.

Glossary

Mediation service/s
A provider of mediation services.

Mediator
A third party who assists the parties to reach a negotiated settlement.

MIAM
See Mediation information assessment meeting.

Mid-nup
A mid-nuptial agreement: an agreement made during the marriage. See Post-nup.

Mirror order
A court order obtained in a foreign court, which reflects exactly the terms of an English court order. Mirror orders are generally obtained to enforce the terms of an English order outside England and Wales.

Mortgagee
This is usually a bank or building society, but it can be anyone who lends you money to buy a property on the security of the property.

Mortgagor
This is the borrower who obtains a mortgage.

MPS
See Maintenance pending suit.

Non-molestation order
An order prohibiting a person from molesting another person. The order usually prohibits one person from using or threatening violence or intimidating, harassing or pestering another person. The order can include the protection of children. Once a respondent is aware of a non-molestation order, breaching it is a criminal offence that is punishable by either a fine or a term of imprisonment. This often goes hand-in-hand with an occupation order or orders relating to the children.

Occupation order
An order regulating the occupation of the family home. A person can be excluded from the family home or from a certain part of it for a set period of time. If the respondent breaches an occupation order, and if a power of arrest has been attached to the order, the police can arrest the respondent and bring them back to court.

Offer to settle
Offers to settle may be "open". This means they can be referred to, openly, in court and especially at any final hearing. Offers to settle may also be without prejudice, which means it is not possible to refer to them openly in court except at the FDR and especially not in any final hearing.

Order
A direction by the court that is legally binding and enforceable.

Parent with care
A term previously used by the Child Support Agency for the parent with whom the child had his or her main home. The Child Maintenance Service now refers to the parent with care as the "receiving parent" (i.e. they receive the maintenance on behalf of the child).

Parental responsibility
If the parents are married, or if the child was born after 1 December 2003 and the father is named on the birth certificate, both parents of a child have joint parental responsibility for that child before, during and after divorce or separation. This term describes all of the rights, duties and responsibilities which, by law, a parent of a child has in relation to that child. Aspects of parental responsibility include decisions about a child's religion, education, name and medical treatment. Parental responsibility can also be granted to a person by order of the Court and in some cases can be restricted or removed.

Glossary

Particulars
In divorce proceedings issued prior to April 2022, if the petition/application was based on unreasonable behaviour or adultery, the applicant had to set out details which were referred to as particulars.

Pension
Cash and/or an income paid by the Government or a private company or arrangement on a person's retirement. Pension funds can be extremely valuable and may be an important part of any financial settlement, especially after longer marriages. There are three ways of resolving issues around pensions and provision on retirement.

Pension earmarking is arranging that, when a pension comes to be paid, a proportion of it is paid to the other party.

Pension offsetting is offsetting the value of the pension against some other asset such as the marital home.

Pension sharing is the splitting of the pension at the time of divorce, giving both parties their own pension fund.

Periodical payments
The technical phrase for maintenance or alimony.

Permission to remove
An application to the court for permission to remove a child permanently from England and Wales. This used to be called leave to remove.

Petition
See Matrimonial order application.

Petitioner
Now called an applicant. This is the person applying for the divorce. Since the law changed in April 2022 both spouses can apply together and will be referred to as applicant 1 and applicant 2.

Post-nup
The aim of a pre-marital agreement is usually to protect the wealth of one or both spouses and, if prepared properly, should dictate the financial settlement on divorce. If you are considering a pre-nup you should seek specialist advice immediately. You can also take steps to protect your position after the wedding, which may involve a post-nup/mid-nup. These are the same as a pre-nup, but made at any time after the marriage ceremony. Nuptial agreements cannot be referred to as binding as a judge will always have discretion to make a different order.

Power of arrest
This allows the police to arrest a person who ignores or breaks an order of the court. If your partner breaks the order and you call the police, they will ask to see a copy of the order to see if it has a power of arrest. Once the police have arrested that person they must bring them back to court within 24 hours. A power of arrest can only be attached to an occupation order and not a non-molestation order because a breach of a non-molestation order is automatically considered to be a criminal offence.

Prayer
The section of the petition that asks the court to make orders in favour of the petitioner.

Pre-nup
A pre-nuptial agreement (also known as a pre-marital agreement or contract) is made in contemplation of marriage, most commonly setting out the terms which are to apply between the spouses in the event of separation or divorce. Sometimes they can deal with arrangements during the marriage, upon separation/divorce and upon death. If prepared correctly then they are likely to be upheld by the family court on divorce.

Glossary

Privilege
The right of a person to refuse to disclose a document or to refuse to answer questions on the ground of some special interest recognised by law.

Process server
This is someone employed to serve court papers. To prove that the papers have been served, the process server will normally swear an affidavit, which will be sent to the court.

Prohibited steps order
An order used to prohibit something being done to a child, for example, changing a child's surname or taking the child out of England and Wales.

Property adjustment order/ property transfer order
The court's power to change the ownership of an asset. Usually, but not always, this will be in relation to property.

Questionnaire
A list of questions asking for further details about a person's financial circumstances. This is usually made in response to any gaps or omissions in someone's Form E in financial proceedings.

Relevant child
A child of the marriage, either aged under 16 at the time of decree nisi/conditional order or aged between 16 and 18 and in full time education or training. A disabled and dependent child of any age will always be considered a relevant child.

Residence
This term is no longer used. We now have "child arrangements orders" which can include with whom, or when a child lives, spends time with or otherwise has contact with a parent.

Residence order
As from April 2014, residence orders no longer exist. They have been replaced with "child arrangements orders".

Respondent
The person who receives the divorce petition/matrimonial order application or other application to court, such as in financial proceedings.

Sale of property order
Where a court makes an order for secured periodical payments (see Maintenance), lump sum or property adjustment, it may make a further order for the sale of property to satisfy the earlier order.

Seal
A mark or stamp that the court puts on documents to indicate that they have been issued by the court.

Section 25 factors
The checklist, set out in section 25 of the Matrimonial Causes Act 1973, of criteria upon which financial remedy applications are decided.

Section 8 order
An order under section 8 of the Children Act 1989: namely a child arrangements order, a prohibited steps order and a specific issue order.

Separation agreement
A contractual document that deals with the arrangements between a couple after their separation. Sometimes this is used when a couple are not yet ready to start divorce proceedings.

Service
The process by which court documents are formally sent to, and received by, the party to whom they are addressed.

Set aside
Cancelling a judgment or order. This will only be available in limited circumstances.

Solicitor
A lawyer who advises a client and prepares a case for court. Specialist family law solicitors may also be trained as mediators, collaborative lawyers or arbitrators. Solicitors are regulated by the Solicitors Regulation Authority.

Glossary

Specific issue order
An order determining a specific issue relating to a child, for example, which school a child is to attend.

Statement in support
A formal statement sworn on oath to be true by the person making it, usually in support of an application to the court. See also Swear.

Statement in support of divorce
This statement poses a number of questions aimed at ensuring that the contents of your petition remain true and correct and that there have been no changes in circumstances that may affect your ability to rely on the irretrievable breakdown of your marriage. This statement has to be filed at court when you apply for a conditional order.

Statement of arrangements
The document that used to be sent to the court with the petition/matrimonial order application if the divorcing couple had children. As of 22 April 2014, it is no longer necessary to submit this document.

Statement of truth
A statement or other document containing facts verified as being true by the person making the statement. If the document is false, proceedings for contempt of court may be brought against the person who made the false statement.

Stay
To place a stop or a halt on court proceedings.

Strike out
The court ordering that written material or evidence may no longer be relied upon.

Swear
To declare on oath that what is being said or what is contained in a document is true. This is usually administered by a solicitor, notary public or a member of court staff. It sometimes incurs a small fee.

Talaq
Dissolves an Islamic marriage under Islamic law. It is a unilateral process whereby a husband rejects his wife by saying words to the effect "I divorce you".

Tenancy-in-common
This is one way of owning property jointly. The separate shares are agreed (usually when the property is purchased). If one of the owners dies, their share will form part of their estate and will not automatically belong to the survivor, unlike joint tenancy.

Term order
Maintenance/periodical payments for a specified period of time. The term (or length) of the order can either be capable of being extended to cater for something unexpected happening or, alternatively, the court can order that the term cannot be extended.

Two-years separation
This used to be one of the five facts or bases for getting a divorce, i.e. the divorcing couple has lived apart for two years and the other spouse consents to divorce. The requirement to rely on facts has since been abolished and will only be relevant for divorce proceedings started prior to April 2022.

Undertaking
An undertaking is a promise given to the court or to the other party. Once an undertaking has been given to the court, it has the same effect as a court order. This means that, if it is broken, it will be seen as contempt of court and (in extreme cases) an application can be made for the person who has broken the undertaking to be committed to prison.

Unreasonable behaviour
This used to be one of the five facts or bases for getting a divorce, i.e. the behaviour of the respondent was such that the applicant should not be expected to live with them. The requirement to rely on facts has since been abolished and will only be relevant for divorce proceedings started prior to April 2022.

Without prejudice
Correspondence or documents that are marked "without prejudice" cannot be shown to the court. The purpose of allowing this is to encourage discussions about settlement. The only time a court can see without prejudice proposals is in the FDR hearing because this is a without prejudice hearing.